Praise for *Enterprise Patterns and MDA*

"The burgeoning field of Model Driven Architecture tools and worldwide support for the Unified Modeling Language are finally being met with high-quality books that explain standard modeling techniques in a way any developer can follow. This book meets an urgent need squarely and clearly, and explains with copious examples a powerful approach to building usable (and reusable!) assets and applications. Every enterprise developer needs this book."

—Richard Mark Soley, Ph.D.
Chairman & CEO
Object Management Group, Inc.

"I've never seen a system of business patterns as detailed as this one. The completeness that Arlow and Neustadt provide in these patterns is impressive. The explanations for why the patterns are formed the way they are and how they're interconnected are incredibly thorough. The patterns presented here have the potential to impact business applications in the same way the 'Gang of Four' patterns have impacted general software development."

—Steve Vinoski
Chief Engineer of Product Innovation
IONA Technologies

"[*Enterprise Patterns and MDA* is a] detailed, yet very readable, guide to designing business applications using reusable model components and Model Driven Architecture. It deserves a place on every application designer's desk."

—Andrew Watson
Vice President and Technical Director
Object Management Group, Inc.

"Design patterns are generally acknowledged as an effective approach to developing robust and highly reusable software. Now that Model Driven Architecture is raising software design to ever-higher levels of abstraction, it is only natural that pattern concepts should find application in advanced modeling techniques. With this book, Arlow and Neustadt have greatly advanced the state of the art of MDA by defining both a theory and a methodology for applying the concept of Archetype Patterns to business software modeling."

—John Poole
Distinguished Software Engineer
Hyperion Solutions Corporation

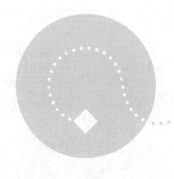

Enterprise
Patterns
and MDA

JIM ARLOW AND ILA NEUSTADT

Enterprise Patterns and MDA

Building Better Software with Archetype Patterns and UML

♦♦Addison-Wesley

Boston • San Francisco • New York • Toronto • Montreal
London • Munich • Paris • Madrid
Capetown • Sydney • Tokyo • Singapore • Mexico City

The publisher offers discounts on this book when ordered in quantity for bulk purchases and special sales. For more information, please contact:

U.S. Corporate and Government Sales
(800) 382-3419
corpsales@pearsontechgroup.com

For sales outside of the U.S., please contact:

International Sales
(317) 581-3793
international@pearsontechgroup.com

Visit Addison-Wesley on the Web: www.awprofessional.com

Library of Congress Cataloging-in-Publication Data

Arlow, Jim, 1960–
   Enterprise patterns and MDA : building better software with archetype patterns and UML / Jim Arlow, Ila Neustadt.
      p.   cm.
   Includes bibliographical references and index.
   ISBN 0-321-11230-X (pbk.)
      1. Computer software—Development.   2. UML (Computer science)   3. Software patterns.   4. Object-Oriented programming (Computer science)   5. Business enterprises—Data processing.   I. Neustadt, Ila.   II. Title.

   QA76.76.D47A735 2003
   005.1'17—dc22   2003062962

ISBN 0-321-11230-X
Text printed on recycled paper
1 2 3 4 5 6 7 8 9 10—CRS—0706050403
First printing, December 2003

To our family

Contents

Part 3   Archetype pattern catalog   117

4   Party **archetype pattern**   119

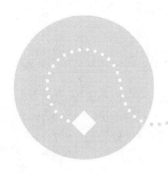

Foreword

Not 200 meters from where I sit, there was a revolution.

Responding to a call from a famous night rider, a handful of men turned out in the middle of the night to protect their families, their lands, and a set of "human rights" they had in fact just discovered. Their intolerable treatment by a distant tyrant caused them to risk everything—their very lives—to protect their way of life. Some paid the ultimate price that morning, sending a message heard around the world, becoming the beacon of revolution that was to reverberate throughout the Age of Enlightenment down to today.

They wanted nothing less than to create a better society, a just society, different than what they saw in the distant tyrant's domain. They wanted to change everything, wipe the slate clean, and dissolve the political bonds that bound them to their past. Leaning on the previous hundred years of political philosophy, they believed themselves to have what would soon be termed "certain inalienable rights," and they meant to assert those rights.

The result was years of painful fighting, a trans-oceanic war between the world's greatest superpower and a band of rebels, led by a figure termed a "traitor" by the ranks of that superpower. Against all odds, the rebels won the war in a mere eight years, winning a place in history and control of their own destinies.

Yet . . . more than 200 years later, here I sit in that same country drinking a cup of coffee in my local coffeehouse, where stood 200 years ago another coffeehouse. Though this country and its former tyrannical, imperial owner have been separated for more than two centuries, we still share the same language. The legal systems are nearly identical; the political systems, while different, have strong and clear similarities. The cultures are closely related, closely enough to share the same sources of entertainment. In fact, these one-time enemies are considered to have a "special relationship" that transcends all other diplomatic relationships, even to the exclusion of the closest neighbors and trading partners of both countries.

The message is clear: sometimes at least, revolutions are evolutionary. The urge to reinvent, to clear the decks and start again, quite often instead reifies an extant system—in this case, personal freedom in the context of a precedent-based legal system structured around a government of the people, for the people, and by the people.

Moving our focus from political history to the structure of scientific and industrial revolutions, we find much the same situation. Thomas Kuhn's view of the world is constantly invoked in the information technology industry, but more often as not, IT "paradigm shifts" are in fact only terminology shifts.

Model Driven Architecture (MDA), the vision of the Object Management Group (OMG) to move software development out of the depths of handicraft up to the heights of engineering, without doubt represents a paradigm shift. By focusing on architecture and encapsulating design "on paper" the way building architects capture blueprints, the OMG aims not only to lower initial software development costs but, more importantly, to decrease the ever-increasing costs of software integration and maintenance (which claim some 90 percent of software lifecycle resources today). At the same time, MDA starts with a graphical language rather than a textual one and forces developers to design before coding (or even instead of coding). Clearly there's a revolution under way.

At the same time, however, MDA represents just another level of abstraction, another level of compilation. The authors of the tome in your hands call MDA a "revolution" akin to the late-twentieth-century move from procedural to object-oriented programming languages; but even that was only another compiler-based level of abstraction (few instruction sets are object-oriented; object-oriented languages must be compiled to those non-OO instruction set architectures). In fact, the MDA revolution is already delivering benefits, without discarding that which came before; that is, it is an evolutionary revolution.

Every revolution, regardless of how well it replaces or expands the existing order, must have a language; political revolutions have their constitutions and declarations, and the MDA revolution focuses on software processes and assets. This book, while it briefly presents a software development process, focuses primarily (and in prescient and clear depth) on filling out a set of patterns to simplify the development of software. This book is, effectively, your dictionary of the new language of MDA, a set of basic blueprints that will accelerate the construction of the building you have in mind. Builders don't all need to reinvent steel I-beams, and software developers don't need to reinvent the product catalog.

In sum, you hold in your hands the keys to an evolutionary revolution, one that is already having its impact on the software development world. I must confess to a personal failing, that I find joy in reading encyclopedias and dictionaries. As I sip my coffee near the site of an evolutionary revolution, it's hard not to enjoy reading the declaration of another.

—Richard Mark Soley, Ph.D.
Lexington, Massachusetts, U.S.A.
October 2003

Introduction

About this book

We have called this book *Enterprise Patterns and MDA—Building Better Software with Archetypes Patterns and UML.* The first part of the title sets the theme for the book as a whole: we aim to provide you with a set of essential patterns for enterprise computing. These are not technical "design patterns"; rather, they are essential business patterns that are found, at least to some degree, in virtually all enterprises. You should find that one or more of these patterns are immediately applicable in software development projects. These patterns are high-value model components that you can easily use in your own UML models. Each pattern provides a solution for understanding and modeling a specific part of a business system. Furthermore, we show you how you can use the emerging discipline of Model Driven Architecture (MDA) to apply these patterns with a high degree of automation.

The second part of the title sets out how we achieve our goal of producing a set of patterns that are useful at the enterprise level. We introduce the new concepts of *archetypes* and *archetype patterns* in order to define a level of abstraction optimized for reuse *and* to the automation possibilities of MDA. These patterns are documented using the technique of *literate modeling*, which embeds the patterns, expressed as UML models, in a narrative such that the patterns can be understood, validated, and adapted even by nontechnical readers.

This is a practical book that gives you a useful set of archetype patterns and the theory you need to use them effectively in an enterprise context. We hope that this will save you a great deal of time and effort in your software development projects.

These patterns are valuable—a similar, but much less mature, set of patterns was recently independently valued at about $300,000 by a blue-chip company.

Using any one of these patterns, or even a pattern fragment, may save you many days or months of work. Perhaps even more important than this saving is the fact that the knowledge engineered into each archetype pattern may prevent you from making costly and time-consuming mistakes!

All of the patterns presented in this volume work together harmoniously and so provide a unified pattern language for talking about selling systems. This harmony greatly adds to their value.

At the time of this writing in 2003, we think we are at the start of a revolution in software development. Much as the 1990s saw an increase in the level of abstraction from procedural to object-oriented (OO) code, we believe that this decade will see a further, and more significant, increase in the level of abstraction. This will be a change from code-centric software development to model-centric software development through MDA.

We hope that the concepts, techniques, tools, and patterns that we describe in this book will help us all to make this revolution in software development a reality.

Our vision

One of the reasons this book came about was through boredom! After modeling for many years, we decided that we were often just doing the same old thing over and over again. At the right level of abstraction, most businesses seem to be made up of the same semantic elements—Customer, Product, Order, Party, and so on. In fact, so pervasive are some of these elements that it led us to the notion of business archetype patterns.

We speculated that most business systems could be assembled, like Lego bricks, from a sufficiently complete set of archetype patterns.

The essence of our vision is that archetype patterns should be treated as a type of "model component" that can be taken off the shelf, customized, and instantiated in your own models. This process can be done manually, but ideally it should be automated to as high a degree as possible by using an MDA tool.

Today, you can use a GUI builder to create graphical user interfaces rapidly from GUI components. The work we describe in Chapter 2 enables you to construct semantically correct and verifiable UML models rapidly from platform-independent, generic model components with a high degree of automation. We believe that this may be the future of software development. We call this *component-based modeling*.

This is reuse writ large—software systems are not considered to be composed of reusable classes, reusable code components, or even reusable subsystems, but rather from the reusable semantic elements that are archetype patterns. In fact, to a great extent the essence of the business system lies in its archetypes and their patterns, rather than in any code or design artifacts. Coding practices, design practices, and even architectures come and go with technology changes, but the archetypes themselves survive, largely unchanged, sometimes over millennia.

Why we haven't done it sooner

We have wanted to write this book for several years, but there have been obstacles that we have only recently overcome.

- The state of the art of UML modeling. Until the recent MDA initiative of the Object Management Group (OMG), we did not really have the conceptual tools necessary to describe archetype patterns in good form.
- The problem of pattern variation. Business patterns often need to adapt their forms to a specific business context. We have now formulated a simple solution to this problem that allows us to create archetype patterns that are adaptable to different business environments.
- The problem of communicating UML models to a wide audience. In fact, we've had a good solution to this for a few years now, in the form of literate modeling (described in Chapter 3).
- UML modeling tool support. It's all very well presenting a theory of archetype patterns, but such a theory is useful to the average software engineer *only* if it can be put into practice. Modeling tools have recently come onto the market that can accommodate our requirements for archetype pattern automation.

The structure of this book

There are four main threads to this book:

1. The theory of archetypes and archetype patterns (Chapters 1 and 2)
2. Pattern automation using MDA (Chapter 2)
3. Increasing the business value of UML models by making them accessible to a wide audience through literate modeling (Chapter 3)
4. A valuable pattern catalog that you can use in your own models (Chapter 4 onward)

Chapters 1, 2, and 3 provide you with the theoretical basis for the rest of the book, and you will find that they cover a lot of new material.

In Chapter 1 we describe a new approach to dealing with the problem of pattern variation—how to adapt patterns for different usage contexts.

In Chapter 2 we show you how you can automate the process of using archetype patterns with an MDA-enabled UML modeling tool. The first two chapters are intimately related. The pattern automation described in Chapter 2 depends on the theory of archetypes and archetype patterns presented in Chapter 1.

Chapter 3 describes the technique of literate modeling that you can use to document your patterns. This chapter is pretty much self-contained. Literate modeling is a powerful way to communicate UML models to a wide audience.

Each of the first three chapters contains a summary that reiterates the key information in the chapter in a very concise outline form. This is great for revision and it is also a useful source of bullet points for presentations.

The pattern catalog can stand alone. If you choose to use the book primarily as a pattern catalog (Chapter 4 to Chapter 12), you can skip much of the theoretical background in the first three chapters. Use the pattern catalog as a valuable resource for your own models. Each of the pattern chapters ends with a brief summary that lists the key concepts and archetypes introduced in that chapter. Again, we do this in outline form.

Having said that the pattern catalog can stand alone, we believe that you will be able to apply the patterns much more effectively if you have at least a basic understanding of archetype theory first. You can find all you need to know in Chapter 1. All the patterns in the pattern catalog are a direct result of the application of the theories and techniques described in the first three chapters. The notions of archetypes, archetype patterns, pattern configuration, and literate modeling have allowed us to create much more complete and robust patterns than otherwise would have been possible.

Finally, we provide a glossary of archetypes, a bibliography, and a complete index.

How to use this book

In this section we present roadmaps for the various ways in which you might wish to use this book and some recommendations about how you might like to approach reading it.

Please be aware that this is *not* a beginner's book, so there may be prerequisites for some of the roads that you may want to travel. None of these prerequisites are particularly difficult to achieve, but it's always worth ensuring that you have what you need, or at least know where to get it, before setting out on the journey!

Table 1

You are	Your goal in reading this book	Prerequisites	Useful references	Roadmap
OO analyst/designer OO programmer Architect	I want to understand the theory of archetypes and archetype patterns	A working knowledge of UML	[Arlow 2001]	Chapter 1
OO analyst/designer OO programmer Architect	I want to see how MDA tools can be used to automate the use of archetype (and other) patterns	A working knowledge of UML (some knowledge of MDA would also be helpful)	[Arlow 2001] [Kleppe 2003]	Chapter 1 Chapter 2
OO analyst/designer Architect	I want to improve my UML models and see how I can make them available to a wider audience	A working knowledge of UML	[Arlow 2001]	Chapter 3
OO analyst/designer Architect	I want to reuse the archetype patterns in my own models in an informal way by taking patterns, pattern fragments, or just ideas	A working knowledge of UML A working knowledge of the business domain in which you intend to apply the patterns	[Arlow 2001]	Pattern catalog
OO analyst/designer Architect	I want to reuse the archetype patterns in my own models in a formal way by understanding the theory behind them	A working knowledge of UML A working knowledge of the business domain in which you intend to apply the patterns	[Arlow 2001]	Chapter 1 Chapter 2 Chapter 3 Pattern catalog
OO analyst/designer OO programmer Architect Business analyst Project manager Software engineer	I want to use the pattern catalog to help me understand a particular business domain	Some knowledge of UML is desirable, but if you don't have this, you should still be able to understand most of the text of the literate models	[Arlow 2001]	Pattern catalog

In Table 1 we (naturally) reference our previous book, *UML and the Unified Process*, as a suitable source for readers who need some introductory material on UML. When we wrote that book, we always had in mind that it could serve as a useful precursor to more advanced texts such as this.

The pattern chapters contain a lot of information, and you may find it helpful to proceed as follows when reading each chapter.

1. Read the chapter's section on business context. As its name suggests, this section provides information that sets the pattern in its context within the business world.
2. Read the chapter's summary section. This will give you a clear idea of exactly what you can find in the chapter.
3. Look at the chapter roadmap. This will give you an overview of the archetypes and their relationships, and where they are discussed in the text.
4. Read the chapter.

Conventions

We have used the following conventions.

Archetypes, pleomorphs, attributes, operations, relationship names, relationship role names, and code fragments are in this font: `AnArchetype`, `APleomorph`, `anAttribute`, `anOperation()`, `aRelationshipName`, `aRoleName`, `some code`.

Archetype definitions look like this:

> The `Money` archetype represents an `amount` of a specific `Currency`. This `Currency` is `acceptedIn` one or more `Locales`.

Term definitions look like this:

> A business process is a sequence of business activities that, when executed, is designed to lead to some business benefit.

Acknowledgments

We'd like to thank our U.K. editor, Simon Plumtree, for seeing the potential of this project. We'd also like to thank our U.S. editor, Mary O'Brien and her team, Brenda Mulligan, Julie Nahil, Kim Arney Mulcahy, Chrysta Meadowbrooke, Kathy Benn McQueen, and Carol Noble for all their work and support.

Thanks to Dr. Wolfgang Emmerich and John Quinn for their contributions to the work on literate modeling described in Chapter 3. We'd like to acknowledge our friends in iO Software, Richard Hubert, Ronald Steinhau, and Marcus Munzert, without whom Chapter 2 would be considerably shorter. Fabrizio Ferrandina of Zuhlke Engineering has been of invaluable assistance by publicizing our work and introducing us to key contacts.

We have received essential help from John Watkins at IBM and Andy Carmichael at Borland, who provided us with tools to do the job. Andrew Watson of the OMG has been of tremendous assistance in bringing our work to the attention of that body. Liz Dobson of Zuhlke Engineering has always been helpful and enthusiastic, even when we had to turn down consulting opportunities in order to work on the manuscript.

Our reviewers, Richard Soley (OMG), John Poole (Hyperion Software), Steve Vinoski (IONA Technologies) and Fred Waskiewicz (OMG) helped us to improve the quality of the final manuscript, and Richard has written a fine foreword for us.

Once again, we have been fortunate to have had excellent support from Sue and David Epstein. In particular, David helped us with some key advice on writing when this book was still in the planning stage.

Finally, we'd like to thank our cats who, as always, have been an important part of the project. We have solved many modeling problems while stroking Homer. Paddy lies on top of our monitors and nonchalantly indicates modeling errors with paws and tail. Meg generates new ideas by juxtaposing unrelated manuscript pages in novel ways.

Part 1

Archetype theory, practice, and Model Driven Architecture

Chapter 1

Archetypes and archetype patterns

1.1 Introduction

In this chapter, we introduce and explain the concepts of business archetypes and archetype patterns. We have found these concepts to be exciting and very useful in our own work in object modeling, and we hope that you will too.

Although an understanding of archetypes and archetype patterns was essential to create the archetype patterns presented in the main part of this book, it is not essential to the pragmatic application of these patterns in business systems. If you just want to use this book as a useful pattern catalog, you may safely skim this chapter, which is mainly theoretical. However, you should at least take a quick look at Section 1.7 to understand the Unified Modeling Language (UML) profile we are using.

If you are involved in capturing business patterns or creating high-level or even enterprise-level object models, you may find the "thought tools" presented in this chapter to be very valuable.

We begin with a general discussion of archetypes (Section 1.2), define what we mean by business archetypes and archetype patterns (Section 1.3), and discuss how we can model archetypes and archetype patterns using UML (Section 1.7). We look at the issue of pattern variation (Section 1.9) and introduce the powerful notion of pleomorphism as a way to understand how archetypes and archetype patterns adapt to specific business environments (Section 1.12).

1.2 What are archetypes?

The word *archetype* comes from the Greek *archetypo* (αρχετυπο), which means "original pattern." Here is a definition.

> An archetype is a primordial thing or circumstance that recurs consistently and is thought to be a universal concept or situation.

According to the psychologist Carl Gustav Jung [Jung 1981], archetypes arise from a common fund of human experiences (the collective unconscious) that uses archetypes as one of its ordering and structuring principles. In fact, wherever there is a commonality of human experiences over extended periods of time, archetypes arise to help structure these experiences.

One of the most intriguing aspects of the Jungian archetypes is that they naturally exhibit *variability*—they change their form to adapt themselves to specific cultural contexts while their core semantics remain fixed. For example, the Hero archetype looks very different in the Native American paradigm than in the Australian Aboriginal paradigm, and yet the Hero is still somehow always recognizable as the Hero. We'll see shortly that this natural variability is an important feature of archetypes.

Because archetypes are a basic human mechanism for organizing, summarizing, and generalizing information about the world, you can reasonably expect them to have some application in the field of software development.

Human beings have been involved in business activities for millennia, and we think it is quite reasonable to suppose that many archetypes have arisen in the business domain. For example, if you think about the basic business activity of selling, the earliest recorded instances of this activity occurred some 5,000 years ago. There's no doubt that this activity was also occurring much earlier than this. All selling over this enormous span of time has in some way involved the basic concepts of product, price (in terms of a notion of the value of the product), seller, and buyer.

You can see that there are some very fundamental (we would say archetypal) concepts here and that there is also an archetypal pattern of relationships between these concepts. For example, the price is always associated in some way with the product.

The agenda of this book is to try to capture some of these archetypes and archetype patterns in UML object models. To do so, we introduce the following new concepts.

1. Business archetypes
2. Business archetype patterns
3. Archetype and archetype pattern variability
4. Pleomorphism
5. Pattern configuration

We'll discuss the first four of these ideas in the next few sections, and we devote much of Chapter 2 to pattern configuration.

1.3 What are business archetypes?

Object-oriented (OO) software systems reflect the business domains in which they operate. You can therefore expect to find archetypes in the business domain, in software systems, and in models of those systems. We call this type of archetype a *business archetype.*

A business archetype is a primordial thing that occurs consistently and universally in business domains and business software systems.

A good example of a business archetype is Party. A Party represents an identifiable, addressable unit that may have a legal status. Usually this represents a person or an organization of some sort. All business systems have some concept of Party. You can look at the actual definition and semantics of the Party archetype in Chapter 4.

The notion of archetypes is very general, and there are certainly archetypes in other domains (such as health care and engineering) as well as in the business domain. You may use the term <domain name> archetype to refer specifically to these other archetypes. However, in this book, we limit ourselves to the business domain.

As well as there being archetypal things in business systems, these things can interact in patterns that are themselves archetypal. For example, the collaboration between the archetypes Party, Product, and Order is the basis of virtually every business that sells goods or services. We refer to these archetypal collaborations as *business archetype patterns*.

> A business archetype pattern is a collaboration between business archetypes that occurs consistently and universally in business environments and software systems.

In this book, for convenience we usually refer to business archetypes and business archetype patterns simply as archetypes and archetype patterns.

The essential characteristics of archetypes and archetype patterns are listed below.

- Universal: for something to be archetypal, it must occur consistently in business domains and systems.
- Pervasive: they occur in both the business domain *and* the software domain. When building OO systems, you should expect to find things and patterns that are archetypal in the business domain occurring in much the same form in the software domain. This is the principle of convergent engineering described in [Taylor 1995] and more recently in [Hubert 2001].
- Deep history: for example, the product archetype has been around ever since people first began to barter and sell.
- Self-evident to domain experts: this is not always the case, but if an archetype isn't obvious to a domain expert, you should certainly question whether it is really an archetype.

A quick word about terminology: the term *archetype* has been used in the context of computing by other authors. Peter Coad and his colleagues define *archetype* as "a form from which all things of the same kind more or less follow" [Coad 1999, p. 2]. Coad uses his archetypes in a way that is in some respects similar to how we use ours, but the Coad archetypes occur at a *much* higher level of abstraction and lack any formal UML profile.

Mellor and Balcer define *archetype* as "a fragment of data access and text manipulation logic that states formally how to embed an executable UML model into text" [Mellor 2002, p. 294]. In other words, the term is used to describe a specific aspect of an executable UML model. This is very different from any dictionary definition of the term.

Both of these uses of the word *archetype* are different from our usage in the term *business archetype*. Generally, whenever we use the term *archetype* in this book, we are using it as a shorthand for *business archetype* unless we explicitly state otherwise.

1.4 Archetypes and analysis classes

In object modeling, there are two fundamentally different types of classes, as shown in Table 1.1.

Table 1.1

Type of class	Semantics
Analysis class	Represents a crisp abstraction in the problem domain
	Maps onto real-world business concepts
Design class	A class whose specification is complete to such a degree that it may be implemented
	Incorporates features from both the problem domain and the solution domain (implementation technology)

We discuss both types of classes in much more detail in an earlier book [Arlow 2001], so we won't repeat that detailed discussion here. But to summarize, an analysis class arises directly from the problem domain (e.g., selling furniture) and has no implementation-specific features. On the other hand, a design class may contain features from both the problem domain and the solution domain (e.g., J2EE, .NET, or Web services). Analysis classes are for understanding the business, while design classes are for understanding the technical solution.

It's important to realize that archetypes are *always* at a higher level of abstraction than normal analysis classes. From a conceptual point of view, this is because archetypes are about consciously recognizing and capturing *universal* concepts, whereas analysis classes are not necessarily concerned with universality at all. From a technical point of view (as you will soon see), archetypes *generate* one or more analysis classes.

1.5 What are patterns?

We'll give a very brief introduction to patterns in this section, but for more details we advise you to refer to the key text on patterns, *Design Patterns—Elements of Reusable Object-Oriented Software*, by Erich Gamma, Richard Helm, Ralph Johnson, and John Vlissides [Gamma 1995].

According to [Gamma 1995], a pattern is a solution to a problem in a context. To be more precise, a pattern consists of a description of a problem, the context of the problem, and a possible solution to that problem in that context. You can think of a pattern as a "recipe" that describes how you may solve a particular problem under particular circumstances.

The idea of patterns originated in the work of Christopher Alexander on the architecture of towns and buildings [Alexander 1977]. Alexander said that a pattern describes a recurring problem and the key elements of the solution to that problem in a way that allows you to apply the solution again and again, each time in a novel but consistent fashion.

Gamma and his colleagues applied this idea to software systems in their book. Each pattern they defined has four elements.

- Pattern name: the name of the pattern. This allows you to talk about the pattern without having to always describe its details. Pattern names define a language that allows designers to communicate about designs at a high level of abstraction.
- Problem: the description of the problem that the pattern solves, for example, how to design an object that may have only a single instance (the Singleton pattern).
- Solution: the design of the pattern itself as a UML model. This design doesn't describe actual classes but rather a collaboration that classes in your model may implement.
- Consequences: the effects of applying the pattern.

Patterns can exist at many different levels of abstraction. [Gamma 1995] describes design patterns that are possible solutions to common problems encountered in OO design. It should be an essential component of your OO designer toolset!

Fowler has extended the idea of patterns into the analysis domain in his book, *Analysis Patterns—Reusable Object Models* [Fowler 1996]. This book contains some interesting patterns, but they are generally quite abstract and need a lot of refinement before you can apply them in a real development situation.

We compare and contrast archetype patterns with analysis patterns in the next section.

1.6 Archetype patterns and analysis patterns

This section is for those of you who want to know how archetype patterns and analysis patterns differ. If you are not interested in this topic, you can safely skip this section.

When we've presented material on archetype patterns at conferences prior to publication, we've sometimes been asked, "Aren't archetype patterns just analysis patterns?" The answer to this is no—archetype patterns have many unique features that make them much *more* than analysis patterns.

As we mentioned above, analysis patterns were first described by Fowler and defined as follows: "Analysis patterns are groups of concepts that represent a common construction in business modeling. It may be relevant to one domain, or it may span many domains" [Fowler 1996, p. 8].

Notice that there is no notion of *archetypal* concepts in this definition. This is the primary conceptual difference between analysis patterns and archetype patterns.

In fact, archetype patterns are much richer than analysis patterns, both conceptually and in terms of technology. These differences are summarized in Table 1.2.

Table 1.2

Feature	Reference	Archetype patterns	Analysis patterns
Is concerned with archetypal concepts	Chapter 1	Always	Sometimes
Incorporates the principle of convergent engineering	[Taylor 1995]	Always	Often
Is supported by a UML profile	Section 1.7	Yes	No
Is sufficiently detailed to feed into the Model Driven Architecture (MDA) development workflow as a platform-independent model (PIM)	Chapter 2	Yes	No
Supports variability of model elements	Section 1.9	Yes	No

Table continued on next page

Table 1.2   (Continued)

Feature	Reference	Archetype patterns	Analysis patterns
Supports pleomorphism	Section 1.12	Yes	No
Introduces pattern configuration rules to support pattern configuration	Section 2.5	Yes	No
Defines a set of platform-independent models	Section 2.3	Yes	No
Applicable across different business domains	Chapter 1	Often	Often
Supplied as literate models	Chapter 3	Yes	No
May be automated using MDA modeling tools	Chapter 2	Yes	No

As you will see in Section 1.15 and in Chapter 2, business archetype patterns are also applied in a very different way than analysis patterns.

1.7 UML profile for archetypes and archetype patterns

You can introduce new modeling extensions into UML by defining a UML profile. This consists of a set of stereotypes, tagged values, and constraints that define the semantics for the new modeling extensions you want to introduce. A profile extends the UML metamodel with a set of new modeling elements.

Our UML profile for archetype patterns is defined in Table 1.3. We've tried to keep it as simple as possible.

Table 1.3

Business archetype UML profile		
Stereotype	**Applies to**	**Semantics**
«archetype»	Class	A primordial thing that occurs consistently and universally in business environments and business software systems
		All archetypes in a business archetype pattern are optional

Table 1.3   (Continued)

Business archetype UML profile		
Stereotype	**Applies to**	**Semantics**
«archetype pattern»	Collaboration Package	A collaboration between business archetypes that occurs consistently and universally in business environments and software systems
«archetype pattern library»	Package	A subtype of the standard UML stereotype «model» The package is a model that contains one or more archetype patterns You should ensure that each archetype pattern library has a globally unique name to avoid namespace clashes—we recommend that you use your domain name as the name of the package, e.g., "clearviewtraining.com"
«o»	Composition Aggregation Attribute Operation	A feature that is optional and may be omitted When «o» is applied to a composition or aggregation relationship, it indicates that the relationship is optional
«pleomorph»	Refinement relationship between archetype patterns	The archetype pattern at the source of the arrow is a variation (pleomorph) of the archetype pattern pointed to by the arrow We discuss pleomorphism in detail in Section 1.12

These stereotypes may be used as illustrated in the following sections.

1.7.1   «archetype»

You can model business archetypes by using the class icon and adding the stereotype «archetype» to indicate that the classifier represents an archetype. Figure 1.1 shows a simple example.

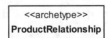

Figure 1.1

By definition, archetypes are optional and can, if wished, be omitted from any model based on the archetype pattern.

1.7.2 «archetype pattern»

You may use package notation for an archetype pattern as shown in Figure 1.2. You may also use collaboration notation (see Figure 1.17 later in this chapter).

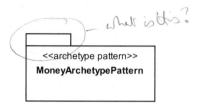

Figure 1.2

1.7.3 «archetype pattern library»

You can model an archetype pattern library as shown in Figure 1.3.

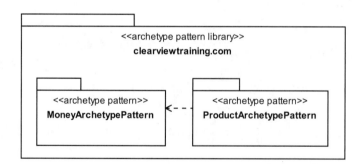

Figure 1.3

1.7.4 «o»

You can use the stereotype «o» (optional) to specify the parts of an archetype or archetype pattern that are optional. We'll discuss the reasons why we need this new stereotype in detail in Sections 1.9 and 1.10.

Figure 1.4 shows examples of the «o» stereotype being used on attributes, operations, and relationships.

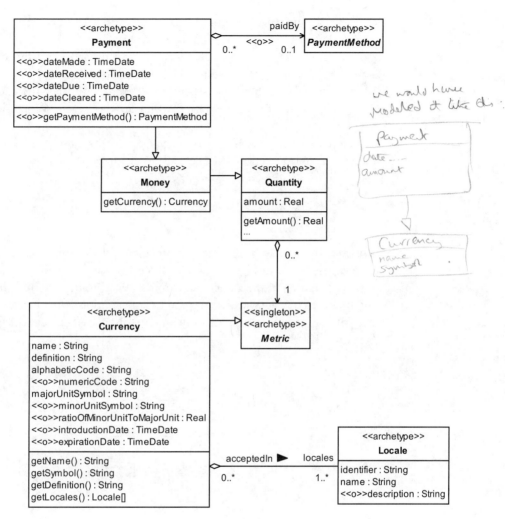

Figure 1.4

Reading Figure 1.4, you can see the following information.

- The Currency attributes numericCode, minorUnitSymbol, ratioOf-
  MinorUnitToMajorUnit, introductionDate, and expirationDate
  are optional.
- All the Payment attributes are optional. This gives you a lot of flexibility
  in how the archetype can be used in different business contexts. For example, a system that makes Payments would usually need the optional

attribute dateMade but not the others. However, a system that accepts Payments would not need dateMade but would include one or more of dateReceived, dateDue, and dateCleared. We discuss this use of Payment more fully in Section 11.9.

- The relationship paidBy between Payment and PaymentMethod is optional, and thus the Payment operation getPaymentMethod() is optional.

Note that the «singleton» stereotype on Metric simply indicates that there needs to be only a single instance of the Metric archetype at runtime. The Singleton pattern is described in [Gamma 1995].

1.7.5 «pleomorph»

This stereotype may be applied to refinement relationships between archetype patterns as shown in Figure 1.5. The archetype pattern at the source of the arrow is a variation of the archetype pattern pointed to by the arrow. In the figure the IdenticalProduct archetype pattern is a variation of the Product archetype pattern for a specific business domain. We discuss pleomorphism in detail in Section 1.12.

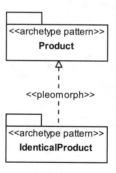

Figure 1.5

1.8 Modeling style

Whenever you create a UML model, it's a good idea to define a modeling style that you then use consistently throughout the model.

The modeling style used to create the models you see in this book arises from the specific requirements listed below.

- Make the models as readable as possible.
- Make the models as useful as possible.
- Make the models as precise as possible.
- Make the diagrams fit harmoniously within the bounds of this book.

We have adopted the following modeling style to satisfy these requirements.

- We usually don't show set and get methods for attributes. You may assume they are there unless an attribute is explicitly marked as private. This modeling style is described in *Convergent Architecture* [Hubert 2001] as the Compact Attribute style. It saves a lot of space on UML diagrams!
- As we described in our UML profile for archetypes in Section 1.7, we indicate that an attribute, operation, composition, or aggregation relationship is truly optional by using the stereotype «o».
- Archetypes are always optional.
- Everything that is not explicitly optional is mandatory.
- We show navigability wherever we can—this reduces the coupling between modeling elements, so we always try to put the maximum amount of navigability on our diagrams.
- We always show multiplicity explicitly. Some modelers assume that when multiplicity is not shown, it automatically defaults to 1, but this is a false assumption—when multiplicity is not shown, it means that it is *undecided*.
- We try to refine each association relationship as much as we can. This means that we use aggregation and composition wherever possible. Aggregation and composition have very specific semantics (see [Arlow 2001] and www.businessarchetypes.com) that are very useful in the models we create.

The goal of our modeling style is to try to create models that are as precise and constrained as it is possible to make them while still maintaining their generality and readability.

Figure 1.6 shows a completely general purpose UML model. This model is so *un*constrained as to be totally meaningless. (Oddly enough, in our consulting work, we do occasionally come across UML models somewhat like this one!) In fact, UML models become *more* meaningful the larger the number of constraints you can apply. This is because constraints capture information.

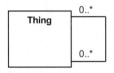

A general purpose model

Figure 1.6

Finally, we are always guided by what we refer to as "the principle of maximum utility"—we consciously strive to make the diagrams and text as useful to you in every respect as possible. Our ultimate aim is to try to make the diagrams talk to you about the business domain.

1.8.1 OCL data types

Ultimately, all models are built up from combinations of a relatively small number of basic data types such as `int`, `float`, `double`, `String`, and so on. In order to make our archetype patterns as universal as possible, we take our set of basic types from the Object Constraint Language (OCL), which is a part of UML that provides a formal language for expressing constraints. OCL defines a set of predefined types that allow us to express business archetype patterns as completely language- and platform-independent UML models.

The advantage of using the OCL types instead of (for example) Java or .NET data types is that the OCL types can be very easily mapped onto those of other languages. This can be done manually when you instantiate an archetype pattern or completely automatically if you are lucky enough to be using an MDA-enabled modeling tool.

The types are summarized in Table 1.4.

Table 1.4

OCL type	Semantics
Real	Represents the mathematical concept of a real number
Integer	Represents the mathematical concept of a whole number

Table 1.4 (Continued)

OCL type	Semantics
String	Represents an ASCII string of characters
	Although OCL specifies an ASCII string, you should assume that String in our models represents a Unicode string so that archetype patterns may be used internationally—this is our only departure from OCL
Boolean	Represents a value that is true or false

These types have exactly the sort of operations (+, -, /, and so on) that you might expect. You can find the full details in the UML specification (www.omg.org/uml).

We add TimeDate to this set of OCL types. This represents a point in time as defined in ISO 8601. You can assume that TimeDate provides a set of operations for performing calculations on time as well as comparison operations. Most programming languages provide a type or library component that maps onto TimeDate, so we don't provide any more details here.

1.9 Variation

One of the unique aspects of the archetype pattern approach is that it explicitly addresses the problem of pattern variation.

Sometimes a specific model of something, such as a model of products, may be suitable for use in one business area but not in another. This is what we refer to as *the principle of variation:* different business domains often seem to require different models of the same thing.

This principle just seems to be a fact of life. Often there is no way around it even if you choose to make some modeling compromises.

Because of variation, the construction of generic, highly reusable object models, such as enterprise object models, has proven to be rather difficult. You may even have heard some pundits say that such activities have failed and are, in principle, impossible.

However, in our experience *you can succeed* at such activities, and we'll tell you how.

Although you can't usually make variation go away, there is always another option. By carefully analyzing and understanding the variation, you can work with it constructively to create archetype patterns that are adaptable and that can change their form to adapt themselves to different business contexts.

The first step in understanding variation is to look at the types of variation possible in archetype patterns. You will find that there are three different kinds of variation.

1. Archetype variation: archetypes may need *different features* (attributes, operations, constraints) to be effective in different business contexts.
2. Archetype pattern variation: optional features in the patterns may be omitted if they are not needed.
3. Pleomorphism: in this special type of archetype pattern variation, the pattern may take on a *different structure* to adapt itself to the specific requirements of a business context. This may mean different archetypes, archetype features, and relationships in each of the variants.

We will look at these types of variation in detail in the next three sections.

1.10 Archetype variation and optionality

This type of variation occurs when an archetype needs to be adapted to a particular business use. There are really only two ways in which an archetype may be varied.

1. Some new features may be added.
2. Optional features may be omitted.

The key to dealing with this kind of variation successfully is to ensure that the core semantics of the archetype *remain fixed* for every variant you create. You therefore need a way to show which parts of the archetype are optional and can be omitted from variants derived from the archetype.

In our models, we indicate that a feature is optional by using the stereotype «o». When we mark an attribute (or operation) as optional, this means that the feature may be *omitted entirely* from the class.

You can see how we indicate variability in the `PartySignature` archetype shown in Figure 1.7. The attribute `reason` is optional and so is the operation `getAuthentication()`. The attribute `when` is not explicitly marked as optional, so it is mandatory. The `PartySignature` archetype itself is optional within the context of the `PartyArchetypePattern` (in which it appears) because all archetypes are optional by default.

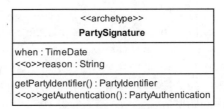

Figure 1.7

To understand optionality fully, consider the example shown in Figure 1.8, which shows a simple archetype pattern that contains only a single archetype, A. This archetype has one mandatory feature (attribute a1) and two optional features (attribute a2 and operation o1()). When this archetype pattern is instantiated in one of your models, there are four possible ways to make this instantiation, as we show in the figure.

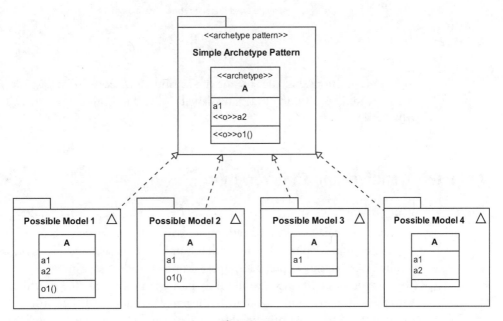

Figure 1.8

We assume that you make the simplest possible instantiation of the pattern—you just turn the archetype into a class in your model. You can instantiate the pattern manually by copying the pattern into your model yourself, or semi-automatically by using a suitably equipped MDA modeling tool (described in detail in Chapter 2). Notice that the optional elements may be *absent entirely from an instantiated pattern.*

This idea of optionality is very important because it allows archetypes (and archetype patterns) to be configurable. Pattern configuration is one of the major topics in Chapter 2.

It's worth noting that UML also has a notion of optionality, but this is at the instance level, rather than at the class level. UML provides a syntax to indicate that a class attribute can take the value null in instances of that class. You can do this by appending the multiplicity [0..1] to the attribute as shown in Figure 1.9.

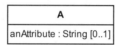

Attribute anAttribute may have the value null

Figure 1.9

However, note that the slot for the attribute *still exists* in an instance even when it holds the value null. This is very different from the attribute being truly optional.

1.11 Archetype pattern variation

As described in Section 1.7, any feature of an archetype pattern that is marked with the «o» stereotype, and anything stereotyped «archetype», is optional.

For example, Figure 1.10 shows the complete Money archetype pattern, which is fully described in Chapter 11.

Suppose that you need to use only part of this pattern. You are concerned with Money but *not* with payments or currency exchange. Furthermore, suppose that you are interested only in ISO currencies. The archetype pattern has optional features, so you can "prune" the pattern down to just the bits you need. In this case, you would have the result shown in Figure 1.11.

You must use your judgment as a modeler to adapt the pattern in such a way that what remains is still semantically well formed. For example, if you

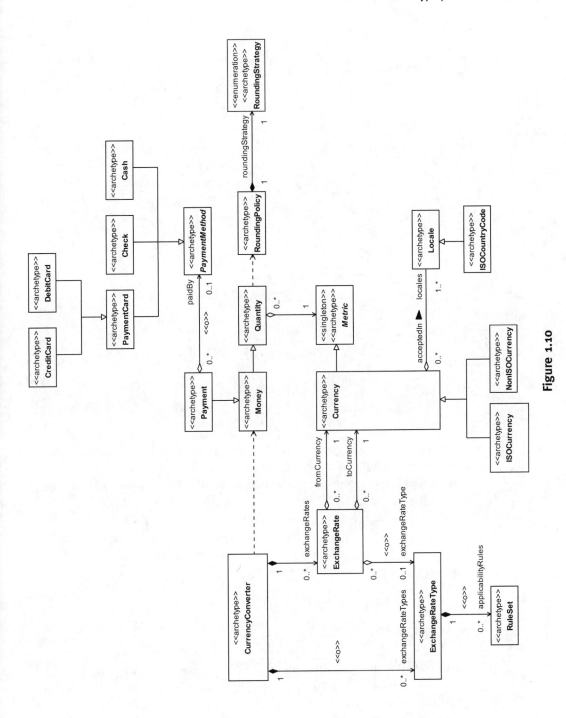

Figure 1.10

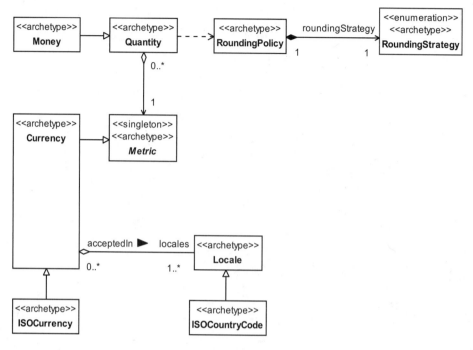

Figure 1.11

were to prune the Money archetype pattern so that you included Money but omitted RoundingPolicy and RoundingStrategy, the pattern would be semantically invalid because Money requires RoundingPolicy and RoundingStrategy for its arithmetic functions.

Adapting a pattern by selecting only those features you need is known as *pattern configuration.* We discuss pattern configuration in considerably more detail in Chapter 2, where we also present an automated approach using pattern configuration rules to ensure that the resultant patterns are well formed.

1.12 Pleomorphism

Perhaps the most unusual aspect of business archetype patterns is that they do not necessarily have a fixed form. In fact, the form of an archetype pattern can depend on its business context. This seems to be a general property of archetypes, including the Jungian archetypes [Jung 1981].

This adaptation to an environment through a modification of form is common to many organisms and is known as *pleomorphism*. For example, in its larval stage the dragonfly is adapted to water, while when mature, it is adapted to air. However, both forms are aspects of the thing that we call a dragonfly.

For modeling software systems using archetypes and archetype patterns, we define pleomorphism as follows.

> Pleomorphism is the adaptation of an archetype pattern to a specific business context by a modification of its form such that its essential semantics remain unchanged.

By "essential semantics" we just mean, for example, that the Product archetype pattern always models products in every variant form and never becomes a model for anything else.

The Product archetype pattern (see Chapter 7) provides a very good example for pleomorphism. This pattern can appear in three distinctly different forms depending on certain characteristics of the products you want to sell. According to our UML profile for archetype patterns, we can model pleomorphism as shown in Figure 1.12. Let's look at this in some depth.

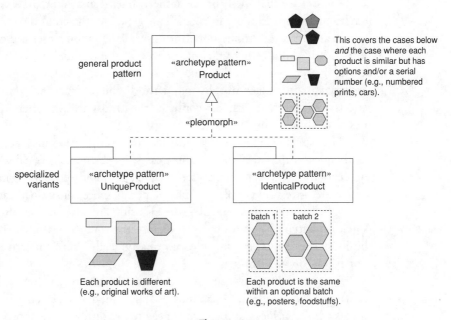

Figure 1.12

Each of the pleomorphs defines a notion of products suitable for a specific business context. As mentioned, we discuss this archetype pattern in detail in Chapter 7, but here is a summary of the essential points.

- General `Product` archetype pattern: use this when each instance of the product is similar but is also uniquely identifiable (e.g., signed and numbered prints of an original painting) or when you have a mix of product types that span the pleomorphs below. If required by the business context, this general pattern can be specialized into one of the following more restricted pleomorphs.
- `UniqueProduct` pleomorph: use this when each instance of every product in your system is unique (e.g., original paintings or other works of art). In this case you can use a very simple pattern that stores all the product information in a single archetype.
- `IdenticalProduct` pleomorph: use this when each instance of every product in your system is identical (e.g., posters for sale on Art.com). All of the instances of the poster are identical, but, for quality control reasons, they may be organized into batches.

In each pleomorph, the high-level semantics of the `Product` archetype pattern remain intact—it always models something that can be bought and sold.

You can see that the `Product` archetype pattern adapts to a specific business environment by changing its form. This generates the child pleomorphs.

Pleomorphism, unlike polymorphism, is *not* about interface conformance; rather, it is about semantic conformance at the particular level of abstraction at which archetype patterns are defined. This is an essential point: even though archetype pattern pleomorphs may have different structural adaptations to be effective in different business contexts, they must always adhere to the semantics of the base archetype pattern.

The base archetype pattern describes the common business semantics across all the pleomorphs and may, in some cases, be abstract. As you'll see, the literate model of the archetype pattern (see Chapter 3) should generally be in terms of the base pattern treating the pleomorphs as special, more constrained cases.

When you design a business system using archetypes, you often use only a single archetype pleomorph—you choose the one that is most suited to your business context. The other pleomorphs typically don't concern you and will not appear on your models.

An exception to this general rule of a single archetype pleomorph may sometimes occur in enterprise object models. These models are often very broad, spanning a whole business, and you may need to use different pleomorphs for specific business contexts.

For example, one business division may use the `IdenticalProduct` pleomorph of `Product` and another may need to use the general `Product` archetype pattern. However, the advantage of modeling with business archetypes is that you can immediately see that each division uses the `Product` archetype (albeit in different variations), and you can also understand the trade-offs and advantages involved in using each pleomorph in the different divisions. This understanding can be very valuable because it leads to greater degrees of interoperability and can help create a unified vision across the enterprise.

1.13 How to find archetype patterns

In order to identify business archetypes and archetype patterns, you need a detailed knowledge of the business domain of interest. Because you are looking for archetypes (rather than classes), your knowledge should ideally span the same business domain across different companies.

Any particular company will generally have only a *partial* view of a particular archetype. As illustrated in Figure 1.13, a bookshop will tend to see the `Product` archetype as books, while an airline will tend to see the `Product` archetype as seats on flights.

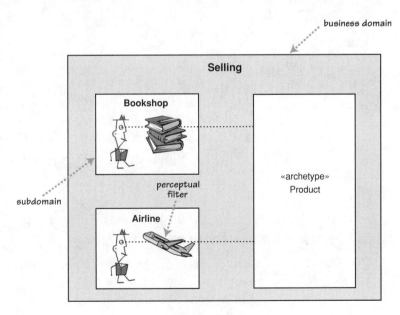

Figure 1.13

What happens is that any subdomain (such as `Bookshop` or `Airline`) of a domain such as `Selling` will add its own perceptual filters that may give a partial or even a distorted view of the true archetypes. This is just like the parable of the blind men and the elephant. The first blind man feels the elephant's tail and thinks it is a rope. The second blind man feels the elephant's leg and thinks it is a tree.

In fact, within the same company, there may be many different partial or distorted views of the same archetype. For example, if a company sells two very different types of products, there can often be (at least) two competing or complementary views of the `Product` archetype. This is particularly the case if the company has different divisions dedicated to each product. Even worse, each partial view may be supported by its own dedicated software systems, and this can be a significant cause of inefficiency and expense to the business. It can also constrain the business when it needs to move into new markets.

A software system itself may act as a powerful perceptual filter that can create grossly distorted views of the business domain and its business archetypes. When business activities are predicated upon particular software systems, the users may "see as through a glass, darkly" the business domain presented only according to the protocols of that system. The software system comes to define and limit their vision of the domain. We refer to this as *system blindness*—it's a bit like snow blindness, but you get it in front of a screen. It is generally not desirable because it tends to encourage and support pathological business processes. It can be particularly prevalent in established companies that have many legacy systems and long-term staff.

So, as an archetype hunter you must have, or cultivate, the ability to "think out of the box"—to perceive how other companies go about essentially the same business activities. But to gain this insight, you don't necessarily have to go to work for a different company! For example, if you are interested in selling systems and you work for a supermarket chain, go on-line and see how other companies sell—see how Amazon sells books or how Art.com sells posters. There are many examples of selling, and selling systems, all around you.

In the next few sections, we show you specific sources of archetypes and archetype patterns.

1.13.1 Domain expert interviews

The primary source of archetypes and archetype patterns is the domain expert. This is a person who knows a particular part, or domain, of the business in great depth. You can discover archetypes by interviewing domain experts and then analyzing those interviews in particular ways that we will discuss shortly.

You have to choose your domain experts with some care! The thing is, some "domain experts" are really just experts in a very small part of the business domain or only in the rather artificial subdomain created by existing business software systems. These are not primarily the people you are looking for, although they may still provide useful input. You really need to find the true domain experts who have a broad *and* deep knowledge of the business.

Once you have found suitable domain experts, you can proceed to interview them about the business domain in question.

We find that it is best to initially ask very general questions. For example, you would ask a question such as, "How do you sell things?" rather than, "How do you sell books?" The latter question presupposes specific details about what is being sold.

You can record the results of the interview in any way you like, but we find mind mapping to be an appropriate and powerful technique [Buzan 1996].

When you interview domain experts, it is often best to do this over a period of time. Initially let them just talk (this is why mind mapping is a good note-taking technique!) so you can get a good overview of the business domain. After each initial interview, you can identify candidate archetypes and patterns in your notes, then arrange to go back to the same domain expert and to others to validate these.

You are always looking for the fundamental concepts that make the business domain tick. These are generally concepts that, if removed, would make business impossible or at least prohibitively difficult.

Once you have a reasonably solid set of candidate archetypes, you can capture these in a UML model and begin to arrange them into any archetype patterns you identify.

1.13.2 Literature

Another excellent source of archetypes and archetype patterns is literature. Books or other external documents about a business domain will invariably introduce archetypal concepts. An advantage of these sources is that they tend to use a neutral vocabulary that is valid across many organizations that operate in the same domain.

Other types of literature, such as in-house publications, are also good sources of archetypes, but be aware that they may use jargon that has developed in your business over time and is *specific* to your organization. You may need to generalize this to a more standard vocabulary if such exists.

1.13.3 Models

Any existing models, both data and object, can be fruitful sources of archetypes and archetype patterns. The important point with models is to be able to generalize to an archetypal case from what might be very specific business solutions. This is a skill you'll develop over time as you inspect more and more models.

1.14 Model management for archetype patterns

We recommend that you manage your archetype patterns as follows.

- Place each archetype pattern in its own package stereotyped «archetype pattern». This package should be named after the key, or central, archetype in the pattern. If the pattern seems to have more than one key archetype, you should choose the one that will give the archetype pattern the most descriptive name. The standard we use for naming archetype patterns is:

  <KeyArchetypeName>ArchetypePattern

  The name is in camel case (mixed uppercase and lowercase letters, no spaces, with each word starting in uppercase), for example, MoneyArchetypePattern.
- Create an archetype pattern library for your patterns. This library should be a package stereotyped «archetype pattern library» that contains all of your archetype patterns. It needs to have a globally unique name so you can mix it with pattern libraries from other sources without namespace clashes. The best way to achieve this is to use your domain name as the name of the package, for example, clearviewtraining.com.
- You may group archetype patterns into sublibraries within your main archetype pattern library. If you do, we recommend that you name each sublibrary according to a significant aspect of your business domain, for example, Marketing, Manufacturing, or ResourceManagement.
- Create a literate model for the archetype patterns. You can find full details of how to do this in Chapter 3 and numerous examples of archetype patterns and their literate models in Part 3 of this book.

Figure 1.14 shows a simple example of our naming conventions.

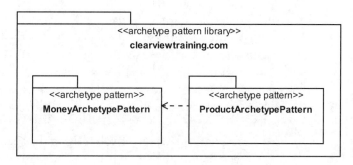

Figure 1.14

1.15 Using archetype patterns in your models

The process of applying a pattern to a model is often called *instantiating the pattern*. In this section we'll look at how you can instantiate archetype patterns manually. We devote Chapter 2 to a discussion of how you may use a suitably equipped modeling tool to automate this process.

All of our archetypes and patterns should be easy to understand because we have described them using literate modeling (see Chapter 3). However, there are a few aspects of their usage that we'd like to make very explicit.

- The key to successfully applying the archetype patterns is first of all to understand them—this means that you should study the UML models and also read the literate model.
- You need to understand your specific business requirements so you can choose which patterns will be useful to you.

Once you have chosen which patterns to use and you understand how they work, you need to figure out how to apply the patterns in your specific domain. For each pattern you should follow these guidelines.

- Choose the right pleomorph (see Section 1.12). The first step in using an archetype pattern is to choose the pleomorph most appropriate to your specific business domain.

- Choose what parts of the pattern you need to use. Don't be scared of "pruning" the archetype patterns to make them fit your purpose. As you know from Section 1.10, our patterns have optional features that provide points of controlled variation. We have tried to provide maximum depth in the patterns, so it is quite likely that the patterns contain elements you may not need. Even if these elements are removed, it's nice to know that the "hooks" are there for them to be added later if necessary.
- Apply (instantiate) the pattern. This is perhaps the most complex step. There are two options that you may consider (we'll look at these in detail in the next section).
  - *Translation:* this simply involves using the adapted pattern as is. Archetypes in the pattern become analysis classes. You may choose to subclass the archetypes if necessary.
  - *Mapping:* this involves mapping the pattern into the domain language of your specific problem. For example, if you are using the Inventory archetype pattern but applying it to a schedule of train journeys, it might make sense to use terms such as Schedule rather than Inventory. Note too that a single analysis class in your model may realize *one or more* archetypes.
- Add to the instantiated pattern. You may need features that we don't provide or discuss. Feel free to add your own extensions. However, read the accompanying literate model thoroughly *first*—we may well have satisfied your requirement in a way you don't immediately recognize, or we may have given a reason why we *haven't* satisfied your requirement.
- When you are applying this manual process, it is often a good idea to first import the pattern into a temporary package in your analysis model. Once you have adapted the pattern to your specific needs, you can then incorporate it into the main body of your analysis model by moving it to whatever package you feel is appropriate.
- Finally, you can create a literate model for your instantiated pattern, explaining how it differs from the standard archetype pattern and any new features or constraints you have introduced.

This process for using archetype patterns is illustrated in Figure 1.15. As you can imagine, applying this manual process is easy, but it can also be rather tedious and error prone. We discuss an automated approach in Chapter 2.

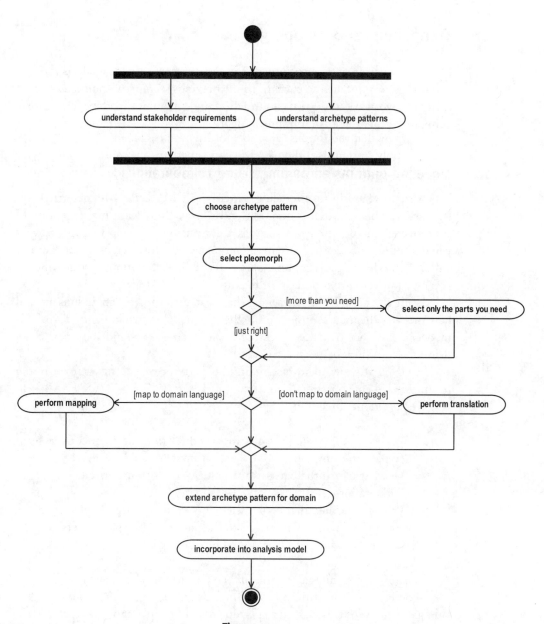

Figure 1.15

1.16 Translation and mapping

In order to use archetype patterns (or other patterns) in your analysis models, you need to instantiate the pattern. In the previous section, we pointed out that there are two ways to do this—translation and mapping. In this section we're going to explore these two options in depth.

1.16.1 Modeling patterns as parameterized collaborations

The basic mechanism for modeling patterns in UML is the parameterized collaboration. This is a useful notation and not at all as fearsome as it sounds! We're using this notation primarily as a convenience to help us explain what you do in the processes of translation and mapping. However, be aware that not all UML modeling tools support parameterized collaborations at this time, so you may not yet have tool support for this.

A simple example illustrates what these parameterized collaborations are and how they may be used. Consider the archetype model shown in Figure 1.16. This model is an archetype pattern because it shows archetypes and the essential semantic relationships between archetypes.

In UML, if we want to instantiate this pattern, we can first turn it into a parameterized collaboration as illustrated in Figure 1.17.

We have done three things.

1. We have encapsulated the classifiers and relationships that constitute the pattern using the UML collaboration icon (a dotted oval).
2. We have named the pattern (the name of the parameterized collaboration).
3. We have specified that certain elements of the pattern are placeholders by naming them as parameters to the pattern in the parameters box of the collaboration icon (the dotted box on the icon).

This formally defines a reusable archetype pattern called Inventory.

In order to use this pattern in your models, you have to instantiate it by providing classifiers (usually classes) to play the roles of the placeholders (parameters). These classifiers must accord with the semantic constraints of the pattern and its parameters.

For example, suppose you needed to instantiate the Inventory archetype pattern for a book inventory system. As we've said, there are two ways you can do this—translation and mapping.

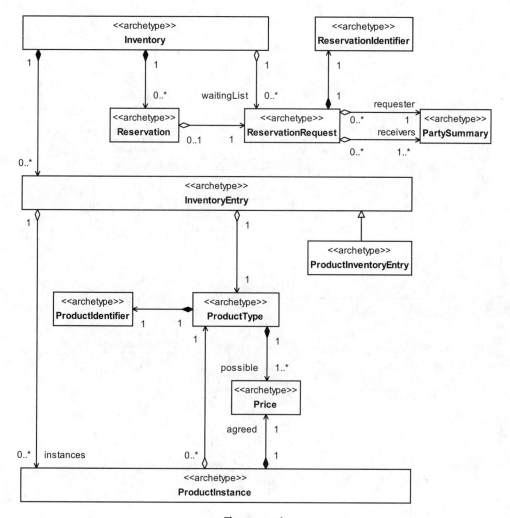

Figure 1.16

1.16.2 Translation

For translation, you just translate the pattern into classes; each archetype simply becomes a class. Translation proceeds as follows.

- Configure the pattern by selecting the optional features you require.
- Copy the archetype pattern into a target package in your model—each archetype in the pattern becomes a class in your target package.

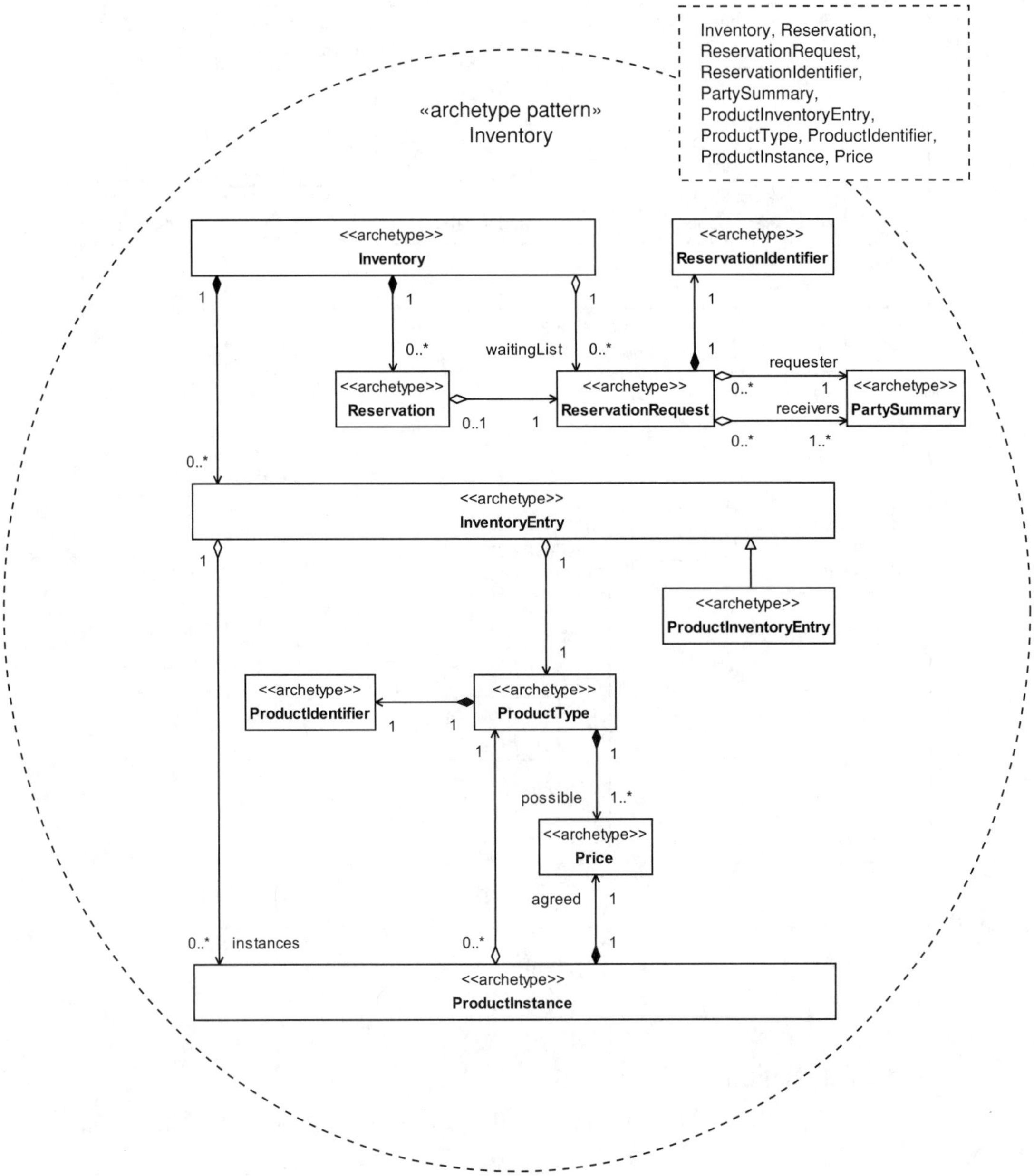
Inventory, Reservation, ReservationRequest, ReservationIdentifier, PartySummary, ProductInventoryEntry, ProductType, ProductIdentifier, ProductInstance, Price
«archetype pattern» Inventory
<<archetype>> Inventory
<<archetype>> ReservationIdentifier
<<archetype>> Reservation
<<archetype>> ReservationRequest
<<archetype>> PartySummary
waitingList
requester
receivers
<<archetype>> InventoryEntry
<<archetype>> ProductInventoryEntry
<<archetype>> ProductIdentifier
<<archetype>> ProductType
possible
<<archetype>> Price
agreed
instances
<<archetype>> ProductInstance
1
0..*
0..1
1..*

Figure 1.17

In this case, your target package has exactly the same structure, down to the detailed model element names, as the archetype pattern. All you are really doing is dropping the «archetype» and «o» stereotypes on the elements you decide to keep!

According to set theory, this is called *isomorphism* (a one-to-one mapping). It is the simplest possible type of instantiation, and it is appropriate in many cases.

1.16.3 Mapping

For mapping, you need to perform a more complex pattern instantiation that is not merely a straight translation. For example, you might want to apply a general archetype pattern to a very specific business domain and use classifier names taken from that domain. Mapping proceeds as follows.

- Select the optional features you require.
- Map each archetype onto one or more classes in your target package. One class in your target package may realize one or more archetypes.

You are creating a *homomorphism* (a many-to-many mapping) between your instantiation and the pattern itself, rather than a straight translation.

Figure 1.18 shows a possible instantiation of the parameterized collaboration of Figure 1.17. We discuss this example in more detail in Section 8.11.

Using the UML parameterized collaboration syntax we can show mapping very clearly. The dotted lines with parameter names on them show you which classes in our target model play the roles of these parameters. Notice the following.

- We have provided classes for each of the parameters, but these classes have names that are more appropriate to the business domain in question.
- We have chosen to simplify the instantiation by allowing one class, BookReservationRequest, to realize two parameters—Reservation-Request and ReservationIdentifier.

Despite these changes, by explicitly instantiating the archetype pattern, you ensure that your domain-specific model has the correct business semantics and is traceable to a fully documented archetype pattern.

Mapping is very useful when you need to map an archetype pattern onto an existing legacy system or onto a commercial off-the-shelf (COTS) package.

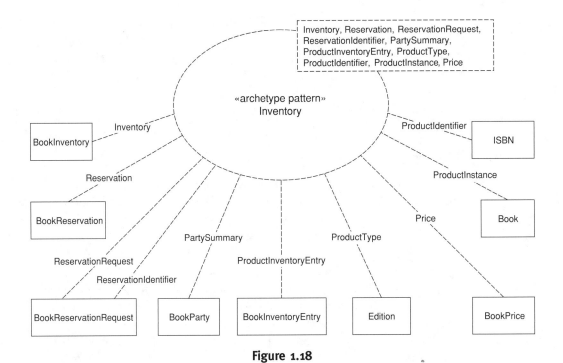

Figure 1.18

1.17 Example applications of archetype patterns

In the next few sections we look at three examples of applying archetype patterns to particular software engineering problems.

- Using archetype patterns for quality: archetype patterns can be used as quality mechanisms in software development, and we explore how to apply them.
- Using archetype patterns with Extreme Programming (XP): although archetype patterns are clearly very useful in model- and architecture-centric software development processes, they also have important applications in lightweight processes, as we describe.
- Archetype patterns and messaging (ebXML): we use the emerging standard of ebXML as a basis to discuss the application of archetype patterns to messaging systems and standards.

1.17.1   Using archetype patterns for quality

One of the problems with object modeling, especially at the analysis and business levels, is that it's quite hard to tell if your models are correct.

This problem may be one of the reasons behind the current popularity of light methods such as XP. After all, if you don't model but jump straight into code, you can get instant feedback about the correctness of that code as soon as you try to execute it. However, this sort of feedback tests only what we call the *micro-correctness* of the system. You might write a component that executes exactly as desired, so that part of the system is correct, but what about the big picture—how does that component fit into the rest of the system?

It is quite possible to assemble a large system that is *incorrect* at the macro level from components that are themselves *correct* at the micro level.

For a good example of this, consider a Lego set. Each individual component is micro-correct, but if, for example, you try to construct a model car, you have to choose the right set of components and stack them up in just the right way to achieve macro-correctness. There are many more arrangements of components that are incorrect than arrangements that are correct, and you can generally achieve macro-correctness only by having some sort of plan, or architecture, in mind.

In fact, XP is predicated on already having an architecture. So XP is not a complete method in itself because there is always the question, "Where does the architecture come from?" As we point out in the next section, business archetype patterns may provide a very agile way to create at least the logical aspects of this architecture.

In our view, the most plausible way to achieve macro-correctness of a system is by modeling, but you are then back to the question of how you know that your models are correct.

There are lots of standard ways to test the correctness of a model, and you can find a good discussion of these in [Arlow 2001]. The essential technique is to apply dynamic modeling—creating use case realizations to illustrate how the static model supports the required system behavior as specified by the use cases.

It is also possible to use archetype patterns as a powerful way to check the correctness of a model, even in the very early stages of modeling. There are two ways you can use archetypes as part of your quality assurance process.

1. Use archetype patterns explicitly: analyze your system looking for specific places where you can apply archetype patterns. Instantiating archetype patterns in your model can help you create a model that is correct and has well-understood semantics. If your system doesn't seem to need

any of the archetype patterns presented in this book, perhaps you should query that! It may be a very unusual system, or perhaps you are missing an opportunity for reuse.

2. Use archetype patterns implicitly: if you are working on an existing model that has *not* been constructed from archetype patterns, you should look for and be able to find parts of the model where an archetype pattern could have been applied. You might say that this part of the model contains implicit archetype patterns. Comparing the implicit archetype patterns of your model with the explicit archetype patterns described in this book may help you substantially improve your model.

So you may use archetype patterns in these two ways—explicitly, as templates to ensure that you achieve at least some degree of macro-correctness in your models, and implicitly, as a basis for the evaluation of something you have already created.

1.17.2 Using archetype patterns with Extreme Programming

XP is a lightweight methodology that focuses on coding. As such, it can be very appropriate for small systems that have to be delivered rapidly.

XP arose to some extent out of the need to deliver software in "Internet time"—that is, quickly. Unlike a completely general purpose methodology, such as the Rational Unified Process (RUP), XP is code intensive and is really suited only to a small and very specific class of software development problems. Nevertheless, XP is a popular methodology, so in this section we'd like to show you how business archetypes can support the key values of XP and also provide a major input to the process.

XP has four key values that are sufficiently general that virtually everyone can agree with them.

1. Communication: promote free discussion without fear of reprisal.
2. Simplicity: choose the simplest design, technology, algorithms, and techniques that will meet the user requirements.
3. Feedback: use code testing, customers' stories, pair programming, code reviews, and so on.
4. Courage: be brave enough to do what is right.

As you will see in Chapter 3, literate modeling with business archetypes shares all of these key values but with a very different emphasis—XP is code-centric but literate modeling is model-centric.

XP also has twelve practices.

1. Planning game
2. Small releases
3. Simple design
4. Testing
5. Continuous integration
6. Refactoring
7. Pair programming
8. Collective ownership
9. Forty-hour workweek
10. On-site customer
11. Metaphor
12. Coding standards

We can't really discuss all of these practices here; otherwise this would be a book about XP! However, if you are interested, there are several good books on XP. We recommend *Extreme Programming Examined* [Succi 2001] as a good reference. You can (as always) find more information on our Web site, www.businessarchetypes.com.

The XP best practices that directly relate to business archetypes are simple design, refactoring, and metaphor.

The idea behind simple design is to keep the code simple. Fair enough! However, there are actually two aspects to this: the simplicity of the code itself, and the simplicity of the business semantics that the code realizes. One criticism of a code-centered approach is that while the code may be simple, it may realize complex or even incorrect business semantics, as we've seen many times in practice. This is because source code is actually a very difficult, inefficient, and expensive way to explore business semantics.

The XP practice of refactoring is a way to change source code so that it is simpler—but refactoring code is one thing, and refactoring twisted business semantics is another. Code refactoring is generally relatively easy, relatively quick, and not too expensive. However, refactoring business semantics is an altogether different matter—it is usually complex, time consuming, and very costly. You can see that even the XP developer needs to understand the business semantics before diving into code.

This brings us to the practice of metaphor. In the XP book we mentioned above, one of the authors states, "This is the real gap in XP, and one that the XPers need to sort out" [Succi 2001, p. 15]. And this is exactly where you may find that business archetypes and literate modeling can really help your XP project.

The typical dictionary definition of a metaphor is "an expression in which a word or phrase that usually denotes one kind of object or idea is used to denote another, thus making an implicit comparison between them." However, XP seems to assign a slightly different meaning to the word *metaphor*.

In XP terms a metaphor is a common language and set of terms used to envision the functionality of a project. There is not necessarily the element of substitution of one idea with another different idea that is the essence of the dictionary definition. In fact, when XP programmers talk about metaphor, they are often really talking about the domain language—the language used by people operating in a particular business domain. Sometimes, when there seems to be no preexisting domain language or that language has not been uncovered through analysis, XP does indeed substitute an existing, known domain language (a true metaphor), but generally, such a substitution is neither necessary nor desirable.

To take a specific example, if your software system needs to work with orders, and your users understand the concept of orders, XP (one hopes) would not then create a metaphor comparing orders to something different—for example, a metaphor comparing order processing to an assembly line—merely because the programmers are already familiar with assembly lines.

Business archetype patterns provide a common and indeed archetypal language and set of terms for describing generalized business systems. Using the XP definition of metaphor, archetype patterns and their associated literate models should provide ready-made metaphors for many XP projects. If developers and customers can understand and agree on the semantics of the archetype patterns by jointly studying existing patterns and perhaps even creating their own patterns and associated literate models, the XP project has its metaphor in a detailed and structured form.

The ideal situation for any XP project would be to take the metaphor off the shelf, customize it for the specific project, and then use it as the basis for launching into code. And this is exactly the capability that we're beginning to put in place with this book.

In fact, we have often argued that XP is not nearly extreme enough! What you really need to do is to dispense with the expensive, time-consuming, and error-prone activity of coding as much as possible. In Chapter 2, we'll show you how you can get *really* extreme by using archetype patterns with a suitably enabled MDA modeling tool.

To summarize, although business archetypes and literate modeling are model-centric and XP is code-centric, you may find that there is a natural match between the two approaches. We think that there are great possibilities for the application of business archetypes and their literate models in the communication and metaphor aspects of XP.

1.17.3 Archetype patterns and messaging (ebXML)

In messaging, business systems communicate with each other electronically by sending and receiving packages of information called messages. In order for messaging to work between systems, they must agree on common standards for:

- The representation of the message itself (e.g., XML)
- The protocols used to send and receive the messages (e.g., SOAP, HTTP)

But this is still not sufficient. The systems must also be able to make sense of the information they receive. In order to achieve this they must share a common agreement on the meaning of the contents of the message.

For example, if system A sends system B a message containing information about a customer, both systems must share some common understanding of the thing "customer" in order for the communication to be meaningful. This common understanding is often referred to as a *common ontology.*

An ontology is an explicit and formal specification of how to represent things of interest. Clearly, archetype patterns constitute ontologies, and as such, they have important applications in the area of messaging.

In order to explore this, we will take a brief look at the relationship between archetype patterns and a specific messaging standard called ebXML.

ebXML is a framework of specifications designed to enable businesses to collaborate electronically using technologies based on XML. You can find out more about ebXML in *Professional ebXML Foundations* [Chappell 2001] or on the ebXML Web site (www.ebxml.org).

The goal of ebXML is to enable XML to be used effectively in business environments. ebXML is likely to become an important standard, possibly replacing existing standards for electronic business such as EDIFACT.

ebXML is the result of a specific project between the United Nations Centre for Trade Facilitation and Electronic Business (UN/CEFACT) and the Organization for the Advancement of Structured Information Standards (OASIS), a not-for-profit consortium that builds and maintains XML-based standards for business interoperability. When the project was completed in summer 2002, it became clear that *much* more work needed to be done in just about every area of the specification. This work has been divided between the two project participants. OASIS is working mostly on technical infrastructure (see www.oasis-open.org) and UN/CEFACT on business processes and core components (see www.uncefact.org). The work is ongoing.

One of the key ideas in ebXML is that of *core components*. These are fragments of XML schemas that may be combined in many different ways to create various electronic documents that can be exchanged in business-to-business (B2B) and customer-to-business (C2B) communications. These core components are modeled in UML. XML document type definitions (DTDs) or schemas are then generated from these UML models.

Although at first glance there may appear to be similarities between ebXML core components and archetype patterns, the two things are for very different but complementary purposes, and you should keep this clearly in mind when comparing and contrasting the two.

The primary difference is that archetype patterns define PIMs (see Chapter 2) for creating software systems, while ebXML defines the structure of messages *sent between* software systems (in fact, the ebXML consortium members explicitly state that they do not address the internal structure of software systems).

So, although ebXML and archetype patterns are different, they often model the same underlying business semantics, albeit for completely different purposes and from different points of view. Because of these common semantics the two systems of patterns can be related through model transformation.

In fact, the business messages flowing between software systems are merely a specific transformation of the information represented inside those systems. The source and target systems have to be semantically congruent in order to be able to process those messages. For example, if a message sent between two systems contains something called an order, there has to be some notion of an order in both the source and target systems.

However, a software system can *never* be considered to be merely a simple transformation of its externalized messages—it always has more complexity and richness, as well as deeper semantics. From an information theoretical perspective this *must* be the case because the software system *generates* and *processes* messages. Archetype patterns capture aspects of these deep semantics of software systems, whereas ebXML core components capture the weaker semantics of possible interactions between those systems.

In our view, it is a mistake to try (as some organizations have already tried) to use ebXML core components as a basis for software systems. This is not what they were designed for.

Archetype patterns *are* designed specifically for software systems, and you can easily generate ebXML messages as simplified views of underlying archetypes and patterns, often just by filtering information.

In summary, archetype patterns are designed to be compatible with ebXML, and we believe that the two technologies are very complementary. Archetype patterns give you the semantics of the underlying business systems, while ebXML gives yu the semantics of messages that can pass between those systems.

1.18 Summary

In this chapter we introduced archetypes and archetype patterns. We covered the topics listed below.

- Archetype: a primordial thing or circumstance that recurs consistently and is thought to be a universal concept or situation.
  - First described by the psychologist Carl Gustav Jung.
  - An ordering and structuring principle of the collective unconscious.

- Business archetype: a primordial thing that occurs consistently and universally in business domains and business software systems.
  - In the book we may refer to these simply as *archetypes* for short.
  - There are certainly archetypes in other domains apart from business.

- Business archetype pattern: a collaboration between business archetypes that occurs consistently and universally in business environments and software systems.
  - In the book we may refer to these simply as *archetype patterns* for short.

- Characteristics of archetypes and archetype patterns:
  - Universal: for something to be archetypal, it must occur consistently in business domains and systems.
  - Pervasive: it occurs in both the business domain *and* the software domain.
  - Deep history: for example, the product archetype pattern has been around ever since people first began to barter and sell.
  - Self-evident to domain experts: this is not always the case, but if an archetype isn't obvious to a domain expert, you should certainly question whether it is really an archetype.

- Archetypes and analysis classes:
  - Archetypes are *always* at a higher level of abstraction than normal analysis classes.
  - Archetypes are about consciously recognizing and capturing *universal* concepts.
    - Analysis classes are not necessarily concerned with universality.

- Pattern: a solution to a problem in a context.
  - A pattern consists of a description of a problem, the context of the problem, and a possible solution to that problem in that context.
  - A pattern is a "recipe" that describes how you may solve a particular problem under particular circumstances.

- The idea of patterns originated in the work of Christopher Alexander on the architecture of towns and buildings.
- A design pattern has four elements:
  - Pattern name: the name of the pattern.
  - Problem: the description of the problem that the pattern solves.
  - Solution: the design of the pattern itself as a UML model.
  - Consequences: the effects of applying the pattern.
- Patterns can occur at different levels of abstraction:
  - Archetype patterns.
  - Analysis patterns.
  - Design patterns.

- Archetype patterns differ from analysis patterns.
  - Archetype patterns model archetypes and relationships between archetypes, not analysis classes and their relationships.
  - Archetype patterns explicitly allow variation.
    - Some parts of the pattern are optional when the pattern is adapted to a specific business domain.
  - An archetype pattern is a special type of platform-independent model (PIM) that describes a *set* of possible PIMs (i.e., it is a meta-PIM).

- UML profile for archetypes and archetype patterns:
  - «archetype»:
    - This stereotype applies to classes.
    - It is a primordial thing that occurs consistently and universally in business environments and business software systems.
    - All archetypes in a business archetype pattern are optional.
  - «archetype pattern»:
    - This stereotype applies to collaborations and packages.
    - It is a collaboration between business archetypes that occurs consistently and universally in business environments and software systems.
  - «archetype pattern library»:
    - This stereotype applies to packages.
    - It is a subtype of the standard UML stereotype «model».
    - The package is a model that contains one or more archetype patterns.
    - We recommend that you use your domain name as the name of the package (e.g., clearviewtraining.com).
  - «o»:
    - This stereotype applies to compositions, aggregations, attributes, and operations.

- A feature is optional and may be omitted. When «o» is applied to a composition or aggregation relationship, it indicates that the relationship is optional.
  - «pleomorph»:
    - This stereotype applies to refinement relationships.
    - The archetype pattern at the source of the arrow is a variation (pleomorph) of the archetype pattern that is at the target end of the arrow.
- Modeling style:
  - Goals:
    - Make the models as readable as possible.
    - Make the models as useful as possible.
    - Make the models as precise as possible.
    - Make the diagrams fit harmoniously within the bounds of this book.
  - Style:
    - We usually don't show set and get methods for attributes.
    - We indicate that an attribute, operation, composition, or aggregation relationship is truly optional by using the stereotype «o».
    - Archetypes are always optional.
    - Everything that is not explicitly optional is mandatory.
    - We always show multiplicity explicitly.
      - When multiplicity is not shown on models it means that it is *undecided*—it does *not* default to 1.
    - We try to refine each association relationship as much as we can.
    - Principle of maximum utility: we consciously strive to make the diagrams and text as useful as possible.
    - We use OCL data types.
      - Real: represents the mathematical concept of a real number.
      - Integer: represents the mathematical concept of a whole number.
      - String: OCL says "an ASCII string of characters"—we assume a Unicode string.
      - Boolean: represents a value that is true or false.
- Variation:
  - Principle of variation: different business domains often seem to require different models of the same thing.
  - Archetype variation:
    - You can add new features.
    - You can omit optional features.
    - The core semantics of the archetype remain fixed for all variants.

- Archetype pattern variation:
  - Pattern configuration: taking only those parts of a pattern that you need.
  - Pleomorphism: the adaptation of an archetype pattern to a specific business context by a modification of its form such that its essential semantics remain unchanged.
    - Pleomorphs exhibit semantic conformance—they have common business semantics.

- Finding archetype patterns:
  - You need a detailed knowledge of the business domain of interest.
  - Different companies may have only a partial view of a broad domain such as "selling."
  - Software systems can act as perceptual filters by presenting a domain in a distorted or specialized way.
  - Sources of archetype patterns:
    - Domain expert interviews:
      - Seek experts with a broad and deep knowledge of the domain.
      - Ask open rather than closed questions.
      - Look for fundamental concepts.
    - Literature:
      - You may need to generalize if the source is specific to your organization.
    - Models—both data and object models:
      - Generalize to an archetypal case from what might be a specific business solution.

- Model management for archetype patterns:
  - Place each archetype pattern in its own package stereotyped «archetype pattern».
    - This package should be named after the key, or central, archetype in the pattern.
  - Create a package stereotyped «archetype pattern library» that contains all of your archetype patterns.
    - Use your domain name as the name of the package.
  - As appropriate, group archetype patterns into sublibraries within your main archetype pattern library.
    - Name each sublibrary according to an aspect of your business domain (e.g., Marketing, Manufacturing, and ResourceManagement).
  - Create a literate model for the archetype patterns.

- Using archetype patterns in models:
  - Prerequisites:
    - Understand the patterns.
    - Understand your business requirements.
  - Application:
    - Choose an appropriate pleomorph.
    - Select what parts of the pattern to use.
    - Apply (instantiate) the pattern in one of two ways:
      - Translation (isomorphism): use the pattern as is.
        - Each archetype becomes a class in your analysis model.
      - Mapping (homomorphism): map the pattern into the domain language of your specific problem.
        - Each archetype maps to one or more classes in your analysis model.
    - Add to the instantiated pattern.
    - Incorporate into your analysis model.

- Using archetype patterns for quality:
  - Micro-correctness: correctness at the component level but not at the system level.
  - Macro-correctness: correctness at the system level.
  - Use archetype patterns explicitly.
    - Apply archetype patterns where possible.
    - This helps you create a model that is macro-correct.
  - Use archetype patterns implicitly.
    - Compare parts of your model with relevant archetype patterns.
    - This helps you understand any limitations in your model.

- Using archetype patterns with XP:
  - Simple design: archetype patterns help XP programmers create code that is both simple and semantically correct.
  - Refactoring: archetype patterns help programmers get it right the first time, reducing costly refactoring.
  - Metaphor: archetype patterns provide "off the shelf" metaphors for XP.
    - The XP definition of metaphor is a common language and set of terms used to envision the functionality of a project—this is *not* the dictionary definition of metaphor.

- Archetype patterns for messaging:
  - For messaging between systems you need:
    - Common representation for the message (e.g., XML).

- – Agreed protocols (e.g., SOAP).
- – Common ontology: a common understanding of the things in the messages.
  - • Archetype patterns can provide common ontologies.
- ebXML: a messaging standard.
  - – Core components: schema fragments that can be combined in many different ways to create different messages.
    - • It is fine to use these for messages but not for software systems.
    - • Use archetype patterns for software systems.
  - – Archetype patterns and ebXML model systems from two complementary perspectives.
    - • Archetype patterns define the structure of software systems.
    - • ebXML defines the structure of the communications between software systems.
- Messages are a transformation of the information embodied in the software system that generates them.

Chapter 2

Model Driven Architecture with archetype patterns

2.1 Introduction

In Chapter 1, we discussed our notion of business archetype patterns and explained how you can use them effectively in your own models.

As you saw, archetypes and archetype patterns provide a language for describing business systems in a general way. Can that language then be converted *automatically* into a specific business system, meeting specific business requirements? We think it can, and in this chapter we will show you how you can begin to automate the use of archetype patterns by using the Model Driven Architecture (MDA) of the Object Management Group (OMG) and a suitably equipped modeling tool. This work moves us very close to the vision of automated software construction from business archetype patterns, which we outlined in the introduction to this book.

We begin with some background on MDA in Section 2.2 and discuss what you need to consider when automating the use of archetype (and other) patterns in Sections 2.3 and 2.4. In Sections 2.5 through 2.9, you'll see how to create configuration rules that describe the set of well-formed configurations of any pattern that exhibits variability.

We also consider a real-world example of archetype pattern automation (Sections 2.10 through 2.14) using the ArcStyler modeling tool from Interactive Objects (www.arcstyler.com). At the time of writing, this example is just a prototype for archetype automation, but it should demonstrate to you that the theory we present here can be realized, quite easily, in practice. Although we use a specific tool in order to give you a concrete example, the principles of archetype pattern automation are quite general and should apply to other MDA-enabled modeling tools.

2.2 Introduction to Model Driven Architecture

In 2001, the OMG launched a new initiative called Model Driven Architecture. You can find out about MDA at www.omg.org/mda and in [Kleppe 2003] and [Frankel 2003]. We provide a brief overview of MDA in this section.

The essence of MDA is that the creation of an executable software architecture should be driven by the formulation of models rather than by manually writing source code. Source code is generated from the models by a compilation step much as machine code is generated from source code. The MDA initiative aims to move software development to a higher level of abstraction.

In order to understand MDA you need to understand the following:

- Models
- Abstraction
- Platform
- Model transformation
- The MDA value proposition

We will look at each of these in the next few subsections.

2.2.1 Models

The OMG defines a model as "a formal specification of the function, structure and/or behavior of a system."[1]

The key point is that the specification must be formal. This means that the modeling elements must have well-defined semantics. A diagram with boxes and lines does not constitute a model unless the boxes and lines all have very clearly defined semantics, as is the case with UML.

Under the OMG's definition, source code can be considered to be a model because it is a formal specification (all coding constructs have precise semantics) and it models executable machine code that is generated from the source code by a compiler or an interpreter. However, in the rest of this chapter we will, for convenience, use *model* to mean a UML model.

---

1. Object Management Group, "MDA Guide Version 1.0.1." Available on-line in October 2003 at www.omg.org/mda.

2.2.2 Abstraction

According to ISO 10746-2, the Reference Model for Open Distributed Computing (RM-ODP), abstraction is "the suppression of irrelevant detail."[2]

A model at a higher level of abstraction has fewer details than a model at a lower level of abstraction.

In MDA, you start by creating a model at a high level of abstraction, which you then transform into models at progressively lower levels of abstraction until you reach source code. This is how models drive the creation of the software architecture.

The whole history of software development has been characterized by a trend toward greater levels of abstraction. The earliest computers were programmed by altering their physical hardware. We then moved to a higher level of abstraction with stored program computers that were programmed in binary. Next came assembler, macro assembler, and the first high-level languages, FORTRAN and COBOL. Nowadays, we program in modern high-level object-oriented (OO) languages such as Java, C#, and C++.

But the basic form and ideas of these "modern" languages were laid down in the 1980s or earlier. So, in truth, none of these languages should be considered *truly* modern.

What's next? Clearly, programming languages can continue to move to higher and higher levels of abstraction and become easier and easier to use. However, this is likely to be an incremental process and probably will not constitute a *radical* shift in the level of abstraction.

MDA proposes an alternative *model driven* approach to software development in which UML models are transformed into source code.

2.2.3 Platform

A platform is an execution environment for models. Remember that in MDA, code can be considered to be a model.

One feature of platforms is that they form platform stacks. One platform runs on top of another. This is illustrated in Figure 2.1, where the model (Java code in this case) executes on the Java 2 platform, which executes on a Java Virtual Machine (JVM), which executes on Windows XP, which executes on a PC. In the figure the base platform is shown as the PC platform. However, you

---

2. Available on-line in October 2003 at www.iso.org.

could drill down even further to the Intel Pentium platform and so on. Ultimately, the bottom-level platform is space, time, and matter.

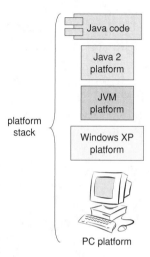

Figure 2.1

One of the problems with platform stacks from the software development perspective is that they are subject to large amounts of churn. Over the last few years we have seen Java 2, Microsoft .NET, and now Web services as possible platforms for software development. If anything, the amount of churn seems to be increasing with new technologies coming along all the time.

In conventional software development the top of the software stack is source code, and this means that in order to move software onto new platforms, you have to port the code. This is horribly expensive and time consuming.

MDA resolves this issue by adding UML models that are at a higher level of abstraction than source code to the top of the stack. These UML models may then be compiled into source code for many different platform stacks, as illustrated in Figure 2.2.

One of the *many* advantages of this approach is that expert platform knowledge can be built into the MDA modeling tool, rather than remaining in the heads of all too few expert software developers. The MDA tool will generate most (or all) of the code for specific platforms from more abstract UML models. However, the MDA tool doesn't just generate code—it will typically also generate documentation, test harnesses, build files, and deployment descriptors where appropriate.

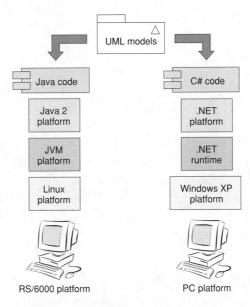

Figure 2.2

The key to making the MDA vision work is model transformation, which we discuss in the next subsection.

2.2.4 Model transformation

MDA generates executable systems by model transformation. This is illustrated in Figure 2.3.

The initial model is a platform-independent model (PIM). This is a model that:

- Represents business functionality undistorted by technology issues
- Is completely independent of any platform stack
- Is a detailed model (usually in UML)
- Is the basis of a platform-specific model (PSM)

The PIM is then transformed into a PSM that has been customized for a particular technology platform, for example, Enterprise JavaBeans (EJBs). The PSM is a model that:

- Contains both business and platform information
- Is created by mapping the PIM to a particular platform stack

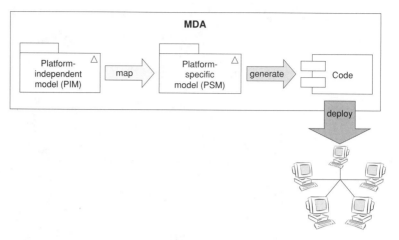

Figure 2.3

- Is a detailed model (always in UML)
- Is the basis of source code and associated artifacts

The PSM is compiled into source code and other artifacts such as deployment descriptors, build files, documentation, and so on.

You can see that MDA separates concerns—the business functionality is represented in the PIM and the platform aspects are represented in the PSM. This makes the PIM reusable over many different platforms, provided that there is a suitable PIM-to-PSM mapping and a PSM-to-code compiler for the target platform.

These two features—separation of concerns through models at different levels of abstraction (the PIM and the PSM) and model transformation—are really the source of all the advantages of MDA. The software engineer is to a large extent freed from platform considerations and can focus on capturing business functionality in the PIM. The MDA tool vendor provides the PIM-to-PSM mapping and PSM compilers that produce expert-level code and related artifacts.

To transform the PIM into the PSM, the MDA developer applies a predefined mapping that requires the developer to specify how each PIM model element should be mapped onto the target platform. For example, should an Account class in the PIM map onto a session EJB or an entity EJB? This sort of decision can't be readily automated and relies on both the business and the platform knowledge of the developer. So MDA doesn't remove the need for platform knowledge entirely. Rather, in MDA the developer needs to know enough about the target platform to specify the desired outcome, and the code for that outcome is automatically generated by the MDA tool.

2.2.5 The MDA value proposition

In MDA, languages such as Java, C#, and C++ become the "machine code" that UML is compiled into. Through this mechanism, UML becomes executable, and the emphasis in software development shifts away from particular languages and deployment platforms to system functionality expressed as UML models. This is why it is called *Model Driven* Architecture.

But why is this a good idea? The thing is, for most of the history of software development, much of the value of a software development project has been delivered as source code. This has several significant disadvantages.

- Code is *often* tied to a particular platform such as Windows XP. So what happens when a new platform comes along, as it invariably will?
- Code is *generally* tied to a specific technical infrastructure such as Java 2. But for some time now, there has been little stability in this area as technologies come and go. This is likely to be true for the foreseeable future, and the rate of change seems to be increasing rather than decreasing.
- Code is *always* written in a specific programming language. But these languages likewise come and go. FORTRAN, Algol, and PL/1 are, for most practical purposes dead; Smalltalk is all but dead; and C++ is giving way to Java and C#. Who knows what will come along in the future?

What this means for the software developer is that value invested in source code tends to depreciate rapidly as the programming language, platform, and technical infrastructure on which the code relies become legacy.

So it seems that source code is not a particularly good repository for value!

These features of code also have an effect on the so-called "agile" methodologies such as Extreme Programming and Agile Modeling. These lightweight methods invariably focus on the creation of source code, and it is therefore ironic that their main deliverable—source code—is itself *not* agile.

In MDA, value is invested in UML models, and the value of a model increases with its level of abstraction. The PIM is the most valuable model; source code is the least valuable model. This is because the PIM provides the basis for the PSM that generates the code. The more abstract PIM is therefore more fundamental and of more value than the less abstract PSM, which in turn is more valuable than the source code. This is illustrated in Figure 2.4.

The «trace» stereotype in the figure is a standard UML stereotype that indicates that the code is traceable back to the PSM, which in turn may be traced back to the PIM.

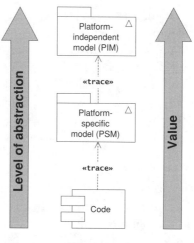

Figure 2.4

The PIM is significantly more agile than source code can ever be because of its platform independence.

You can see that creating a PIM is a crucial first step in the MDA process. But where do you get your PIM? This is where archetype patterns come in.

2.3 Archetype patterns and MDA—creating a PIM

You could create your PIM through a standard process of OO analysis. MDA specifies a computationally independent model (CIM) that is a model of the concepts in the business domain completely independent of any idea of computability. If your company has such a high-level model, it may prove useful as input to the OO analysis and design process.

However, it will always be quicker and easier to generate the PIM by adapting archetype patterns where these are available, as shown in Figure 2.5. Again, if you have a CIM, it may provide valuable guidance to help you choose the most appropriate patterns.

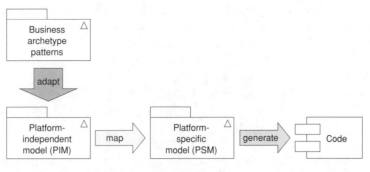

Figure 2.5

You treat archetype patterns as "model components" from which you can construct your PIM. This is the idea of component-based modeling, which we discussed in the introduction to this book. The process of adaptation is simply one of applying the types of archetype variation and archetype pattern variation covered in Sections 1.10 through 1.12, according to your specific business requirements.

For some types of business systems, it may be possible to generate most of the PIM from the archetype patterns presented in this book. However, for other types of systems, either the archetypes may be unexplored or the system may be so particular that no meaningful archetypes can be said to exist for it. This simply means that you fall back onto conventional OO analysis and design strategies.

2.4 Archetype pattern automation

In order to automate the use of business archetype patterns with an MDA-enabled modeling tool, there are several things you need to achieve.

1. Archetype pattern availability: simply prepare the archetype patterns as model files, for example, XML Metadata Interchange (XMI) files or Rational Rose files. You can enter the patterns into your modeling tool from this book or you can check our Web site (www.businessarchetypes.com) for the availability of model files in various formats.
2. Archetype pattern configuration: this involves working out which combinations of optional pattern elements constitute semantically valid pattern configurations.

3. Archetype pattern instantiation: in Sections 1.16.2 and 1.16.3, we discussed two variants on pattern instantiation.

- Isomorphism is where you take the pattern more or less as is—archetypes and their relationships simply become classes and relationships.
- Homomorphism is a more complex mapping where an archetype in the archetype pattern may be mapped onto one or more classes in the pattern instantiation.

In this chapter, we consider only pattern instantiation by isomorphism. Instantiation by homomorphism is also quite straightforward, but it is future work for us.

As you will soon see, each of these steps may be easily accomplished with the ArcStyler modeling tool because of its built-in capabilities for model-to-model transformation. To give you some idea of how easy this can be, the prototype we describe later in this chapter was created from scratch in about 14 days of work.

The key to achieving high levels of archetype pattern automation is step 2—pattern configuration. This involves taking an archetype pattern and configuring it by selecting only those bits you want to use, in such a way that you preserve the semantic correctness of the final configuration. We describe this in detail in the next section.

2.5 Pattern configuration

Any archetype pattern that has optional elements can have many possible instantiations, each of which is a specific combination of all the mandatory features and zero or more of the optional features. We call each of these possible instantiations of a pattern a *pattern configuration* (or just *configuration* for short).

Some archetype pattern configurations are semantically valid, and some are not. We call semantically valid configurations *well-formed configurations*. All other configurations are *ill-formed configurations*. For example, if you are working with the Money archetype pattern, a semantic constraint on the business domain is that all money is expressed in a currency. If, therefore, you want to use the Money archetype from the pattern, you *also* need to include the Currency archetype and the relationship between the two.

When using an archetype pattern in your analysis model, you generally need to limit yourself to those configurations that constitute a semantically well-formed pattern.

In Section 1.15, we discussed instantiating archetype patterns manually and left it entirely up to you, the modeler, to use your judgment to select well-formed pattern configurations. This is usually very straightforward to do provided you know something about the business domain in question!

However, in order to automate the use of archetype patterns using a modeling tool, you need to enable the tool so that it can recognize well-formed and ill-formed configurations. This amounts to enabling the tool with some limited knowledge about the business domain of the archetype pattern.

You can capture the knowledge about the business domain that the tool requires by defining a *pattern configuration rule* (PCR) for each archetype pattern. This rule is a set of invariants (things that must be true) that describes to the modeling tool exactly what constitutes well-formed configurations of that specific archetype pattern, based on the semantics of the business domain.

PCRs may be applied in one of three ways by the tool.

1. The modeling tool *constrains* the user to create only well-formed configurations.
2. The modeling tool *guides* the user toward the creation of well-formed configurations.
3. The modeling tool *validates* configurations created by the user and provides a warning if a configuration is ill formed.

Using the ArcStyler modeling tool, we can realize any or all of these options.

In practice, option 1 is usually far too restrictive—sometimes you may wish to extend an archetype pattern in such a way that you need to start from an ill-formed configuration.

Option 3 works fine but occurs only at the end of the configuration process—it tells you you're wrong once you've done all the work!

In our opinion, option 2 is the ideal solution, with just the right combination of flexibility versus constraint. This is the one we have chosen for the prototype we describe later in this chapter.

A PCR for an archetype pattern may select from a very large set of possible configurations. If an archetype pattern has n optional features, and all of these features are independently variable, then combinatorics tells you that:

$$C_p = 2^n$$

where C_p is the number of possible configurations. You can see that the number of possible configurations increases rapidly with the number of optional features.

However, the optional features of a pattern are generally *not* independently variable. There are two types of dependencies between pattern features.

- Syntactic dependencies: for example, an attribute can't be included in a configuration without its owning class, so all configurations that specify attributes without their owning classes are syntactically ill formed.
- Semantic dependencies: for example, Money is an amount of a Currency, so configurations that include Money but not Currency are semantically ill formed.

Syntactic dependencies arise directly from UML syntax and generate hard constraints on the model that cannot be broken. It's quite feasible for a suitably equipped MDA modeling tool to automatically generate the parts of the PCR that correspond to these constraints.

Semantic dependencies arise from the rules of the business domain. These dependencies generate soft constraints that may be broken under certain circumstances. It is difficult for any modeling tool to automatically generate these soft constraints because the tool would have to contain extensive domain knowledge. It *may* become feasible in the future for a modeling tool linked to a knowledge base to automatically suggest (if not generate) these soft constraints.

There is also another intermediate class of constraints that may be automatically generated provided consistent naming conventions are adopted for classes, attributes, and operations. For example, if the JavaBean naming standard is adopted for attributes and their associated set and get operations, then a tool can automatically infer that an operation called getX() requires an attribute x to be present if such an attribute optionally exists. Notice that naming conventions such as these are *not* enforced by UML.

If C_w is the number of well-formed pattern configurations, then, because of feature dependencies:

$$C_w <= C_p$$

where C_w may be quite small relative to C_p.

You arrive at C_w by defining a PCR for the archetype pattern that selects all the *well-formed* configurations from the set of all *possible* configurations. This PCR has to take into account the hard and soft dependencies between pattern features.

Figure 2.6 illustrates this selection process. On the left side of the figure you can see an archetype pattern that has two optional (configurable) features.

Using the equation $C_p = 2^n$, this variability gives rise to a set of four possible configurations of the pattern (middle of the figure).

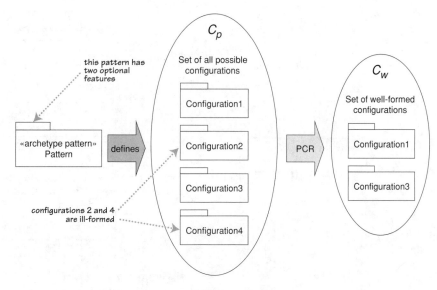

Figure 2.6

You should construct the PCR so that it selects the set of two well-formed configurations from the set of all possible configurations. This gives rise to the set of well-formed configurations shown on the right side of the figure.

2.6 A simple example

For an example, we will use a simplified version of the Money archetype pattern (Chapter 11) that collapses the Quantity and Metric archetypes into Money and Currency, respectively. The reason we are using this simplified Money pattern is purely historical—we began development and testing of our prototype before the Money pattern was finalized.

We'll take a look at a PCR for the fragment shown in Figure 2.7.

Money is defined as an amount of Currency, so the Money archetype depends on the Currency archetype and is incomplete without it. Similarly, Currency needs its Locale.

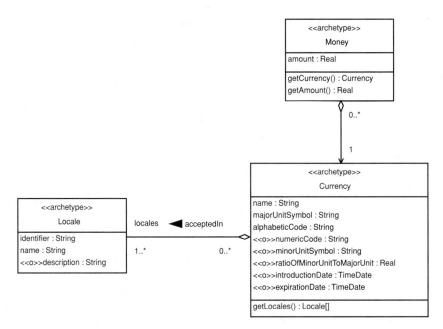

Figure 2.7

These business semantics tell you that *all* valid configurations of the Money archetype pattern must have the following characteristics.

- Any configuration that includes Money *requires* Currency to be included.
- Any configuration that includes Currency *requires* Locale to be included.
- Any configuration that includes any of the optional attributes of Currency *requires* Currency to be included.
- Any configuration that includes description *requires* Locale to be included.
- All the correct semantic relationships between Money, Currency, and Locale must be included.

These statements of fact define the PCR for this fragment of the Money archetype pattern.

In the next section we discuss PCRs in detail and illustrate how you may state them in a formal, machine-readable way that is suitable for use in MDA tools.

2.7   Pattern configuration rules

A PCR consists of a series of statements of truth about what combinations of pattern features constitute well-formed configurations of a specific pattern. By *pattern feature*, we simply mean *any* UML modeling element that is part of the pattern.

As you've already seen, PCRs capture information about the semantic constraints of the business domain in which the archetype pattern operates. In this section, we show you how to construct a formal representation of PCRs.

We would very much have liked to use the Object Constraint Language (OCL) to express PCRs because it is already a part of UML. Unfortunately, at the moment, OCL doesn't give us the support we need for this sort of meta-modeling, and we therefore introduce our own formal language for this purpose. It is called *pattern configuration language* (PCL).

We define PCL as follows:

> PCL is a formal language for expressing well-formedness rules for pattern configurations.

A configuration rule for an archetype pattern consists of a sequence of PCL expressions of the form:

```
f requires (f₁,..., fₙ)
```

In other words, a feature f in the archetype configuration requires the existence of features f_1 to f_n in order for that configuration to be well formed.

There is also the logical negation of the above:

```
f !requires (f₁,..., fₙ)
```

This means that a feature f in the archetype configuration requires the *non-existence* of features f_1 to f_n in order for that configuration to be well formed.

You generally only need this negated rule when there are several optional places for a specific feature but you must locate the feature in just one of these places. You would state this as one `requires` rule positioning the feature and one or more `!requires` rules excluding it from all other optional places.

The whole configuration rule *must* evaluate to `true` for a configuration to be well formed. This happens when every PCL statement in the configuration rule evaluates to `true` because the rule just `AND`s together all of its PCL statements.

The syntax we use for PCRs is summarized in Table 2.1. You can see an example of this syntax in the PCR note in Figure 2.9 in the next section.

Table 2.1

Syntax	Semantics
`requires`	The feature on the left side of the expression requires the existence of the set of features on the right side for the pattern configuration to be well formed
`ClassName`	The name of a class in the pattern
`ClassName::attributeName`	Attribute `attributeName` of class `ClassName`
`ClassName::operationName(p1, p2)`	Operation `operationName` with parameters `p1` and `p2`, of class `ClassName`
`name`	A relationship identifier such as a role name or a relationship name
`path`	If a feature `f1` is in package `p2` and `p2` is itself inside package `p1`, the path to `f1` is `p1::p2`
	Every feature in a PCR needs to be prefixed with a path in order to uniquely locate it in the package hierarchy

The syntax shown in Table 2.1 imposes a reasonable constraint on archetype patterns such that within a specific pattern, each relationship referred to in the rule *must* have a unique identifier. This is either a role name or a relationship name—in our prototype, we always use relationship names.

As well as using the notation just described, we can express PCRs in UML. This has some advantages, as you'll see in the next section.

2.8 Pattern configuration rules in UML

When we use UML to model a PCR, we call it the *configuration model* for that pattern.

There are several ways that you might model a PCR in UML. Taking into account the limitations of the most commonly used UML modeling tools, a pragmatic approach seems to be to extend the UML metamodel by defining some new stereotypes, as shown in Figure 2.8.

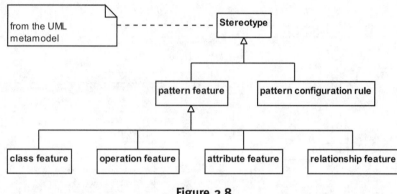

Figure 2.8

The semantics of each of these stereotypes is given in Table 2.2.

Table 2.2

Stereotype	Applies to	Semantics
«pattern configuration rule»	Package	The stereotyped package contains a model that represents a PCR
	Class	The stereotyped class represents a PCR
«pattern feature»	Class	The stereotyped class represents a feature such as a class, operation, attribute, or relationship of a pattern
«class feature»	Class	The stereotyped class represents a class that is part of a pattern
«operation feature»	Class	The stereotyped class represents an operation that is part of a pattern
«attribute feature»	Class	The stereotyped class represents an attribute that is part of a pattern
«relationship feature»	Class	The stereotyped class represents a relationship that is part of a pattern

You can show that one pattern feature requires another to be included by using a dependency relationship stereotyped «requires», as shown in Figure 2.9. Similarly, you may use the stereotype «notRequires» to show that a feature requires another feature to be absent.

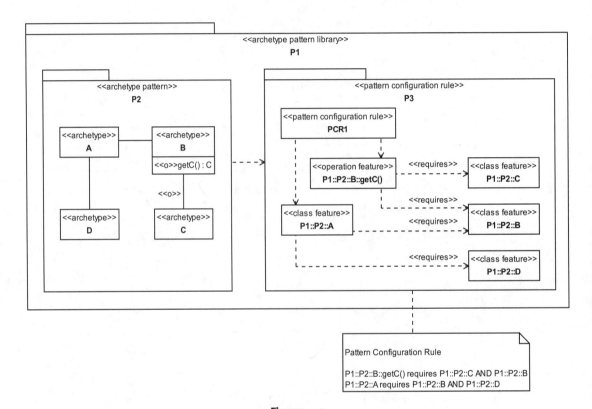

Figure 2.9

The UML syntax we have chosen is straightforward. You can see that the configuration rule is made up of a number of features. Each of these features may depend on a set of other features. The PCR thus has a simple hierarchical structure that is very easy to parse in an MDA modeling tool.

Notice how we have used fully qualified names to specify pattern features. For example, the operation getC() on the class B is specified as P1::P2::B::getC(). The operation name is prefixed by the class name, which is itself prefixed by the names of each containing package in turn.

As you can see, the UML configuration model is reasonably succinct and has the distinct advantage that it may be shipped as part of the same UML model as the archetype pattern. For this reason, we chose to use UML configuration models in the prototype we describe later in this chapter.

2.9 How to create pattern configuration rules

In order to create PCRs, you first need to analyze the pattern to discover which combinations of pattern elements make sense and which combinations do not. This process demands detailed knowledge of the problem domain, so at this time it is not possible to automate it.

You analyze the pattern as follows.

- Look at each class in turn.
  - If the class was included in a configuration, would it necessitate the inclusion of any other features? For example, in the Money archetype pattern, if a configuration contains Money, it must *also* contain Currency.
- Consider the features of each class. You need to consider all attributes and operations. You also need to consider the parameter types and return types of the operations because these can generate dependencies on other classes.
  - Do any of these features imply the existence of other features within the class? For example, in the Money archetype pattern, the Currency archetype has the optional attributes Currency::minorUnitSymbol and Currency::ratioOfMinorUnitToMajorUnit. Clearly, if Currency::minorUnitSymbol exists, we are creating a model of money that can handle minor units (e.g., cents), so we also need to know the ratio of the minor unit to the major unit.
  - Do any of these features imply the existence of features outside of the class? For example, the existence of the operation getExchangeRateType() in ExchangeRate (see Figure 2.13 in Section 2.12) implies the existence of the relationship exchangeRateType.
- Consider the relationships in the pattern. Remember that everything that is not marked as optional is mandatory. If two classes exist, all mandatory relationships between those classes must also exist, and you don't need to state their existence explicitly in the PCR. But if a feature of the pattern implies the existence of an *optional* relationship, you must state this explicitly.

Depending on the size of the pattern, PCRs can be quite complex to draw as UML diagrams. We recommend first writing down the PCR using the simple syntax we described in Section 2.7 and then carefully entering it into your modeling tool.

Because PCRs in UML map directly onto PCRs in PCL it is possible to create a simple utility that reads in PCL syntax and creates a UML version of it automatically. This could save a lot of work—it is much easier to write PCL than to draw a UML model! Perhaps we (or others) will create such a utility at some point.

2.10   Archetype pattern automation with ArcStyler

In the next few sections we will show you how you can enable an MDA modeling tool to support archetype patterns. There are several MDA tools on the market at the moment—see www.omg.org/mda for an up-to-date list. The tool we have chosen for this project is ArcStyler from Interactive Objects (www.arcstyler.com). This tool is currently the best match for our work.

ArcStyler is one of the first modeling tools to fully support MDA. If you browsed to this section and don't know what MDA is, read the brief description in Section 2.2 before continuing with this section. You can also find lots of information about MDA on the OMG Web site (www.omg.org).

ArcStyler extends the Rational Rose UML modeling tool from IBM (www.rational.com) with advanced MDA facilities. From the Rational Rose perspective, ArcStyler is an add-on to Rose. From the ArcStyler perspective, ArcStyler encapsulates Rose. When we talk about ArcStyler in the rest of this chapter, it is always this Rational Rose/ArcStyler combination to which we refer. As we go to press, ArcStyler version 4 is just entering beta testing, and this version of the tool now incorporates its own UML modeler.

As Richard Hubert (CEO of Interactive Objects) has pointed out [Hubert 2001], ArcStyler defines a completely new class of modeling tools that focuses on *model*-centric development in contrast to the more usual *code*-centric development. Hubert calls this class of modeling tools an *Architectural IDE*—an integrated development environment for doing architecture.

Through its support for architectural styles, ArcStyler enables what Hubert calls a holistic approach to architecture, where an architectural style can be applied consistently from high-level business modeling right down to code. You can read *Convergent Architecture* [Hubert 2001] for full details.

The ArcStyler architecture is shown in Figure 2.10.

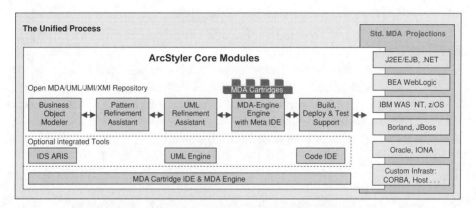

Figure 2.10 (Reproduced by permission of Richard Hubert from *Convergent Architecture* [Hubert 2001])

The steps in ArcStyler development are as follows.

1. Create a business object model (BOM) using the business object modeler. In MDA terms, this BOM is a PIM. Actually, this step is optional; you may bypass the ArcStyler business object modeler and create your PIM directly in Rational Rose. That is what we will do in the example we give in this chapter.
2. The BOM is then transformed by the pattern refinement assistant and by the UML refinement assistant into a PSM in Rational Rose.
   - The pattern refinement assistant applies the convergent architectural style defined in [Hubert 2001] to the BOM.
   - The UML refinement assistant adds platform-specific details to create a PSM.
3. Finally, the MDA-engine generates source code from the PSM. Typically, users of ArcStyler can generate between 80% and 90% of the source code for their projects—and this is very high quality, expert-level code.

From our perspective, the key feature of ArcStyler is that the MDA-engine is not just a code generator but is actually a generalized *model* transformer. It performs model-to-model transformations where (if you think of code as being another type of model) code generation is just a special case.

There are several MDA modeling tools on the market, but it's worth noting that many of them do *not* (as yet) support true UML model–to–UML model transformations. Many are currently limited to UML model–to–code transformations. The ability to perform true model-to-model transformations is essential to pattern automation as we describe it in this chapter.

Another significant feature of ArcStyler is that it has a modular architecture. New architectural styles, code generators, and other model transformers can be added very easily, simply by creating new plug-in cartridges.

Enabling ArcStyler with archetype pattern support involves creating a new ArcStyler cartridge to support archetype patterns and pattern configuration. We'll look at how you can do this next.

2.11 Enabling ArcStyler with archetype patterns

Before we discuss how to enable ArcStyler to support archetype patterns, we need to point out that there are two distinct roles involved in working with these patterns. Our ArcStyler archetype cartridge has to support *both* of these roles:

1. Archetype pattern producer: produces archetype patterns in a specific domain
2. Archetype pattern consumer: uses prepackaged archetype patterns to solve analysis problems

The archetype pattern producer produces archetype patterns and their associated PCRs. The archetype pattern consumer uses the archetype patterns in their UML models. You will see shortly how these roles interact with the ArcStyler cartridge.

The architecture we adopted for archetype automation with ArcStyler is illustrated in Figure 2.11.

The archetype pattern and its configuration model exist in packages in a UML model in ArcStyler. Archetype automation is realized by a special ArcStyler cartridge that has two main features.

1. A pattern configuration GUI: this allows the archetype pattern consumer to select only those elements of the archetype pattern that he or she wants to use. Because the GUI is automatically generated by the cartridge from the archetype pattern *and* from its configuration model, the GUI knows what constitutes a well-formed pattern configuration. It uses this information to guide the archetype pattern consumer to create

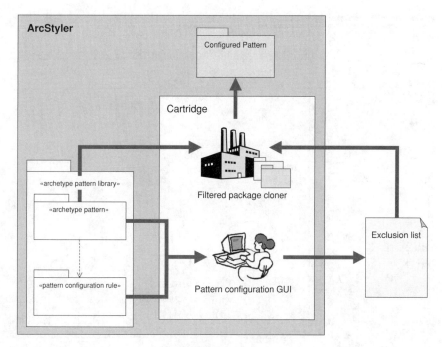

Figure 2.11

well-formed configurations. The output of the configuration GUI is an exclusion list that specifies the pattern features that should *not* be included.

2. A filtered package cloner: this is a simple utility class that traverses a source package hierarchy and copies all elements into a target package hierarchy *except* for those listed in an exclusion list. While the pattern configuration GUI knows about PCRs, the filtered package cloner knows about UML rules. For example, if classes A and B are related by an association a, the package cloner knows that if A is included but B is excluded, the association a must also be excluded. These rules arise from the UML metamodel.

We were able to use ArcStyler itself to implement this cartridge because the architect edition comes complete with a cartridge development environment. Figure 2.12 shows a screenshot of the ArcStyler model for our archetype package.

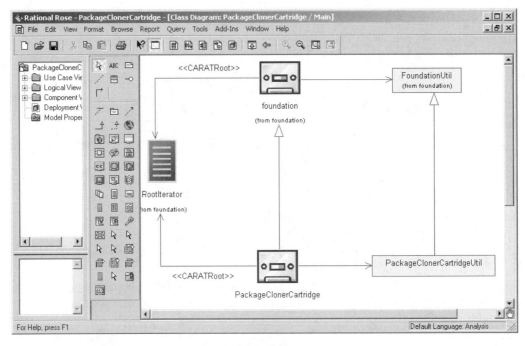

Figure 2.12

We don't want to go into the intricacies of cartridge development here, but just to give you some idea of what's going on, here's a brief overview of what's shown in the figure.

- The icons that look like cassettes are cartridges.
- All cartridges should be subclassed from the foundation cartridge.
- The RootIterator allows your cartridge to traverse the UML model using a simple API.

We are describing the first version of our proof-of-concept prototype, so there are a couple of issues we haven't addressed yet.

- When the pattern consumer modifies the instantiated pattern, the consumer's changes should be preserved if the pattern is then reinstantiated.
- Dependencies of patterns on each other need to be accounted for.

In fact, we already know how to resolve both of these issues and hope to develop solutions at some future date.

2.12   Entering the archetype pattern into ArcStyler

Having put the cartridge in place, the next step is to enter the archetype pattern into Rational Rose.

Figure 2.13 shows our development version of the Money archetype pattern entered into ArcStyler. Over time, we hope to enter all of our archetype patterns into ArcStyler.

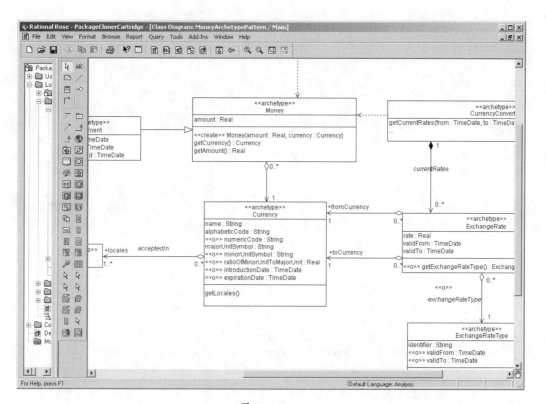

Figure 2.13

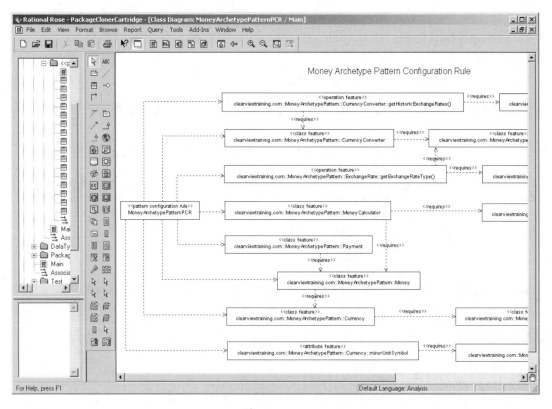

Figure 2.14

The final step is to enter in the PCR using the UML profile we described in Section 2.8. This is shown in Figure 2.14. Again, this is just a partial rule that we use for testing. It is listed in full below.

```
CurrencyConverter::getHistoricExchangeRates()
  requires( historicRates, CurrencyConverter )
CurrencyConverter requires( ExchangeRate )
ExchangeRate::getExchangeRateType()
  requires( ExchangeRate, ExchangeRateType )
MoneyCalculator requires( RoundingPolicy, Money )
Payment requires( Money )
Money requires( Currency )
Currency requires( Locale )
Currency::minorUnitSymbol
  requires( Currency::ratioOfMinorUnitToMajorUnit )
```

Our simple proof-of-concept prototype can process PCRs with hundreds of elements very quickly. In fact, the limiting factor on the size of the PCR (and hence the size of the pattern) seems to be the usability of the generated pattern configuration GUI. In our prototype, this GUI is just a table, so we prefer to work with smaller PCRs to keep things manageable!

2.13 The pattern configuration GUI

The pattern configuration GUI must fulfill the following responsibilities.

- It must allow the archetype pattern consumer to select from the set of configurable features for the archetype pattern.
- It must indicate to the archetype pattern consumer when a selected feature requires one or more other features.
- It must feed information into the package cloner so that the cloner copies only the selected set of features to the target package—this information is in the form of an exclusion list that specifies those features that should *not* be copied.

The pattern configuration GUI for our development version of the Money archetype pattern is shown in Figure 2.15. For our proof-of-concept prototype, we have adopted a very simple table-based GUI. This was quick to program and is very efficient to use. However, other types of GUIs are certainly possible, including tree views of the configurable features and even UML class diagram–based views.

The pattern configuration GUI shown in Figure 2.15 has three columns.

- Include: if this is checked, the configurable feature will be included in the pattern instantiation.
- Configurable feature: this lists all of the optional (configurable) features in the pattern.
- Requires: this tells you what other features a particular configurable feature requires for a well-formed pattern.

As we've said, the GUI uses the PCR to make intelligent suggestions about which configurable features should be included in pattern instantiation.

For example, notice that the feature clearviewtraining.com::Money-ArchetypePattern::Money (the Money archetype) requires the feature clear-viewtraining.com::MoneyArchetypePattern::Currency (the Currency archetype)

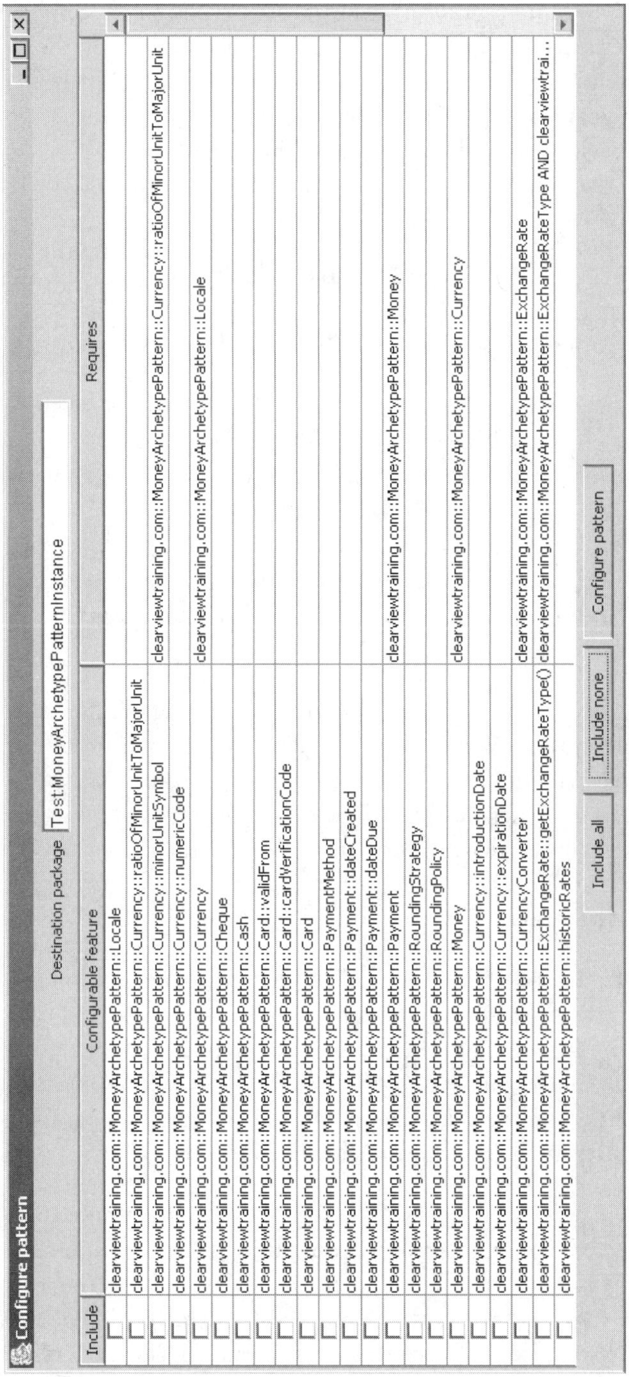

Include	Configurable feature	Requires
☐	clearviewtraining.com::MoneyArchetypePattern::Locale	
☐	clearviewtraining.com::MoneyArchetypePattern::Currency::ratioOfMinorUnitToMajorUnit	
☐	clearviewtraining.com::MoneyArchetypePattern::Currency::minorUnitSymbol	clearviewtraining.com::MoneyArchetypePattern::Currency::ratioOfMinorUnitToMajorUnit
☐	clearviewtraining.com::MoneyArchetypePattern::Currency::numericCode	
☐	clearviewtraining.com::MoneyArchetypePattern::Currency	clearviewtraining.com::MoneyArchetypePattern::Locale
☐	clearviewtraining.com::MoneyArchetypePattern::Cheque	
☐	clearviewtraining.com::MoneyArchetypePattern::Cash	
☐	clearviewtraining.com::MoneyArchetypePattern::Card::validFrom	
☐	clearviewtraining.com::MoneyArchetypePattern::Card::cardVerificationCode	
☐	clearviewtraining.com::MoneyArchetypePattern::Card	
☐	clearviewtraining.com::MoneyArchetypePattern::PaymentMethod	
☐	clearviewtraining.com::MoneyArchetypePattern::Payment::dateCreated	
☐	clearviewtraining.com::MoneyArchetypePattern::Payment::dateDue	
☐	clearviewtraining.com::MoneyArchetypePattern::Payment	clearviewtraining.com::MoneyArchetypePattern::Money
☐	clearviewtraining.com::MoneyArchetypePattern::RoundingStrategy	
☐	clearviewtraining.com::MoneyArchetypePattern::RoundingPolicy	
☐	clearviewtraining.com::MoneyArchetypePattern::Money	clearviewtraining.com::MoneyArchetypePattern::Currency
☐	clearviewtraining.com::MoneyArchetypePattern::Currency::introductionDate	
☐	clearviewtraining.com::MoneyArchetypePattern::Currency::expirationDate	
☐	clearviewtraining.com::MoneyArchetypePattern::CurrencyConverter	clearviewtraining.com::MoneyArchetypePattern::ExchangeRate
☐	clearviewtraining.com::MoneyArchetypePattern::ExchangeRate::getExchangeRateType()	clearviewtraining.com::MoneyArchetypePattern::ExchangeRateType AND clearviewtrai...
☐	clearviewtraining.com::MoneyArchetypePattern::historicRates	

Configure pattern

Destination package Test:MoneyArchetypePatternInstance

Include all   Include none   Configure pattern

Figure 2.15

and this in turn requires clearviewtraining.com::MoneyArchetypePattern::Locale (the Locale archetype). Selecting Money in the GUI (shown by the circled check box in Figure 2.16) automatically selects the required features, Currency and Locale (the other two checked boxes).

However, the pattern configuration GUI only makes suggestions. If you really wanted to, you could deselect Currency and Locale, even though this might lead to an ill-formed pattern configuration.

Pressing the Configure pattern button instantiates the configured archetype pattern into the destination package Test:MoneyArchetypePatternInstance. The result for the configuration selected in Figure 2.16 is shown in Figure 2.17.

2.14 Generating source code

In MDA, code generation is a compilation phase much like generating Java byte codes from Java source code, and each MDA tool has its own particular code generation facilities. As such, we don't spend a lot of time on it here.

However, it's worth pointing out that when we say *code generation* we don't mean just source code for the UML model elements; we also mean deployment descriptors, build files, test harnesses, documentation, and other development artifacts. This is one of the big advantages of MDA—many of the other development artifacts that are time consuming to produce can be automatically generated.

Before you can generate code, you always need to annotate the instantiated pattern in some way to add platform-specific information to turn the PIM into a PSM. How you do this depends on the MDA tool you are using. With ArcStyler, you need to perform the following steps.

1. Apply the convergent architectural style [Hubert 2001]. This partitions the classes in the model into organizations, processes, and resources. This style indicates to ArcStyler how it should interpret the classes when it generates code.
2. Load a technology projection (e.g., a technology projection for BEA WebLogic or .NET). This adds "slots" to the classes in the PIM where you can record platform-specific information.
3. Annotate the PIM with platform-specific information to create a PSM. You must decide how the PIM elements map onto the target technology. For example, for EJBs, what persistence model do you use, bean managed or container managed? In ArcStyler the PSM is *not* a separate

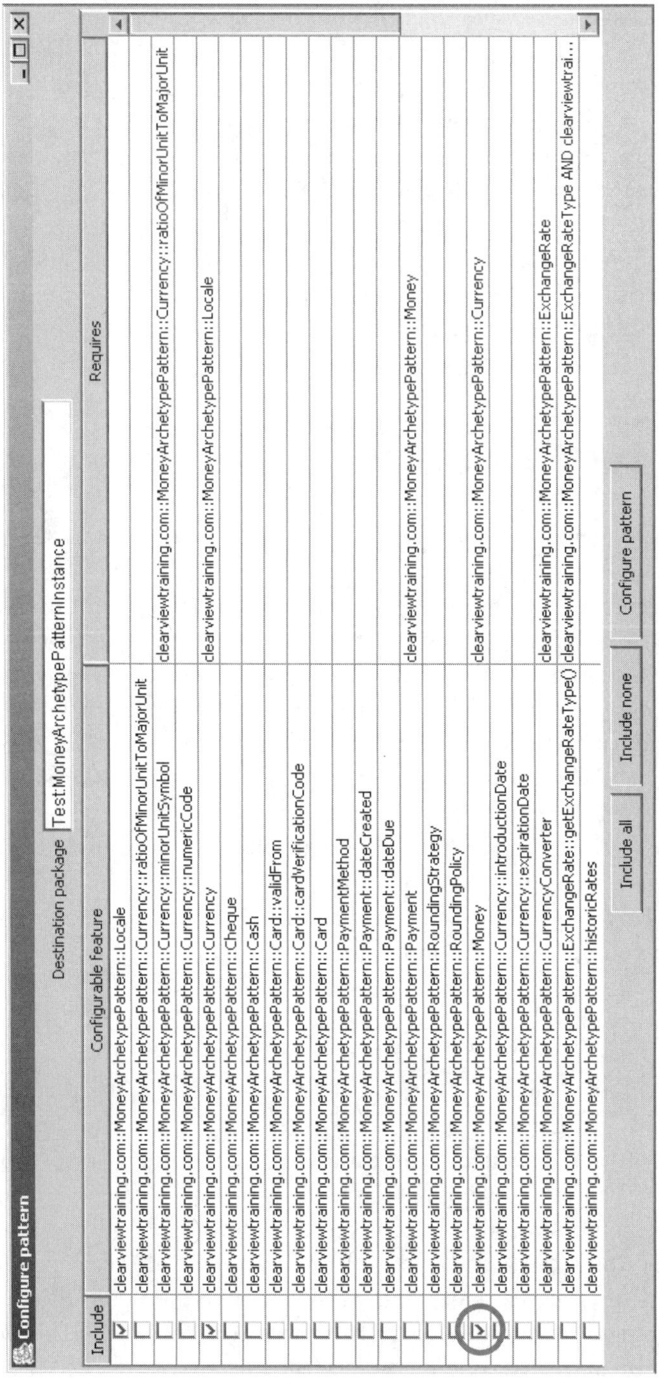

Figure 2.16

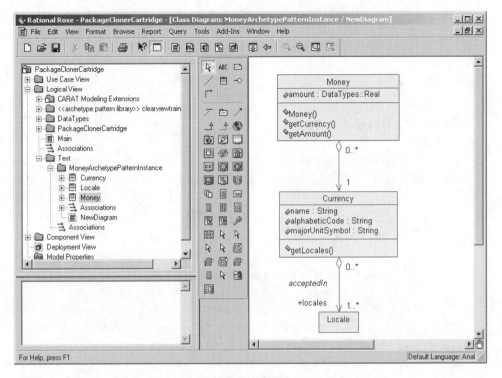

Figure 2.17

model; it is just the PIM with a specific technology projection and annotations. This is sometimes referred to as an *implicit PSM*. It can make
model management easier because there is only the PIM to manage.

4. Generate the code. ArcStyler generates source code, deployment descriptors, test harnesses, and documentation.

5. Edit the code to add business logic. ArcStyler doesn't generate all of the
source code, and you still have to add some code manually in protected
areas. Each time you regenerate, all changes you have made to the protected areas are preserved.

See [Hubert 2001] or www.arcstyler.com for a detailed description of code
generation with ArcStyler. Other MDA tools have different approaches to code
generation, and you should refer to the documentation for whatever tool you
are using for full details.

The advantage of generating code early in the MDA development process is that you can validate your UML models as you construct them and can see how the archetype patterns work and interact.

2.15 Summary

In this chapter we introduced pattern configuration using pattern configuration rules and looked at how the use of archetype patterns can be automated by using a suitably equipped Model Driven Architecture (MDA) tool. We covered the topics listed below.

- Model Driven Architecture:
  - An initiative by the Object Management Group (OMG).
  - Intent: to move software development to a higher level of abstraction.
  - Key concepts:
    - Model: a *formal* specification of the function, structure, and/or behavior of a system.
      - Source code can be considered to be a model.
      - In this chapter we use *model* to mean a UML model.
    - Abstraction: the suppression of irrelevant detail.
      - Each generation of programming languages has historically moved source code to a higher level of abstraction—this will continue but will probably be incremental rather than radical.
      - MDA proposes an alternative *model driven* approach to software development in which models at a high level of abstraction are transformed into models at progressively lower levels of abstraction until you reach source code.
    - Platform: an execution environment for models (including code).
      - Platforms form platform stacks—these are subject to increasing levels of churn.
      - Because source code is at the top of the stack, we have to port code in order to move software onto new platforms.
      - MDA adds UML models at a higher level of abstraction than source code to the top of the stack.
        - Source code for many *different* platform stacks can be generated by an MDA modeling tool from these models.
        - Expert platform knowledge can be built into the MDA tool rather than remaining in the heads of expert software developers.

- Model transformation: the transformation of one model into another model, usually at a different level of abstraction.
  - MDA generates executable systems by model transformation— platform-independent model (PIM) to platform-specific model (PSM) to code.
  - A PIM has the following characteristics.
    - It represents business functionality undistorted by technology issues.
    - It is completely independent of any platform stack.
    - It is a detailed model (usually in UML).
    - It forms the basis of the PSM.
  - A PSM has the following characteristics.
    - It contains both business and platform information.
    - It is created by mapping the PIM to a particular platform stack (e.g., Enterprise JavaBeans).
    - It is a detailed model (always in UML).
    - It forms the basis of source code and associated artifacts.
  - Transformation to code:
    - The PSM is compiled into source code in the target language for the target platform.
    - The MDA tool also generates documentation, test harnesses, build files, and deployment descriptors.
- MDA value proposition:
  - Code has several disadvantages.
    - Code is often tied to a particular hardware platform.
    - It is generally tied to a specific technical infrastructure (e.g., J2EE).
    - It is always written in a specific programming language.
    - Value invested in source code tends to depreciate rapidly as the programming language, platform, and technical infrastructure become legacy.
    - Code isn't "agile."
  - In MDA the value of a model increases with its level of abstraction.
    - The PIM is more fundamental (and therefore more valuable) than the PSM.
    - The PSM is more valuable than the code (which is generated on demand).
- Where do you get your PIM?
  - Use the normal process of object-oriented analysis.
  - Use archetype patterns when they are available.
    - This is a great time saver!

- Archetype pattern automation:
  - Get the pattern into your modeling tool.
  - Configure the pattern by selecting only those bits you want to use.
  - Instantiate the pattern:
    - Isomorphism: archetypes and their relationships become classes and their relationships.
    - Homomorphism: an archetype may map to one or more classes, and archetype relationships may collapse into zero or more class relationships.

- Pattern configuration:
  - Any archetype pattern that has optional features may have more than one instantiation.
  - Each possible instantiation is called a *pattern configuration.*
  - Some configurations are semantically valid; some are not.
    - Well-formed configurations are semantically valid.
    - Ill-formed configurations are semantically invalid.
  - A pattern configuration rule (PCR) describes the set of well-formed configurations of a pattern.
    - PCRs may be applied by a modeling tool in three ways:
      - To *constrain* the user to create only well-formed configurations.
      - To *guide* the user toward the creation of well-formed configurations—the best choice!
      - To *validate* configurations created by the user.
    - A PCR may select from a very large set of possible configurations. This set of configurations is limited by:
      - Syntactic constraints: UML syntax generates hard constraints for the well-formedness of a model.
      - Semantic constraints: for example, Money is an amount of a Currency, therefore all well-formed configurations that contain Money must also contain Currency.
      - Constraints based on naming standards: for example, you can check whether the attributes referenced by get and set operations exist.

- Pattern configuration rules:
  - Pattern configuration language (PCL): a formal language for expressing well-formedness rules for pattern configurations.
  - A PCL expression takes one of two forms:

    `f requires (f₁,..., fₙ) or f !requires (f₁,..., fₙ)`

- – f is a pattern feature (i.e., a class, attribute, operation, or relationship).
- – Features are named using path names (e.g., ClassName::attributeName).
- – To reference a feature in a PCR, the feature must be named.
- The rule evaluates to true for well-formed configurations, otherwise it evaluates to false.
- PCRs may be expressed in UML.
  - – This can be parsed by an MDA modeling tool.

- How to create pattern configuration rules:
  - Analyze the pattern as follows:
    - – Look at each class in turn.
      - • If the class was included in a configuration, would it necessitate the inclusion of any other features?
    - – Consider the features of each class.
      - • Do any of these features imply the existence of other features within the class?
      - • Do any of these features imply the existence of features outside of the class?
    - – Consider the relationships in the pattern.
      - • Everything that is not marked as optional is mandatory.
      - • If two classes exist, all mandatory relationships between those classes must also exist, so you don't need to state their existence explicitly in the PCR.
      - • If a feature of the pattern implies the existence of an *optional* relationship, you must state this explicitly.

- Archetype pattern automation with ArcStyler:
  - ArcStyler:
    - – An MDA tool that extends Rational Rose.
    - – An architectural integrated development environment.
  - Software development with ArcStyler:
    - – Create a business object model (BOM); in MDA terms, this is a PIM.
    - – Transform the BOM into a PSM by applying the convergent architectural style.
    - – Transform PSM into code by using the MDA-engine.

- Enabling ArcStyler with archetype patterns:
  - ArcStyler may be extended by adding a cartridge to:
    - Take a pattern and its configuration rule and automatically generate a GUI to allow the user to configure the pattern (the pattern configuration GUI).
    - Create an exclusion list of features to be excluded from the instantiation.
    - Clone the pattern into a target package, excluding features in the exclusion list.
  - ArcStyler itself was used to build the cartridge.
- The pattern configuration GUI:
  - Allows the archetype pattern consumer to select from the set of configurable features for the archetype pattern.
  - Indicates to the archetype pattern consumer when a selected feature requires one or more other features.
  - Feeds an exclusion list into the package cloner so that the cloner copies only the selected set of features to the target package.

- Generating code:
  - In MDA, generated code is just the "machine language" of UML models.
  - Each MDA tool generates code differently.
  - With ArcStyler, you follow these steps.
    - Apply the convergent architectural style.
    - Load a technology projection.
    - Annotate the PIM with platform-specific information to create a PSM.
    - Generate the code.
    - Edit the code to add business logic.
  - Generating code early in the MDA development process allows you to validate UML models as they are constructed.

Part 2
Literate modeling

Chapter 3

Literate modeling

3.1 Acknowledgments

We'd like to acknowledge Dr. Wolfgang Emmerich of University College London and Mr. John Quinn of British Airways for their help in the work we present in this chapter. We initially presented the core ideas of literate modeling in a paper titled "Literate Modelling—Capturing Business Knowledge with the UML" [Arlow 1998] at the «UML» '98 conference.

3.2 Introduction

In this chapter we're going to discuss literate modeling. This is a way to enhance a UML model by embedding it in an easy-to-read narrative. In Sections 3.3 through 3.7, we examine the problems with UML and other visual modeling languages. In Sections 3.8 through 3.18, we look at a solution and describe the specific techniques that allow you to alleviate these problems.

3.3 The problem with visual modeling

UML and other visual models capture valuable information about the business and business systems in a concise, elegant manner, but this information is accessible only to those who understand the visual syntax and semantics of the visual modeling language. In most businesses, the people who know UML are in the minority and so, in a way, the UML model encrypts important business information so that it is accessible only to those few who are "in the know."

There are also other issues with visual models.

- To access the information embedded in a model, you may also need to know how to work a modeling tool. All modeling tools can generate reports, often in HTML format, but you may find these reports difficult to read and navigate. They are (at least in our experience) of limited practical use.
- Unless you are already familiar with the general "shape" of a model, it can be difficult to know precisely where to start, either when reading the model in a modeling tool or when reading a generated report.
- You may find it difficult, and often impossible, to uncover the important business requirements and imperatives that shaped the model and provide its business value. This is true even if you know UML syntax and are comfortable working the modeling tool.

The last point is worth close examination. When key information is taken out of its business context and expressed in UML or some other abstract visual notation, it often becomes invisible. In our paper [Arlow 1998] we call this the *trivialization of business requirements*. We discuss this in detail in Section 3.7.

3.4 A solution—literate modeling

Our solution to the problems outlined in the previous section is to extend the UML model by providing a narrative description that is accessible to many different readers, not just those in the know. This is what we call a *literate model*.

We got the idea for literate modeling from our own experiences of trying to explain complex UML enterprise object models to a wide spectrum of stakeholders. These stakeholders ranged from those with detailed knowledge of UML modeling to those with no knowledge at all.

We call this technique *literate modeling* because it is in some ways similar to literate programming as discussed in [Knuth 1984]. Literate programming tried to make programs more comprehensible by embedding them in an explanatory narrative. Literate modeling essentially tries to do the same thing, but for UML models.

In practice, literate programming, although a very good idea, didn't really take off too well. This was partly because of its reliance on special text-processing tools that were not widely available and partly because programmers generally prefer to write code rather than narrative!

In contrast to this, literate modeling has proven to be *very* popular with those who have tried it. This is because a literate model not only provides a context for a UML model that is otherwise lacking but also helps the modeler do his or her work.

Creating a literate model as part of the process of creating a UML model will actually improve the quality of your thought processes and of your modeling. You will also achieve enhanced communication with both technical and nontechnical stakeholders.

We'll give you specific techniques for literate modeling shortly, but first we're going to take a look at the issues of the comprehensibility and accessibility of UML models in more depth.

3.5 The comprehensibility and accessibility of UML models

In this section we show you our assessment of how well different groups of people involved in a software development project are able to access and comprehend the various types of UML models.

This assessment is based on *experiential* evidence that we have accumulated over many person-years of using the UML in various substantial and mission-critical projects. We first discussed these ideas in [Arlow 1998], and since then we have had many letters supporting these results. We are confident that, although subjective, this assessment is pretty accurate. However, it's a big world, and if you've had other experiences, we'd like to hear from you!

We're going to consider two aspects of UML models, their comprehensibility and their accessibility.

1. *Comprehensibility* is the ability to understand the semantics of the model. Comprehensibility is the key to obtaining business value from UML models, and it is often contingent on accessibility.
2. *Accessibility* is the ability to access the information contained in a UML model.

There are two components to accessibility.

1. The ability to understand UML's visual syntax
2. The ability to drive the modeling tool to navigate around the model

In order to make an assessment of comprehensibility and accessibility, we need to define *who* we are considering and *what* it is they are trying to understand.

For the purposes of this consideration, you can divide stakeholders who could benefit from access to UML models into six broad categories, as shown in Table 3.1.

Table 3.1

Role	Semantics	Type
Nontechnical manager	A project management role Needs only a very high-level understanding of the technical aspects of the project—does not need to have any UML knowledge	Nontechnical
User	Someone who uses the delivered system Does not need to be technical but may have some knowledge of analysis or requirements capture Does not need to have any UML knowledge	Nontechnical
Domain expert	An expert in the problem domain of the project Does not need to have any UML knowledge	Nontechnical
Analyst	A creator of analysis-level UML models	Technical
Designer	A creator of design-level UML models	Technical
Programmer	A creator of source code	Technical

These categories of people can be thought of as very broad roles within the project, and any individual project participant may play more than one of these roles at any point or over time.

We also need to consider the various types of UML models as represented by their diagrams (class diagrams, sequence diagrams, and so on), and how accessible and comprehensible these are to the people in various roles.

Figure 3.1 shows our estimates for the comprehensibility of the main UML artifacts in an analysis-level model. We do *not* consider design models or physical models (deployment and implementation diagrams). This is because our focus in this book is on using literate models to convey business information. It is certainly possible to use literate modeling at more concrete levels of abstraction, but we feel that its main benefit is at the analysis level.

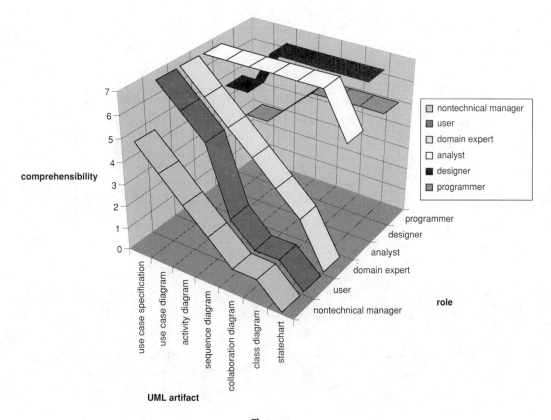

Figure 3.1

For each of our roles, we have rated their comprehension of the various UML artifacts on a scale of 0 to 7. On this scale, 0 means virtually no comprehension, while 7 denotes virtually complete comprehension. We arrived at these estimates based on our private communications with many individuals performing roughly these roles over the course of many different UML projects in many different businesses. The chart is not (and we're not sure it ever could be) quantitative, but as we've already said, we believe that it illustrates the trends in comprehension correctly.

In the next few subsections, we'll look at each of the UML artifacts and their comprehensibility in a bit more detail.

3.5.1 Use case specifications

Considering all roles, use case specifications have the highest overall comprehensibility for the following reasons.

- They are usually written in plain English, so there is no comprehensibility issue arising from a need to know a visual syntax.
- They are often written in a word processor because support for use case specifications in the current crop of modeling tools is generally limited to plain text. There is no accessibility problem because no modeling tool is involved.
- They often feel familiar to non-OO practitioners because they are just descriptions of business processes from the point of view of the actor. It is quite easy to "step inside" the use case specification and role-play in order to enhance understanding.

Despite this high level of comprehensibility, there can still be some problems with use case specifications.

- A use case is a description of a specific business process from the perspective of a particular actor. As such, they typically don't give a clear picture of the *overall* business context and imperatives that generate the need for the business process in the first place.
- Use cases are often written using domain-specific jargon. This means that they can sometimes be quite incomprehensible to people who are not domain experts. As we discuss in [Arlow 2001], there are ways to get around this issue. Because of this need for a certain amount of domain knowledge, the more technical designer and programmer roles may have problems understanding the real business meaning of some use case specifications.
- The business context that gives rise to a set of business requirements is not well captured or explained by use cases or by *any* UML construct.

Unfortunately, UML provides no *formal* mechanism to capture and present important contextual information. You can't easily embed this information in the use case specifications themselves because the business context is generally orthogonal to any particular use case. You can always use notes, free-text annotations to diagrams, and constraints. This isn't a particularly good solution because the notes and free text are distributed throughout the model.

3.5.2 Use case diagrams

UML use case diagram syntax is very simple, and this leads to high levels of comprehensibility, similar to that of use case specifications. However, the following features may cause particular problems:

- Use case generalization
- «include»
- «extend»

Use case generalization is not widely used (unless the parent use case is abstract), largely because its effect on use case specifications can be very complex. See [Arlow 2001] for a discussion of this.

«include» is easy to understand for anyone who has some background in programming, and «extend» can be understood even by nontechnical users if the explanation is clear enough. Again, we refer you to our previous book [Arlow 2001] for the semantics of these relationships.

The main comprehensibility problem is that use case diagrams are semantically very weak. You may find that the real business meaning of a use case diagram is not apparent without detailed explanation or reference to the use case specifications themselves. We have therefore given use case diagrams a lower comprehensibility than use case specifications for the nontechnical roles (i.e., nontechnical manager, user, and domain expert).

The technical roles may not have sufficient business domain knowledge to infer business semantics from the sparse syntax of the use case diagram.

3.5.3 Activity diagrams

One of the nice features of activity diagrams is that you can use them for almost anything! They can model use case flows, business processes, or even the detailed specification of a method. Because we are focusing on the analysis domain, we will consider only two uses for activity diagrams here—modeling use case flows and modeling business processes.

Essentially, activity diagrams are just OO flowcharts. Most people are familiar with flowcharts, so activity diagrams tend to have high levels of comprehensibility. We have positioned them on our chart as having slightly lower comprehensibility for nontechnical roles than use case specifications and use case diagrams because there is significantly more visual syntax to learn for activity diagrams. However, activity diagrams have a high level of comprehensibility for technical roles.

3.5.4 Sequence diagrams

We are now in the realm of object orientation, and comprehensibility falls sharply for non–OO literate participants. We have found that nontechnical managers and users find raw sequence diagrams very difficult to follow because they don't really understand the semantics of object interaction.

Comprehension may be slightly higher for domain experts; people in these roles often have some exposure to object orientation through working with analysts.

If you adorn sequence diagrams with scripts, this will increase comprehensibility markedly for the nontechnical group. But comprehension is now of the script, rather than of the visual syntax, which remains largely obscure.

Because sequence diagrams show the interaction between objects, designers and programmers tend to naturally understand them. However, they might not be so sure about the underlying business semantics that drive the interactions!

3.5.5 Collaboration diagrams

Nontechnical roles typically find these confusing. Unlike sequence diagrams, there is no reasonable possibility for you to adorn them with a script to increase their comprehensibility. We give these a low comprehensibility for the nontechnical audience although, again, comprehension may be higher for the domain expert.

The technical roles find these diagrams both useful and comprehensible.

3.5.6 Class diagrams

For comprehension, these require the following:

- Some basic OO training
- Knowledge of UML syntax
- Ability to use the modeling tool to uncover class and relationship semantics

We have found that comprehensibility of these diagrams is typically very low for nontechnical managers and users. Again, it may be slightly higher for domain experts.

For the technical group, analysts and designers in particular, comprehensibility is very high. Analysts tend to understand the class diagram from the business perspective, while designers often know less about the business, so that their comprehension may be more in terms of OO design issues such as patterns, idioms, APIs, and technical infrastructure.

In many organizations, programmers tend to be more junior than analysts and designers. As such, they may not have sufficient understanding of the business and of UML and OO analysis and design to fully appreciate class diagrams. You may therefore find that programmers' comprehension of many of the key aspects of the UML model is lower than that of analysts and designers.

3.5.7 Statecharts

Statecharts are quite specialized and have a very elegant yet terse syntax that is rarely understood by the nontechnical group. On our scale, comprehensibility is effectively zero for these stakeholders.

Generally, we have found that it is designers, and not all designers at that, who have a good grasp of statecharts.

The problem is that statecharts attempt to capture a dynamic system in a static notation. This obviously makes them quite hard to understand because it is left up to the reader to imagine the dynamic flow between states. This can happen only if the reader understands object interaction semantics.

Statecharts increase in comprehensibility if they can be executed and animated in a modeling tool, but this functionality is still quite rare.

3.6 The problem of comprehensibility

You can see that several important issues arise from the above discussion.

1. Moving through our seven diagrams along the UML artifact axis of Figure 3.1 from use cases to statecharts, the nontechnical group is gradually left behind. The people in those roles lose comprehension as the diagrams become more technical and the emphasis shifts from a focus on business requirements to a focus on the intricacies of implementation.

2. There is a traceability issue. The people in the nontechnical group understand the business requirements best, but they have little comprehension of UML sequence, collaboration, class, and state diagrams. Traceability of high-level requirements to these diagrams therefore relies mainly on the fidelity of the modeling transformations and lacks essential feedback from the nontechnical group.

3. We have found that designers and programmers may have little understanding of the actual business and its needs. You may not be able to rely on them to capture business requirements correctly in their models and code.

4. Key business requirements are expressed as elements in UML diagrams, but there are so many elements in these diagrams that the *important* requirements become lost. We call this process *trivialization* because key requirements are translated into a context in which their importance is no longer apparent.

The last point about trivialization of requirements is very important, and we discuss it in more detail in the next section.

3.7 The trivialization of business requirements in visual modeling

We all know that some business requirements are more important than others. Often, though, you can't tell from a blunt statement of the requirement just *how* important it is to the overall operation of the business. In order to appreciate the true importance of a requirement, you need to see it in its business context, but it is precisely this business context that is lacking in conventional UML models.

In the real world, you may notice that important business requirements are often highlighted by a certain amount of activity and ceremony—there may be papers, working groups investigating the requirement, and discussion at the managerial level. This activity is a key indicator that those in charge perceive something to be important to the business.

All of this valuable contextual information is absent from the UML model. Although you may have a statement of a particular business requirement as part of a UML use case, you have no formal mechanism to highlight the importance of this requirement or to set it in its true business context.

Worse, when the requirement is expressed in a class diagram, it becomes merely a cluster of modeling elements much like any other.

Rather than being *highlighted* in the UML model, essential business requirements tend to fade into the background. This is what we mean by trivialization.

In our paper [Arlow 1998] we present the following example from British Airways (BA) that illustrates trivialization.

The last decade has been that of the global airline. Globalization often involves forming alliances so that one partner may sell seating capacity on another partner's flight. This practice is known as codeshare.

As an example of codeshare, consider a single operating flight from London Heathrow to Barcelona on June 2, 2003, at 3:40 P.M. This is sold by BA as flight number BA7075 and by Iberia as flight number IB4187, and the flight is operated by Iberia. It also has an *operational* flight number (usually that of the carrier who operates the flight) that is the "real" flight number as far as air traffic control is concerned.

Codeshare is good for an airline because it extends the airline's network, and it is good for passengers because they can complete a complex journey using a set of cooperating carriers. Codeshare can also improve customer service. In fact, codeshare can generate new business worth millions of dollars.

You can see that it is an essential business requirement for alliance partners to be able to support codeshare in their systems. The key to this support is that each flight must be able to have *many* flight numbers.

But how do you represent this key business requirement in a UML model?

From the use case perspective, it's not entirely clear where the requirement gets captured. There will be a use case involving a BA customer flying on a BA flight. But it is unlikely that there will be any mention of codeshare in this use case because the principle of codeshare is that it is meant to be *transparent* to the customer.

In the class diagram, codeshare is represented as a many-to-many relationship between `Flight` and `FlightNumber`, as shown in Figure 3.2.

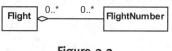

Figure 3.2

So a multimillion dollar business requirement, affecting an alliance of companies together worth billions, is represented as a multiplicity on a UML analysis class diagram!

This sort of trivialization is surprisingly common when you begin to recognize it.

3.8   Literate modeling

As you saw in the last few sections, although UML models can have a high degree of precision and conciseness, they may be difficult to access and comprehend—especially by nontechnical people. Literate modeling provides one solution to this problem.

Literate modeling applies Knuth's idea of literate programming [Knuth 1984] to UML models. The approach is very simple—you interleave UML diagrams with a narrative text that explains the model to both the author of the model and all the roles listed in Table 3.1.

Literate modeling addresses all of the issues we have raised: the accessibility and comprehensibility of the UML models and the trivialization of business requirements. It does this by providing the missing business context in the form of a document that anyone can read.

So the core idea of literate modeling is very simple—you simply extend your UML modeling by adding new documents we call *business context documents* (BCDs) that explain the model in light of the business context and forces that have shaped it. This is illustrated in Figure 3.3.

You can use BCDs to:

1. Explain the rationale behind the UML model in terms that business users can understand
2. Highlight important business requirements
3. Map important business requirements to specific features of the model
4. Explain how the business requirements and context caused particular modeling choices to be made

In our experience, the literate model increases the business value of a UML model by making it accessible and comprehensible to a very wide audience.

3.9   Structuring the business context document

BCDs discuss the background, general principles and concepts, essential requirements, and forces that shape a specific part of the business. They consist of a narrative with embedded UML diagrams. Any description of any part of these diagrams is *always* from the perspective of the business.

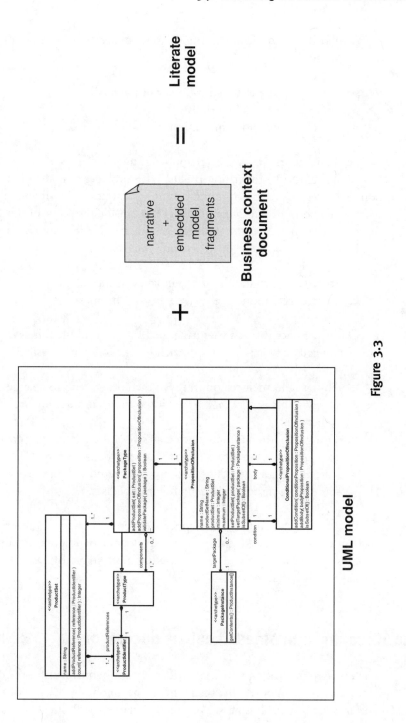

Figure 3.3

A good BCD can be quite difficult to write because you need quite a range of knowledge and skills:

- A very sound and broad overview of the business
- Good UML modeling skills
- Good writing and communication skills

For many years we have been applying the techniques of Neuro-Linguistic Programming (NLP) to writing BCDs. NLP provides a model of communication and a set of specific communication techniques to improve the quality of communication. A full discussion of NLP is outside the scope of this book, and we refer you to *The Structure of Magic* [Bandler 1990] for more information.

You have two options for structuring the BCD.

1. Structure it around the *things* in your business.
2. Structure it around the *processes* in your business.

Our experience is that structuring the BCD around the things in your business (e.g., `Products`) is the best approach for the following reasons.

- Things, and their relationships to each other, tend to change quite slowly—this is *particularly* true if the things in question are business archetypes!
- Things tend to naturally form cohesive clusters (e.g., `Person`, `Organization`, `Address`) that provide an excellent focus for the BCD.
- Things support processes (and processes require things), so things are in some sense more fundamental than processes.

On the other hand, business processes tend to change quite rapidly and may cut across clusters of things. You can document important business processes as a narrative, but you should use the more stable BCDs as the building blocks for this narrative.

3.10   Creating a business context document

The first step in creating a BCD is to identify a suitable focus for the document. As we mentioned above, this focus should be a cohesive cluster of things that deliver value to your business. We generally name the BCD after the key thing in that cluster. For example, if you consider the `Money` archetype pattern presented in Chapter 11, you can see that the cluster of things (archetypes in this case) includes the following:

- `Money`
- `Currency`
- `ExchangeRate`
- `CurrencyConverter`
- `Locale`

The key thing is `Money`, so in this case we call the BCD the `Money` archetype pattern.

Each BCD has the following minimal structure.

- Business context
  - General discussion of the business context that this document describes
- Compliance to standards
  - Existing standards that anyone working in this area needs to know about
- `<patternName>` archetype pattern and roadmap
  - Roadmap UML model showing all of the main things and relationships with cross-references to the appropriate sections (see Section 3.14 for more details)
- `<thing>`
  - Narrative, referencing one or more model fragments and containing:
    - UML diagrams constructed to illustrate the narrative
    - Informal diagrams
- `<thing>`
  - Narrative, referencing one or more model fragments and containing:
    - UML diagrams constructed to illustrate the narrative
    - Informal diagrams
- and so on . . .

We find that class diagrams, use case diagrams, and sequence diagrams are referenced most often in the BCD. In rare cases, you may find it useful to include a few state diagrams for the more technical readers.

You can use *informal* diagrams wherever they enhance the text, but they should never be a substitute for a UML diagram.

The structure shown above is not fixed, and you can add things to it or remove things from it as you see fit. However, the core semantics of the BCD—that it explains the model in light of the business context and forces that have shaped it—must always be preserved.

3.11 Developing a business nomenclature

One key advantage of the BCD is that it can begin to regularize the language used in a particular business domain. To achieve this, you should highlight definitions of things and terms, as we do in the literate models presented later in this book.

You will find that most businesses use terms quite loosely. For example, airlines often use the term *flight* to mean four distinctly different things.

1. The physical deployment of an aircraft between a particular origin and destination at a particular time and date
2. The physical deployment of one or more aircraft between a particular origin and destination at a particular time of day over a range of dates
3. A marketing entity that describes travel between an origin and a destination that may be realized by one or more physical flights, available at a particular time and date
4. A marketing entity that describes travel between an origin and a destination that may be realized by one or more physical flights, available at a particular time of day over a range of dates

This is an example of a *homonym*—a single word that has two or more different meanings.

You will also encounter examples of *synonyms*, that is, two different terms that have the same meaning. For example, many Web sites use the terms *customer* and *user* to mean the same thing.

Synonyms and homonyms are a reality of business life, yet you can (and must) resolve them in your BCDs. You can mention synonyms and homonyms in your narrative, explaining why you have chosen one term in preference to another. You can also create a glossary to go with your BCDs, giving a single entry for each preferred term with all synonyms and homonyms listed underneath.

If BCDs had no other benefit, they would still be worth creating just because they introduce the possibility of regularizing business terminology!

3.12 Business context documents and packages

The UML grouping mechanism is the package, and in a well-constructed UML model you will find that packages contain cohesive clusters of things. This tells you that there should be a simple relationship between your BCDs and the package structure of your UML model.

In the simplest case, there is one BCD per package. However, it is also quite common for a business context to describe a cluster of closely related packages such as a package and its nested packages.

Just as there are dependencies between packages, there are corresponding dependencies between BCDs. A client document will often have to refer to a thing in a server document. You can resolve this as follows.

- You can include the definition of the thing you are referring to in the client document.
- You can reference the server document where the thing is covered in detail.
- You can include definitions in a global glossary.

Replicating the same definition in different documents is clearly a bad idea from a maintenance perspective. However, from a readability perspective, it helps your readers to have all the information at their fingertips. Word processors such as Microsoft Word or Adobe FrameMaker allow you to put commonly used text, such as definitions, in a library where you can reuse them. This reduces your maintenance overhead.

If you find that your BCDs imply a package structure *different* from that of your UML model, you need to resolve this. Go back to the business and find out what the true clustering of things is. You will find that the truth *is* out there!

3.13 Business context document conventions

Always write BCDs using the names of the things in the UML model. In this way you tie the narrative to the UML model. These names may be highlighted in a specific typeface (as in this book).

An additional benefit of using model element names directly in the text is that this provides a very stringent test for the quality and comprehensibility of your model. Parts of the narrative that domain experts find hard to understand may indicate where you have named something poorly or even where you might be using the wrong abstraction.

Consider the following description of the Money archetype (see Chapter 11).

The Money archetype represents an amount of a specific Currency. This Currency is acceptedIn one or more Locales.

The Money, Currency, and Locale archetypes are shown in Figure 3.4.

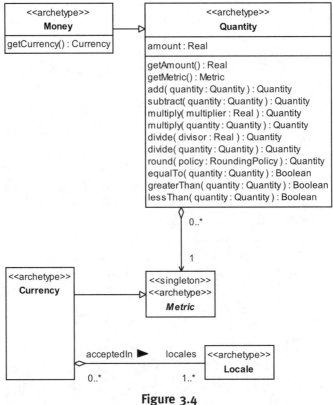

Figure 3.4

Notice the following points, illustrated in Figure 3.5.

- The text refers to one or more specific UML model elements.
- The names of all model elements are written in a special font—you can refer to any model element on the diagram that has a name.

- Use plurals where necessary—for example, if you need to talk about more than one Locale, use the term Locales.
- Use apostrophes appropriately—for example, you can talk about a Currency's Locale.
- The text reads well and is comprehensible whether the UML model is present or not.

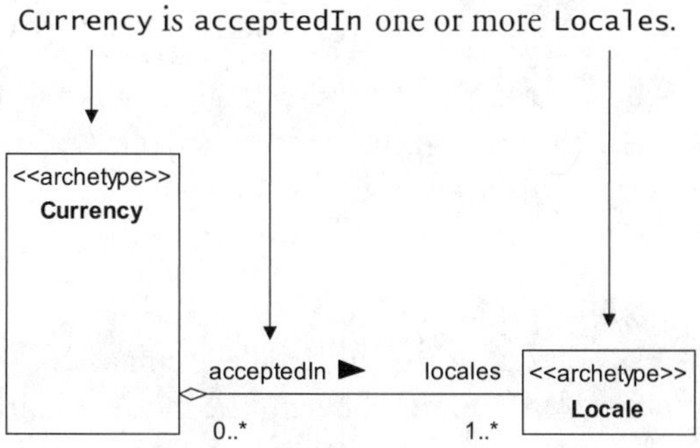

Currency is acceptedIn one or more Locales.

Figure 3.5

The last point is very important. The text should be comprehensible whether you can read the UML model or not. In fact, a good test of a BCD is to cover up all the UML models and see if it is still readable. It should be!

3.14 UML tags for literate modeling

UML doesn't provide built-in support for linking models to external documents. However, it is very easy to implement this capability using the UML extension mechanism called *tagged values*.

Tagged values are fully discussed in [Arlow 2001], but to summarize, they are name (tag) and value pairs that can be applied to a model element to record extra information about that element.

For literate modeling we define the tags shown in Table 3.2.

Table 3.2

Tag	Semantics
document	A unique identifier for the key document that describes the model element
section	The section number for the key section within the document that describes the model element

The document and section tags for a model element should refer to the *key document* for the tagged element and the *key section* within that document, respectively. The key section must contain:

- A definition of the model element
- A description of its detailed semantics
- A UML model showing the model element and all of its attributes, operations, and associations
- References to other relevant sections, perhaps in other documents

To use the section tags, the literate model should be numbered like this book. Here, each chapter is given a consecutive number and each section is numbered consecutively within the chapter as follows:

```
chapterNumber.sectionNumber
```

An inherent constraint of the literate modeling tags is that there is *one document tag and one section tag per model element*. We feel that this is a very desirable constraint because the model element tags should provide a single starting point for information about the element, rather than an exhaustive set of references.

You can see an example of the literate modeling tags applied to the roadmap diagram of the Money archetype pattern in Figure 3.6.

For the models in this book, we need to show only the section tags because the document tag is always the same—it is the ISBN of this book.

These section tags are generally used only on the roadmap diagrams so that the other models are not cluttered.

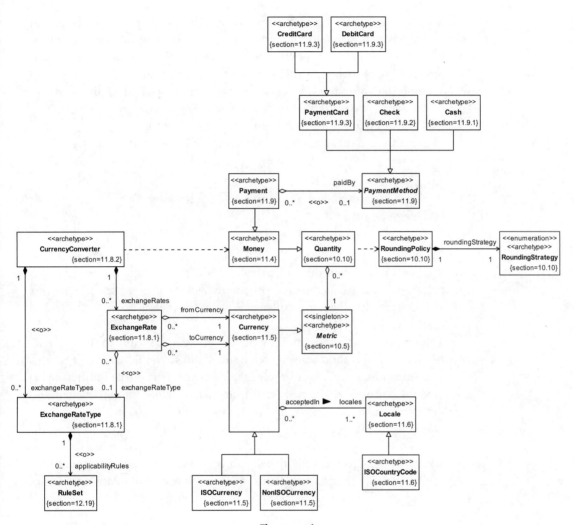

Figure 3.6

3.15 Readability

We encourage you to believe that boredom is always optional!

Ever wondered why some texts put you to sleep? It's probably due to the use of the passive voice.

Passive voice disassociates the reader from the story line of the document and leads to boredom and low comprehension. Dr. Richard Bandler (one of the world's greatest hypnotists) pointed out in [Bandler 1990] that using the passive voice is one of the best ways to induce trance in a reader.

Combining the passive voice with long, rambling, and ambiguous sentences can be truly devastating! In fact, if you *want* to write something that no one will ever really read, this is a sure-fire way to achieve it.

We've observed that a surprising number of corporate documents are

- Written in the passive voice
- Have long, rambling, ambiguous sentences
- Are never read

We advise you to write the BCD as though you are talking to someone—much as we have written this book. Try to make the document as engaging as possible. Given the subject matter, you are unlikely to ever make the *New York Times* best-seller list, but you will make your documents more readable and therefore useful.

Perhaps the most important tip we could give you is simply to "tell a story." Your UML diagrams should always tell a story, and so should your BCDs. This story explains to the reader, in simple language, how part of the business operates and why it operates in that way. Your literate model should explain and highlight important business things, processes, and requirements.

We find that we get the best results when the BCD is lively, involving, direct, provocative, precise, concise, and, if possible, humorous. However, it can be difficult to incorporate humor well, and you should avoid it if in doubt.

This isn't really the place to discuss good writing style in depth, so we refer you to *Bugs in Writing* [Dupré 1998] for more information.

3.16 Use concrete examples

It's important to make the BCDs as concrete and "real world" as possible.

One of the best ways to do this is to include real-world examples throughout the text. For example, if you are discussing product specification, give a real business example in your text.

If you are working in a situation where your literate models may also be used by business partners, consider giving some examples from your partners' business. We have done this several times, and it is always very well received. It shows your partners that you have been taking their needs into consideration, and it helps bypass the "not invented here" syndrome.

Another tactic that we find useful in BCDs is to include more than one example in areas that cover difficult material. You might start with a simple example to give the reader the general idea and then go on to a more complex example. In one literate model we created for a transport company, we chose the most complex journey in its timetable and demonstrated how our UML model could accommodate that. This gave our literate model a *lot* of credibility within that business.

Apart from the credibility issue, another very good reason for choosing a difficult example is to stress-test your UML model. We have often found that something that works for a simple case breaks down for more complex cases. In fact, many of the UML models you find in UML textbooks work only for very simple cases. You can greatly improve your modeling skills by providing worked examples that illustrate how your model supports complex real-world business situations.

3.17   Precision and correctness

Combining a narrative text with a UML model gives you something that is more than the sum of its parts.

The reason for this is that the narrative is free to explore the entire business context in which the UML model must operate, while the UML model enforces precision on the narrative. We often find that a good literate model is much more detailed and precise than either the model or the narrative would be if they stood alone.

The UML model highlights errors in the narrative, and the narrative highlights errors in the UML model. You may be surprised at how often a UML model that looks fine on paper reveals problems when you begin to write about it!

3.18   The future of literate modeling

The most significant enhancement we can make to literate modeling will be to define an XML schema for the BCD. The schema will incorporate special tags containing information that links the tag contents directly to elements in a

UML model. Our work is ongoing as we go to press, but we provide some thoughts in this section that you might find useful.

You can do most of what you need to do in literate modeling with only four new XML tags:

```
<modelElement>
<modelElementDefinition>
<umlDiagram>
<keySection>
```

For example, the tag `<modelElement>` might look something like this:

```
<modelElement pathName = nameOfElement, identifier =
  identifierOfElement>
nameOfElementUsedInNarrative
</modelElement>
```

This tag contains the path name of a model element and (optionally) its unique identifier in the UML modeling tool. The content of the tag should be the name of the element as used in the narrative. For example, if the path name of the element is `clearviewtraining.com::Money Archetype Pattern::Currency`, then at one point in the narrative, `nameOfElementUsedInNarrative` might be `Currency` and in another part, `Currencies`. The tag identifies a reference to a UML model element within the text.

The `<modelElementDefinition>` tag is used as follows:

```
<modelElementDefinition pathName = nameOfElement, identifier =
  identifierOfElement>
Definition of the model element
</modelElementDefinition>
```

The body of this tag contains a definition of a specific model element.

Here is the tag to identify embedded UML diagrams:

```
<umlDiagram pathName = nameOfDiagram, identifier =
  identifierOfDiagram>
embeddedUMLDiagram
</umlDiagram>
```

This tag refers to a specific UML diagram in the model. To include a UML diagram in a document, you usually have to export it from the modeling tool in a graphics format such as JPEG. The body of this tag should contain the URL to this exported graphic.

Finally, we can use <keySection> to identify the key section in the document that refers to a particular archetype:

```
<keySection pathName = nameOfElement, identifier =
  identifierOfElement>
The key section of the document for a model element
</keySection>
```

The body of this tag is the section in the document most relevant to the model element (see Section 3.14).

In addition to these literate modeling specific tags, you need tags for things like paragraphs, tables, and so on. A commonly used XML schema for documents is the DocBook schema (www.docbook.org). This provides an excellent base for the literate modeling extensions.

Once the BCD is expressed in XML it can be processed by XML parsers and accessed by XML query tools such as those based on XML Query (XQuery). The UML model may also be saved as XML in XML Metadata Interchange (XMI) format. This opens up several interesting possibilities for working with the two XML documents.

- You can write simple tools to automate consistency checking between the BCD and the UML model. You can check model element names and definitions.
- One document may be designated as the master source of all model element definitions (probably the UML model). You can then use simple XML-based tools to automatically update these definitions in the BCD.
- By processing the <keySection> tags within a BCD, you can automatically update UML models with document and section tags (see Section 3.14).
- The literate models themselves could provide the user interfaces for the archetype automation technology that we described in Chapter 2. For example, a nontechnical stakeholder could begin to configure an archetype pattern by checking boxes in a BCD next to the pattern features pertinent to his or her business requirements. We hope to do some work on this in the near future.

3.19 Summary

In this chapter we introduced literate modeling. We covered the topics listed below.

- The problems with visual modeling:
  - You need to know how to work the modeling tool.
  - It's hard to know where to start reading a model.
  - UML models lack a business context.
    - They encrypt important business information.
    - It's hard to uncover the business requirements and imperatives that shaped the model.

- The problem of comprehensibility:
  - Nontechnical stakeholders lose comprehension as the focus of UML diagrams shifts from business requirements to implementation.
    - They understand the business requirements but have little comprehension of UML sequence, collaboration, class, and state diagrams.
    - Traceability of high-level requirements to these diagrams relies mainly on the fidelity of the modeling transformations and lacks essential feedback from the nontechnical group.
  - Designers and programmers may have little understanding of the actual business and its needs.
  - Key business requirements are expressed as elements in UML diagrams.
    - *Trivialization of business requirements*: there are so many elements that key requirements may become hidden.

- A solution—literate modeling:
  - It is based on Knuth's idea of literate programming.
    - Literate programming relies on special tools—literate modeling doesn't.
  - Interleave UML diagrams with an explanatory narrative to create a business context document (BCD).
    - UML model + BCD = literate model
  - Use the BCD to:
    - Explain the rationale behind the UML model to business users.
    - Highlight important business requirements.
    - Map key business requirements to specific features of the model.
      - Explain how the business requirements and context caused particular modeling choices to be made.

- There are several advantages to the literate modeling approach.
  - It makes the model available to a wide audience.
  - Even those who don't know UML or the modeling tool can access and read the literate model.
  - It provides a valuable business context for the model.
  - It helps modelers to do their job.
    - The discipline of writing a narrative helps clarify the understanding of the domain.
    - Literate modeling leads to enhanced communication between the modeler and the technical and nontechnical stakeholders.

- Creating a business context document:
  - BCDs can be hard to write because you need:
    - A very sound and broad overview of the business.
    - Good UML modeling skills.
    - Good writing and communication skills.
  - Consider using Neuro-Linguistic Programming (NLP) techniques to improve communication.
  - Structure the BCD around key things that deliver value to your business.
    - Things, and their relationships to each other, tend to change quite slowly.
      - This is *particularly* true if the things in question are business archetypes!
    - Things tend to naturally form cohesive clusters (e.g., `Person`, `Organization`, `Address`) that provide an excellent focus for the BCD.
      - Name the BCD after the key thing in the cluster.
    - Things support processes (and processes require things), so things are in some sense more fundamental than processes.
    - Business processes tend to change quite rapidly and provide an unstable base for the BCD.
  - Each BCD has the following base structure:
    - Business context: a general discussion of the business context that this document describes.
    - Compliance to standards: existing standards that anyone working in this area needs to know about.
    - A roadmap UML model showing all of the main things and relationships, with cross-references to the appropriate part of the document.

- – A number of sections, each describing a thing or related things and comprising:
    - Narrative, referencing one or more model fragment.
    - UML diagrams constructed to illustrate the narrative—typically, class diagrams, use case diagrams, and sequence diagrams.
    - Informal diagrams.
  - You can add to or remove things from this structure as appropriate.

- Developing a business nomenclature:
  - The BCD helps regularize the language used in a particular business domain.
    - – It highlights definitions of things and terms.
    - – It resolves synonyms and homonyms.
      - Synonym: two different terms have the same meaning.
      - Homonym: one term has two or more different meanings.
      - Strategy: choose a single preferred term and mention any common synonyms and homonyms in your narrative, explaining why you have chosen the preferred term.
  - Create a glossary to complement your BCD.
    - – This contains the key terms and any synonyms and homonyms.

- BCDs and packages:
  - Expect a simple relationship between the package structure of your UML models and your BCDs.
    - – A BCD may describe one package or a cluster of closely related packages.
  - There are dependencies between BCDs corresponding to package dependencies. Some ways to resolve these are as follows:
    - – Include a definition of the thing you are referring to in the client document.
    - – Reference the server document where the thing is covered in detail.
    - – Include definitions in a global glossary.

- BCD conventions:
  - Always write BCDs using the names of things in the UML model.
    - – Use class, attribute, operation, and association names or role names to tie the narrative to the UML model.
    - – This provides a very stringent test for the quality and comprehensibility of the model.

- Ensure that:
  - The names of all model elements are written in a special font—you can refer to any model element on the diagram that has a name.
  - Plurals are used where necessary (e.g., `Locale`, `Locales`).
  - Apostrophes are used appropriately (e.g., a `Currency's Locale`).
  - The text reads well and is comprehensible whether the UML model is present or not.

- UML tags for literate modeling:
  - Tagged values are name (tag) and value pairs that may be applied to model elements to record extra information.
  - Literate modeling has two tags:
    - Tag = `document`
      - Value = a unique identifier for the key document that describes the model element.
    - Tag = `section`
      - Value = the section number for the key section within the document that describes the model element.
    - Constraint: there can be only one `document` tag and one `section` tag per model element.
  - The document should be numbered like this book— `chapterNumber.sectionNumber`
  - The key section must contain:
    - Definition of the model element.
    - Description of its detailed semantics.
    - UML model showing the model element and all of its attributes, operations, and associations.
    - References to other relevant sections, perhaps in other documents.

- Writing style:
  - Readability:
    - Avoid passive voice—it has trance-inducing qualities.
    - Write the BCD as though you are talking to someone.
    - Try to make the document as engaging as possible.
    - Tell a story that explains to the reader, in simple language, how part of the business operates and why it operates in that way.
  - Concrete examples:
    - Use real-world examples throughout to illustrate the BCD.
      - You can start with a simple example to illustrate the basic concepts.
      - Choose more complex examples to "prove" the pattern.

- Precision and correctness:
  - A narrative text with a UML model is more than the sum of its parts.
    * The narrative is free to include the business context for the model.
    * The model enforces precision on the narrative.
  - Writing about a UML model can highlight semantic errors in the model.
  - Modeling a narrative can highlight semantic errors in the narrative.
- The future of literate modeling:
  - Future work will involve defining an XML schema for the BCD.
  - You need four XML tags:
    - `<modelElement pathName = nameOfElement, identifier = identifierOfElement>`
      * The body of the tag is the name of the model element as used in the narrative.
    - `<modelElementDefinition pathName = nameOfElement, identifier = identifierOfElement>`
      * The body of the tag is the definition of the model element.
    - `<umlDiagram pathName = nameOfDiagram, identifier = identifierOfDiagram>`
      * The body of the tag is the URL to the diagram stored as a graphic.
    - `<keySection pathName = nameOfElement, identifier = identifierOfElement>`
      * The body of the tag is the section most relevant to the archetype.
  - In addition to literate modeling tags, you need tags for document structure (e.g., paragraphs, tables, and so on).
    * Consider using the DocBook schema extended with the four literate modeling tags.
  - An XML representation of the BCD allows:
    - Processing of the document by XML tools such as parsers.
    - Querying of the BCD by XML tools such as XML Query (XQuery).
    - Consistency checking with the UML model, especially when the model is saved in XML Metadata Interchange (XMI) format.
    - Automatic updating of definitions in the BCD (using definitions in the model) and of `document` and `section` tags in the UML model (using `<keySection>` tags from the BCD).

Part 3

Archetype
pattern catalog

Chapter 4

Party **archetype pattern**

4.1 Business context

The Party archetype pattern describes how to represent essential information about people and organizations. We use Party as a general term for a person or an organization such as a business.

Almost every business is concerned to some degree with maintaining information about parties and about the roles that these parties play in various relationships with them. This concern is as old as business itself. Even in very early business activities based around barter, transactions were predicated on trust, and that was based on having some knowledge, whether formally represented or not, of your trading partners.

One very common problem is that many businesses have no standard and unified way to represent information about parties. This omission creates many problems:

- Redundancy in systems (leading to high maintenance costs)
- Poor data quality (leading to service failures)
- Lost business opportunities
- Poor quality of service
- Legal issues

For example, customer information is often replicated and held in many different formats in many different systems. It may even be distributed across multiple systems. It's a useful exercise to assess how customer information is held in your own business. You may find that a standard, unified view of the customer and his or her details, requirements, preferences, buying patterns, relationships to you, and so on is simply not available. What specific problems does this create for you?

In this chapter, we look at a standard way to represent information about parties across business domains. Although the archetype pattern for this solution is very simple in principle, in practice it may take years to apply it uniformly across all the business systems in your organization.

We discuss the important issue of party roles and relationships in Chapter 5.

4.2 Compliance with standards

The models presented in this chapter comply with the standards listed in Table 4.1.

Table 4.1

Standard	Contents	Reference
OMG Party Management Facility Specification	A standard that supports party management	www.omg.org/technology/ documents/formal/ party_mgmt
ISO 3166	Two- and three-letter country codes and country names	www.iso.org
ISO 5218	A representation of human sexes	www.iso.org
ITU-T Recommendations	Standards for telecommunications addresses	www.itu.int

4.3 Party archetype pattern overview and roadmap

As the Party archetype pattern is quite large, we have broken it down into the main pattern (Figure 4.1) and PartyRelationships (see Chapter 5).

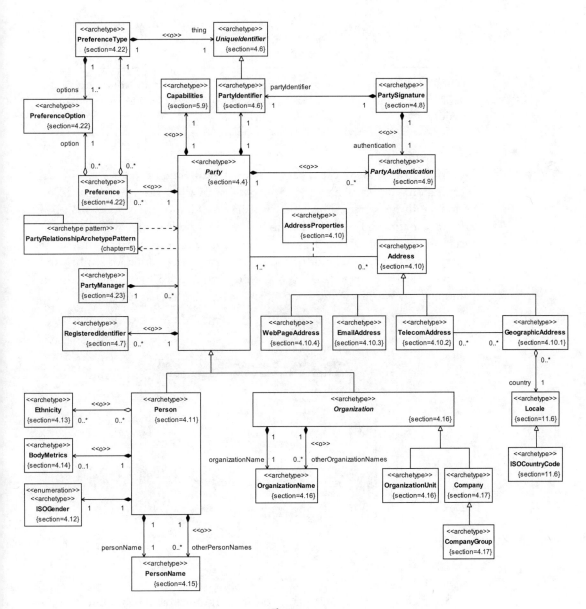

Figure 4.1

4.4 **The** Party **archetype**

> The Party archetype represents an identifiable, addressable unit that may have a legal status and that normally has autonomous control over (at least some of) its actions.

Usually, the Party archetype captures essential information about a person or an organization—but it is merely a *representation* of that person or organization within a software system. This representation holds information *pertinent to your business activities*, and it's important to be clear about this to maintain the correct focus. You should never, under any circumstances, confuse a Party with a *real* person or organization. This distinction between a representation, or symbol, and the thing itself was made famous by the Belgian surrealist René Magritte in his painting *The Treachery of Images*, on which we have loosely based Figure 4.2.

Figure 4.2

Being clear on this point helps you to work out exactly what information the Party archetype *needs* to contain and maintain for your business systems in order to achieve your specific business goals, and what information is extraneous. This is illustrated in Figure 4.3.

The Party archetype is shown in Figure 4.4.

A real person or organization is represented in business systems
by an instance of the Party archetype

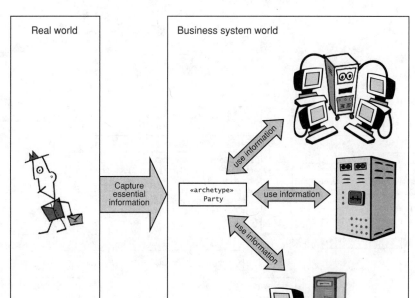

Figure 4.3

The information maintained by the Party archetype normally includes:

- Unique identifier
- Name
- Address

It may also include:

- Registered identifiers (passports, identity cards, and so on)
- Preferences
- Any other information that your company needs

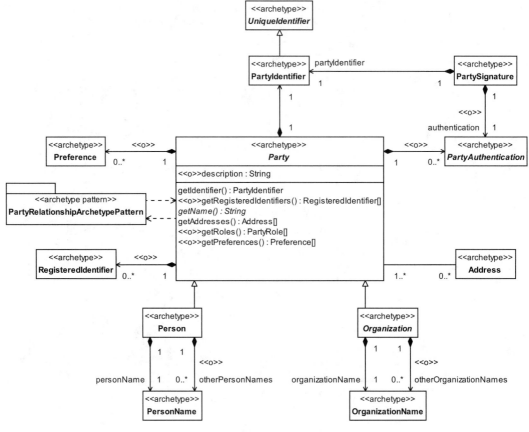

Figure 4.4

A little later in this chapter we'll look in more detail at how you can represent all these types of information.

4.5 Types of Party

The Party archetype itself is a very abstract thing, with only the most rudimentary semantics—most of the semantics are actually captured by the Person and Organization subclasses of Party.

Typically, there is no need to subclass Person (Section 4.11)—people seem to come in only one type as far as software systems are concerned! However, there are many different types of Organization (Section 4.16).

As a general rule, `Parties` have no interesting behavior—they simply hold information. This is an important point to grasp because it makes the `Party` reusable across many different business domains. If you were to add significant amounts of behavior to the `Party`, or to any of its subclasses, this behavior might be appropriate for some domains but not for others. Your best strategy, therefore, is to treat the different types of `Party` mostly as passive data stores and to allow other things to act upon them.

4.6 PartyIdentifier

The `PartyIdentifier` archetype represents a unique identifier for a `Party`.

The `UniqueIdentifier` archetype represents an identifier that is unique within a given context.

One of the first issues you encounter when working with `Parties` is that of identification. How can you uniquely identify a `Party` across your business and, perhaps, across different businesses?

Unfortunately, there is no single, internationally accepted way to uniquely identify `Parties`. So the best approach is to assign each `Party` instance a unique `PartyIdentifier` that you generate yourself, as shown in Figure 4.5.

Using database terminology, the `PartyIdentifier` acts as a *primary key* for accessing the `Party` information. In fact, this information is normally stored in some persistent store, such as a database. According to the principles of data quality, this identifier must have the following characteristics.

- It must be unique across your whole business.
- It should usually be an alphanumeric string. (We have seen systems that use integers, but this is not a robust option because integers can have different sizes on different platforms.)
- It must *not* be null.
- It must be created when a new `Party` object is saved to persistent storage (such as a database).
- It must *not* be changed.
- It must have *no* significance.

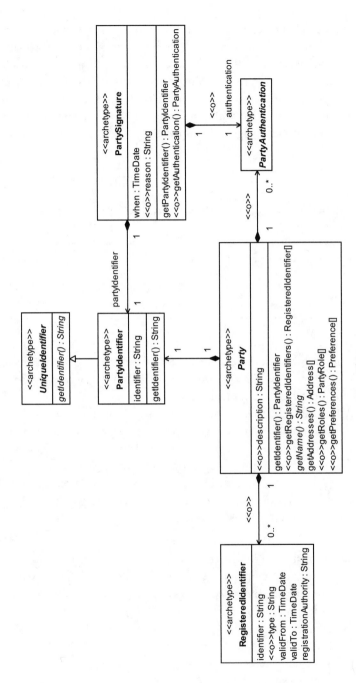

Figure 4.5

The last point is important. It is generally a very bad idea to encode *any* information about a Party into the key used to access that information. There are several good reasons for this.

- You may not know requisite Party information at the point at which the Party object is saved to persistent storage.
- You may have gathered the Party information incorrectly (this is quite common, especially when information is collected over the telephone).
- Any of the Party information may change over time (because of real changes to the Party data or as errors are corrected), but it is important that the unique identifier does not change.

The PartyIdentifier archetype can deliver great benefit to your business. Having a single, unique identifier for a Party will help to increase the quality of your Party data. In particular, duplicated and inconsistent data can be identified and cleaned up, and Party relationship management will become much easier.

4.7 RegisteredIdentifier

The RegisteredIdentifier archetype represents an identifier for a Party that has been assigned by a recognized or statutory body.

The RegisteredIdentifier archetype is shown in Figure 4.5. Notice that a RegisteredIdentifier is not a UniqueIdentifier. This is because Registered-Identifiers are not necessarily guaranteed to be unique.

Each RegisteredIdentifier can hold the following:

- The identifier itself
- An optional type that can be used to classify the Registered-Identifier (e.g., VATRegistrationNumber)
- A date that the RegisteredIdentifier is validFrom
- A date that the RegisteredIdentifier is validTo
- The registrationAuthority

As we pointed out in Section 4.6, there is no single, internationally accepted way to uniquely identify `Parties`. However, a variety of identifiers have widespread application and validity within the context of a country, industry, or activity. For example, different statutory bodies register nations' citizens and companies and may issue some kind of `RegisteredIdentifier`, while other `registration-Authorities` such as sporting federations and trade associations may register individuals or organizations and likewise assign `RegisteredIdentifiers`.

A widespread use of `RegisteredIdentifiers` is to capture tax identity codes (such as VAT Registration Numbers within the European Community) for businesses of all sorts, from sole proprietors to various types of companies, that are registered for sales tax purposes.

`RegisteredIdentifiers` are considered for `People` in Section 4.11.1, for `Companies` in Section 4.19, and for `OrganizationUnits` in Section 4.20.1.

4.8 PartySignature

Sometimes in business systems it is important to identify that an action or decision has been passed by an appropriate `Party` or to identify formally which `Party` has taken a particular action or decision.

> The `PartySignature` archetype represents the identifying mark of a `Party`.

The `PartySignature` archetype is shown in Figure 4.5. It specifies when the signature was created along with an optional `reason` for the `PartySignature`. For example, a `PartySignature` may be associated with an `AssignedResponsibility` (see Section 5.8) to indicate who did the assigning.

The `PartySignature` can optionally reference a `PartyAuthentication` that proves that the `PartySignature` is authentic. We discuss this in the next section.

4.9 PartyAuthentication

Once you have arrived at a scheme for uniquely identifying a `Party` within your business systems, you will need to consider the issue of authentication. This is about providing a way to verify that the `Party` is who they say they are. It implies that you have some sort of security mechanism in place.

You can model authentication by associating each Party with zero or more PartyAuthentications (see Figure 4.5).

> The PartyAuthentication archetype represents an agreed and trusted way to confirm that a Party is who they say they are.

In our model, PartyAuthentication is just a placeholder to show how authentication relates to the other archetypes. This is because there are many possible ways to provide authentication.

A PartyAuthentication may be as simple as a user ID and password combination, or it could be your own in-house security tokens or a secure digital certificate from a trusted third party such as VeriSign (www.verisign.com) or Thawte (www.thawte.com).

For example, on many Web sites, I (Jim) have only a user name and password. If I forget either of these, I can get the information sent to my registered e-mail address by entering a pass phrase. This generally provides an adequate level of security for personal use.

However, on some very secure Web sites that I access, I use SecurID from RSA Security (www.rsasecurity.com). This consists of a user name and a two-part password. The first part of the password remains fixed, but I get the second part from a small electronic device that presents me with a constantly changing number. This provides a level of security sufficient for corporate security requirements.

The whole notion of authentication is predicated on the existence of some sort of security system. Most security systems work according to the general mechanism illustrated in Figure 4.6.

Here is a brief walkthrough of the process in Figure 4.6, which we provide to highlight some of the issues you need to consider. For a more complete discussion of security see [Bishop 2002].

identify party
This activity obtains the identity of the user. There are several options.

1. The Party may enter a user name, user number, or some other unique string (this is *not* the same as the PartyIdentifier) or may use some physical token such as a card (e.g., in an ATM).
2. The Party may enter some personal identification that the system resolves into its own internal unique identifier.
3. The system may automatically identify the Party (perhaps by obtaining a cookie or some other persistent identifier from the Party's machine).

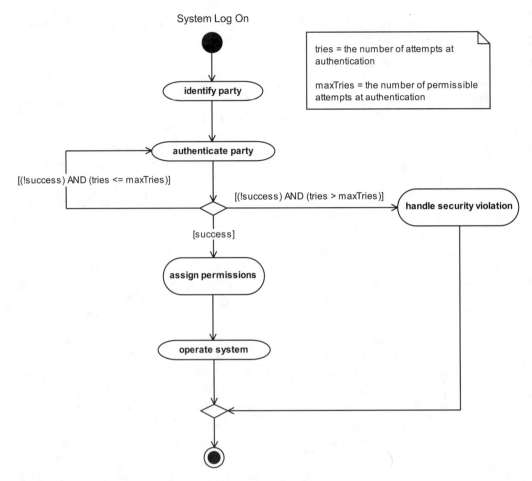

Figure 4.6

The degree of security you require will determine which of these options is appropriate.

Option 1 is the most secure if the Party is required to keep the user string secret, but it is predicated on the Party remembering this string.

Option 2 tries to take away the requirement to remember a user string, by attempting identification based on common personal information such as name and postal code, or perhaps a passport number. This can be a less secure approach because common personal information may be readily available to anyone, not just the Party in question. Also, depending on the personal information requested, there may be more than one Party instance returned.

Option 3, automatically obtaining the `Party`'s ID from his or her machine, is always attractive in selling systems because it provides the lowest barrier to entry of the system. But from the user's perspective it is the least secure. Depending on how `authenticate party` is implemented, this approach may allow other people to buy goods or access services on the user's account without his or her knowledge or permission.

authenticate party

Authentication is about establishing that a `Party` is who, or what, the `Party` claims to be. Usually, this is done by exchanging a secret token such as a password, or even a security certificate, across a secure channel. On-line selling systems may give the `Party` the option to store this password in a persistent form on his or her machine so that the system can access it automatically. Again, this is the least secure option—you should *always* give your users advice about the security implications of this, and *always* give them the option to turn the feature off.

handle security violation

Most systems allow a maximum number of authentication attempts, perhaps in a fixed time period, and then treat failure as a security violation. This violation may result in actions with varying degrees of severity.

1. Do nothing.
2. Log the violation.
3. Log the violation and immediately notify the security administrator.
4. Log the violation, immediately notify the security administrator, and suspend the user's account (in the case of a physical token, such as a card in an ATM, the token may be confiscated or otherwise rendered invalid).

Your least extreme option is to do nothing—but this is rarely, if ever, appropriate! The least extreme *realistic* option is simply to log the violation for inspection by a security administrator. This is not a very secure approach because it may leave your system open to brute-force cracking if the administrator doesn't handle the violation in a timely way. Options 3 and 4 above provide more secure approaches.

assign permissions

This activity assigns to the `Party` permissions to access various system resources.

`operate system`
The Party operates the system in some way.

4.10   Address

> The Address archetype represents information that can be used to contact a Party.

This is illustrated in Figure 4.7 where you can see that:

- A Party may have zero or more associated Addresses.
- There are four kinds of Addresses—we will discuss each of these in the next four subsections. Business rules should be applied to determine which Address to use in a particular situation.
- Each time an Address is associated with a Party, there is an associated AddressProperties object (defined below). This object should at least specify the use of the Address (i.e., limit the context in which the Address is applicable—business, home, out-of-hours contact, emergency contact, and so on). You can also employ use to identify whether an Address is a preferred address for the Party. Other properties may be added to AddressProperties according to your business requirements.

> The AddressProperties archetype specifies information about an Address assigned to a specific Party.

4.10.1   GeographicAddress

> The GeographicAddress archetype represents a geographic location at which a Party may be contacted. It is a postal address for the Party.

The semantics of the attributes of GeographicAddress (see Figure 4.7) are summarized in Table 4.2 on page 134.

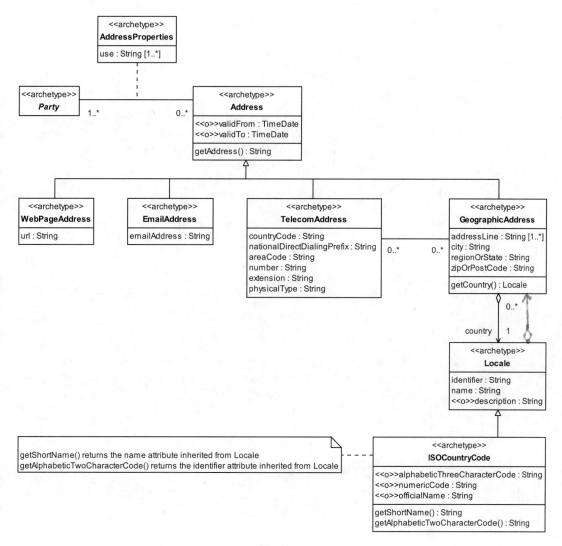

Figure 4.7

Each GeographicAddress has exactly one Locale (see Section 11.6). This is often an ISOCountryCode (also discussed in Section 11.6) that represents the alphabetic and numeric country codes and English language country names defined in ISO 3166.

ISO 3166 is an international standard published by the International Organization for Standardization (ISO). You can find out about ISO standards at

Table 4.2

GeographicAddress **archetype**	
Attribute	**Semantics**
addressLine[1..*]	One or more address lines
	The first line of an address is often a building name, a building number and street, or a postal box number; the other address lines are for location information that is best placed on its own line
city	The name of a city or town
regionOrState	The name of a geographical region within a country—in America this would be a state; in England, a county; and in Switzerland, a canton
zipOrPostCode	A code used to identify a geographic area

the ISO Web site, www.iso.org. This site allows you to purchase ISO standards documentation and has complete and up-to-date lists of country codes and country names available for download, in HTML and semicolon-delimited text formats.

4.10.2 TelecomAddress

The TelecomAddress archetype represents a number that can contact a telephone, mobile phone, fax, pager, or other telephonic device.

In the future there may be types of telephonic devices that we don't know about yet. For example, there are already home automation systems that allow you to phone up the controller and instruct or interrogate it using your telephone's touch tone keypad.

The International Telecommunication Union (www.itu.int) provides standards for TelecomAddresses. Each address is made up of the parts shown in Figure 4.8.

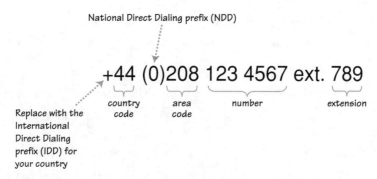

National Direct Dialing prefix (NDD)

Replace with the
International
Direct Dialing
prefix (IDD) for
your country

country
code

area
code

number

extension

Figure 4.8

Each part of the number, except the IDD, is represented by an attribute in the `TelecomAddress` archetype as described in Table 4.3. The IDD is not part of the `TelecomAddress` because it is the number you have to *add* to the `TelecomAddress` to access international direct dialing. This number depends on which country you are in when you try to direct dial out, so it is usually represented by a plus sign. For example, in the United Kingdom the IDD is 00, in the United States it is 011, and in France and several other countries it varies depending on which telecom provider you want to use for your international call. (See www.kropla.com for detailed listings of country codes, IDDs, and NDDs.)

Table 4.3

TelecomAddress **archetype**	
Attribute	**Semantics**
countryCode	The number you must use to direct dial a particular country—this is *not* the same as the ISO 3166 country code, which is an alpha code
nationalDirectDialingPrefix	The prefix you use to make a call within a country between different cities or areas—generally dropped when dialing from outside the country (exceptions include Italy, where the `national-DirectDialingPrefix` is included when dialing from outside; and Spain, which does not currently use a `nationalDirectDialingPrefix`)

Table continued on next page

Table 4.3 (Continued)

TelecomAddress **archetype**	
Attribute	**Semantics**
areaCode	The code for an area or city
number	The telephone number—this may be arbitrarily broken into one or more sequences of digits depending on local standards
extension	An extension accessible via the number
physicalType	The type of device accessed by the TelecomAddress

TelecomAddresses may connect to different physical devices, so each TelecomAddress has a physicalType that describes the device to which the TelecomAddress connects (not the logical type such as home number, work number, and so on—this is represented by the use attribute on the associated AddressProperties).

Some possible values for physicalType are

- "phone"
- "fax"
- "mobile"
- "pager"

Expect there to be more values in the future!

4.10.3 EmailAddress

The EmailAddress archetype specifies a way of contacting a Party via e-mail.

EmailAddresses (see Figure 4.7) have the following form:

username@domainName

They are usually represented as a text string because generally there is no advantage in separating the two parts of the address. It is very easy to extract the domain name if you need this—it is just the part after the @ symbol.

4.10.4 WebPageAddress

> The WebPageAddress archetype represents the URL for a Web page related to the Party.

This consists of a Uniform Resource Locator (URL) that locates a page on the World Wide Web. URLs have the following form:

www.domainName/resourceName

where the resourceName is optional.

WebPageAddresses (see Figure 4.7) are normally represented as a text string. Again, there is no real advantage in storing the parts separately.

4.11 Person

> The Person archetype represents information about a human being.

The Person archetype pattern is shown in Figure 4.9.

Each Person has an optional dateOfBirth. Although every individual was born on a specific date, we model this as an optional attribute in Person because this information is not important to every business system.

We discuss the other archetypes associated with Person in the next sections.

4.11.1 Identifiers for People

There is no internationally recognized, universally applied, single unique identifier for people. Each country may optionally adopt its own identification scheme, and some countries, such as the United States and the United Kingdom, have no scheme at all.

We conclude that the best approach to identifying People is to assign each Person a unique PartyIdentifier that you generate yourself.

There are, however, a variety of RegisteredIdentifiers, as discussed in Section 4.7, that exist outside of (and independent of) your business. You may

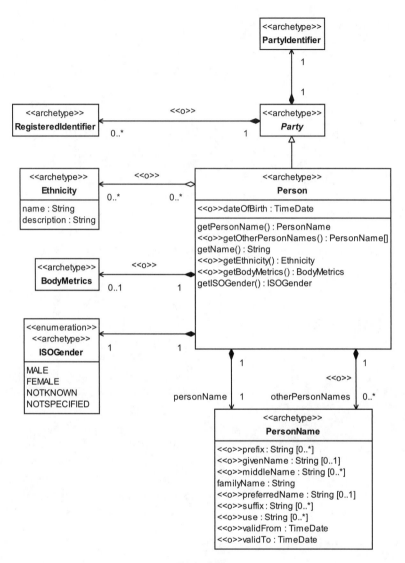

Figure 4.9

need to use these too, for legal or business reasons or to aid the exchange of information with other organizations. Some examples for People are

- Passport number
- Social security number
- Identity card number

We look at each of these in turn below and discuss why they are best treated as RegisteredIdentifiers rather than as unique PartyIdentifiers.

Passport number: If an individual has a passport, the passport number can act as an identifier. However, this may not be suitable for People generally for the following reasons.

- An individual might not have a passport.
- An individual might have more than one passport (e.g., he or she holds multiple citizenships).
- In some countries, more than one individual may be covered by a passport (increasingly rare).

Social security number: Many companies use a social security number issued by the government as a unique identifier. In the United States, this number is known as the SSN (Social Security Number); in the United Kingdom, its equivalent is the NI (National Insurance) number.

However, this strategy has problems and may be a *very* bad idea. The problems with this approach were nicely summarized in [Garfinkel 1995], which pointed out that the common business uses of a social security number—authentication and identification—are actually antithetical to each other.

The fundamental problem is that for a social security number to be used as a unique identifier, it must be widely known, but for it to be used for authentication, it must be secret! In fact, both the governments of the United States and the United Kingdom explicitly state that the SSN and NI number should *not* be used for identification purposes. Rather, these are actually intended to be account numbers that give individuals access to certain information and services.

For example, in the United Kingdom the NI number may be used in this spirit by:

- The Inland Revenue
- Employers, for the deduction of tax and NI contributions
- Employment Services, to administer Jobseekers' Allowances
- Local Authorities, to administer Housing Benefits

Because social security numbers may be used by governments to grant access to specific information about a person, if you have access to someone's SSN or NI number, this may allow you to access sensitive information that the person may regard as private.

Although there is no law in the United Kingdom or the United States that makes it illegal for companies to use social security numbers for whatever they like, our view is that the SSN, NI number, and similar numbers should *not* be used as a unique identifier for an individual within business systems.

Identity card number: Some governments issue identity cards that have numbers that may be used as unique identifiers for individuals within a particular country. However, there is no international standard in this area, and implementation varies widely from country to country. Some countries never issue these cards, some countries make such cards optional on request, and some countries make cards mandatory.

4.12 ISOGender

> The ISOGender archetype represents a classification of a Person according to their gender using the ISO 5218 standard.

Every Person has an ISOGender (see Figure 4.9). We have based this on ISO 5218 (see www.iso.org), which specifies four possible values for gender:

- MALE
- FEMALE
- NOTKNOWN—the gender is not known
- NOTSPECIFIED—the person has chosen not to specify his or her gender

There is an important business distinction between NOTKNOWN and NOTSPECIFIED. NOTKNOWN simply means that the gender information has not been gathered, whereas NOTSPECIFIED means that the individual has specifically chosen not to specify his or her gender.

4.13 Ethnicity

> The Ethnicity archetype represents a classification of one or more People according to common racial, national, tribal, religious, linguistic, or cultural origin or background.

Each `Person` may have zero or more `Ethnicities` (see Figure 4.9). It can be useful to capture this information for customer relationship management (CRM) and marketing reasons, with the permission of the individual. For example, some ethnic groups may have specific product needs, service requirements, or preferences—Jains, for example, are strict vegetarians.

You can see that we have modeled `Ethnicity` simply as a `name` and a `description`. You may choose to add more information to `Ethnicity`, including business rules and preferences, as appropriate to your application.

4.14 BodyMetrics

> The `BodyMetrics` archetype provides a way to store information about the human body such as size, weight, hair color, eye color, measurements, and so on.

We don't go into any specific detail about this in our model (see Figure 4.9), first because there is a very wide range of `BodyMetrics` that could be captured, and second because `BodyMetrics` are generally needed only in very specialized applications. For more information on body measurements and on BodyXML, an XML standard for capturing this information, see www.bodymetrics.com.

4.15 PersonName

> The `PersonName` archetype represents a name for a `Person`.

`PersonName` is shown in Figure 4.9.

When you model names for `People`, it is important to be as international and culturally neutral as possible. For example, you should avoid culturally charged terms such as "Christian name." Every name, in every part of the world, can be broken down into the components listed in Table 4.4.

Table 4.4

PersonName **archetype**		
Attribute	**Multiplicity**	**Semantics**
«o»prefix	Zero or more	An honorific such as Mr., Miss, Dr., Rev., and so on
«o»givenName	Zero or one	The first name in Western countries—this can include hyphenated names (e.g., Jean-Paul) and names including more than one word (e.g., Kwai Lin)
«o»middleName	Zero or more	Any name other than the given name and the family name
familyName	One	The last name in Western countries—this is the only mandatory component of the name and the only one used if a Person has but a single name
«o»preferredName	Zero or one	A name that the person is commonly known by—this is often a contraction of one of the other names (e.g., "Jim" is short for "James," "Bill" is short for "William")
«o»suffix	Zero or more	Each suffix may be: • A generational label (e.g., Jr., III) • A qualification (e.g., BSc., bachelor of sciences; Ph.D., doctor of philosophy) • A title (e.g., FRSC, Fellow of the Royal Society of Chemistry; Bart, Baronet; KG, Knight of the Garter)
«o»use	Zero or more	A short description of what the name is used for (e.g., a stage name or a legal name)
«o»validFrom	One	The date from which the PersonName is valid
«o»validTo	One	The date until which the PersonName is valid

The only mandatory attribute is the familyName. The other elements may or may not be needed, depending on the information you need for your business and the information you are able to collect.

Each `Person` has one legal `personName` at any point in time. However, a person may have many `otherPersonNames`. These may be names that are no longer valid (historic names) or aliases of various kinds.

Police systems certainly need to record aliases and their uses. However, a business may also find it useful to record aliases and their uses so that it can address an individual in the most appropriate way. For example, occasionally people will use a completely different name from their legal name for religious reasons, while some people with names from non-Western countries may employ Anglicized versions of their names in particular circumstances.

In communications with a `Person`, you should use business rules that take account of context and culture to determine which names are used and in which order. We don't discuss this explicitly here, but we do provide a simple rules engine in Chapter 12.

4.16 Organization

The `Organization` archetype represents an administrative and functional structure.

The `OrganizationName` archetype represents a name for an `Organization`.

The `OrganizationUnit` archetype represents an `Organization` that is part of another `Organization`.

Whereas there is only one type of `Person`, there are many different types of `Organizations`. You can see some common examples in Figure 4.10, although you can probably find other examples in your own business.

Notice that not everything in Figure 4.10 is an archetype. We think that the notions of `CompanyGroup`, `Company`, and `OrganizationUnit` are certainly archetypal but that different *types* of `OrganizationUnits`, such as `Divisions` and `Departments`, are not. This is because a `Company` may call its parts anything it likes—see Section 4.20 for further discussion of company structure.

In the next few sections, we will look at `Companies`.

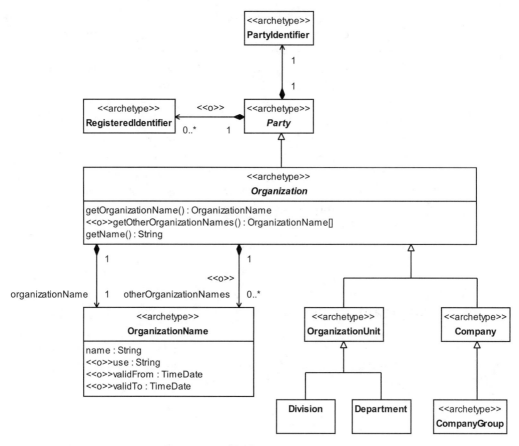

Figure 4.10

4.17 Company

The Company archetype represents an Organization created to make money by selling goods or services, with a legal identity that is separate from its owners.

The CompanyGroup archetype represents an Organization comprising a collection of Companies that have a legal relationship.

Different countries recognize different types of Companies. For example, in the United States, there are currently four types of Companies, although not all of these are available in all states. Although Company is an archetype, the types of U.S. Companies illustrated in Figure 4.11 are not. This is because they are contingent on U.S. federal and state law, are not universal, and are subject to change.

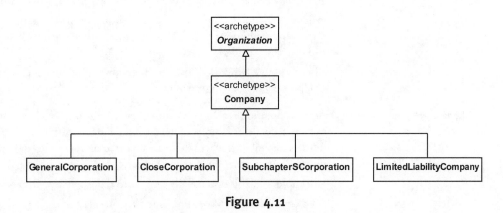

Figure 4.11

The semantics of these different types of U.S. Companies are summarized in Table 4.5.

Table 4.5

Type of U.S. Company	Semantics
GeneralCorporation	A GeneralCorporation (also known as a C corporation) is a Company that is allowed to issue more than one class of stock and that can have unlimited stockholders
	Stockholders' liability is usually limited to their investment in stocks
	Federal corporate income tax is paid on profits prior to making dividend distributions to stockholders (i.e., both company income and dividends paid are taxed)
	This is the corporate structure most usually chosen by companies planning large public stock offerings

Table continued on next page

Table 4.5   (Continued)

Type of U.S. Company	Semantics
CloseCorporation	A CloseCorporation has a maximum of around 30 to 50 stockholders (depending on the state); new shares must usually first be offered to existing stockholders
	Stockholders' liability is usually limited to their investment in stocks
	Federal corporate income tax is paid on profits prior to making dividend distributions to stockholders (i.e., both company income and dividends paid are taxed)
	This corporate structure is usually chosen by an individual or small group of people starting a company
SubchapterSCorporation	An S corporation is a Company with a special tax status such that it does not pay federal corporate income tax but passes profits or losses directly to the stockholders, where these are reported on their personal tax returns (ensures that tax is paid only once)
	Stockholders' liability is usually limited to their investment in stocks
	An S corporation is allowed to issue only one class of stock, and the number of stockholders is limited to 75
	This corporate structure is usually chosen by small business owners who prefer to be taxed as if they were sole proprietors or partners
LimitedLiabilityCompany	This is a less restricted form of Company than a corporation. It has both the limited liability protection of a company and taxation similar to a sole proprietorship or partnership

4.18 Company names

Most countries or states require a company to register with a designated body (e.g., Companies House in the United Kingdom) before they are permitted to start trading.

Each Company has an organizationName that is registered with the designated body. This often includes a postfix that indicates its legal status, for example, PLC (United Kingdom), Inc. (United States), or AG (Germany). You can set the value of the use attribute of OrganizationName to "legal name" to capture this (see Figure 4.10).

In many countries, Companies are allowed to trade under more than one name. You can model these as separate otherOrganizationNames and identify them by setting use to "trading name".

4.19 Identifiers for Companies

There is no internationally recognized, universally applied, single unique identifier for Companies. As with People, we therefore conclude that the best approach to identifying Companies is to assign each Company a unique PartyIdentifier that you generate yourself.

However, you may also need to capture a variety of RegisteredIdentifiers (see Section 4.7) for legal or business reasons or to aid the exchange of information with other organizations.

We examine some common candidates for identifiers below and discuss why they are best treated as RegisteredIdentifiers rather than as unique PartyIdentifiers.

DUNS number: This unique, nine-digit identification code—issued free of charge by Dun & Bradstreet (see www.dnb.com for more details)—references a single business entity. There are currently about 70 million businesses around the world that have a DUNS (Data Universal Numbering System) number.

DUNS numbers are used by the United Nations, the U.S. federal government, the Australian government, and the European Commission, among others. They are also used as a unique identifier by VeriSign (www.verisign.com) for assigning digital IDs. Some businesses insist that *all* their business partners have a DUNS number. If this is the policy of your business, you may already have a robust, ready-made unique identifier for these partners, which can be captured as the PartyIdentifier. Many organizations, though, are not in a position to do this.

Domain names: You might think that domain names (e.g., www.clearviewtraining.com) are candidate identifiers for Companies because they are guaranteed to be unique by ICANN (the Internet Corporation for Assigned Names and Numbers—www.icann.org). However, you can't rely on domain names to provide a unique, universally applied identifier for a company for a number of reasons.

- A company might have more than one domain name (e.g., the U.K.-based company BT has www.bt.com, www.btplc.com, and www.britishtelecom.com).
- Some smaller companies might not have a domain name or might have only a subdomain.
- A company might need to change its domain name because of a change of company name, marketing reasons, or a domain name dispute.

Stock exchange symbols: Only companies listed on a stock exchange have a stock exchange symbol.

National IDs: Companies may have national ID numbers. For example, within the United Kingdom, the company number issued by Companies House is a unique identifier for a company. However, these numbers cannot be guaranteed to be unique outside of national boundaries.

Registered name and office address: Companies may be uniquely identified at a particular time by their registered name and registered office address, but either of these could be changed at some point.

4.20 Company **organizational units**

In principle, a Company may structure its OrganizationUnits however it pleases—there is no legal restriction on this. In practice, you will find that certain organizational structures are commonly used. For example, a Company is commonly divided into one or more Divisions, where each Division has one or more Departments that may consist of one or more Teams. This is shown in Figure 4.12. Be aware, though, that Companies may have other structures, often depending on their size.

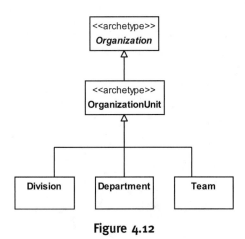

Figure 4.12

4.20.1 Identifiers for organizational units

Often, OrganizationUnits have a unique name within their parent Organization. But even where this is the case, it can be a risky strategy to use that name alone as the identifier. At some time in the future, there may be a reorganization that leads to a change of name.

Also, it's quite possible for more than one unit within an Organization to have the same name. For example, a company may have several Divisions, *each* with a customer service Department, as shown in Figure 4.13.

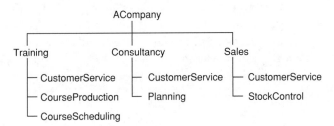

Figure 4.13

To address these problems, a unique identifier that you generate yourself can be assigned to each OrganizationUnit. However, there is another approach that can be adopted.

A unique identifier can be created by generating a path name starting from the top of the organization and working down, for example:

ACompany.Training.CustomerService

This path name strategy works because it never makes sense for two OrganizationUnits with the same parent to have precisely the same name. Note, though, that there is some maintenance overhead if units are moved around within the organizational structure (a surprisingly common occurrence in business) and a further problem if an OrganizationUnit changes its name but remains *unchanged* in all other respects. Clearly, in this case, the unique identifier should remain unchanged, but if you have adopted the organization paths identification strategy, you may *have* to change it.

We conclude, again, that the best approach is to assign to each OrganizationUnit a unique PartyIdentifier that you generate yourself.

4.21 Partnerships and sole proprietors

If your organization does business with partnerships or sole proprietorships, these can be accommodated by the Party pattern.

A partnership can be modeled as an `Organization`. The partnership's name and any alternative trading names can be captured as an `organizationName` and `otherOrganizationNames`, with the appropriate use noted in each case.

A sole trader or proprietor can be modeled as a `Person`. If the name under which the `Person` trades differs from their own name, this can be captured as an `otherPersonName`, with the use noted as `"trading name"`.

You can use the `PartyRole` archetype (see Chapter 5) to identify whether the partnership or sole proprietor is acting as a supplier, partner, and so on. Use `RegisteredIdentifier` to note any tax identity code for the business that your own organization needs to know (e.g., VAT Registration Numbers within the European Community).

4.22 Preferences

> The `Preference` archetype represents a `Party`'s expressed choice of (or liking for) something, often from a set of possible or offered options.

This definition implies that there can be a range of options that a `Party` may choose between. We'll see how to model this a bit later.

There are at least two different types of `Preferences` that you can capture:

- General `Preferences` held by a `Party` (e.g., dietary preferences)
- Specific `Preferences` held by a `Party` playing a particular `PartyRole`

Most preferences are of the second type—that is, they arise when a `Party` is in a particular context that provides options. Our model of `Preferences` (Figure 4.14) provides for both types.

Each `Party` and each `PartyRole` may optionally have zero or more `Preferences`. We discuss `PartyRole` in Section 5.3.

Every `Preference` has a `PreferenceType`.

> The `PreferenceType` archetype specifies the name, a `description`, and a range of `PreferenceOptions` for a `Preference`.
>
> The `PreferenceOption` archetype specifies the name of a possible option and its `description`.

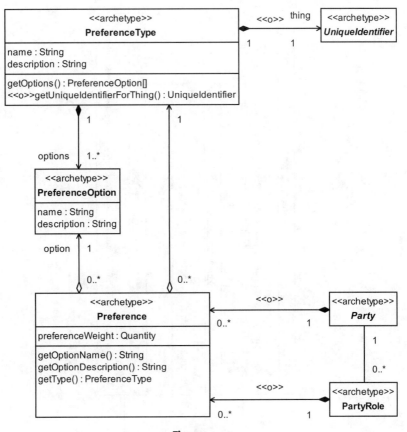

Figure 4.14

Each Preference specifies exactly one option from the range of options listed in its PreferenceType.

For example, Figure 4.15 shows a PreferenceType for a meal on an economy class flight, along with some available PreferenceOptions.

An actual Preference would select one of the PreferenceOptions defined by the PreferenceType, as shown in Figure 4.16.

PreferenceTypes may be related to a specific product or service. This tends to be the case when PreferenceTypes are used with the Customer PartyRole. To show this link, the PreferenceType may optionally specify a product or service as the thing it concerns. If this is the case, the names of the PreferenceOptions

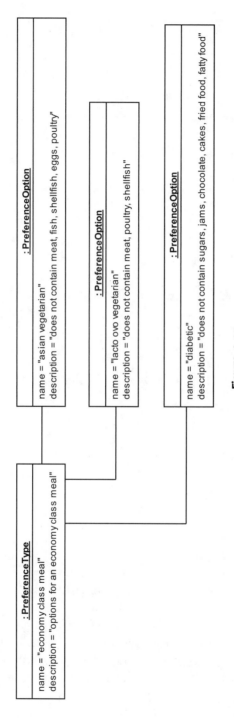

Figure 4.15

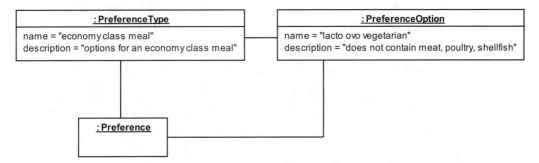

Figure 4.16

will typically refer to specific product features of the product or service (see Section 7.10 for full details of these).

You may also optionally assign a `preferenceWeight` to a specific `Preference`. This is a measure of how important the `Preference` is to the `Party` or `PartyRole` that owns it. Weighting `Preferences` in this way may help you make intelligent CRM decisions in cases where only a subset of `Preferences` can be allowed or where there is a conflict between the `Preferences` expressed.

4.23 PartyManager

It is generally a good idea for your business to centralize the management of `Parties` in one place. This feature is represented in our model as the `PartyManager` archetype, shown in Figure 4.17.

The `PartyManager` archetype manages a collection of `Parties`.

The `PartyManager` archetype provides services to add and remove `Parties` from your company's records. It also provides a set of "finder" operations that allow you to locate a specific `Party`. You can add further operations as needed to meet the specific requirements of your business.

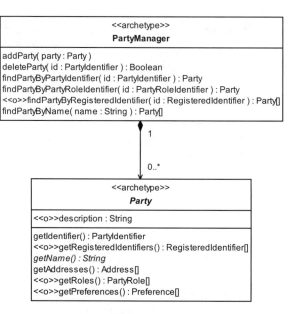

Figure 4.17

4.24 Summary

In this chapter we looked at the Party archetype pattern, which is a pattern for representing essential business information about people and organizations. We covered the topics listed below.

- Party: how to represent a person or an organization
  - PartyIdentifier: how to uniquely identify a Party
  - RegisteredIdentifier: how to represent identifiers for a Party that have been assigned by recognized or statutory bodies
  - PartySignature: how to represent the identifying mark of a Party
  - PartyAuthentication: how to represent a trusted way to confirm the identity of a Party
- Address: how to represent contact information for a Party
  - GeographicAddress
  - TelecomAddress
  - EmailAddress

- WebPageAddress
- AddressProperties: how to specify arbitrary properties of an Address (e.g., the context in which it should be used)

- Person: how to represent information about human beings
  - Identifiers for people
  - ISOGender: how to represent gender information
  - Ethnicity: how to represent a Person's ethnic background
  - BodyMetrics: how to represent information about the human body
  - PersonName: how to represent names of people

- Organization: how to represent an administrative or functional structure
  - OrganizationName: how to represent the name of an Organization
  - OrganizationUnit: how to represent an Organization that is part of another Organization

- Company: how to represent companies
  - CompanyGroup: how to represent a related group of companies
  - Company names
  - Identifiers for companies
  - Identifiers for company organizational units

- Partnerships and sole proprietors

- Preference: how to represent a Party's choice of or liking for something, typically selected from a range of options
  - PreferenceType: how to represent a range of options available to a Party
  - PreferenceOption: how to represent a specific option from the range available to a Party

- PartyManager: how to represent and manage collections of Parties

Chapter 5

PartyRelationship archetype pattern

5.1 Business context

In the last chapter, you saw how to capture information about people and organizations using the `Party` archetype and its subclasses `Person` and `Organization`. In this chapter we will look at the much more complicated issue of relationships between `Parties`.

As you will see, modeling `Party` relationships can become quite complex and abstract. Parts of this chapter may therefore be more appropriate for software developers than businesspeople. If you *are* a businessperson rather than a software developer, our advice is simply to skim over those sections that appear to be abstract.

It can be very important to understand and capture relationships between `Parties`. For example, you may need to understand your customer base and the various relationships a customer has to you and perhaps to other customers—this is a big part of customer relationship management. Or you may need to model an organization such as a business or a team and to understand the relationships within that organization.

To achieve any of these goals, you need to model not just the `Parties` themselves but also the relationships between those `Parties`.

These relationships can be many and complex. Perhaps you have heard of the game "Six Degrees of Kevin Bacon." In this game the object is to relate the actor Kevin Bacon to another actor by using no more than six relationships, where each relationship is a movie in which two of the actors in the chain both appeared. For example, you can easily link Kevin Bacon to Sigourney Weaver as shown in Figure 5.1.

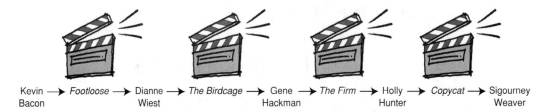

Kevin → *Footloose* → Dianne → *The Birdcage* → Gene → *The Firm* → Holly → *Copycat* → Sigourney
Bacon   Wiest   Hackman   Hunter   Weaver

Figure 5.1

Each of us is connected to almost everyone else on the planet by a surprisingly small number of relationships. No one knows precisely what the average number of relationships in such a chain is, but recent research indicates that it is probably no more than about ten. This figure is very low because a few people are very highly connected. Once a chain gets to one of these highly connected people, he or she creates a shortcut to many other people. Such a network is known as a *scale-free network:* most nodes (e.g., actors) have very few relationships (e.g., shared films) but some nodes (such as Kevin Bacon) have many, and these nodes create shortcuts through the network.

Another example of a scale-free network is the World Wide Web. Web traversal is dominated by a relatively small number of highly connected nodes such as Yahoo! and Google.

The other type of network is the *random network*, where every node has the same average number of relationships (a measure of its "scale").

Because we all live our lives in a web of very complex relationships, the key point from the perspective of the object-oriented analyst/designer is to work out exactly which of these relationships are significant for business systems and which are not. You can't exhaustively capture all relationships around a given Party, so you must use business requirements to decide which part of the network of relationships you *need* to capture.

5.2   PartyRelationship **archetype pattern overview and roadmap**

The PartyRelationship archetype pattern model is shown in Figure 5.2. This is the more common and useful AsymmetricPartyRelationship pleomorph of this pattern (see Section 5.3 for details of the two pleomorphs).

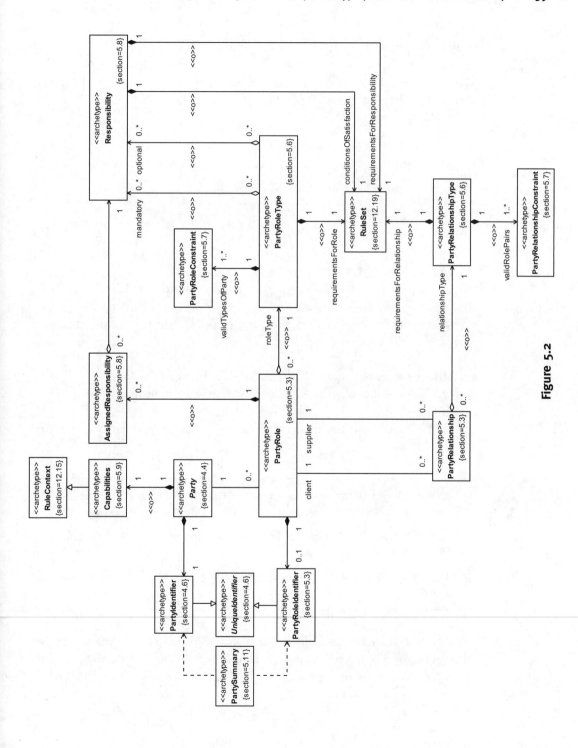

Figure 5.2

5.3 PartyRole **and** PartyRelationship

There are several ways you can model the fact that a Party is related to another Party. The simplest approach is shown in Figure 5.3.

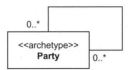

Figure 5.3

All that Figure 5.3 *really* tells you is that Parties are related in some undefined way to zero or more other Parties. Because you already knew that, this is not a particularly useful model!

You generally need at least two extra pieces of information to make this useful from the business perspective.

1. The exact semantics of the relationships between the Parties
2. The specific roles the Parties play in these relationships

You can easily capture this information by introducing the new archetypes defined below.

> The PartyRelationship archetype captures the fact that there is a semantic relationship between two Parties in which each Party plays a specific role.
>
> The PartyRole archetype captures the semantics of the role played by a Party in a particular PartyRelationship.
>
> The PartyRoleIdentifier archetype represents a unique identifier for a PartyRole.

The PartyRole archetype is always used to store information that pertains to the PartyRole itself, *not* information about the Party or the PartyRelationship. This is an important point, and one that modelers often miss.

You will find that the English language does not always distinguish clearly between relationships and roles. This is partly because some relationships are symmetrical (as described below), so the role and the relationship become somewhat confused, and partly because in normal English usage the difference between the two often just isn't relevant. However, it is very important when interviewing stakeholders to analyze their language patterns, to try to distinguish the possibly implicit roles and relationships in their business domain.

There are two variants, or pleomorphs, of the `PartyRelationship` archetype pattern, shown in Figure 5.4.

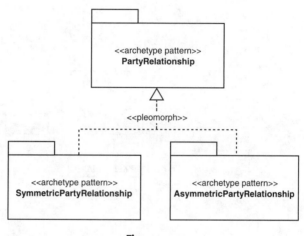

Figure 5.4

A relationship is symmetrical if the roles on each end are identical—that is, they may be substituted for each other *without* changing the semantics of the relationship in any way.

In this case, there is only *one* set of role information, and this information may be attached to the relationship itself. This gives rise to a simple pleomorph that we call `SymmetricPartyRelationship`, as shown in Figure 5.5. In this symmetric case, the `PartyRole` is just an attribute of the `PartyRelationship`.

A good example of this sort of symmetric relationship is the sister/sister relationship between two female siblings (see Figure 5.6).

However, if you need to capture any information that relates to just one of the roles—for example, if you wish to indicate which sister is the elder and which the younger—this cannot be attached to the relationship, and it is therefore no longer symmetrical.

In the real world, most `PartyRelationships` are *asymmetrical* because each `Party` plays a different role in the relationship. This asymmetry is typically what

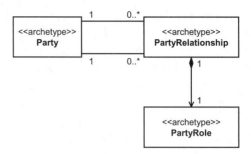

Figure 5.5

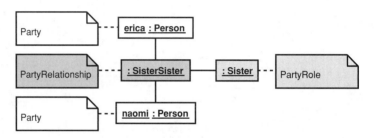

Figure 5.6

gives the relationship its value—one Party has capabilities and/or requirements that complement those of the other Party.

Asymmetry gives rise to the most useful pleomorph, AsymmetricParty-Relationship, of which SymmetricPartyRelationship is just a special case. Because of this, we will concentrate on the AsymmetricPartyRelationship pleomorph in the rest of this chapter.

The AsymmetricPartyRelationship pleomorph is shown in Figure 5.7. (The attributes and operations of the PartyRole and PartyRelationship arche-types will be discussed as appropriate in subsequent sections.)

The semantics of this model match the natural language description of roles and relationships perfectly: a party plays a role in a relationship with another party that plays a complementary role.

In Figure 5.7 you can see that one PartyRole is acting as the client in the PartyRelationship, and the other PartyRole is acting as the supplier. You can use the terms *client* and *supplier* to emphasize the fact that the relationship is asymmetrical, but the particular assignment of a pair of PartyRoles to the client and supplier sides of the PartyRelationship may not always be clear cut.

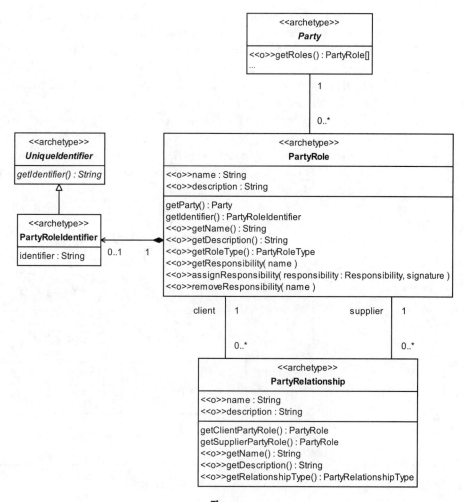

Figure 5.7

For example, in a producer/consumer business-to-business relationship, it is clear which of the roles is the supplier (producer) and which is the client (consumer). In relationships such as father/son, however, the decision as to which role is connected to the supplier side and which is connected to the client side depends on your particular interpretation of that relationship. Nevertheless, you should always make the assignment consistently. As we've already mentioned, in any relationship where both roles are *exactly* the same (e.g., the sister/sister relationship) there is simply no decision to be made and the notion of client and supplier is redundant.

The level of abstraction at which you are working becomes very important when you are finding roles and relationships. For example, if you consider the father/son relationship in an abstract way, you could conceivably introduce a symmetric party relationship called `FamilyRelationship`. This is clearly a very abstract type of relationship that could also be applied to father/daughter, father/mother, sister/sister, and so on.

As relationships get less abstract, they tend to become more asymmetrical. Thus, if you make the `FamilyRelationship` relationship less abstract, in the case of father/son it first becomes `ParentChild`, then (even less abstract) `ParentSon`, and finally `FatherSon`. All these more concrete relationships are asymmetrical. You can see this illustrated in Figure 5.8.

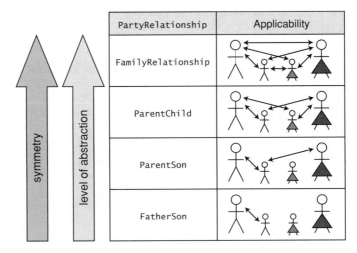

Figure 5.8

5.4 N-ary relationships

You may notice that we are only modeling the case where there is a relationship between exactly two `Parties`. This is known as a *binary relationship*. There are also other types of relationships, known as *n-ary relationships*, that involve many `Parties` simultaneously.

You can reduce every n-ary relationship to two or more binary relationships. In this sense, n-ary relationships can be considered to be just a summary of a set of binary relationships in the special case where each binary relationship has a PartyRelationship object that is equivalent to that of all the others. Because of this—and the fact that binary relationships are more flexible, conceptually cleaner, and easier to understand—we'll stick with binary relationships in our models.

5.5 A simple example

Before we go on to discuss the detailed semantics of PartyRole and PartyRelationship, we'll look at a very simple example to illustrate how these archetypes can be used in practice. In this example, we use PartyRoles and PartyRelationships to express structural relationships—see Section 6.3 for an example of a nonstructural use of PartyRole.

We will model a small software development project called the Archetype Cartridge Project, a real project we were involved in. (We described some of the results of this work in Chapter 2.)

In order to use the PartyRelationship archetype pattern, we first need to identify the following:

- The Parties involved
- The PartyRelationships that connect these Parties together
- The PartyRoles that these Parties play in those PartyRelationships

You may remember from the last chapter that Parties come in two basic types, People and Organizations. In this example, we have one Organization (the archetypeCartridgeProject) and several People who are members of the project.

- jim
- ila
- ronald

The PartyRoles that the People play in the project are shown in Table 5.1.

You can see that jim plays two PartyRoles in the project—ProjectManager and Architect. The archetypeCartridgeProject itself plays a PartyRole with respect to its People. This PartyRole is called EmployingProject.

Finally, we need some PartyRelationships to link these PartyRoles together in the right way. In this case, all of the interesting information can be captured

Table 5.1

Party	PartyRole				
	ProjectManager	Architect	Developer	TechnicalConsultant	EmployingProject
jim	X	X			
ila			X		
ronald				X	
archetypeCartridgeProject					X

in the PartyRoles themselves, so the PartyRelationship is just acting like glue to stick these PartyRoles together. We introduce a very simple and generic relationship called MemberOfProject to do this job.

Having defined all the types of Parties, PartyRoles, and PartyRelationships necessary for the project, we can extend the AsymmetricPartyRelationship pattern as shown in Figure 5.9.

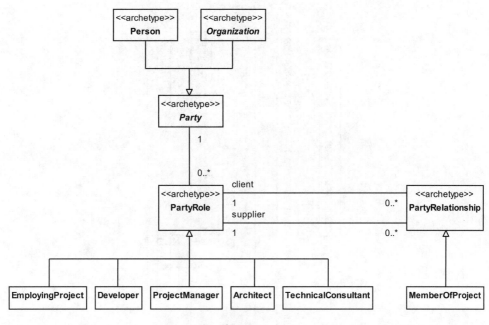

Figure 5.9

Using these classes and archetypes, we can model the actual structure of the team as a set of objects, shown in Figure 5.10. We've shaded in the various types of things (PartyRoles, PartyRelationships, and Parties) to help you see what is going on.

At first glance, you might think that this is a rather verbose way to model a project structure. Notice, though, how it allows you to uniquely capture the details of each Person's role in the project as a PartyRole object. It also allows you to capture any unique details of each Person's relationship to the project itself as a PartyRelationship object. This is the most complete and flexible way to model the project structure.

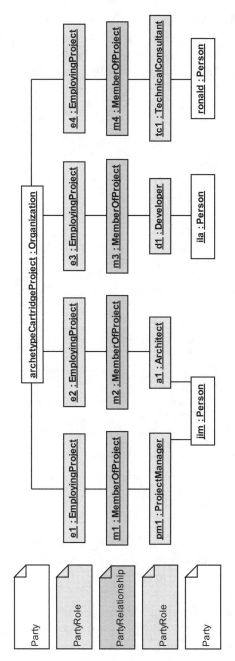

Figure 5.10

However, the project structure is not the only thing of interest about this project. It also has a rather interesting reporting structure.

To model the reporting structure, we need to extend the AsymmetricPartyRelationship pattern in a slightly different way. We add two new PartyRoles and one new PartyRelationship, as shown in Figure 5.11.

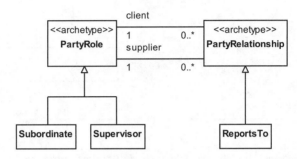

Figure 5.11

Now we can construct the reporting hierarchy shown in Figure 5.12. Again, you can see that you can explicitly capture all the PartyRoles and Relationships for each Party. Notice that ronald has a dual chain of reporting! We have introduced richard, who is ronald's supervisor.

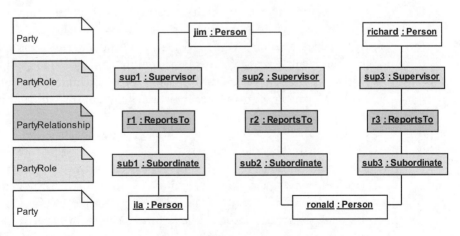

Figure 5.12

In fact, in this project, jim and ila work for clearViewTraining, and richard and ronald work for interactiveObjects (makers of the ArcStyler architectural IDE that we discuss in Chapter 2). The archetypeCartridgeProject is a joint project between clearViewTraining and interactiveObjects. We can model this collaboration by defining some new types of PartyRoles and PartyRelationships, as shown in Figure 5.13.

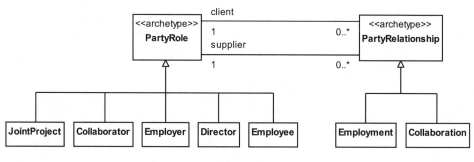

Figure 5.13

Using these new PartyRoles and PartyRelationships, the relationship between clearViewTraining, interactiveObjects, and the archetypeCartridgeProject can be modeled as shown in Figure 5.14.

However, there is yet another relationship between clearViewTraining and interactiveObjects—there is a formal partnership agreement between the two Organizations. Again, we need to introduce some new types of PartyRoles and PartyRelationships (as shown in Figure 5.15) to capture this.

Notice that the Partnership relationship is asymmetrical. This is normal; one Party (the PrinciplePartner) is usually responsible for running the partnership program.

Using these new PartyRoles and PartyRelationships, we can model the partnership as shown in Figure 5.16.

As you can see, even with this simple example involving only four people (jim, ila, ronald, and richard) and three organizations (archetypeCartridgeProject, clearViewTraining, and interactiveObjects), there is a very complex network of relationships. The key to managing this effectively is to model only those relationships that are important for your business.

Don't try to model relationships exhaustively!

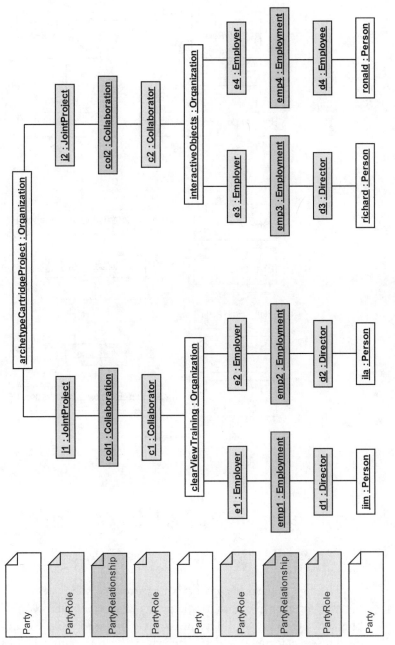

Figure 5.14

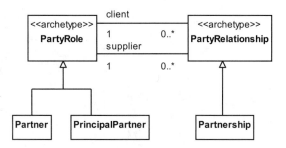

Figure 5.15

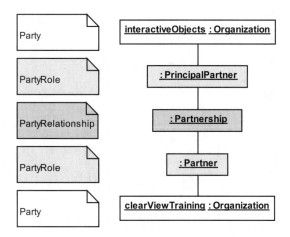

Figure 5.16

5.6 PartyRoleType **and** PartyRelationshipType

There are essentially two ways you can model different types of PartyRoles and PartyRelationships.

The first and simplest way is to introduce subclasses of PartyRole and PartyRelationship for each type of role and relationship you wish to model. This is exactly what we did in the example in the previous section.

This is a reasonable approach when the roles and relationships you are modeling are simple and don't contain much information, as is typically the case if you use PartyRoles and PartyRelationships in order to capture a network of relationships between Parties but nothing else.

However, when you are interested in the detailed semantics of the Party-Roles and PartyRelationships themselves, you may find that you need to store a lot of information. This information may include detailed descriptions, responsibilities, preferences, and so on. Much of this information is *common* across all instances of particular PartyRole and PartyRelationship types. In this case, you can introduce two new archetypes, PartyRoleType and PartyRelationshipType, to store all of the common information once only. This information can then be referenced from PartyRole and PartyRelationship instances.

> The PartyRoleType archetype provides a way to store all of the common information for a set of PartyRole instances.
>
> The PartyRelationshipType archetype provides a way to store all of the common information for a set of PartyRelationship instances.

The model for PartyRoleTypes and PartyRelationshipTypes is shown in Figure 5.17.

Notice that the PartyRoleType and PartyRelationshipType are shown as optional. You can see that they each have name and description attributes that capture the basic information about a PartyRole or PartyRelationship respectively. If you choose to include these optional archetypes, you should *omit* the name and description attributes from PartyRole and PartyRelationship (otherwise, you would be storing these names and descriptions twice).

In the next few sections we'll look at how you can use PartyRoleType and PartyRelationshipType to manage the roles and relationships between Parties.

5.7 Managing PartyRoles and PartyRelationships

When managing the network of PartyRoles and PartyRelationships, one of the key things you have to decide is, "Which things can be connected together, and which things can't?"

This question breaks down into two parts.

1. Which types of Parties (e.g., People, Companies) can play which PartyRoles?
2. Which PartyRoles can participate in which PartyRelationships?

A good way to capture this information is simply to add constraints to the PartyRoleType and the PartyRelationshipType, as shown in Figure 5.18.

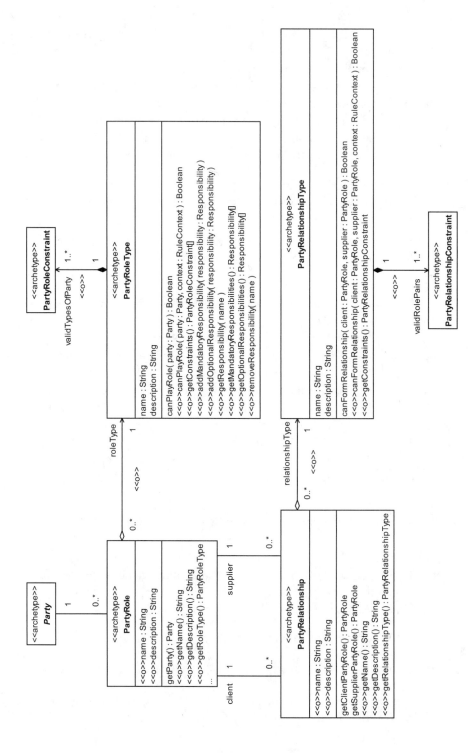

Figure 5.17

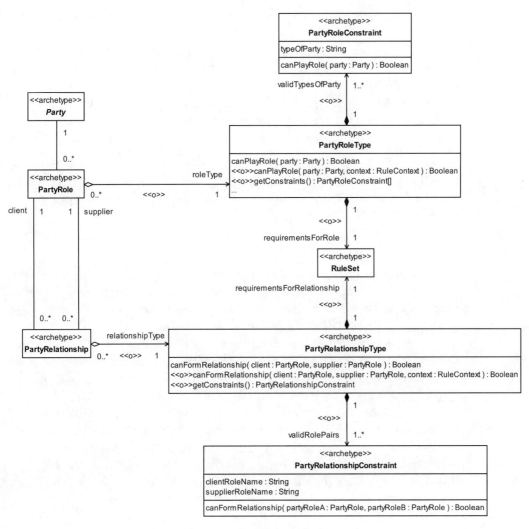

Figure 5.18

One or more PartyRoleConstraints are associated with each PartyRoleType.

The PartyRoleConstraint archetype specifies the typeOfParty that is allowed to play a PartyRole of a specific PartyRoleType.

For example, if there is a `PartyRoleConstraint` on a particular `PartyRole-Type` where the `typeOfParty` is `"Organization"`, any `Party` of type `Organization` can adopt a `PartyRole` of that type. You can see that, taken together, `PartyRole-Constraints` limit or constrain the type of `Party` that may assume a `PartyRole` of a particular type.

PartyRelationshipConstraints work in much the same way. Each `Party-RelationshipType` has one or more `PartyRelationshipConstraints`.

> The `PartyRelationshipConstraint` archetype specifies the names of `PartyRoles` that may adopt the `client` and `supplier` sides of a `PartyRelationship` of a specific `PartyRelationshipType`.

A `RuleSet` that specifies a set of arbitrary `requirementsForRole` is optionally associated with `PartyRoleType`. These are a set of requirements that must be met before a `Party` can play a `PartyRole` of a specific type. An example might be `"age > 18"`. See Chapter 12 on `Rules` for more information.

We do exactly the same thing for `PartyRelationshipType`. The optional `requirementsForRelationship RuleSet` defines a set of conditions that must be true before two specific `PartyRoles` can engage in a particular type of `Party-Relationship` with each other.

You should *always* use `PartyRoleConstraints` and `PartyRelationship-Constraints` to model the *basic* constraints on the type of `Party` that can adopt a particular type of `PartyRole` or the type of `PartyRoles` that can form a specific type of `PartyRelationship`. The `requirementsForRole` and `require-mentsForRelationship RuleSets` model a set of requirements for the `Party` and `PartyRole` that are *supplementary* to the `PartyRoleConstraints` and `Party-RelationshipConstraints` and that are about completely arbitrary aspects of the `Party` or `PartyRole`. We'd like to stress again that `requirementsForRole` and `requirementsForRelationship` are optional, and you are likely to use them only in quite advanced applications of this pattern!

Let's take a concrete example to show how `PartyRoleConstraints` and `PartyRelationshipConstraints` work: we will model the `Marriage` relationship. We first need to introduce the appropriate `PartyRoles` (`Husband` and `Wife`) and `PartyRelationship` (`Marriage`), as shown in Figure 5.19.

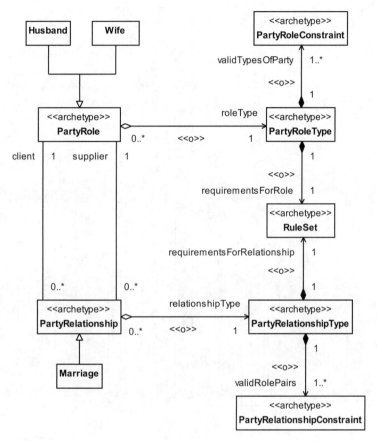

Figure 5.19

Using our model, you can represent the following set of facts, as shown in Figure 5.20.

1. The Husband PartyRole must always be played by a Party of type Person.
2. The Wife PartyRole must always be played by a Party of type Person.
3. In this view of Marriage, the Marriage PartyRelationship must always be between a Husband and a Wife.

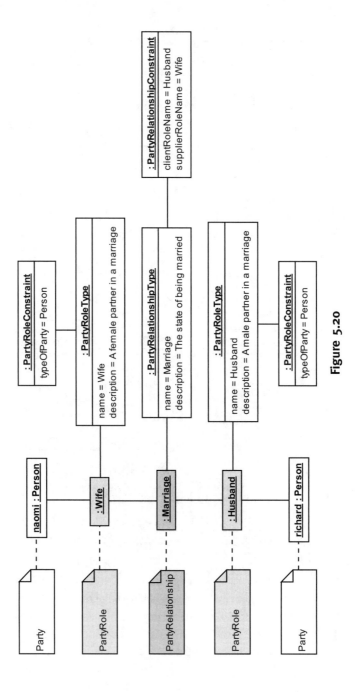

Figure 5.20

From Figure 5.20, you can see that naomi is married to richard. Note how we have captured the constraints on the PartyRoles and PartyRelationship. The PartyRoleConstraints state that only Parties of type Person may adopt PartyRoles of type Husband or Wife. The PartyRelationshipConstraint states that the PartyRoles that can participate in a Marriage PartyRelationship are Husband and Wife. We have quite arbitrarily let the Wife fulfill the supplier side of the relationship and the Husband fulfill the client side.

It's worth pointing out that there is more than one type of Marriage, but for this example we kept things simple and assumed that it is always between a Husband and a Wife. Again, for simplicity, we excluded requirementsForRole and requirementsForRelationship from our example. However, note that in most countries there is a legal age at which marriage becomes possible, and this age could be specified as one of the requirementsForRole constraints. Likewise, a Husband could be constrained by the requirementsForRole to be male and a Wife constrained to be female.

5.8 Responsibilities

One of the primary reasons for defining PartyRoles is so that you can assign Responsibilities to them. This capability is an optional part of the Party-Relationship archetype pattern; there are some cases, as you've seen above, where you may be using PartyRoles and PartyRelationships to capture purely structural information.

> The Responsibility archetype represents a description of an activity that a PartyRoleType may be expected to perform.

A Responsibility usually results in, or contributes toward, the delivery of some expected outcome as defined by optional conditionsOfSatisfaction for the Responsibility. These conditionsOfSatisfaction are a set of Rules that define the conditions under which a Responsibility is fulfilled. See our Rule pattern in Chapter 12 for one approach to capturing business rules.

Each PartyRoleType defines a set of optional Responsibilities and a set of mandatory Responsibilities as shown in Figure 5.21 (also see Figure 5.17 on page 174 for the related operations in PartyRoleType). Any Party adopting a PartyRole of this type must assume all of the mandatory Responsibilities and may assume some or all of the optional Responsibilities.

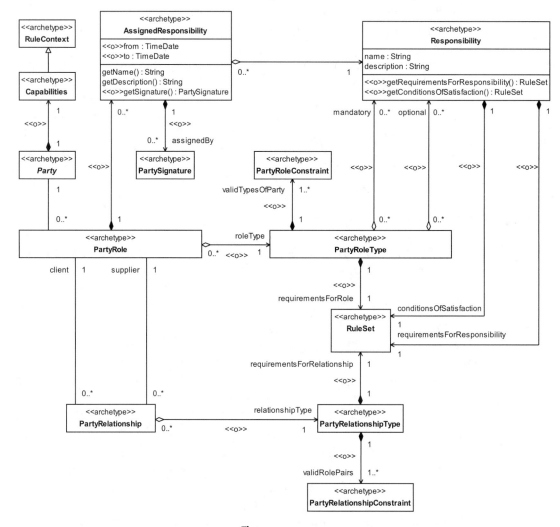

Figure 5.21

For example, one of us, when taking on the PartyRole of TeamLeader, once had the mandatory and optional Responsibilities described in Table 5.2.

Table 5.2

PartyRole = TeamLeader			
	Responsibility	requirementsFor-Responsibility	conditionsOfSatisfaction
mandatory Responsibilities	Motivating the team		Average score for staff motivation >= 7 out of 10 on staff feedback form
	Assigning tasks to team members		Average staff utilization >= 80% over previous 6-month period
optional Responsibilities	Carrying out formal review of staff performance	Team leader grade > team member grade	Formal reviews completed and written up

It's quite common for businesses to assign Responsibilities without having any concrete way to assess whether the Responsibilities are carried out or not! However, in Table 5.2, you can see that the business assigned measurable conditionsOfSatisfaction to each mandatory Responsibility.

You can model the assumption of a Responsibility by a PartyRole as an AssignedResponsibility.

The AssignedResponsibility archetype represents an instance of a Responsibility assigned to a specific PartyRole.

The AssignedResponsibility gets its name and description from its parent Responsibility. The AssignedResponsibility may have an optional period of operation starting at from and proceeding until to and optionally may be signed with a PartySignature that records who made the assignment (see Section 4.8 for further discussion of PartySignature).

Each Responsibility may also have a set of requirementsForResponsibility that defines the constraints that *must* be satisfied before the Responsibility may be assigned to a PartyRole. In our TeamLeader example, the requirementsForResponsibility for the optional performance review Responsibility specify that the TeamLeader is of a more senior grade than the team member under review.

Sometimes it appears that a responsibility is given to an individual, rather than assigned to the role he or she is carrying out. For example, a manager may have a responsibility, additional to that of managing his or her own area, for collating and validating the monthly reports for the entire department. Our view is that the manager in this case has actually been assigned the additional PartyRole of ReportsCoordinator, and it is this role that has the responsibility.

5.9 Capabilities

> The Capabilities archetype represents a collection of facts about what a Party is capable of doing.

For example, a Party might have a capability:

`"Java programming skill level = 8 out of 10"`

In our model, we have captured Capabilities as a type of RuleContext (see Figure 5.21). This means that the Party Capabilities may be matched with the requirementsForRole and requirementsForResponsibility, both of which are RuleSets, to create a simple rules-based approach to PartyRole and Responsibility assignment. You can find out more about business rules in Chapter 12.

A full discussion of the assignment of Roles and Responsibilities is beyond the scope of this book. This is a complex area, and we intend to address it in more detail in a future volume, when we discuss Activities and Resource allocation.

5.10 Using the PartyRelationship archetype pattern

As you have seen, the PartyRelationship archetype pattern is very flexible, and there are many ways in which you could use it. In this section, we give you some hints on how you can apply this pattern effectively.

The golden rule, as we have pointed out, is that you capture a relationship only if there is a business need to do so. The web of possible relationships between even a small number of Parties can be very large, and you generally need to capture only a small fragment of this web to meet your business requirements. The first step in applying this pattern is therefore to understand your business requirements for capturing PartyRelationships.

Once you understand your requirements, you can analyze them to work out what types of Parties, PartyRelationships, and PartyRoles you need to introduce to model the relationships. Proceed as follows.

1. Identify the types of Parties that you need to relate to each other.
2. List the different types of relationships that exist between these types of Parties—this will give you your PartyRelationships.
3. Check that each of these PartyRelationships meets some identifiable business need.
4. Work out what roles different types of Parties play in these Party-Relationships—this will give you your PartyRoles.
5. If you are using PartyRoleConstraints and PartyRelationship-Constraints, formulate rules that describe which typesOfParties can play which PartyRoles and which PartyRoles can participate in which PartyRelationships.

5.11 PartySummary

As you have seen, our model of Parties and PartyRelationships is quite detailed and contains a lot of information. However, in certain circumstances you will need to take a snapshot of a small subset of this information for a specific purpose. You can handle this using the PartySummary archetype (see Figure 5.22).

Figure 5.22

> The PartySummary archetype represents a snapshot of summary contact information about a Party, in relation to a particular context.

You can see that this captures a very small subset of the possible Party or PartyRole information. You can extend this archetype with whatever information you need in your circumstances. Our model recognizes that a PartyIdentifier may not always be available or known in a specific instance, although a name and address should be known. Each business needs to decide whether to capture roleIdentifiers, telephoneNumbers, or emailAddresses as part of the PartySummary.

A good example of where you would use the PartySummary archetype is on an Order. When an Order is raised, you have to capture Party information for each of the Parties involved in the Order. This needs to be a snapshot of the required contact information because once an Order has been raised, it can be changed only by an amendment process (discussed in Section 9.13). You can't just record a PartyIdentifier (or PartyRoleIdentifier) on the Order because the information to which these identifiers point is subject to change outside of the Order amendment process. The Order itself would then be subject to change in unpredictable ways and would no longer represent a stable record of the sales transaction.

5.12 Summary

In this chapter we looked at the PartyRelationship archetype pattern. This is a pattern for representing relationships between Parties. We covered the topics listed below.

- PartyRole and PartyRelationship: how to represent relationships between Parties and the roles the Parties play in those relationships
  - PartyRoleIdentifier: how to uniquely identify a PartyRole
- N-ary relationships: how to represent a relationship between three or more Parties
- PartyRoleType and PartyRelationshipType: how to represent different types of PartyRoles and PartyRelationships

- Managing `PartyRoles` and `PartyRelationships`: how to manage complex networks of `PartyRelationships`
  - `PartyRoleConstraint`: how to constrain the types of `PartyRoles` that a particular type of `Party` can play
  - `PartyRelationshipConstraint`: how to constrain the types of `PartyRoles` that can act as the `client` and `supplier` sides of a specific `PartyRelationshipType`
- `Responsibility`: how to describe a particular activity that a `PartyRoleType` may be expected to perform
  - `AssignedResponsibility`: how to capture the fact that a particular `Responsibility` has been assigned to a particular `PartyRole`
- `Capabilities`: how to model the facts about what a `Party` is capable of doing
- The `PartyRelationship` archetype pattern: how to use this pattern effectively
- `PartySummary`: how to take a snapshot of summary information about a `Party` when the full set of information is not required

Chapter 6

Customer relationship management archetype pattern

6.1 Business context

Although the best businesses have always realized that their relationships with their customers are important, it is only more recently that customer relationship management (CRM) has become a hot topic. This is because with the advent of the Internet, your competition is now only a few mouse clicks away for your customers! Similarly, sharing a good (or bad) customer experience with thousands of others is very easy to do. The physical barriers to acquiring new customers *from* the competition, or to losing your existing customers *to* the competition, are lower than they have ever been.

CRM is about actively managing the relationships between your business and your customers, in order to understand and increase customer value, motivation, and loyalty. Increasingly, CRM is about recognizing and treating the customer as an *individual*. This is known as *relationship marketing* because the marketing activity is based on an established relationship to a known customer.

CRM can work only when the right business information has been collected and is made easily available to the right people, at the right time, in the right place, and in the right way to allow them to manage customer relationships effectively. This business information aspect of CRM needs to be supported by technology, and that's what we'll examine in this chapter.

However, there is more to CRM than technology, despite what some CRM vendors may have you believe. CRM usually necessitates a strategic change in business culture and philosophy, to center business activities around the customer.

The goals of CRM are to:

- Assess the business value of the customer
- Increase the business value of the customer
- Increase customer satisfaction
- Gain and maintain customer loyalty (i.e., decrease customer churn)
- Motivate customers to repeat business
- Attract new customers
- Understand which customers to keep and which to lose
- Save money by streamlining customer interactions

All CRM is predicated on having a *unified* view of the customer—unless you have this, your attempts at CRM are likely to be ineffectual or to fail.

This unified view of the customer should include:

- Customer information (name, address, and so on)—see Chapter 4
- Customer needs (preferably anticipating these needs!)
- Customer preferences—see Chapter 4
- Customer value to the business
- Customer buying patterns (behaviors)
- Customer communications with the business

In this chapter we are going to take two existing archetype patterns, `Party` and `PartyRelationship`, and show you how to combine them to create a new archetype pattern, called the CRM archetype pattern. This new pattern captures some key business information aspects of CRM. In particular, we address the following issues.

- What is a customer?
- How do you manage customer communications?

If you are not familiar with the `Party` and `PartyRelationship` archetype patterns, we suggest you read (or at least skim) Chapters 4 and 5 before proceeding with this chapter.

As we have mentioned, CRM is much more than business information, but the other aspects are outside the scope of this book. However, if you are interested in the many other dimensions of CRM, please check out our Web site (www.businessarchetypes.com) for useful references.

6.2 CRM archetype pattern overview and roadmap

Figure 6.1 shows our model for the CRM archetype pattern.

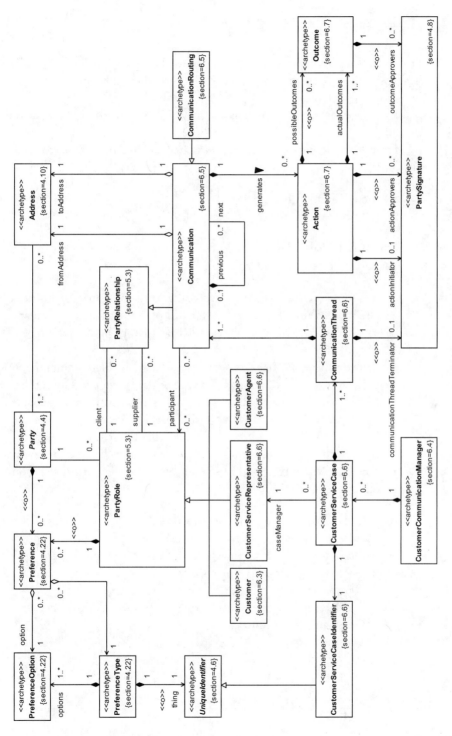

Figure 6.1

6.3 Customer

From an information point of view, one of the key questions in CRM is, "What is a customer?" A customer is defined by most dictionaries as "a person who buys goods or services."

In other words, a customer is a `Party` involved in the process of buying products.

From a modeling perspective, there are two potential ways to look at a customer.

1. A customer is a type of `Party`.
2. A customer is a role that a `Party` plays in a sales process.

Option 1 is plausible, and we know many businesses that have gone down that route! However, it suffers from some major drawbacks.

- It is semantically incorrect—according to the dictionary definition, the essential feature of a customer is that it participates in a particular activity, that is, *customer* describes a role that a `Party` plays, not a type of `Party` per se.
- Your business may have different parts, each of which maintains a list of its customers—if a customer is a type of `Party`, you end up replicating `Party` information, possibly even across several business systems. (In Chapter 4 we explained why this is a *very* bad idea.)
- It is a very simple and inflexible model that doesn't scale well with complexity—you may find that a `Party` needs to be able to play many possible roles in relationship to your business, where *customer* is only one such role.

In fact, this option is so bad that we won't discuss it further, except to say that it provides a very poor basis for *any* CRM system. We find that most companies that have adopted this approach move from it at some point to option 2.

Option 2 is more complex but correct. A `Party` may play *many* roles in respect to your business, one of which may be the `Customer` role.

We model `Customer` as a type of `PartyRole` (see Section 5.3), and we define the `Customer` archetype as follows.

> The `Customer` archetype is a type of `PartyRole` that a `Party` may play on the purchasing side of a sales process.

This approach has the major advantage that you can store Party information for People or Organizations just once, then let these Parties play the role of Customer (or other roles) with respect to your business in as many ways as you find useful. All of these roles may be easily related back to the specific Party that is playing the role.

For example, suppose your company sells PCs and you have a business division and a home division. Each division may maintain its own list of Customers, but these roles *always* relate back to a specific Party that is stored only once.

This can give you some very useful flexibility in CRM. Let's say that you'd like to give any Party who is a business Customer of high value special treatment if he or she also appears as a home Customer. This CRM opportunity will be available to you only if you can "join the dots" and work out that the business Customer and the home Customer correspond to the same Person. Many businesses find it hard to do this!

Figure 6.2 shows our model of Customer as a type of PartyRole. Notice that you may assign an optional customerValue to the Customer that indicates the value of the Customer to your business. We don't recommend any particular way to measure customerValue—your business needs to devise its own metrics. However, by using the Quantity pattern (Chapter 10) to express customer-Value, our model can support any standard of measurement (Metric) that makes sense to your business. Refer to [Dyché 2001] for more information about assessing the business value of a Customer.

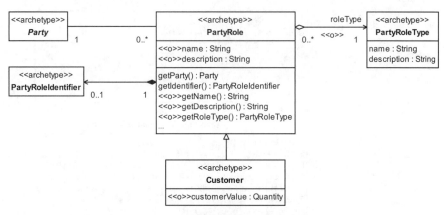

Figure 6.2

Finally, it's worth noting that a customer can assume different roles for specific interactions with the business. See Section 9.6 for details of the roles that a customer can take within the Order process.

6.4 CustomerCommunicationManager

> The `CustomerCommunicationManager` archetype manages all `Customer` Communications as a set of `CustomerServiceCases`.

Figure 6.3 shows the relationship of `CustomerCommunicationManager` to `CustomerServiceCases`. We'll look at the `Communication` and `CustomerServiceCase` archetypes in more detail in the next sections.

There are many aspects to CRM, but without doubt one of the most important of these is managing `Customer` Communications effectively. There are several aspects to this:

- Knowing who you are communicating with, even if the `Customer` is represented indirectly by an agent
- Maintaining a record of all `Communications`
- Making the `Communication` history available to `Parties` authorized to interact with the `Customer`
- Generating `Actions` based on `Customer` Communications
- Tracking `Actions` generated from `Customer` Communications
- Monitoring the `Outcomes` of `Actions` generated by `Customer` Communications

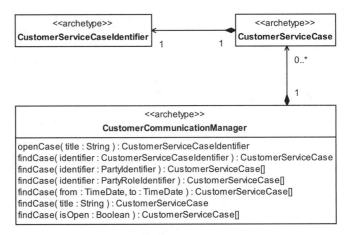

Figure 6.3

Whether initiated by the business or by the `Customer`, communication always has a purpose. From the business perspective, this purpose is ultimately to achieve business benefit by increasing the loyalty or value of the Customer. In order to achieve this benefit, communication must be seen to be effective by all Parties concerned. This is why it is so important to track Communications and their generated Actions and Outcomes.

6.5 Communication

 The Communication archetype represents a type of PartyRelationship that captures details of a communication between two PartyRoles.

Our model of Communication is shown in Figure 6.4. The PartyRelationship archetype is described in Chapter 5.

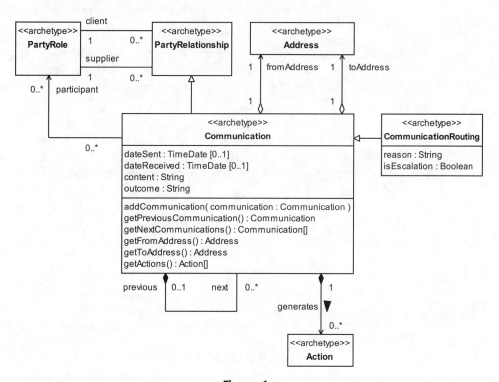

Figure 6.4

Note that `Communications` are not only complaints! Your business may well wish to track and manage formally those `Communications` that detail a customer's requests or requirements or that convey appreciation for service received.

A `Communication` has the attributes described in Table 6.1.

Table 6.1

Communication **archetype**	
Attribute	**Semantics**
dateSent	The time/date of the `Communication`—use this if your business initiates the `Communication`
dateReceived	The time/date of the `Communication`—use this if the `Customer` or their `CustomerAgent` initiates the `Communication`
content	The actual content of the `Communication`—this may be the text of a letter or e-mail or a summary of a phone conversation
	You may be able to hyperlink this field to actual documents such as e-mails and faxes
outcome	A summary of the outcome of the `Communication`—every `Communication` should have some outcome (this may be something other than an `Action`, e.g., agreement that an issue has been resolved)

Each `Communication` has a `fromAddress` representing the `Address` where the `Communication` originated and a `toAddress` representing the `Address` where the `Communication` was received. These `Addresses` can be any of the types discussed in Section 4.10.

Finally, some `Communications` represent handovers between `Customer-ServiceRepresentatives`. These special types of `Communications` are called `CommunicationRoutings`.

> The `CommunicationRouting` archetype is a special type of `Communication` that represents a handover between `CustomerServiceRepresentatives`.

Every `CommunicationRouting` has a `reason`, along with a flag called `isEscalation` to indicate whether the `CommunicationRouting` represents an escalation of the `Communication` to a higher authority.

6.6 CustomerServiceCase

When a new Communication begins, a CustomerServiceCase is opened. You can think of this CustomerServiceCase as being a casebook in which all of the Customer Communications will be recorded. The CustomerServiceCase has the attributes listed in Table 6.2.

> The CustomerServiceCase archetype represents a collection of all Communications about a specific topic related to a specific Customer.

Table 6.2

CustomerServiceCase **archetype**	
Attribute	**Semantics**
title	The title of the case—this should summarize the nature of the case, e.g., "Complaint about call out service"
briefDescription	A short description of the case, e.g., "The customer complained about the response time on DD:MM:YYYY"
raisedBy	The PartyRoleIdentifier of the PartyRole that raised the case—this is usually the PartyRoleIdentifier of a Customer
start	The time/date on which the case began—usually, that of the first Communication in the case
end	The time/date on which the case ended—usually, that of the last Communication in the case or when a decision was made to close the case
isOpen	This is true if the case is still open and false if the case has been closed
priority	This is an indication of the importance of the case from the per-spective of the business, e.g., cases may be prioritized as "low", "medium", or "high" priority

Our model for CustomerServiceCase is shown in Figure 6.5.

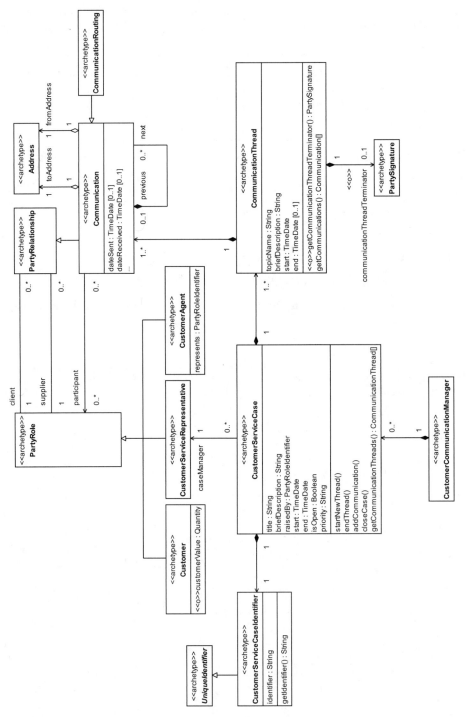

Figure 6.5

Each `CustomerServiceCase` has its own unique `CustomerServiceCaseIdentifier` and is managed by a `caseManager` who is a `CustomerServiceRepresentative` (another type of `PartyRole`).

> The `CustomerServiceCaseIdentifier` archetype represents a unique identifier for a `CustomerServiceCase`.

A `CustomerServiceCase` may contain one or more `CommunicationThreads`.

> The `CommunicationThread` archetype represents a sequence of `Communications` about a particular `topic`.

Each of these threads has a `topicName` that indicates the topic of the thread and a `briefDescription` of the topic and is made up of one or more `Communications`.

The `start` of a `CommunicationThread` is usually the date of the first `Communication`. The end of the thread may be the date of the last `Communication` or the date a decision was made to close the thread (a `PartySignature` can optionally be captured in this instance to identify the `communicationThreadTerminator`).

Each `Communication` relates a `Customer` or `CustomerAgent` to one or more `CustomerServiceRepresentatives`.

> The `CustomerAgent` archetype represents a `PartyRole` played by someone who acts on behalf of a `Customer`.
>
> The `CustomerServiceRepresentative` archetype represents a `PartyRole` played by someone who acts on behalf of, and with the authorization and authority of, the customer services department.

The `PartyRole` that initiates the `Communication` is always assigned to the supplier side of the relationship. For example, if a `Customer` phones a help desk, the `Customer` initiated the `Communication` and would be put on the supplier side of the `Communication` relationship.

Where a `Customer` or `CustomerAgent` initiates a `Communication`, the `Communication` `dateReceived` is noted; if a `CustomerServiceRepresentative` is the initiator, a `dateSent` is noted.

For simplicity, `Communications` always originate from exactly one `supplier` and are received by exactly one `client`. However, many other `PartyRoles` may also be `participants`.

Each `Communication` within a `CommunicationThread` may be linked to zero or one `previous` `Communication` and to zero or more `next` `Communications`. This forms a hierarchical tree of `Communications`, rooted in the initial `CommunicationThread`, as illustrated in Figure 6.6.

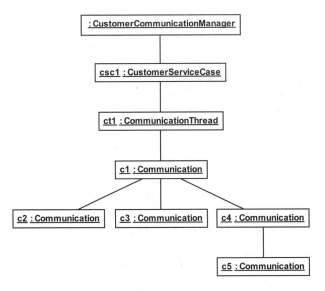

Figure 6.6

This kind of threaded `Communication` structure will be familiar to you if you have used any kind of Internet bulletin board. It has proven to be a very robust and intuitive way to manage even complex conversations.

6.7 Actions **and** Outcomes

As we mentioned earlier, it's not enough simply to record `Customer` `Communications`—to achieve effective CRM, you have to do something about them! Each `Communication` may generate zero to many `Actions`, as illustrated in Figure 6.7.

The `Action` archetype represents a description of something that can happen.

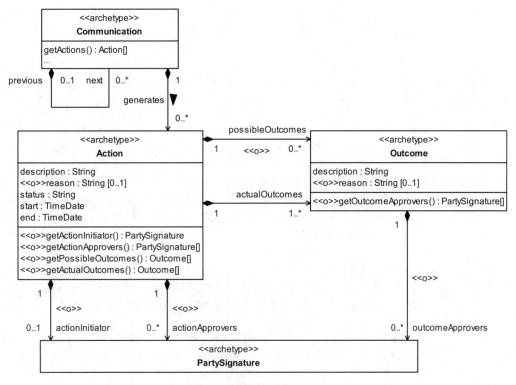

Figure 6.7

Actions have the attributes described in Table 6.3.

Table 6.3

Action **archetype**	
Attribute	**Semantics**
description	A short description of the Action—this should focus on what the Action is trying to achieve
«o»reason	An optional reason for the Action
status	This is the status of the Action—typically this will be one of "pending", "open", or "closed"
start	The time/date on which the Action was started
end	The time/date on which the Action was concluded

The `Party` who is the `actionInitiator` optionally may be captured by a `PartySignature`, as may one or more `Parties` acting as `actionApprovers`.

> The `Outcome` archetype describes the possible or actual result of an `Action` (the `description`) and an optional `reason` for that specific `Outcome`.

Every `Action` may optionally have zero to many `possibleOutcomes` that describe the range of possible results that the `Action` can generate. This is useful when you know in advance all the `possibleOutcomes` for a given `Action`.

For example, a specific `Communication` such as "Ordered goods not received" may generate the `Action` "Check despatch status of goods", and this may have one of two `possibleOutcomes`—"Goods despatched" or "Goods not despatched". Either of these `possibleOutcomes` may generate further `Communications` and `Actions`.

Every `Action` must have one or more `actualOutcomes`, otherwise there is no point in performing the `Action`. (The `description` of this `Outcome` may be "Pending" when first created.)

You can improve your CRM processes by tracking the one or more `actualOutcomes` of each `Action` against any `possibleOutcomes` you may have identified.

If necessary for auditing purposes, each `actualOutcome` may be signed off by zero or more `outcomeApprovers` as represented by their `PartySignatures`.

6.8 Summary

In this chapter we looked at the customer relationship management (CRM) archetype pattern. This is a pattern for representing information about a company's relationships with its customers. We covered the topics listed below.

- What is a customer?
  - Should you represent it as a type of `Party`?
  - Should you represent it as a role that a `Party` plays?
  - The `Customer` archetype: how to represent the `PartyRole` that a `Party` may play on the purchasing side of a sales process

- `CustomerCommunicationManager`: how to represent the business function of managing `Customer Communications` as a set of `CustomerServiceCases`

- Communication: how to capture details of a communication between two PartyRoles as a type of PartyRelationship
  - CommunicationRouting: how to represent the handover of a Communication between CustomerServiceRepresentatives

- CustomerServiceCase: how to capture all of the Communications about a specific topic related to a specific Customer
  - CustomerServiceCaseIdentifier: how to uniquely identify a CustomerServiceCase
  - CommunicationThread: how to capture a sequence of Communications about a particular topic

- CustomerAgent: how to represent the role of someone who acts on behalf of a Customer

- CustomerServiceRepresentative: how to represent the role played by someone who acts on behalf of the customer services department

- Action: how to represent an action that is taken as the result of a Communication

- Outcome: how to represent the actual or possible result of an Action

Chapter 7

Product
archetype pattern

7.1 Business context

All businesses make money by selling some product, either goods or services.

The notion of "product" is very ancient. As soon as humankind developed the concept of ownership, there was the possibility of barter—exchanging one good or service for another to gain some real or perceived benefit. The exchanged goods or services were types of products.

In this chapter we describe the Product archetype pattern, taking a selling rather than a manufacturing perspective on products. The pattern provides a way to model goods and services effectively.

If you have a very clear and explicit notion of the Product archetype pattern, this will lead to flexible business systems that are easy to adapt to new business opportunities. However, if you ignore the Product archetype pattern, it is quite possible to create systems that can sell some things but not others. In today's increasingly volatile business environment, this has to be a dangerous and expensive restriction, yet we have seen examples of it time and again. By understanding and incorporating the Product archetype into object-oriented analysis models, you can avoid this mistake.

7.2 Compliance with standards

The models presented in this chapter comply with the standards listed in Table 7.1.

Table 7.1

Standard	Contents	Reference
EAN.UCC System	Product identification standards	www.uc-council.org www.ean-int.org
ISO 2108	International Standard Book Number (ISBN)	www.iso.org
ISO 10957	International Standard Music Number (ISMN)	www.iso.org

7.3   Product **archetype pattern overview and roadmap**

Figure 7.1 shows the model for the Product archetype pattern.

There are two variants (pleomorphs) of the Product archetype pattern, as we discuss in the next section.

7.4   **Variation in the** Product **archetype pattern**

Products can take a number of different basic forms, and the Product archetype pattern has to accommodate all of them.

If you think about the types of things you can sell, these things fall into three broad categories based on their degree of uniqueness.

1. Unique things
2. Identical things
3. Identifiable things—things that are similar but individually identifiable (e.g., a car of a particular make)

7.4.1   **Unique things**

Consider an artist such as Salvador Dali. Some of his paintings may have originally sold for the same price, but that is just coincidental—each of the paintings themselves is unique. If you imagine a catalog of Dali's paintings, there is a one-to-one relationship between a catalog entry and a specific painting. For example, the catalog entry for the painting *Persistence of Memory* maps directly onto the painting itself.

Artisan-produced products tend to be unique, with a one-to-one correspondence between a catalog entry and the artifact itself.

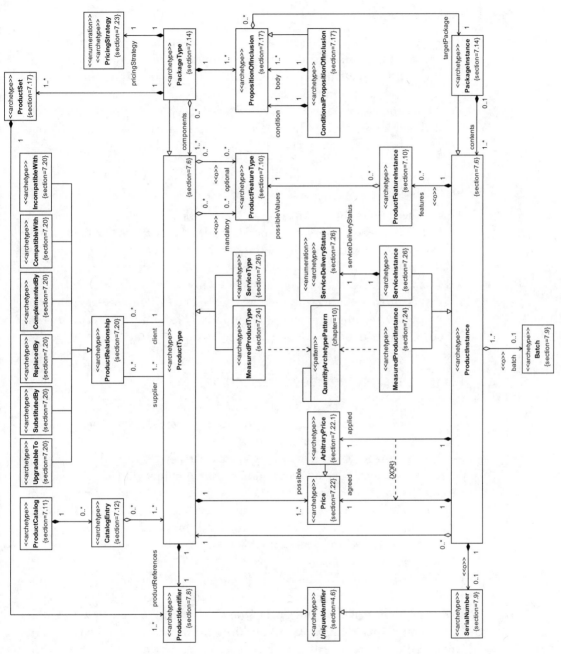

Figure 7.1

7.4.2   Identical things

If you now consider a Dali *poster* for sale on Art.com, the catalog entry for that poster has a one-to-many relationship with instances of the poster held in some inventory. All of these instances are identical but, for quality control reasons, they may be organized into batches.

Mass-produced products are, by their nature, copies of some original (even if this is only a prototype or design). In this case, we have a one-to-many correspondence between a catalog entry and a set of identical artifacts.

7.4.3   Identifiable things

This is the most complex situation of all. Consider a signed and numbered print of a Dali painting. This corresponds to the common case of a limited edition of something. Each instance of this product is similar to all the others, but it has a serial number for tracking purposes and to establish its identity, uniqueness, and rarity. Again, we have a one-to-many relationship with many instances of the product held in some inventory, but this time we have to treat every instance as being unique. Although unlikely for prints, this category can include instances that may have one or more optional features.

7.4.4   Product **archetype pattern pleomorphs**

You can see that a generalized model for products needs to be able to handle the three cases described above, as well as the situation where the product is sold by quantity (e.g., electricity, fabric, flooring).

We call this generalized model the Product archetype pattern.

If your business system needs to deal with *only* unique things, you may find it more appropriate to use a specifically optimized Product archetype pattern pleomorph called UniqueProduct. On the other hand, if your business system needs to handle *only* the special case of identical things, it may be more appropriate to use a specifically optimized Product archetype pattern pleomorph called IdenticalProduct.

The main point of confusion when modeling products arises directly from the fact that the Product archetype pattern has these specialized pleomorphs as well as the more general form. There is no *single* way to model products that is optimal in *all* circumstances. Generally, the standard Product archetype pattern will be sufficient, but the specific business context may determine that one of the other variants should be used instead.

The Product archetype pattern, with its UniqueProduct and Identical-Product pleomorphs and their basic semantics, is illustrated in Figure 7.2.

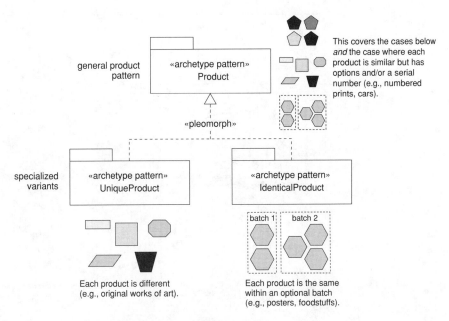

This covers the cases below *and* the case where each product is similar but has options and/or a serial number (e.g., numbered prints, cars).

Each product is different (e.g., original works of art).

Each product is the same within an optional batch (e.g., posters, foodstuffs).

Figure 7.2

We will discuss the UniqueProduct pleomorph in Section 7.27.1 and the IdenticalProduct pleomorph in Section 7.27.2. The main focus of this chapter is on the general Product pattern, rather than either of its more constrained pleomorphs. However, you will find that much of the material presented may be used, with only minor modification, with either pleomorph.

7.5 **The** Product **archetype pattern**

The Product archetype pattern represents a generalized model for products. Figure 7.3 illustrates its basic semantics.

In this figure, you can see a ProductCatalog (discussed in Section 7.11) that contains descriptions for one or more ProductTypes. A description is shared by many ProductInstances, each of which has its own unique identifier and may have optional features.

When you go into a shop to buy one of these products, the ProductType represents the information the salesperson gives you verbally or in a catalog or leaflet, and the ProductInstance represents the actual thing you walk out the door with.

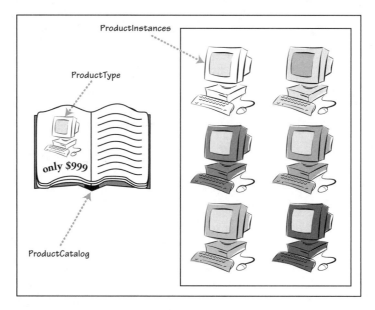

Figure 7.3

7.6 ProductType **and** ProductInstance

The ProductType archetype describes the common properties of a set of goods or services.

For example, the name "Epson Stylus C80" and its associated specification describe a type of printer—this is a ProductType. There are many specific instances of this printer, including the one in our office—these are represented by ProductInstances.

The ProductInstance archetype represents a specific instance of a ProductType.

This split between ProductType and ProductInstance is essential whenever you have many instances of the same type of thing that you need to track individually. You can record the specification for the thing once in the Product-Type, and then each of the ProductInstances can refer back to this specification for the common features. The ProductInstances are generally flyweights [Gamma 1995]—lightweight objects that represent an instance of the Product-Type. However, each ProductInstance may also add its own unique features.

The basic relationship between ProductType and ProductInstance is shown in Figure 7.4. The attributes and operations of these archetypes will be discussed in subsequent sections of this chapter (note that reservation of ProductInstances is covered in Section 8.9).

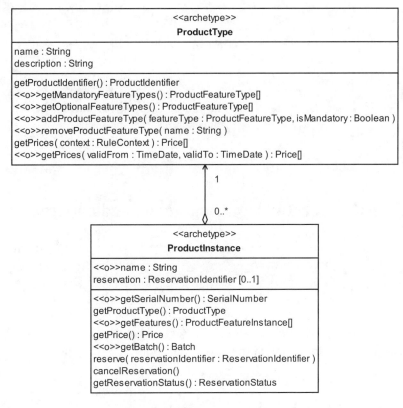

Figure 7.4

For each ProductInstance, there is exactly one ProductType that describes the common properties of the set of similar instances. When you think about it, the *relationship* between a ProductType and its ProductInstances represents stock or inventory—we'll come back to this interesting point in Chapter 8. Because you can get all of the ProductInstances for a specific ProductType by querying the Inventory, we've modeled a unidirectional relationship from ProductInstance to ProductType.

If you consider the process of selling, ProductTypes and ProductInstances play very different roles. Some of these roles are summarized in Table 7.2.

Table 7.2

	ProductType **and** ProductInstance **roles**		
	Manufacturer perspective	**Seller perspective**	**Customer perspective**
ProductType	What you specify	What you advertise in a catalog for sale What you sell	What you browse in a catalog What you order
ProductInstance	What you manufacture	What you hold in inventory What you deliver	What you receive

7.7 Uniquely identifying goods and services

We introduce two new archetypes to act as identifiers for ProductType and ProductInstance.

As you can see in Figure 7.5, both ProductIdentifier and SerialNumber are types of UniqueIdentifiers. These, as their name suggests, represent identifiers that are unique within a given context.

We discuss the semantics and use of ProductIdentifier and SerialNumber in more detail in the next two sections.

7.8 Candidates for ProductIdentifier

> The ProductIdentifier archetype represents a unique identifier for a type of product (a ProductType).

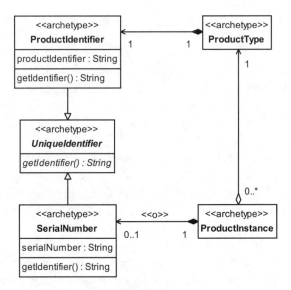

Figure 7.5

Each `ProductType` *must* have a `ProductIdentifier`. If the `ProductTypes` are stored in a database, this `ProductIdentifier` acts as the primary key. Each `ProductType` also has a `name` (see Figure 7.4). This `name` is usually unique (in fact, we can't really think of an example where it isn't), but it doesn't have to be.

There are several sources of unique identifiers.

7.8.1 Create your own identifier

This is the simplest approach, and it may be sufficient if you are not interested in interoperating with other businesses or in using standard bar codes. The key thing you must ensure is that the identifiers you create for yourself are unique within the context in which you intend to use them.

7.8.2 Use a GTIN data structure

The advent of bar codes drove the development of product identification standards during the 1970s—in the United States with the Universal Product Code (UPC) and in Europe with European Article Numbering (EAN).

These systems are compatible and have been increasingly cooperating, most recently in the combined EAN.UCC System, to ensure the availability of unique, internationally recognized identifiers covering both goods and services, for use in the management of global, multi-industry supply and demand chains.

Today, the EAN.UCC System provides a unique Global Trade Item Number (GTIN) that accommodates four different data structures—UCC-12, EAN/UCC-13, EAN/UCC-8, and EAN/UCC-14—while maintaining every identifier's uniqueness across the board.

The four data structures covered by the GTIN are of different lengths and have different internal organization. However, they all include a number of digits representing a company prefix, digits representing an item reference number, and a check digit (see either of the Web sites indicated below for further details).

Although North American companies typically use UCC-12 (known more widely as the UPC), by January 1, 2005, they will be able to capture, store, and use the 14-digit GTIN structure.

In the United States and Canada, the Uniform Code Council (UCC, www.uc-council.org) allocates company prefixes. Elsewhere in the world, this is done by member organizations of EAN International (www.ean-int.org). Item reference numbers are then assigned by the owner of the company prefix to uniquely identify a type of good or service within the company.

Any of the data structures covered by GTIN can provide a standard way to identify products and thus a more robust approach than creating your own identifiers.

Advantages offered by the GTIN approach include those listed below.

- GTINs are internationally recognized standard identifiers.
- This system creates globally unique identifiers.
- The identifiers may be used in all business and public sectors.
- The identifiers include a check digit—this gives them a degree of robustness.
- The identifiers may be easily encoded in a standard way into a bar code symbol and should be compatible with emerging tagging technologies such as radio frequency identification (RFID).
- There are now services that allow you to look up a bar code symbol to find out information about the owning company and its products.

7.8.3   Use an ISBN, ISSN, or ISMN

For books, you may obtain a unique International Standard Book Number (ISBN) as defined in ISO 2108.

The identifier is preceded by the letters ISBN and is a ten-digit number that is divided into four parts of variable length. These parts must be separated clearly by hyphens or spaces. The four parts are shown in Figure 7.6 and de-scribed in Table 7.3.

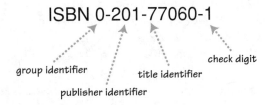

Figure 7.6

Table 7.3

ISBN part	Semantics
Group identifier	Identifies a grouping of publishers by geographic or language area, e.g., the English language grouping (groups 0 and 1) includes the United States, the United Kingdom, Canada, Australia, and so on; the Caribbean is covered by group 976; Switzerland is covered by French language group 2, German language group 3, and Italian language group 88
Publisher identifier	Refers to a particular publisher within a group
Title identifier	Refers to a specific edition of a title published by the publisher
Check digit	Used to ensure data integrity—value is from 0 to X (representing 10)

ISBNs are assigned by ISBN group agencies, coordinated by the International ISBN Agency (www.isbn-international.org).

Once you have been assigned an ISBN, it becomes the edition's unique identifier, and you *don't* need to get a GTIN identifier (see Section 7.8.2). The ISBN makes it very easy to identify virtually any publication in or out of print, and most on-line booksellers (such as Amazon.com) base their whole book-selling systems on ISBNs. This well-constructed and robust identification system has stood the test of time and is used universally by publishers, book sellers, and libraries.

The International Standard Serial Number (ISSN) provides a unique eight-digit identifier for serials, which are publications such as magazines that are issued in parts. Assignment of ISSNs is coordinated by the ISSN International Centre in Paris (www.issn.org). Unlike the ISBN, the ISSN has no structure or meaning, and so cannot be used directly to identify the publisher.

The International Standard Music Number (ISMN), as defined in ISO 10957, provides a unique ten-digit identifier that is becoming standard for all printed music publications. The ISMN, like the ISBN, contains a publisher identifier, item identifier, and check digit. Assignment of these numbers is coordinated by the International ISMN Agency (www.ismn-international.org).

ISBNs, ISSNs, and ISMNs can all be translated in standard ways into bar code symbols.

7.9   SerialNumber **and** Batch

ProductInstances optionally have a name (see Figure 7.4), but this is rarely used and does not have to be unique. It does not therefore provide a reliable way to identify individual ProductInstances.

> The SerialNumber archetype represents a unique identifier for a specific instance of a product (a ProductInstance).

The concept of SerialNumber is very easy to grasp for goods—it is just the number that identifies a specific thing. For services, the SerialNumber identifies a specific delivery of a service and usually relates to some record of that delivery (see Section 7.26).

The SerialNumber archetype is shown in Figure 7.7.

Each ProductInstance *may* have a SerialNumber. There are circumstances where ProductInstances do not have individual identifiers, although the trend toward unique identification of goods seems to be increasing. This is fueled in part by the availability of low-cost identification mechanisms such as ID chips and the development of printers that can mark almost anything, and in part by concerns about security and quality control.

One situation where ProductInstances may not have SerialNumbers is when the instances are identified only by batch number. Here, the actual identity of each instance is unimportant, but it *is* important to know which batch of

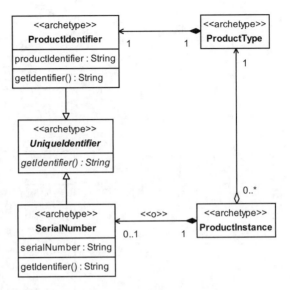

Figure 7.7

instances it came from, for quality or safety purposes. (This is very common with foodstuffs and chemicals.)

If your business is concerned with batches of instances, you can introduce an optional Batch archetype, shown in Figure 7.8.

> The Batch archetype describes a set of ProductInstances of a specific Product-Type that are all to be tracked together, usually for quality control purposes.

To this end, each Batch may be optionally checkedBy zero or more Parties, as represented by their PartySignature.

The concept of a Batch is important when manufacturing products. On the selling side, batchIdentifiers provide a means of communicating information from manufacturer to retailer to consumer, typically about safety or quality control issues. One example of the use of batchIdentifier is by manufacturers who need to recall defective products; another is by customers who want to ensure color matches when buying several rolls of wallpaper.

Each Batch has attributes that record information about it. These attributes are listed in Table 7.4.

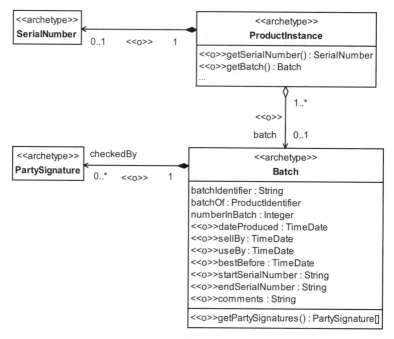

Figure 7.8

Table 7.4

Batch **archetype**	
Attribute	**Semantics**
batchIdentifier	A unique identifier for the Batch
batchOf	The ProductIdentifier for the Batch
numberInBatch	The number of ProductInstances in the Batch
«o»dateProduced	The date that the Batch of ProductInstances was produced—if the Batch is produced over a period of time, this is the date on which the Batch was completed
«o»sellBy	The latest date on which the ProductInstances in the Batch may be sold

Table 7.4 (Continued)

Batch **archetype**

Attribute	Semantics
«o»useBy	The latest date on which the ProductInstances in the Batch may be used—this indicates the date by which the ProductInstances will have spoiled (for perishable goods) or become obsolete or otherwise unusable (for nonperishable goods)
«o»bestBefore	The date on which the ProductInstances pass their best quality
«o»startSerialNumber	The serialNumber of the first ProductInstance in the Batch
«o»endSerialNumber	The serialNumber of the last ProductInstance in the Batch (note the assumption that serial numbers are consecutive within the batch)
«o»comments	Comments about this Batch

As you can see in Table 7.4, a number of attributes are associated with periods of validity. Some products effectively become unsellable after a period of time. There are two main reasons for this.

1. The goods are perishable. The dates sellBy, useBy, and bestBefore are usually associated with Batches of perishable goods such as foodstuffs. Local trading standards probably make one or more of these dates mandatory.
2. The goods are related to a specific date or period of time (e.g., newspapers, diaries, calendars) and have no market once this has passed. The sellBy date can be used to represent this.

A SerialNumber range can optionally be noted against the Batch as a convenient way to summarize serial information. Generally, SerialNumbers are *not* used in conjunction with Batches. However, there are some circumstances where goods are both serialized (because they are of high individual value and vulnerable to theft) and batched (for quality control purposes). An example of this is the hard drive in a PC.

If you are dealing with large numbers of identical instances of a specific `ProductType` and are concerned only with knowing the *total number* of instances you have, you can either sum the `numberInBatch` across all `Batches` of that `ProductType` or create a single `Batch` for the `ProductType` to keep track of the total number.

7.10   Product specification

For any product you wish to sell, you need some way to capture the specifications for that product. These specifications describe all the features of the product pertinent to your selling process *except* price, which needs to be handled separately (see Section 7.22). Examples of such features include size and color.

One way to specify a product is to create attributes in the `ProductInstance` or `ProductType` for each feature. However, if you create attributes in the `ProductInstance` to capture features, it's very likely that you will store the same data many times. Creating attributes in the `ProductType` for each feature also has several significant problems.

- Attributes are part of the static semantics of the model and are *very* hard to change. You have to remodel to make changes.
  - Different types of goods and services have to be represented as subclasses of `ProductType` and `ServiceType`—this can lead to many subclasses.
  - Introducing new types of goods or services means introducing new subclasses.
- If there are many `ProductTypes`, and each `ProductType` has a different set of attributes, it becomes very difficult to create a system that can handle them all in a uniform way.

Despite the serious disadvantages of this simple approach, we often see it adopted in books on UML modeling and even in real systems. It *may* work in the following limited circumstances.

- The features of the goods or services never change, or change only very infrequently.
- There are very few different types of goods or services.

However, most businesses have many different types of goods and services that change over time.

A better approach is needed. You can model product features *explicitly* by introducing the new archetypes shown in Figure 7.9, with their semantics summarized below.

The ProductFeatureType archetype represents a type of feature (such as color) of a good or service and its range of possible values (e.g., {blue, green, yellow, red}).

The ProductFeatureInstance archetype represents a specific feature (such as color) of a good or service and its value (e.g., blue).

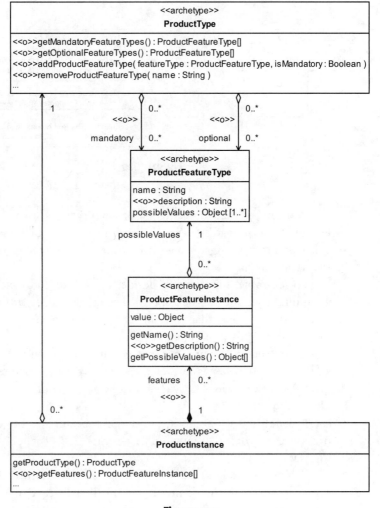

Figure 7.9

The basis of the whole model is the `ProductType`. This has a set of manda-tory plus a set of optional `ProductFeatureTypes`.

For example, looking at the Web site of IKEA, an internationally known furniture store (www.ikea.com), you can buy a Karlanda leather sofa with the following types of features:

- Upholstery color—can be sand, black, blue, or red
- Legs—can be birch or aluminum

You can model this as shown in Figure 7.10.

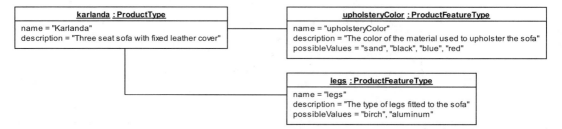

Figure 7.10

You can see that the Karlanda `ProductType` has two mandatory `Product-FeatureTypes`—`upholsteryColor` and `legs`. Each of these `ProductFeature-Types` specifies a range of `possibleValues` that a `ProductFeatureInstance` of that type may have.

For example, suppose you decide to go retro and have black leather with aluminum legs. You choose a specific `ProductInstance` that meets your require-ments, that is, one that has the right `ProductFeatureInstances`. You can model this as shown in Figure 7.11.

Each `ProductFeatureInstance` gets its name from its `ProductFeatureType` and has a `value` that is one of the `possibleValues` defined by its associated `ProductFeatureType`. This `value` may be any type of object but often is a sim-ple `String`.

`ProductType` is only meant to model the simple, atomic features of a good or service. In particular, our model assumes that `ProductFeatureTypes` *do not* interact.

When you have to handle cases where product features do interact (e.g., the existence of one feature is predicated on the existence of another feature), the simplest solution is to represent the complex product as a `PackageType`. Depen-

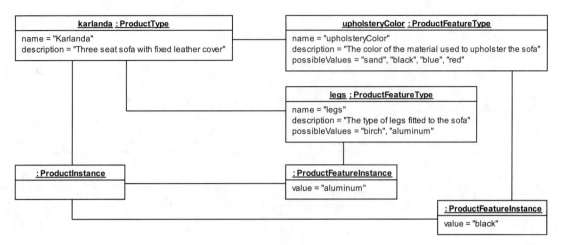

Figure 7.11

dent product features can then be represented as `ProductTypes` within the `PackageType`. Note that, unless any of the components of a package formed in this way can be sold separately, it is only the `PackageType` that appears in the `Inventory` and `ProductCatalog`, not the product features that have been represented as `ProductTypes`. We describe this approach in Section 7.13.

While representing a product with interacting features as a `PackageType` perhaps is not ideal, it does have the enormous advantage of confining the use of configuration rules to the level of the package. If you employ these rules at both product and package levels, you run a significant risk of complex interactions between the two levels.

7.11 ProductCatalog

In selling systems, you need somewhere to store your collection of `Product-Types`. This is modeled by the `ProductCatalog` archetype (see Figure 7.12).

The `ProductCatalog` archetype represents a persistent store of product information used in the selling process.

A `ProductCatalog` has the set of *manager operations* described in Table 7.5.

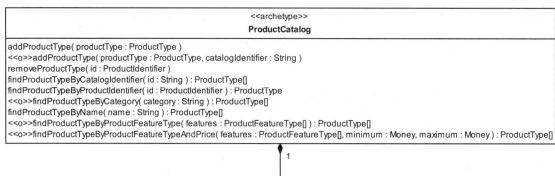

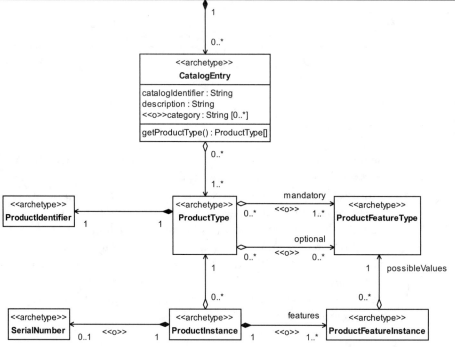

Figure 7.12

Table 7.5

ProductCatalog **manager operations**	
Operation	**Semantics**
addProductType(productType : ProductType)	Adds a ProductType to the ProductCatalog by creating a unique CatalogEntry for it
«o»addProductType(productType : ProductType, catalogIdentifier : String)	Adds a ProductType to the ProductCatalog by assigning it to an existing CatalogEntry This operation is required *only* where a business system must allow for one-to-many mappings of CatalogEntries to ProductTypes

Table 7.5 (Continued)

ProductCatalog **manager operations**	
Operation	**Semantics**
removeProductType(id : ProductIdentifier)	Removes a ProductType from the ProductCatalog
	Removes the CatalogEntry provided there are no more ProductTypes associated with that entry

You can see from Table 7.5 that the addProductType(...) operations you need depend on whether your business system needs to handle CatalogEntries that map to more than one ProductType (see Section 7.12).

A ProductCatalog also has the set of *finder operations* described in Table 7.6.

Table 7.6

ProductCatalog **finder operations**	
Operation	**Semantics**
findProductTypeByCatalogIdentifier(...)	Returns a set of ProductTypes that have the given catalogIdentifier
	Where a business system only has one ProductType per CatalogEntry, this set contains a single ProductType
findProductTypeByProductIdentifier(...)	Returns a single ProductType that has the given ProductIdentifier
«o»findProductTypeByCategory(...)	Returns a set of ProductTypes in the specified category
findProductTypeByName(...)	Returns a set of ProductTypes—will return a single ProductType if every ProductType has a different name (the usual case)
«o»findProductTypeByProductFeatureType(...)	Returns a set of ProductTypes that match the specified set of ProductFeatureTypes
«o»findProductTypeByProductFeatureTypeAndPrice(...)	Returns a set of ProductTypes that match the specified set of ProductFeatureTypes and are in the given price range

While all the operations in Table 7.6 are important, it is often the last two that determine the business value of the ProductCatalog. Just how easy is it to find a suitable ProductType for a customer, given an incomplete list of the features the customer desires?

In our model we have shown the simplest case, where the ProductCatalog is passed a set of mandatory and optional ProductFeatureTypes that the customer wants. In many cases, this is an adequate strategy, but it is also possible to consider other search algorithms based on a list of prioritized customer requirements or fuzzy customer requirements (e.g., "Find me a two-week vacation somewhere hot").

Whatever search algorithm is used, it should return a list of possible matches that is usually ordered according to the fidelity of the match and may be ordered according to business constraints such as a policy of offering the best match with the highest price first.

7.12 CatalogEntry

> The CatalogEntry archetype represents information about a specific type of product held in a ProductCatalog.

When a ProductType is stored in a ProductCatalog, it is stored as a CatalogEntry. This CatalogEntry has a unique catalogIdentifier, a description, and zero or more optional categories (see Figure 7.12).

Categorizing ProductTypes can aid navigation in the ProductCatalog. For example, a catalog of books might order them under the categories "Crime fiction", "Science fiction", and so on. In our model, a category is just an optional label assigned to a CatalogEntry. For flexibility, each CatalogEntry may be assigned more than one category.

In most business systems, each CatalogEntry represents exactly one ProductType. In this case it may be possible to give the catalogIdentifier the same value as the ProductIdentifier for that ProductType.

Sometimes, however, a CatalogEntry must represent more than one ProductType. For example, in the United Kingdom, many drugs are available as "generics" rather than as branded drugs, so a drugstore might supply aspirin as "Aspirin, 100 g, 16 tablets". This (or some shorter representation that maps onto this, such as a number) would be the catalogIdentifier. However, the generic CatalogEntry must ultimately be resolved into an aspirin product from a specific manufacturer. The manufacturer's `ProductIdentifier` will almost certainly be different from the `CatalogEntry`'s `catalogIdentifier`. In fact, there may be aspirin products from more than one manufacturer in stock, all represented by the same generic `CatalogEntry`.

If this is the case, you are making a very profound statement about aspirin! You are saying that from the point of view of selling it (the `ProductCatalog` perspective) there is *no* difference between the various products, but from the point of view of holding stock, there *is* a difference between the products. This is the essence of the distinction between `ProductIdentifier` and `catalogIdentifier`—the `ProductIdentifier` relates to inventory management, and the `catalogIdentifier` relates to sales.

Another good example of a situation where a single `CatalogEntry` may map onto one or more `ProductTypes` comes from the electronics industry. Suppose you need a 74HC00 chip (a simple logic chip). You would look under 74HC00 in the `ProductCatalog`. However, what is delivered to you might be an SN74HC00N from Texas Instruments or an MM74HC00N from Fairchild. As a purchaser and user of the chip, you don't really care because the two chips are functionally identical. However, as a seller of the chip, you might be very concerned about the manufacturer of the chips for reasons of cost and availability.

This can be true for many different types of products. What you advertise for sale can be a more generalized description of what you hold in stock.

7.13 Packages

A common business practice is to sell selections of products grouped together as a unit. These selections are often known as *packages*. An example is a vacation package, where a number of different travel-related products are sold as a unit.

There are many commercial reasons for packaging products together. For example, you may wish to create a package of two or more products so that the customer gains some benefit from buying the package rather than the individual products. This benefit might be added convenience, added value (some free components or a price reduction), or a reward through a loyalty program such as Continental Airlines' OnePass (www.onepass.com). For example, a grocer could offer added convenience and value with a "buy two papaya and get a free lime" package, and a travel agent might advertise a reward such as "buy a flight and book a hotel and get 1,000 extra OnePass miles."

There can be a legal side to product packaging—you may need to create a `PackageType` because one `ProductType` must *always* be combined with another

ProductType. An example of this might be a car rental ProductType and an insurance ProductType. The PackageType's package specification rules can enforce this legal constraint.

As we mentioned in Section 7.10, a package can be a good way to represent a complex product that has dependencies between its features. You represent each feature as a ProductType and the complex product as a PackageType containing these ProductTypes. We show you an example of this in Section 7.19.

7.14 PackageType **and** PackageInstance

Like products, packages can be represented as a PackageType and a PackageInstance. These are defined below.

> The PackageType archetype specifies a set of component ProductTypes and rules about how these may be combined to create PackageInstances. A PackageType is a kind of ProductType.
>
> The PackageInstance archetype represents a collection of one or more ProductInstances sold together to increase the business benefit generated by the sale. A PackageInstance is a kind of ProductInstance.

Each PackageInstance has an associated PackageType that contains rules about what combinations of ProductTypes the PackageInstance can contain.

The package model is shown in Figure 7.13.

To illustrate the relationship between PackageType and PackageInstance, consider the example of the set menu offered in many French restaurants. We will assume that this set menu consists of a starter, main course, and dessert and that there are a number of possible choices for each. This can be modeled as PackageTypes and PackageInstances as follows.

- The PackageType references a set of component ProductTypes that comprise all the possible starter, main course, and dessert ProductTypes.
- The PackageType contains a rule that states that a PackageInstance can contain exactly *one* starter, *one* main course, and *one* dessert—in other words, the PackageInstance can contain a ProductInstance of one of the ProductTypes in each of the starter, main course, and dessert ProductSets.

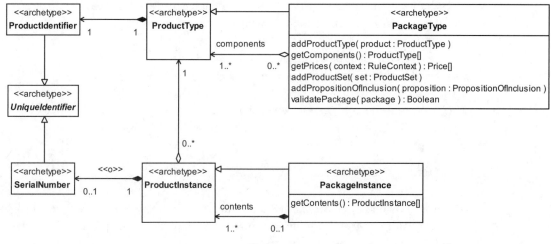

Figure 7.13

You can see that the PackageType defines a set of possible configurations for its PackageInstances by specifying:

- The allowed ProductTypes for the ProductInstances in the PackageInstance
- The number of ProductInstances in the PackageInstance for each specified ProductType

We'll see exactly how it does this in Section 7.17, after we've looked at product combinations and the package specification process in a bit more depth.

7.15 Combining ProductTypes

Even a relatively small number of ProductTypes may be combined in Package-Types in a large number of ways, but generally only very few of these possible PackageTypes make sense from the business perspective. For example, while it might make great business sense to package a PC and a printer together, it would make little sense to package a printer with a VCR.

It's worth taking a little time here to look at the implications of product combination.

Suppose that a `PackageType` contains a choice of k `ProductTypes` from a set of n `ProductTypes`, where the following constraints apply.

- k is less than or equal to n.
- Duplicate objects are not allowed.

The number of possible combinations of `ProductTypes` and hence the number of possible `PackageInstance` configurations, Np, is given by:

$$Np = \frac{n!}{(n-k)! \ -k!}$$

This is known as a *k-combination* in the theory of combinatorics. If we plot this out for values of n and k ranging from 0 to 9, you can see in Figure 7.14 that the number of possible configurations increases rapidly even in this rather constrained case.

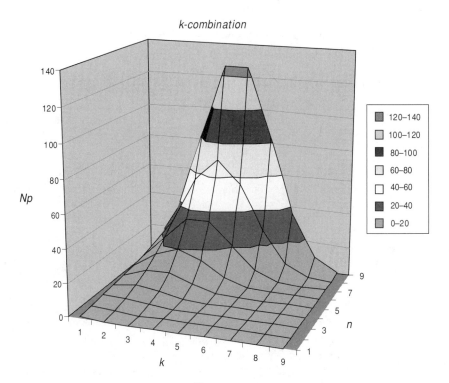

Figure 7.14

Naturally, the fewer the constraints, the larger the possible number of combinations of `ProductTypes`, and hence the larger the number of `PackageInstance` configurations allowed by the `PackageType`.

Consider the following less constrained case.

- *k* is less than or equal to *n*.
- Duplicates *are* allowed.

In this instance, the number of possible configurations, *Np*, is given by:

$$Np = \frac{(n + k - 1)!}{k!(n - 1)!}$$

This is known as a *k-selection*.

The k-selection over the same range of *n* and *k* plotted earlier is shown in Figure 7.15. You can see immediately that the range of possible configurations for even moderate values of *n* and *k* is huge and increases very rapidly.

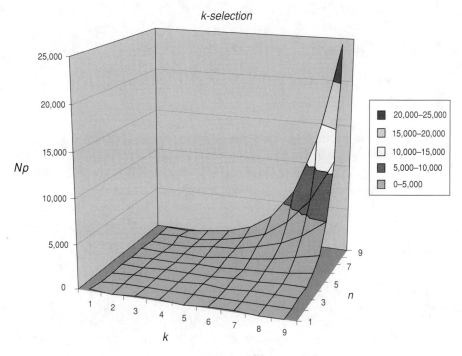

Figure 7.15

If you were to relax the remaining constraint, that k must be less than or equal to n, the number of possible configurations would become, in principle, infinite.

To prevent this combinatorial explosion, the formulation of PackageTypes must be driven by the following requirements and constraints:

- Customer requirements (e.g., the combination of pasta and pasta sauce in a package offer)
- Business requirements (e.g., the need to sell more of a specific ProductType)
- Legal constraints (e.g., the need to always combine two ProductTypes)
- Supply constraints (e.g., insufficient ProductType availability to market the package)
- Financial constraints (e.g., the need to offer the package at a competitive price)
- Product combination constraints (e.g., possible incompatibilities among the proposed ProductTypes—see Section 7.20)

These requirements and constraints feed into a package specification process that we discuss in the next section.

7.16 Package specification process

The package specification process defines a PackageType. The requirements and constraints identified in Section 7.15 feed into this process, as shown in Figure 7.16.

The package specification process (Figure 7.17) is often a highly iterative and creative business process that requires detailed negotiations between the marketing, business strategy, stock control, and legal forces within the business. Depending on the nature of the ProductTypes involved, there may also be an operational factor or product combination constraints to consider. A detailed study of this business process is outside the scope of this book.

Once a PackageType has been defined by the package specification process, specific PackageInstances are created by a package configuration process. This can take one of two forms.

1. The business assembles one or more PackageInstances based on the PackageType and offers these for sale—the customer is offered a PackageInstance with a predetermined configuration.
2. The customer is allowed to construct a PackageInstance at the point of sale based on the rules defined in the PackageType and possibly constrained by the availability of package components.

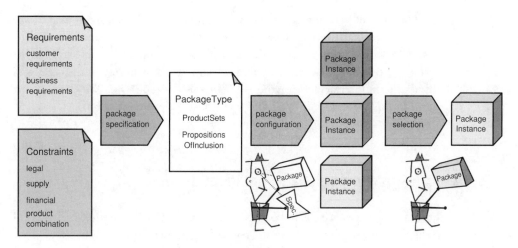

Figure 7.16

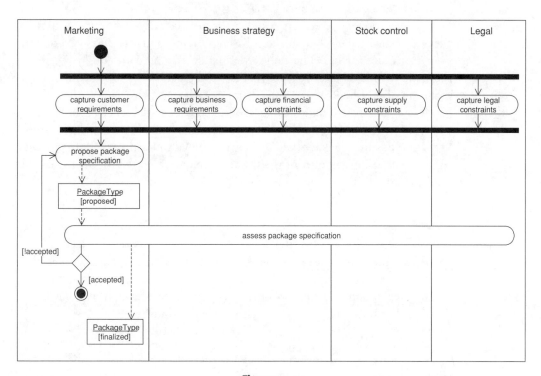

Figure 7.17

Creation of `PackageInstances` according to the rules specified in the `Pack-ageType` is primarily a user interface issue, whether it is performed by the business or by the customer. As such, we don't cover it in any detail here, but it is certainly possible to use Model Driven Architecture to automate the creation of suitable user interfaces from the rules in the `PackageType`. We present some ideas on this issue on our Web site (www.businessarchetypes.com).

7.17 Rule-driven package specification

Product packaging needs to be very fluid to respond to changing market conditions, so it makes sense to express packaging strategies as *rules* that are external to the selling applications. This allows them to be changed easily.

We discuss the general notion of rules and present a simple `Rule` archetype pattern in Chapter 12. If you haven't already read that chapter, you should at least get an overview of it before reading the rest of this section.

Many marketing and business strategy goals can influence the formulation of a `PackageType`. These goals could be expressed as rules, but these rules are generally outside the scope of the software systems, and we don't need to consider them any further. The only type of rules we need to consider here are those that comprise the `PackageType` itself. These are rules for the inclusion or exclusion of specific `ProductTypes` from `PackageInstances`.

In our rules-based model, `PackageTypes` contain a number of `Propositions-OfInclusion`. These are statements of truth that define constraints about how `ProductTypes` in a `PackageType` may be combined to form `PackageInstances`.

You can see our model of these rules in Figure 7.18. We don't discuss this model in any depth for several reasons.

- There is complete source code for a working implementation of this pattern on our Web site.
- We prefer to concentrate on the concepts behind this model, rather than the implementation details, because the concepts are very important.
- Depending on what sort of rules engine you are using, there may be other ways to implement package specification.

For completeness, however, the new archetypes are defined on the next two pages.

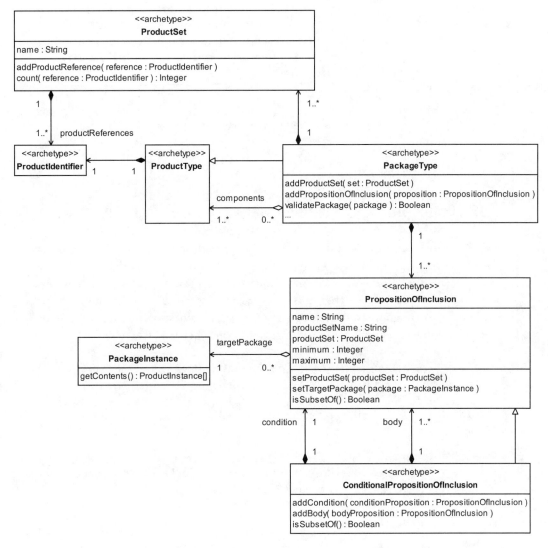

Figure 7.18

The ProductSet archetype represents a set of ProductIdentifiers that refer to ProductTypes.

The PropositionOfInclusion archetype determines the ProductTypes of the ProductInstances that may be included in a PackageInstance based on selections from a ProductSet.

The ConditionalPropositionOfInclusion archetype determines the Product-Types of the ProductInstances that may be included in a PackageInstance based on selections from a ProductSet. The inclusion can occur only if the condition PropositionOfInclusion is true.

These definitions will begin to make sense when you have read the next section.

7.18 Concepts of rule-driven package specification

In this section we're going to focus on the *concepts* of our rules-based approach to package specification, rather than the details of the model in Figure 7.18. This is because there are some important ideas that we need to get across, particularly to software engineers. Other readers may wish to skim this discussion.

We're going to introduce some very simple notation that we will use in the rest of this section to help us to reason about PackageTypes.

set—a collection of zero or more things where each thing is unique

{}—an empty set

S: {}—an empty set called S

S: { p1, p2, p3 }—a set of ProductTypes p1, p2, and p3

We use the following notation to specify a PackageInstance T, containing ProductInstances i, that have ProductTypes p1, p2, and p3:

T: [i_{p1}, i_{p2}, i_{p3}]

Note that PackageInstances are *not* sets—they can contain duplicate elements.
A PropositionOfInclusion takes the form:

P: isSubsetOf(T, S, min, max)

This states that the target PackageInstance T must contain between min and max ProductInstances whose ProductTypes are specified in the ProductSet S.

Here, we use *set* in its strict mathematical sense—it is a collection of Product-Types that meets the following conditions.

- A specific ProductType object may occur only once in the set (no duplicates).
- No two ProductType objects in the set may be equivalent. Equivalence is where two (or more) ProductType objects have exactly the same attribute values.

The PropositionOfInclusion is always subject to the following constraint:

```
min <= max <= |S|
```

where |S| is the number of unique elements in set S. In set theory, this is known as the *cardinality* of S.

Using ProductSets and PropositionsOfInclusion, you can state Package-Type rules very simply. For example, here is set menu from a French restaurant, expressed as a PackageType, where we list the ProductSets first, followed by the PropositionsOfInclusion.

```
S: { "Petite assiette de crudités", "Potage du chef", "Calamars
    marinés aux feuilles de citron", "Salade de chèvre chaud" }
M: { "Plat du jour", "Fricassée de suprême de poulet", "Médaillons
    de veau aux graines de sésame", "Côtes d'agneau braisées aux
    amandes" }
D: { "Sélection de fromages fins", "Tarte aux fraises", "Crème brulé
    à la vanille", "Assortiment du chariot de desserts" }
```

P_S: isSubsetOf(T, S, 1, 1)
P_M: isSubsetOf(T, M, 1, 1)
P_D: isSubsetOf(T, D, 1, 1)

In the example above, S is a set of starter ProductTypes, M is a set of main course ProductTypes, and D is a set of dessert ProductTypes. The Proposition-OfInclusion P_S controls how many elements you may select into the target PackageInstance T from set S, and P_M and P_D do the same for sets M and D.

Looking at min and max for each PropositionOfInclusion in the Package-Specification, you can see that you can have exactly one choice from each of the sets S, M, and D. In other words, you can have one starter, one main course, and one dessert.

Notice the structure of the `PackageType`:

- A set of `ProductSets`
- A set of `PropositionsOfInclusion` that operate on the `ProductSets`

Think of the `ProductSets` as being a pool of "raw material" out of which you may construct an actual `PackageInstance` by adhering to the constraints specified in the `PropositionsOfInclusion`. This is pretty much how you construct packages in real life—you have a set of options (represented by the `ProductSets`) and a set of constraints (represented by the `PropositionsOfInclusion`) controlling how you can put together valid combinations of those options.

While by definition the `ProductSets` can't contain duplicate elements, a `PackageInstance` certainly can.

For example, this is how you can specify that the target `PackageInstance` must contain between two and four `ProductInstances`, where each must be of a *different* `ProductType` chosen from the `ProductSet` S:

```
S: { p1, p2, p3, p4 }
P: isSubsetOf( T, S, 2, 4 )
```

You can specify that `ProductInstances` with the same `ProductType` *are* allowed in a `PackageInstance`, simply by having multiple `PropositionsOfInclusion` operating on the same `ProductSet`:

```
S: { p1, p2 }
P₁: isSubsetOf( T, S, 1, 1 )—select exactly one element from S
P₂: isSubsetOf( T, S, 1, 1 )—select exactly one element from S
P₃: isSubsetOf( T, S, 0, 1 )—select zero or one element from S
P₄: isSubsetOf( T, S, 0, 1 )—select zero or one element from S
```

The above rule states that, "The target `PackageInstance` T must contain between two and four `ProductInstances` whose `ProductTypes` are from the set S, where the `ProductInstances` may have the same `ProductType`." Note that if `ProductInstances` may have the same `ProductType`, the number of `ProductInstances` in the target `PackageInstance` can exceed the number of `ProductTypes` in the source `ProductSet`.

A more concise way to express this rule might be to define a proposition of multiple inclusion as follows:

```
P: isSelectionOf( T, S, 2, 4 )
```

Although isSelectionOf(...) can be useful as an idiom, we prefer to stick to isSubsetOf(...) because we find it easier to understand, even though it makes the package specification rules a bit more verbose.

For more advanced package specification, you may wish to make the inclusion of some rule elements conditional. This is a ConditionalProposition-OfInclusion, and you can express it as a simple if statement as follows:

```
P: if isSubsetOf( T, S, min, max )
        P₁: isSubsetOf( T, S, min, max )
        P₂: isSubsetOf( T, S, min, max )
        ...
        Pₙ: isSubsetOf( T, S, min, max )
```

This states that if the condition P is true, the PropositionsOfInclusion P_1, P_2, ..., P_n must also be true.

The ConditionalPropositionOfInclusion is particularly useful because it allows you to express rules such as, "If the target PackageInstance contains a ProductInstance of type i_{p1}, the target PackageInstance must also contain a ProductInstance of type i_{p2}." You can express this rule very simply, as follows:

```
S₁: { p1 }
S₂: { p2 }
P₁: isSubsetOf( T, S₁, 0, 1 )
P₂: isSubsetOf( T, S₂, 0, 1 )
P₃: if isSubsetOf( T, S₁, 1, 1 )
        P₄: isSubsetOf( T, S₂, 1, 1 )
```

This PackageType specifies a set of three legal PackageInstances:

```
{
T₁: [ iₚ₁, iₚ₂ ],
T₂: [ iₚ₂ ],
T₃: [],
}
```

The notation T_n refers to a target PackageInstance T in configuration n. Notice that T_3 is an empty configuration. This is legal according to the specification defined by the PackageType.

Here is an example of a PackageType specification with multiple propositions after the condition P_4:

```
S₁: { p1, p2 }
S₂: { p3, p4 }
S₃: { p5 }
P₁: isSubsetOf( T, S₁, 0, 1 )
P₂: isSubsetOf( T, S₂, 0, 1 )
P₃: isSubsetOf( T, S₃, 0, 1 )
P₄: if isSubsetOf( T, S₁, 1, 1 )
          P₅: isSubsetOf( T, S₂, 1, 1 )
          P₆: isSubsetOf( T, S₃, 0 , 0 )
```

This states that, "The target PackageInstance T may contain zero or one ProductInstance whose ProductType comes from the set S_1, zero or one ProductInstance whose ProductType comes from S_2, and zero or one ProductInstance whose ProductType comes from S_3. If the PackageInstance contains a ProductInstance with a ProductType from the set S_1, it must also contain a ProductInstance with a ProductType from the set S_2 and it must *not* contain any ProductInstance with a ProductType from set S_3."

This PackageType specifies the set of possible legal PackageInstances shown below:

```
{
T₁: [ iₚ₁, iₚ₃ ],
T₂: [ iₚ₁, iₚ₄ ],
T₃: [ iₚ₂, iₚ₃ ],
T₄: [ iₚ₂, iₚ₄ ],
T₅: [ iₚ₃ ],
T₆: [ iₚ₃, iₚ₅ ],
T₇: [ iₚ₄ ],
T₈: [ iₚ₄, iₚ₅ ],
T₉: [ iₚ₅ ],
T₁₀: [],
}
```

7.19 An example of a PackageType

Let's look at a real-world example of a PackageType. Some of the options available when we recently bought a new PC are shown in Table 7.7.

Table 7.7

New PC		
	Options	**Price adjustment**
Standard features	2GHz Intel Pentium 4 Processor with 256K Cache 3.5" 1.44 Floppy Drive Mini Tower Chassis Keyboard Mouse	£0.00
Memory	256MB Rambus RDRAM	£0.00
	384MB Rambus RDRAM	£80.00
	512MB Rambus RDRAM	£160.00
	768MB Rambus RDRAM	£280.00
	1024MB Rambus RDRAM	£450.00
	2048MB Rambus RDRAM	£1000.00
Hard drive	40GB Hard Drive	£0.00
	40GB Turbo Hard Drive (7200 rpm)	£30.00
	60GB Turbo Hard Drive (7200 rpm)	£110.00
	80GB Hard Drive	£150.00
	120GB Hard Drive	£300.00
Monitor	Standard 17" (15" viewable) FST Monitor	£0.00
	Professional 17" (16" viewable) Monitor	£80.00
	Standard 19" (17" viewable) FST Monitor	£85.00
	Professional 19" (18" viewable) Monitor	£200.00
	Professional 21" (20" viewable) Trinitron Monitor	£400.00
	Flat Panel 15" Analog Monitor	£120.00
	Flat Panel 17" Analog Monitor	£450.00
	Flat Panel 19" Monitor	£650.00
Video card	64MB nVidia GeForce MX Video Card (TV Out)	£0.00
	64MB nVidia GeForce3 Ti200 Card	£80.00
	64MB nVidia GeForce3 Ti500 Card	£230.00

Table continued on next page

Table 7.7   (Continued)

	Options	Price adjustment
Device 1	16x DVD Drive	£0.00
	18x DVD/CDRW Combo Drive	£85.00
Device 2	Not Included	£0.00
	24/40 IDE CDRW	£130.00
	250MB Zip Drive, Built In	£65.00
Device 3	Not Included	£0.00
	250MB Zip Drive, Built In	£65.00
Sound card	Creative Labs Sound Blaster Live Sound Card	£0.00
Speakers	2-piece Stereo Speakers	£0.00
Operating system	Microsoft Windows ME	£0.00
	Microsoft Windows XP	£0.00
	Microsoft Windows XP Pro	£75.00
	Microsoft Windows 2000	£75.00

Table 7.7 shows a set of standard features for the PC and a range of categories from which you must choose exactly what options you want. Associated with each option is a price adjustment applied to the base cost of the package, which we will ignore in this discussion. Options that have a zero price adjustment are the default options. If the category has "Not Included" as an option, the category itself is optional and may be omitted; otherwise, exactly one of the options must be chosen from each category.

As well as the above options, there are some constraints.

1. Standard features are mandatory.
2. If you choose a DVD drive, you can add both a CDRW and a Zip drive.
3. If you choose a combo drive (DVD/CDRW), you can add only a Zip drive.
4. If you choose Windows ME, you can have a maximum of 512MB of RAM—this is all that Windows ME can access.

Notice how the choices you *can* make depend on the choices you *have* made. This is quite common in package configuration.

As shown below, you can express the PC PackageType rule by using the simple notation for ProductSets and PropositionsOfInclusion that we introduced in the last section.

```
PackageType rule for PC

StandardFeatures: { 2GHzPentium, Floppy, MiniTowerChassis, Keyboard,
  Mouse }
WinMEMemory: { 256MB, 384MB, 512MB }
WinOtherMemory: { 256MB, 384MB, 512MB, 768MB, 1024MB, 2048MB }
HardDrive: { 40GB, 40GBTurbo, 60GBTurbo, 80GB, 120GB }
Monitor: { Standard17, Professional17, Standard19, Professional19,
  Professional21, LCD15, LCD17, LCD19 }
VideoCard: { GeForceMX, GeForceTi200, GeForceTi500 }
Device1: { DVD, ComboDrive }
Combo: { ComboDrive }
Zip: { Zip }
DVD: { DVD }
CDRW: { CDRW }
SoundCard: { SBLive }
Speakers: { Stereo }
Win: { WinME, WinXP, WinXPPro, Win2000 }
WinME: { WinME }
WinOther: { WinXP, WinXPPro, Win2000 }
IncludeAllStandardFeatures: isSubsetOf( T, StandardFeatures, 5, 5 )
IncludeOneHardDrive: isSubsetOf( T, HardDrive, 1, 1 )
IncludeOneMonitor: isSubsetOf( T, Monitor, 1, 1 )
IncludeOneVideoCard: isSubsetOf( T, VideoCard, 1, 1 )
IncludeDVDOrComboDrive: isSubsetOf ( T, Device1, 1, 1 )
IncludeSoundCard: isSubsetOf( T, SoundCard, 1, 1 )
IncludeSpeakers: isSubsetOf( T, Speakers, 1, 1 )
IncludeWindowsOS: isSubsetOf( T, Win, 1, 1 )
IfOSIsWinME: if isSubsetOf( T, WinME, 1, 1 )
      IncludeWinMEMemory: isSubsetOf( T, WinMEMemory, 1, 1 )
IfOSIsNotWinME: if isSubsetOf( T, WinOther, 1, 1 )
      IncludeOtherMemory: isSubsetOf( T, WinOtherMemory, 1, 1 )
IfComboDrive: if isSubsetOf( T, Combo, 1, 1 )
      IncludeZip1: isSubsetOf( T, Zip, 0, 1 )
IfDVDDrive: if isSubsetOf( T, DVD, 1, 1)
      IncludeCDRW: isSubsetOf( T, CDRW, 0, 1 )
      IncludeZip2: isSubsetOf( T, Zip, 0, 1 )
```

We've used a simple standard here for `ProductIdentifiers`, where the identifier is a contraction of the product name.

You can use sets of `ProductTypes` to perform Boolean algebra. For example, three of the sets we defined are:

```
Win: { WinME, WinXP, WinXPPro, Win2000 }
WinME: { WinME }
WinOther: { WinXP, WinXPPro, Win2000 }
```

The set `Win` contains all possible operating systems for the computer. It is the union of the sets `WinME` and `WinOther`, which are two disjoint sets (i.e., they have no elements in common). The Boolean expression for this is:

```
Win = WinME AND WinOther
```

Once you have selected an operating system from `Win`, the following Boolean expression must be true.

```
isSubsetOf( T, WinME 1, 1 ) XOR isSubsetOf( T, WinOther, 1, 1 ) = true
```

You have performed a logical XOR by constructing the appropriate `Product-Sets` and then making a selection from them.

7.20   ProductRelationships

We advocate always modeling `PackageType` specifications as a set of rules. However, the package specification process described in Section 7.16 can be affected by more stable relationships between `ProductTypes`. We can model these stable relationships in static semantics by introducing a new archetype called `ProductRelationship` with several subclasses. This is shown in Figure 7.19.

> The `ProductRelationship` archetype represents a fixed relationship between `ProductTypes` that is not a packaging or containment relationship.

The semantics for these `ProductRelationships` are summarized in Table 7.8.

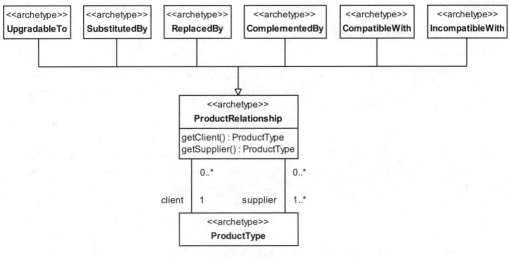

Figure 7.19

Table 7.8

ProductRelationship		Archetype definition
UpgradableTo		The UpgradableTo archetype provides a way to show that the suppliers in a ProductRelationship represent upgrades to the client.
SubstitutedBy		The SubstitutedBy archetype provides a way to show that an instance of the client in a ProductRelationship may be substituted by an instance of one of the suppliers.
ReplacedBy		The ReplacedBy archetype provides a way to show that the client in a ProductRelationship has been superseded by the suppliers—this means that the client is now obsolete and must be replaced by one of the suppliers.

Table continued on next page

Table 7.8   (Continued)

ProductRelationship	Archetype definition
ComplementedBy	The ComplementedBy archetype provides a way to show that the client in a ProductRelationship may be complemented in some way by one of the suppliers.
CompatibleWith	The CompatibleWith archetype provides a way to show that the client in a ProductRelationship is compatible with all of the suppliers.
IncompatibleWith	The IncompatibleWith archetype provides a way to show that the client in a ProductRelationship is not compatible with any of the suppliers.

Note that ProductRelationships do *not* themselves specify a package. Rather, they define rules and constraints that are applied as input to the package specification process. The PackageType specification *must* be compatible with all of the ProductRelationships between ProductTypes in the PackageType.

In some UML texts, we have seen packages defined completely in terms of ProductRelationships by adding a Contains subclass to ProductRelationship. This approach, while simple, is often problematic. It embeds and hides package specification rules inside the source code and (depending on how it is implemented) can lead to inflexible systems where changes to a package structure may necessitate source code changes. Our view is that ProductRelationships are semantically *different* from package specification, and we have modeled the archetypes accordingly. Any model that confuses the semantics of these two things may well be wrong.

7.21 Up-selling and cross-selling

When you want to purchase a product, you are sometimes offered an upgrade to a higher specification product, possibly at a reduced price. This activity, known as *up-selling*, is an important way for businesses to maximize both the business benefit and the customer satisfaction generated from each sale.

An example of up-selling is when you order a small coffee and the vendor says, "Do you want the large size? It is only 25¢ more." Up-selling is very important for service industries such as car rental, as a way to move low-profit customers into higher and more profitable price brackets at the point of sale.

In our model, the `ProductRelationship UpgradableTo` captures the possibility of an upgrade to a higher specification `ProductType`.

Cross-selling is a related activity that is sometimes confused with up-selling, although the two are really quite different. Cross-selling occurs when you choose a product and are then offered a compatible product, possibly at a reduced price. For example, you order a burger and the vendor asks, "Do you want fries with that?" Another example might be that you book a vacation package and the agent asks if you also want to rent a car.

In our model, we capture the possibility of cross-selling with the `Product-Relationship ComplementedBy`.

Notice that in up-selling the `ProductType` is replaced by one of higher specification, whereas in cross-selling the `ProductType` is combined with another different but complementary `ProductType`. Although the two activities sometimes get confused because they tend to happen in parallel, it is important to get this right in the supporting systems; otherwise, the ability of the business to exploit both approaches may be hampered.

When up-selling and cross-selling are practiced with integrity, they can generate advantages for both the buyer and the seller. However, if they degenerate into merely steering the customer into paying a higher price for no real advantage (usually by instilling FUD—fear, uncertainty, and doubt) or if the price of extra components does not reflect their true value, these practices can lead to a loss of customer confidence and ultimately to a loss of business.

7.22 Price

> The `Price` archetype represents the amount of money that must be paid in order to purchase a good or service.

Every product needs a price. In this section we present a model of the `Price` archetype that can cover the full spectrum of pricing strategies, from the simplest to the most complex. You can add or remove components of this archetype as necessary, according to how complex prices are in your business.

In Table 7.9 you can see that there are several pricing cases to cover.

Table 7.9

Pricing case	Example
A single, fixed price	A can of soup in a supermarket
A reserve (minimum) price and a higher price determined at the point of sale	An item for sale on an auction site such as eBay
A price that shows some periodicity	Seasonal rates for hotel accommodation
Multiple prices that depend on the application of business rules	CD prices that may be reduced if you are a club member (our local CD shop does this)
Multiple prices that depend on the application of business rules and that show some time dependence	An airline ticket

Clearly, a single, fixed price that varies infrequently is the simplest case and is quite common. Most items that you buy in a supermarket fall into this category. However, many products (especially relatively high-value products such as airline seats and hotel accommodation) have different prices whose validity varies by time, according to some business rules, or both. For example, if you consider an airline's economy class return ticket from London (LHR) to New York (JFK), the price for the seat can vary according to a number of factors:

- Your date of departure
- The number of days before your date of departure that you purchase the ticket
- How long you intend to stay before you return
- Whether your stay includes a weekend or not
- Where you purchased the ticket (e.g., on-line or from an agency)
- Whether your stay includes a hotel reservation or car rental (e.g., as part of a package)

- The degree of flexibility you require (e.g., whether you want your ticket to be valid only for a particular flight or valid for a range of flights)
- Whether you want your ticket to be refundable

As you can see, pricing rules can be very complex, and unless both business systems and software systems have a way to deal with this complexity, the rules may be inconsistent or may even fail.

As a specific example of failure, consider the story of someone who bought a *nonrefundable* economy class return ticket between two European cities and then decided not to travel. To get around this restriction, he telephoned the airline and upgraded the ticket to a business class ticket by paying the difference between the economy class and business class fares. However, business class tickets *are fully refundable*, so the person called the airline again, cancelled the business class ticket, and got a full refund.

When you think about it, there is a logical inconsistency in the business rules here.

```
R1: Can refund economy class fare = false
R2: Can upgrade economy class fare to business class fare = true
R3: Can refund business class fare = true

(R2 AND R3) implies (R1 == true)
```

This sort of failure arises because the pricing rules have either been insufficiently formulated by the business (e.g., missing conditions about when a refund can be made), which is the most common case in our experience, or incorrectly realized in the software systems. Either way, the formal rules-based pricing that we discuss in this section can help enormously.

The essence of our model of pricing (shown in Figure 7.20) is that each `ProductType` may have one or more `Prices`, and each `Price` has an associated `RuleSet` (see Chapter 12) that defines the `preconditions` for the availability of that `Price`. So if, for example, you want to get `Price X`, you must first satisfy `RuleSet Y`.

If several `Prices` are available, the selling system often filters these `Prices` by deciding which to offer to the customer and in what order to present them. Filtering is generally based on a combination of customer requirements and specific business drivers, such as the need to sell more of a particular product or to maximize profit on the sale.

On the whole, the more constraints that the customer is prepared to accept, the lower the `Price`. This is because flexibility typically results in more

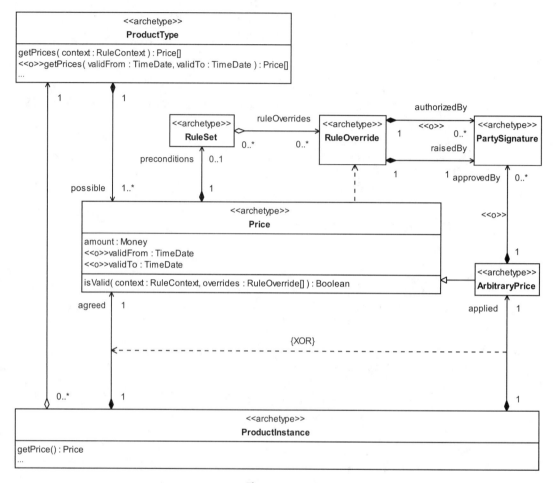

Figure 7.20

overhead costs for the business—for goods, these costs stem from keeping a wider range of inventory, while for services, they represent greater uncertainty about required resourcing levels.

Prices have optional validFrom and validTo attributes that can be used by a RuleSet to decide whether a Price is available and can also be used to get current or historic prices for a ProductType.

A particular ProductInstance is associated with an agreed Price from the set of possible Prices for its ProductType or an applied ArbitraryPrice (see Section 7.22.1). In either case, the Price for the ProductInstance can be obtained by its operation getPrice().

7.22.1 Price reductions

Price reductions can arise in different circumstances and are modeled accordingly.

A price reduction that applies to *any* instance of a ProductType is modeled as one of the ProductType's Prices and may have preconditions.

Individual ProductInstances may also have an ad hoc Price applied that overrides all the other possible Prices—for example, a price reduction for a shop-soiled item. An ad hoc Price is modeled as an ArbitraryPrice.

> The ArbitraryPrice archetype represents an ad hoc Price applied to a specific ProductInstance that overrides all other possible Prices.

An ArbitraryPrice may be approvedBy one or more Parties as represented by their PartySignatures. Your specific business requirements will dictate whether approval is needed.

Finally, price reductions may be applied as Discounts to a whole Order rather than to individual ProductTypes or ProductInstances—see Section 9.17.

7.22.2 Rules-based pricing

The activity diagram in Figure 7.21 captures the basics of a rules-based pricing process. We model pricing rules using the Rule archetype pattern, which we discuss in Chapter 12.

Here is a walkthrough of this pricing process.

get business constraints, get customer details,
get customer requirements

The first three activities are about collecting information—finding out who the customer is, what their requirements are, and any pertinent business constraints that might affect the sales process. The outputs of these activities are a set of customer requirements (these might specify a category, a set of required features, or a set of features and a price range—see Section 7.11), a RuleContext that contains customer information, and a RuleContext that contains any business constraints.

find possible ProductTypes based on requirements

One or more suitable ProductTypes are found for the customer by searching the ProductCatalog for ProductTypes that are a good fit with the customer requirements.

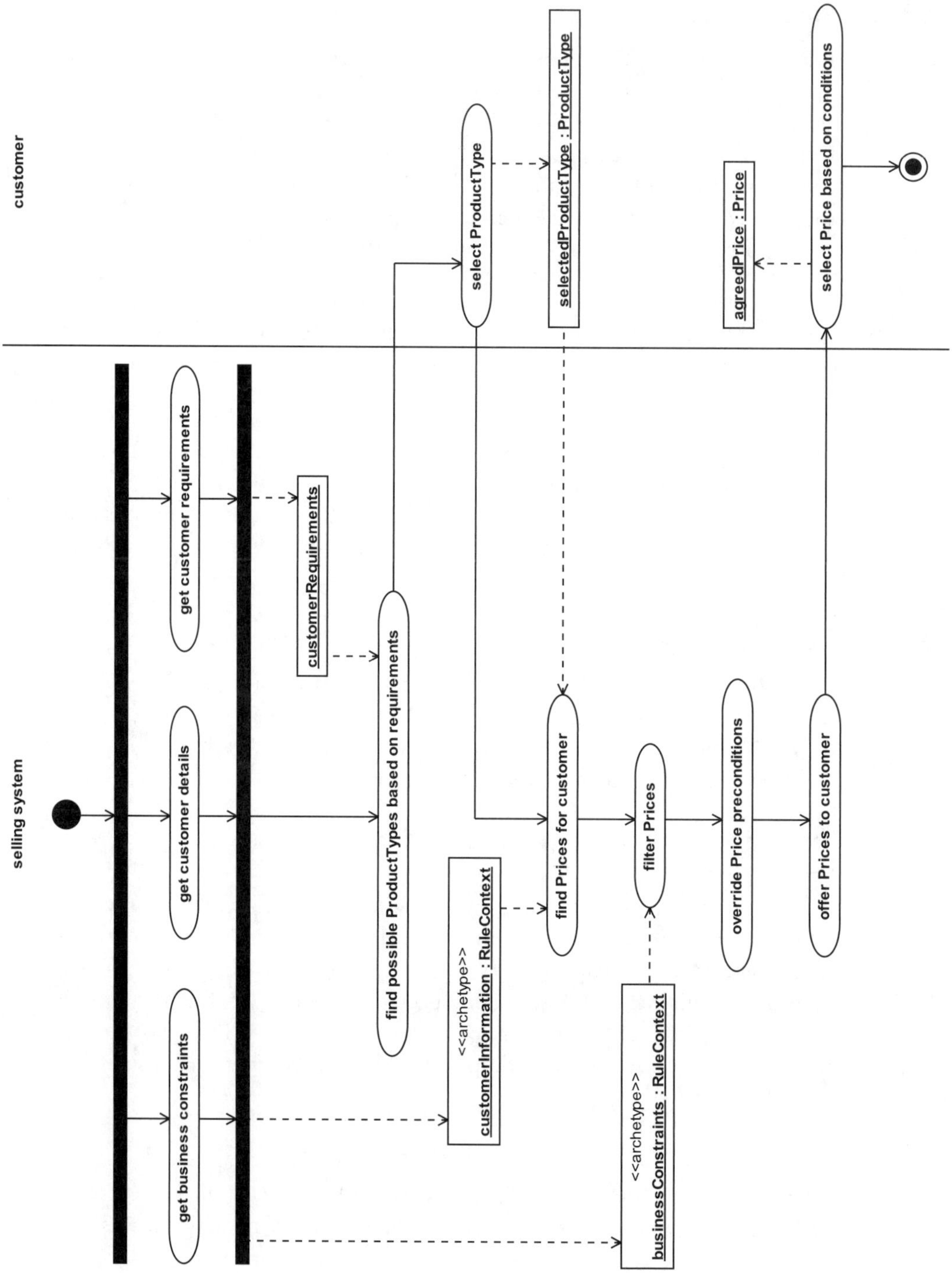

Figure 7.21

select ProductType
The customer selects a single `ProductType`.

find Prices for customer
The `customerInformation` is used to find a set of `Prices` that are appropriate for the customer. This is done by matching the `customerInformation` `RuleContext` against the `Price` `preconditions` to see what `Prices` may be offered.

filter Prices
`Prices` offered to the customer may be filtered according to business constraints. For example, `Prices` may be presented in a particular order to encourage the customer to take a particular `Price` or may be withheld if the business decides it doesn't want to offer a particular `Price` under the prevailing circumstances. The latter is done quite often by organizations such as railways, as part of capacity management (see Section 8.7).

override Price preconditions
This is the point at which `RuleOverrides` may be created if there is a compelling business reason to offer the customer a particular `Price` that would otherwise not be offered.

offer Prices to customer
The `Prices` are presented to the customer.

select Price based on conditions
The customer selects a specific `Price`. This choice is often based on the conditions associated with the `Price`. Customers may well pay more for flexibility.

An important aspect of this process is the explicit provision for `RuleOverrides` (see Section 12.20). Consider the following story: the CEO of a large company was flying economy class between Europe and the United States with three of his salesmen. Because the salesmen were frequent flyers, they were upgraded to business class, while the CEO was not. Then the CEO asked to sit with his employees. What do you do? The rules say "No" to an upgrade, but the CEO gives over $100,000 of business to the airline each year, so common business sense says "Yes, sir!"

Many business systems fall over when presented with issues like this, and this is exactly the reason why a `RuleOverride` is necessary. It allows `Rules` to be overridden in a structured, controlled, and auditable way by capturing the following information:

- The business objective of the `RuleOverride`
- Who the `RuleOverride` was `raisedBy`
- Who the `RuleOverride` was `authorizedBy` (optional)
- When the decision was made
- Which `Rule` was overridden

7.23 Package pricing

How do you assign a `Price` to a package? `PackageType` is a subclass of `Product-Type`, and `PackageInstance` is a subclass of `ProductInstance`, so the pricing model described in Section 7.22 largely applies. Figure 7.22 shows how this model is adapted to cover package pricing, with the addition of a `Pricing-Strategy` archetype that determines how to calculate `PackageType` `Prices`.

> The `PricingStrategy` archetype determines how a `Price` is calculated for a `PackageType`.

Each `PricingStrategy` works as shown in Table 7.10.

Table 7.10

PricingStrategy	Algorithm	Equation
ASSIGNED	The `PackageType` is a `ProductType` and may have one or more possible `Prices` (P)—see Section 7.22	$P = x$
	The business sets each possible `Price` to a specific value (x)	
	Note that a possible `Price` does not depend on the exact `PackageInstance` composition—e.g., a set menu	
AGGREGATED	The `PackageType` calculates a `Price` (P) by summing the appropriate `Price` (p_i) for each of its component `ProductTypes`—preconditions indicate the `Price` at which a `ProductType` is offered when included in this `PackageType`	$P = \sum_{i=1}^{n} p_i$

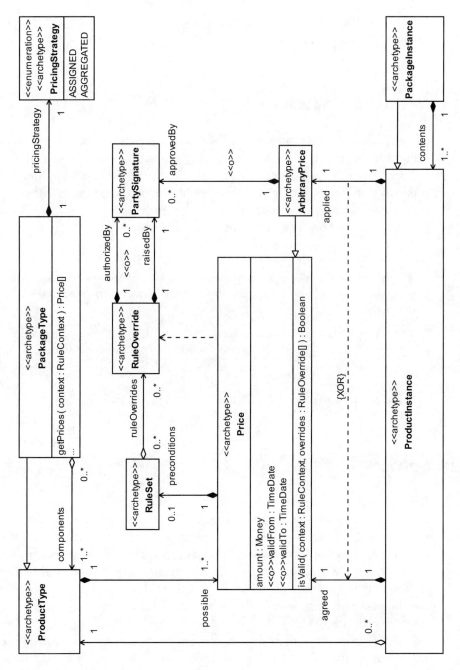

Figure 7.22

Price reductions are handled in the same way as with `ProductTypes` and `ProductInstances` (see Section 7.22.1).

7.24 Measured products

Some products are not sold as predefined units but rather as measures of something. For example, flooring may be sold by the square foot, gasoline by the gallon, fresh produce by the pound, and electricity by the kilowatt hour. Measured products provide a way to handle this type of product, using the `Quantity` pattern that we describe in Chapter 10.

We introduce two new archetypes to handle measured products.

> The `MeasuredProductType` archetype represents a kind of `ProductType` that specifies possible `Metrics` and a single preferred `Metric` for measuring `Quantities` of the product.
>
> The `MeasuredProductInstance` archetype represents a kind of `ProductInstance` that specifies an amount of some `Metric` (a `Quantity`) of the product to be sold.

The model for measured products is shown in Figure 7.23.

7.25 Services

A service represents a process or activity that is offered for sale.

Many modelers consider goods and services to be two different things. This approach is justified to some degree, but there are definite advantages to treating a service as a special case of the more general product. A unified approach allows you to design business systems that can accommodate both goods and services. In fact, only in inventory management (which we discuss in Chapter 8) is there any difference between goods and services that makes a difference from the *modeling* perspective.

The primary *semantic* difference between goods and services is that a good usually represents a thing (such as a computer system) that is more or less concrete, while a service represents a process or an activity (such as a haircut or a stay at a hotel) that is not concrete.

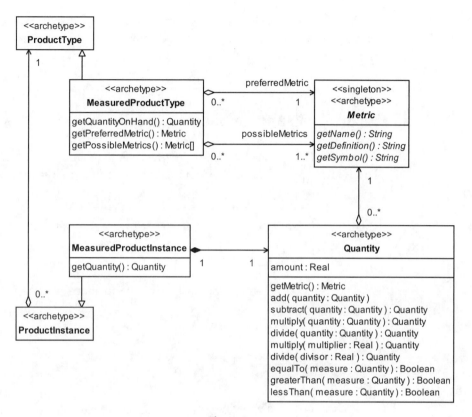

Figure 7.23

When you consider services as being a kind of product, you have to think very carefully about what you are actually selling.

For example, consider a barbershop. What are you selling? Are you selling haircuts? You can't go into a barbershop and find a haircut sitting on the shelf! A haircut is not a thing in itself—it is a process. Still, natural language allows you to refer to the haircut process as though it is a noun. This is known as *nominalization*, and most languages are littered with nominalizations. In common usage, we may often refer to many processes (verbs) as though they are things (nouns). It's important to be very aware of nominalizations when considering services; otherwise, you can get very confused about what is actually being sold!

In practice, if you own the barbershop, you are selling a slot of a barber's time to perform the activity of cutting the customer's hair according to an agreed specification.

When you are selling services, rather than selling things, you are actually selling part of your business's capacity to deliver the service. We discuss capacity in more depth in Section 8.7.

7.26   ServiceType **and** ServiceInstance

We can model a particular type of service, such as a haircut, as a ServiceType. This is just a special kind of ProductType that describes the essentials of a service.

> The ServiceType archetype is a kind of ProductType that represents a type of service.

Each ServiceType may optionally have two attributes, shown in Table 7.11.

Table 7.11

ServiceType **archetype**	
Attribute	**Semantics**
<<o>>startOfPeriodOfOperation	The start of the period over which the ServiceType is available
<<o>>endOfPeriodOfOperation	The end of the period over which the ServiceType is available

When a Party actually receives an execution of the service, we can model this as a ServiceInstance.

> The ServiceInstance archetype represents an instance or execution of a Service-Type delivered to one or more Parties.

You can see our model of ServiceTypes and ServiceInstances in Figure 7.24. ServiceInstances have an actual start and end as well as an optional scheduledStart and scheduledEnd for performance monitoring purposes.

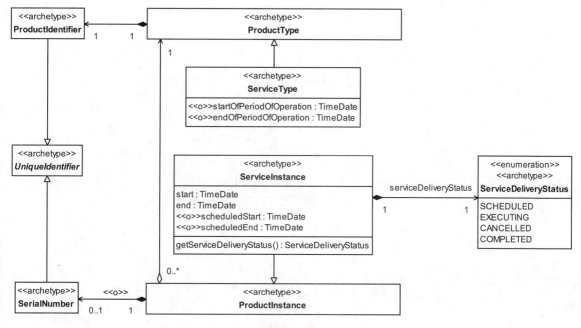

Figure 7.24

The delivery of a ServiceInstance is recorded by ServiceDeliveryStatus.

The ServiceDeliveryStatus archetype records the status of the delivery of a particular ServiceInstance.

This can take one of the values shown in Table 7.12.

Table 7.12

ServiceDeliveryStatus **values**	
Value	**Semantics**
SCHEDULED	The ServiceInstance has been scheduled for delivery
EXECUTING	The ServiceInstance is in the process of delivery
CANCELLED	The ServiceInstance has been cancelled
COMPLETED	The delivery of the ServiceInstance has been completed

These statuses reflect the fact that ServiceInstances are executions of a process, with the lifecycle shown in Figure 7.25.

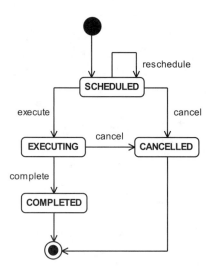

Figure 7.25

7.27 **The specialized** Product **pleomorphs**

We finish this chapter by taking a quick look at the specialized Product pleomorphs. As we stated at the beginning of the chapter, the generalized Product archetype pattern provides the most flexible model, and is what we expect to be used in most cases. In this section we show you how you can arrive at the specialized pleomorphs by simple modifications to the Product archetype pattern.

7.27.1 **The** UniqueProduct **pleomorph**

This variant of the Product archetype pattern applies when all goods or services represented in a business system are custom-made or "one-offs." This is quite rare because most goods (and effectively, many services) are now mass-produced.

This is a very constrained model, so be careful—use it if, and only if, *every* product in the business system is completely unique. If there are exceptions to this rule, consider using the more flexible general Product pattern instead.

For this pleomorph, you simply collapse the ProductType and the Product-Instance archetypes in the particular way shown in Figure 7.26—changed archetypes are indicated by gray shading. (Note that the ProductInstance's getPrice() operation returns either an agreed Price or an applied ArbitraryPrice—see Section 7.22.1.)

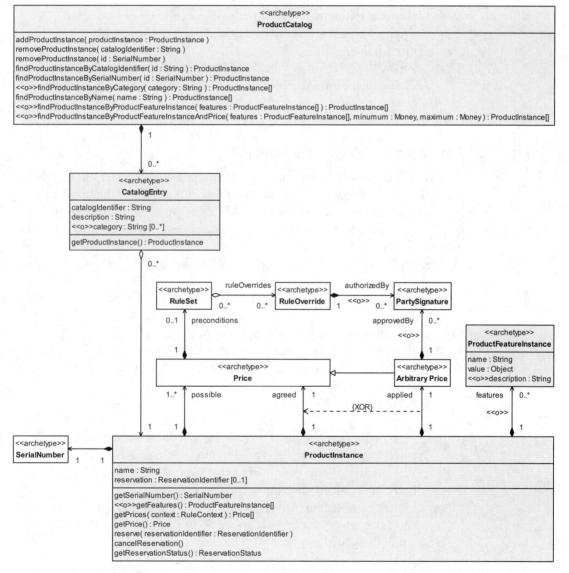

Figure 7.26

This creates a simple but inflexible model.

- You have lost any notion of there being "types" of product. In fact, you don't need this because, by definition, every product is now unique.
- It is not possible to have batches of unique products.
- There can be no concept of optional features. Instead, each unique product has a set of actual features.
- It is not meaningful to define packages. Because every product is unique, any package would be a one-off (i.e., not repeatable or customizable).
- ProductRelationships should not be defined for unique products because each combination of unique products (i.e., of individual items) is itself unique.

7.27.2 The IdenticalProduct pleomorph

This variant of the Product archetype pattern applies when *every* product that you sell is an identical instance of some ProductType. An example might be cans of baked beans on a supermarket shelf. Each can of beans is identical (we hope) to all other cans. However, batches of cans may be tracked by a batch number for quality control reasons.

Again, this is a constrained model that should be used only when a business system exclusively deals with *types* of things, where every instance of a type is exactly the same. If any instances of a type differ because of customization, or if individual instances need to be tracked for commercial, security, or legal reasons, use the more flexible general Product pattern instead.

For this pleomorph, you again collapse the ProductType and Product-Instance archetypes, but in the way shown in Figure 7.27. Changed archetypes are indicated by gray shading.

Again, this creates an inflexible model.

- You have lost any notion of there being individually identifiable instances of product. You don't need to model instances explicitly because every instance is now described by its ProductType and its Batch.
- It is not possible to track instances separately.
- It is not possible to record an ad hoc price reduction to a specific instance (i.e., an ArbitraryPrice—see Section 7.22.1) because instances cannot be individually identified by the system.

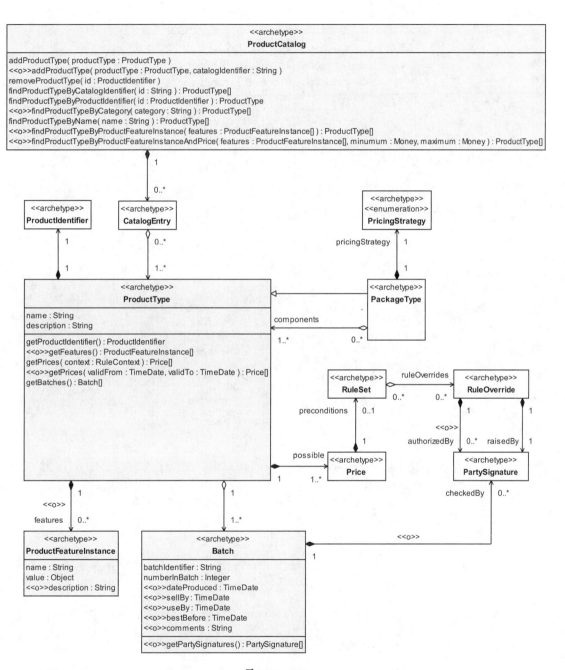

Figure 7.27

- There can be no concept of optional features. Instead, every instance of a ProductType has an identical set of features.
- Note that this pleomorph does not cover measured products because these do not consist of identical instances.

7.28 Summary

In this chapter we looked at the Product archetype pattern. This is a pattern for representing information about a company's goods and services. We covered the topics listed below.

- The Product archetype pattern: a generalized model for representing products
  - Managing variation in the Product archetype pattern: how to use pleomorphs
  - UniqueProduct pleomorph: how to adapt the Product archetype pattern for the case where every product instance in a business system is completely unique
  - IdenticalProduct pleomorph: how to adapt the Product archetype pattern for the case where a business system exclusively deals with types of products and every instance of a type is identical

- ProductType and ProductInstance:
  - ProductType: how to represent types of products (e.g., a type of LCD monitor)
    - ProductIdentifier: how to uniquely identify a ProductType
  - ProductInstance: how to represent specific instances of a product type (e.g., a particular LCD monitor)
    - SerialNumber: how to uniquely identify a ProductInstance
    - Batch: how to represent a set of ProductInstances, all of the same type, that are to be tracked together

- Product specification: how to represent the specification for a ProductType
  - ProductFeatureType: how to represent a type of feature associated with a ProductType
  - ProductFeatureInstance: how to represent a specific feature of a ProductInstance

- `ProductCatalog`: how to represent a persistent store of product information
  - `CatalogEntry`: how to represent the information about a particular type of product in a `ProductCatalog`
- Packages: how to sell selections of products grouped together as a unit
  - `PackageType`: how to specify the possible contents of a particular type of package
  - `PackageInstance`: how to represent a particular instance of a `PackageType`
- Combining `ProductTypes`: an investigation of the mathematics of combining `ProductTypes`
- Package specification process: how a business may specify a `PackageType`
- Rule-driven package specification: how to express packaging strategies as a collection of `Rules`
  - `ProductSet`: how to represent a set of `ProductTypes` from which selections may be made
  - `PropositionOfInclusion`: how to describe the possible contents of a package in a rule of the form:
    - `P: isSubsetOf( T, S, min, max )`
      - States that the target `PackageInstance` T must contain between `min` and `max` `ProductInstances` whose `ProductTypes` are specified in the `ProductSet` S
  - `ConditionalPropositionOfInclusion`: how to describe the possible contents of a package in a rule of the form:
    - `P: if isSubsetOf( T, S, min, max )`
      `P₁: isSubsetOf( T, S, min, max )`
      `P₂: isSubsetOf( T, S, min, max )`
      `...`
      `Pₙ: isSubsetOf( T, S, min, max )`
      - States that if the condition P is true, the `PropositionsOfInclusion` $P_1, P_2, \ldots, P_n$ must also be true
- An example of a `PackageType`: a real-world example of a `PackageType` and the set of rules that describe it

- `ProductRelationships`: how to represent fixed relationships between `ProductTypes`
  - `UpgradableTo`: how to represent an upgrade relationship
  - `SubstitutedBy`: how to represent a substitution relationship
  - `ReplacedBy`: how to represent a replacement relationship
  - `ComplementedBy`: how to represent a relationship where one `ProductType` complements or enhances another
  - `CompatibleWith`: how to represent a relationship that shows that one `ProductType` is compatible with another
  - `IncompatibleWith`: how to represent a relationship that shows that one `ProductType` is incompatible with another

- Up-selling and cross-selling: how `ProductRelationships` can enable increased sales
  - Up-selling: upgrading a sale from one `ProductType` to a more profitable one—"Large is only 25¢ more"
  - Cross-selling: extending a sale by adding another `ProductType` that is an enhancement of the customer's original selection—"Do you want fries with that?"

- `Price`: how to represent the amount of money that must be paid in order to purchase a good or service
  - Pricing approaches
  - `Price` reductions: how to represent different types of price reduction
    - `ArbitraryPrice`: how to represent an ad hoc `Price` applied to a specific `ProductInstance`
  - Rules-based pricing: a walkthrough of a pricing process that is driven by business rules

- Package pricing: how to represent the `Price` of a package
  - `PricingStrategy`: how to represent a pricing algorithm for a package

- Measured products: how to represent products sold by measure
  - `MeasuredProductType`: how to represent a `ProductType`, such as gasoline, that is sold by measure
  - `MeasuredProductInstance`: how to represent the amount of a `MeasuredProductType` (e.g., 10 gallons of gasoline) involved in a specific sale

- Services: how to represent processes or activities that are offered for sale
  - ServiceType: how to represent a type of service
  - ServiceInstance: how to represent an instance or execution of a type of service
  - ServiceDeliveryStatus: how to record the status of the delivery process for a particular ServiceInstance

Chapter **8**

Inventory
archetype pattern

8.1 Business context

An inventory is a stock or store of goods. You can also use inventory to manage the delivery of services.

There are three reasons why a business may concern itself with inventories.

1. It needs to maintain a stock of items for sale.
2. It needs to maintain a stock of parts or materials to supply a manufacturing process or to support the delivery of services.
3. It needs to sell and deliver services.

Inventory has different functions in different business domains. These functions are listed in Table 8.1.

In essence, there are two different business perspectives about inventory: the selling perspective and the manufacturing perspective. Nevertheless, inventory always tends to be handled in a similar way—a stock of items is created and maintained at an appropriate level, or, in the case of services, the capacity to deliver the service is maintained.

Holding inventory of goods is expensive. If you are in a retail or wholesale business, most of your assets may well be tied up in inventory. Similarly, if you are in manufacturing, you may have significant amounts of money tied up in parts or raw materials that you keep on hand.

Table 8.1

Business domain	Purpose of inventory
Selling	To meet expected demand
	To ensure sales are not lost because items have gone out of stock
Manufacturing	To feed the production process
	To decouple production steps by creating a buffer of work in progress between them
	To create a buffer of finished goods in case of production downtime
	To create a buffer of finished goods to cope with peaks in demand (e.g., seasonal fluctuations)
Selling and manufacturing	To allow stock ordering to occur in cycles (e.g., to optimize ordering costs)
	To gain quantity discounts or to hedge against price increases

The equation for estimating the cost of goods inventory is simple:

$$C = \sum_{i=1}^{m} c_i n_i t_i r$$

where:

C = total estimated cost of inventory
m = number of different types of items in the inventory
c_i = unit cost of item i
n_i = total number of item i in the inventory
t_i = average time these items have been in the inventory
r = average interest rate

You should assume that the interest rate is the average cost of money to your company, that is, the average interest rate on your loans.

This equation is only a very rough estimate and takes no account of other important but less visible costs of inventory, such as the cost of storage, warehousing, security, and other maintenance activities. Doing this calculation for your business can be quite enlightening!

Holding inventory of services means having sufficient capacity to deliver services at a predefined rate. This is also expensive, and it can be much harder to estimate the costs. For example, here are some of the equipment and staff costs a rail operator must pay to maintain the capacity to deliver a service between Toronto and Vancouver:

- Engines and rolling stock
- Equipment maintenance
- Drivers
- Guards and other on-board staff
- Station staff
- Track maintenance
- Administration

Inventory management, whether of goods or services, is about minimizing the costs of inventory while maximizing its benefit to the business. Usually this involves keeping inventory of goods and the capacity to offer services to the lowest possible level that still allows the business to operate according to its efficiency and quality requirements.

To understand inventory, you need to understand how we model goods and services. This is described in Chapter 7, Product archetype pattern. If you haven't read Chapter 7 yet, you need to at least skim it before proceeding with this chapter.

8.2 Inventory **archetype pattern overview and roadmap**

The Inventory archetype pattern is shown in Figure 8.1.

8.3 Inventory **and the** Product **archetype pattern pleomorphs**

If you have read Chapter 7, you know that, in addition to the generalized Product archetype pattern, there are two specialized pleomorphs for Product that optimize it for very specific business constraints. The Product pattern variants are summarized again in Figure 8.2.

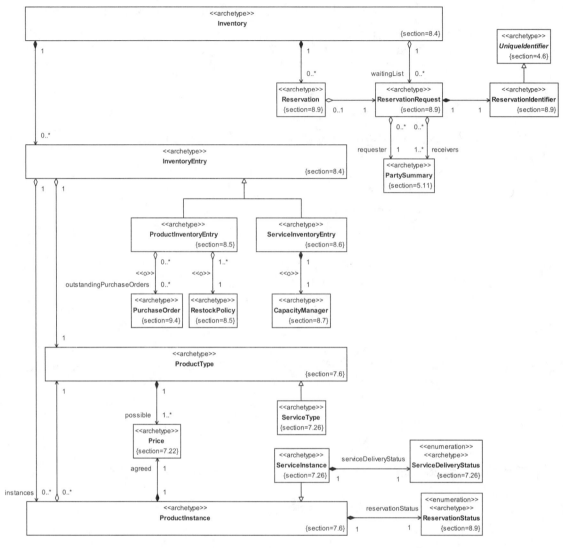

Figure 8.1

Although the Inventory archetype pattern must work for each of the cases illustrated in Figure 8.2, we will focus on making it work with the generalized Product pattern. If you need to apply Inventory to one of the other Product pleomorphs, you can simply collapse ProductType and ProductInstance appropriately, as described in Section 7.27.

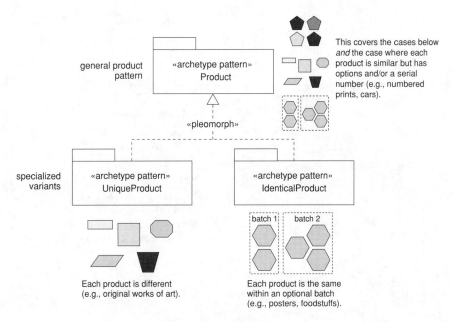

general product
pattern

«archetype pattern»
Product

This covers the cases below
and the case where each
product is similar but has
options and/or a serial
number (e.g., numbered
prints, cars).

«pleomorph»

specialized
variants

«archetype pattern»
UniqueProduct

«archetype pattern»
IdenticalProduct

batch 1   batch 2

Each product is different
(e.g., original works of art).

Each product is the same
within an optional batch
(e.g., posters, foodstuffs).

Figure 8.2

8.4 The Inventory archetype

The Inventory archetype represents a collection of InventoryEntries held in
stock by a business.

The InventoryEntry archetype records a type of good or service and the number
of instances of that good or service that are available.

The essential services offered by an inventory system and realized by Inventory
and InventoryEntry are summarized in Figure 8.3. These services fall into two
categories, inventory management services and reservation (booking) services,
used by the InventoryManager and ReservationAgent actors, respectively, in
Figure 8.3.

The semantics of the first category of services, inventory management services, are summarized in Table 8.2.

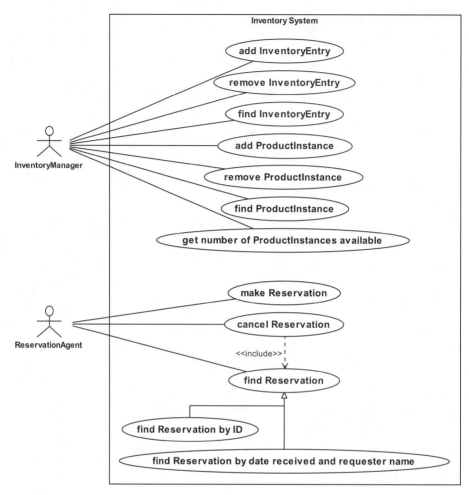

Figure 8.3

Table 8.2

Inventory **management service**	**Semantics**
add InventoryEntry	Adds an InventoryEntry representing a ProductType to the Inventory
remove InventoryEntry	Removes an InventoryEntry from the Inventory This happens when the business decides to no longer sell a particular ProductType

Table 8.2 (Continued)

Inventory **management service**	Semantics
find InventoryEntry	Finds one or more InventoryEntries
add ProductInstance	Adds new ProductInstances to the Inventory If an InventoryEntry for the ProductType already exists, the new ProductInstances are simply added to the existing InventoryEntry; otherwise, a new InventoryEntry is first added for the new ProductType
remove ProductInstance	Removes a ProductInstance from the Inventory when it is sold The number of ProductInstances in the appropriate InventoryEntry is decremented
find ProductInstance	Finds one or more ProductInstances in the Inventory
get number of ProductInstances available	Counts how many ProductInstances of a particular Product-Type you have available or what your current capacity to offer a specific ServiceInstance is (ServiceInstance is a type of ProductInstance)

In the second category, reservation services take requests from Reservation-Agents and resolve these requests into actual items of Inventory, that is, Product-Instances or ServiceInstances. The semantics of these services are summarized in Table 8.3. We'll discuss reservations in much more detail in Section 8.9.

Table 8.3

Inventory **reservation service**	Semantics
make Reservation	Accepts a ReservationRequest from a ReservationAgent and resolves this into a Reservation against an actual ProductInstance or ServiceInstance
cancel Reservation	Cancels an existing Reservation This will succeed only if the reserved item or service has not already been delivered and if there are no terms and conditions preventing cancellation

Table continued on next page

Table 8.3   (Continued)

Inventory **reservation service**	**Semantics**
find Reservation	Finds one or more existing Reservations
	Reservations can be located by their ReservationIdentifier or by a combination of the date the ReservationRequest was received and the name of the requester

Our model of Inventory is shown in Figure 8.4.

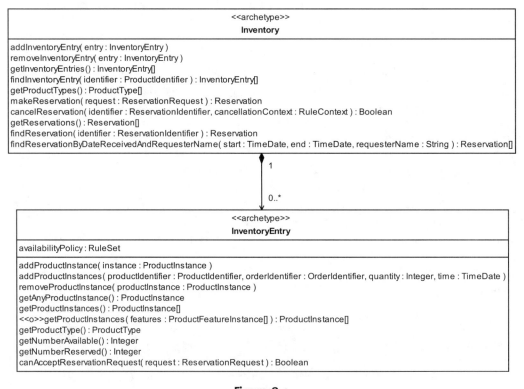

Figure 8.4

There are two types of InventoryEntry, ProductInventoryEntry for goods and ServiceInventoryEntry for services. We'll discuss these types of Inventory-Entry in the next couple of sections.

8.5 ProductInventoryEntry

> The `ProductInventoryEntry` archetype represents an `InventoryEntry` that holds a set of `ProductInstances` all of the same `ProductType`.

`ProductInventoryEntry` is shown in Figure 8.5.

Because `ProductInventoryEntry` deals with goods, rather than services, it usually provides mechanisms to perform the following actions.

- Recognize when stock levels are running low.
- Track information about items on order by linking to the appropriate `PurchaseOrders`. (`PurchaseOrders` are discussed in detail in Section 9.4.)

Inventory information about items on order typically needs to be up-to-date. In our model, you get this information by querying the outstanding-`PurchaseOrders` against a specific `ProductInventoryEntry`. These outstanding-`PurchaseOrders` are `PurchaseOrders` that conform to the following constraints.

- They have one or more `OrderLines` for items of the same `ProductType` as the `ProductInventoryEntry`.
- At least one of these `OrderLines` is not yet fully delivered.

By examining the `outstandingPurchaseOrders` against a particular `ProductInventoryEntry`, you may calculate the quantity on order (`getQuantityOnOrder()`) and the quantity expected by a particular date (`getQuantityExpectedByDate(...)`).

We discuss `OrderLines` in Section 9.5 and receiving items against `OrderLines` in Section 9.19. You need to at least skim Chapter 9 to appreciate the relationship between orders and inventory.

Each `ProductInventoryEntry` may have a `RestockPolicy`.

> The `RestockPolicy` archetype represents a set of rules determining when inventory items need to be reordered.

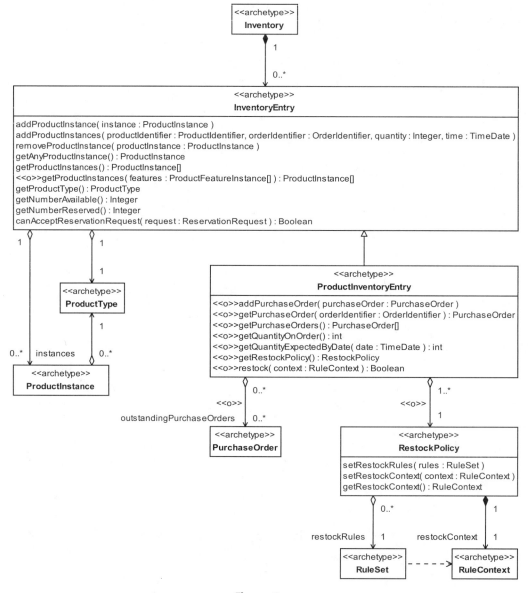

Figure 8.5

This `RestockPolicy` has `restockRules` that define the following:

- What level of `Inventory` of `ProductInstances` of a particular type is optimal (the actual level is defined by the `restockContext`)
- What level of `Inventory` of `ProductInstances` of a particular type triggers an order for more `ProductInstances` (the actual level is defined by the `restockContext`)
- How the existence of outstanding orders (as represented by `outstandingPurchaseOrders`) should affect the restocking process

In fact, maintaining the optimal level of `Inventory` can be a very difficult task because it may also depend on supply and demand forecasts. This is why we have used `restockRules` in our model. These `restockRules` can cope with the simplest case of tracking the number of `ProductInstances` on hand and then reordering if this number falls below a preset value, as well as much more complex cases. Typically, each business creates its own policies for restocking different types of `ProductInstances`. These policies should always be expressed as business rules so that they are made explicit and can be updated easily.

See our `Rule` archetype pattern in Chapter 12 for more information on encoding business rules.

8.6 ServiceInventoryEntry

> The `ServiceInventoryEntry` archetype represents an `InventoryEntry` that holds a set of `ServiceInstances` all of the same `ServiceType`.

The `ServiceInventoryEntry` manages the release for sale of its stock of `ServiceInstances` through a `CapacityManager`, as shown in Figure 8.6.

With services, you may have already scheduled some slots (i.e., `ServiceInstances` with a `ServiceDeliveryStatus` of SCHEDULED—see Section 7.26) in which a `ServiceType` can be delivered, so you effectively have a quantity on hand that can be sold. However, you may also schedule services on demand, according to the capacity of your business to offer these. For example, in a dentist's

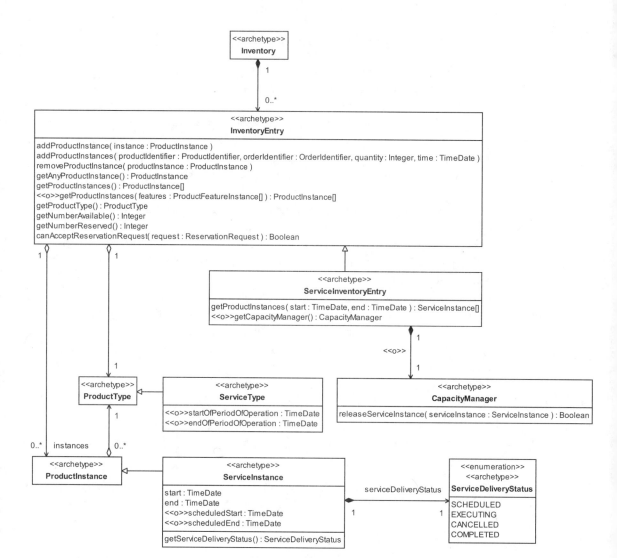

Figure 8.6

office most appointments are made in advance, but walk-in patients may be offered free slots in the schedule. Emergency patients may also be treated outside the regular schedule if the capacity to accommodate this can be found (i.e., a dentist who is willing to work outside of office hours).

Capacity is a complex issue, so we devote the next few sections to it.

8.7 Capacity planning and management

Capacity is the measure of a service provider's ability to provide a specific service.

Capacity is generated when resources are assigned to perform ServiceInstances. We plan to discuss resource allocation in a future book.

If the service provider is treated as a discrete operating unit, capacity is a measure of the upper limit on the load that the operating unit can carry.

To further understand capacity, consider a very simple example—a barbershop employs three barbers (shown in Figure 8.7). A suitable measure of capacity of the barbershop might be "number of haircuts per working day." In more complex cases, where there might be a range of possible but mutually exclusive activities (such as haircuts, facials, and manicures), it can be quite difficult to come up with a suitable metric for capacity. The best solution probably is to use a general metric such as "customer person-hour" that represents one hour of a barber's time spent with a single customer.

Capacity planning is about matching the capacity to perform a service to the demand for that service at a point in time.

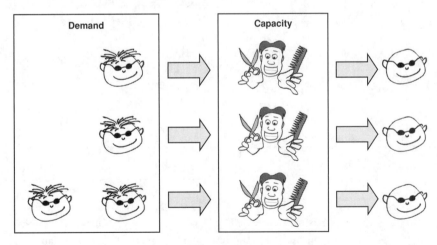

Figure 8.7

The ideal situation for any business is when capacity is exactly matched to demand. If the business has excess capacity, some will go unsold. On the other hand, if a business has too little capacity, there will be loss of business. Optimizing capacity for one or more operating units is known as *capacity planning*.

Apart from capacity planning, there is also the more complex issue of *capacity management*. Capacity management is about constraining capacity in order to achieve some business benefit.

Notice in Figure 8.6 that each ServiceInventoryEntry has access to a CapacityManager if you implement this feature.

> The CapacityManager archetype manages the utilization of capacity by releasing ServiceInstances.

The CapacityManager archetype is really just an interface that represents the capability of your business to carry out capacity management and how that relates to Inventory.

Let's look at an example of capacity management. Suppose your business offers a ServiceType that is a flight from London to Paris in a particular class of travel. Your capacity for any instance of that ServiceType depends on the number of seats on the aircraft you have allocated to that flight in that class of travel. This illustrates, as we've already mentioned, that resource allocation generates capacity. Suppose an Airbus A320 is allocated to the flight from London to Paris. This plane has about 130 seats, and let's assume that they are distributed among two classes of travel as shown in Table 8.4.

Table 8.4

Class of travel	Capacity
Business class	50
Economy class	80

For simplicity, we'll just consider the economy class. Now, depending on when you book an economy class ticket relative to the date of departure of your flight, you can get different prices. These are listed in Table 8.5.

Table 8.5

Fare type	Days before departure	Price
Super Apex	Booked more than 21 days before departure	£30
Apex	Booked between 7 and 21 days before departure	£40
Full fare	Booked within 7 days of departure	£90

Each of these types of fares grants you slightly different terms and conditions, with the more expensive fares having fewer constraints. Also, from the airline's point of view, each of these fares has a different yield (profit). The cheapest fares may make only a small profit for the airline, while the highest fares may in some cases (especially on long distance flights) make significantly more.

Obviously, the customer would like to buy a low fare whenever possible, and the airline would like to sell a higher fare whenever possible.

Capacity management allows the airline to optimize this equation, so that it makes money while the customer still gets a competitive deal. The airline achieves this by constraining capacity as a function of time.

This works as follows. If the airline were to put all its economy seats up for sale more than 21 days before departure, its demand forecasts indicate that it would sell them all. However, it would sell them at the lowest possible price and make the lowest possible profit.

But the airline predicts that it can generally sell about 20 seats between 7 and 21 days out and an even more profitable 10 seats at less than 7 days out. The airline therefore initially *withholds* a certain number of seats to ensure that it retains sufficient capacity to meet this later (but more profitable) predicted demand. This is capacity management.

Capacity management can be a very complex area, and a detailed discussion is beyond the scope of this book. You can find a good introduction to capacity planning and management in [Stevenson 2001].

The `CapacityManager` archetype can implement *arbitrarily* complex capacity management algorithms depending on your specific business needs. These algorithms are often rule based, so you may find our `Rule` pattern in Chapter 12 useful.

8.8 Availability

One of the key functions of `Inventory` is to decide whether `ProductInstances` or `ServiceInstances` are available for sale. This is often known as *availability*. There are three distinct issues that availability needs to address.

1. Can you meet a request for goods or services? In the case of goods this means, "Do you have the goods in stock?" In the case of services this means, "Do you have sufficient capacity to deliver the service?"
2. Are you prepared to meet the request for `Inventory` in this specific case? For example, you may wish to withhold `Inventory` so that you can sell it later.
3. Is the customer entitled to buy the goods or services? For example, a customer must be over a certain legal age to buy alcohol or must have a valid driver's license to rent a car.

The first two issues are related to the ability to sell. For goods, issue 1 is resolved simply by seeing how many goods are in stock or will be in stock within an acceptable time frame. Issue 2 does not generally apply because if you have goods, you tend to sell them. However, if necessary, this issue may be accommodated by using the `availabilityPolicy` of the `InventoryEntry` that we discuss below.

Issues 1 and 2 are addressed quite differently for services. They are both handled by the `CapacityManager` archetype that we discussed in Section 8.7.

Issue 3 is qualitatively different from issues 1 and 2 for both goods and services. This is because issue 3 is not about the ability to sell but rather about the customer's right to buy. To deal with this issue, each `InventoryEntry` has an `availabilityPolicy` (see Figure 8.8 in the next section). This is a set of rules that must be fulfilled before the `InventoryEntry` can accept a `ReservationRequest`. The information needed for these rules is provided by the context of the `ReservationRequest`.

8.9 Reservations

One reason businesses maintain formal inventory is to allow items in the inventory (goods or services) to be reserved for `Parties`.

You begin the reservation process with the creation of a ReservationRequest.

The ReservationRequest archetype represents a request for a Reservation to be made.

Each ReservationRequest has a ReservationIdentifier.

The ReservationIdentifier archetype represents a unique identifier for a ReservationRequest.

ReservationRequests are resolved into Reservations.

The Reservation archetype represents the assignment of one or more Product-Instances to one or more Parties via PartySummaries—that is, an arrangement by which a ProductInstance is kept for the use of a specific Party at some point in time.

Each ProductInstance has a ReservationStatus.

The ReservationStatus archetype indicates whether a ProductInstance is AVAILABLE to be reserved or has already been RESERVED.

The relationships between Inventory, Reservation, and ReservationRequest are shown in Figure 8.8.

Notice that the ReservationRequest has a requester PartySummary and receivers PartySummaries. Each PartySummary references a Party or a Party-Role. (Parties are described fully in Chapter 4, PartyRoles in Chapter 5, and PartySummaries in Section 5.11.) The requester is the originator of the ReservationRequest, and the receivers are the recipients of the goods or services being reserved.

A ReservationRequest provides the information listed in Table 8.6.

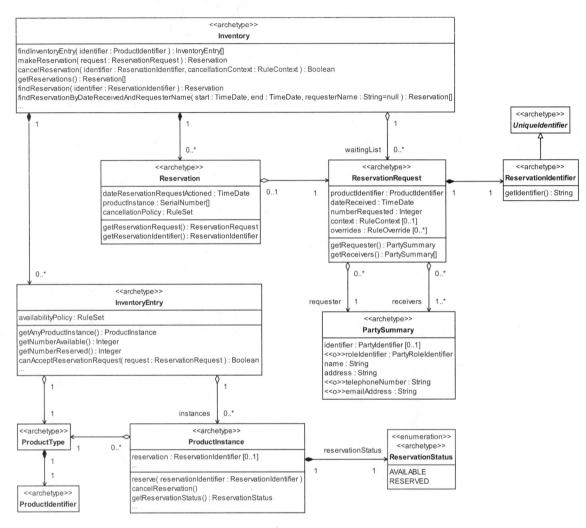

Figure 8.8

Table 8.6

ReservationRequest information	Semantics
requester	A PartySummary for the Party (or PartyRole) making the request
receivers	One or more PartySummaries for the receivers of the reserved item The requester may also be one of the receivers

Table 8.6 (Continued)

ReservationRequest information	Semantics
productIdentifier	The unique identifier for the ProductType or ServiceType requested
dateReceived	The TimeDate on which the system received the ReservationRequest
numberRequested	The number of instances of the ProductType or ServiceType requested
context	A set of information used to determine whether the ReservationRequest can be made into a Reservation or not—see the Rule model in Chapter 12 for more details
overrides	A set of information that may override some of the Rules governing the making of Reservations

This ReservationRequest is passed as a parameter to the makeReservation(...) operation of the Inventory to create the Reservation itself. The Reservation records the following:

- The ReservationRequest
- The date the request was resolved into an actual Reservation (dateReservationRequestActioned)
- One or more ProductInstances

The reservation process is quite straightforward. It is illustrated in Figure 8.9, which shows how the various archetypes collaborate to make the reservation. Once the ReservationAgent has collected applicable information (shown in Table 8.6) from the requester, the process proceeds as follows.

1. «create»—the ReservationAgent creates a ReservationRequest based on this information.
2. makeReservation(request)—the ReservationAgent passes the ReservationRequest to the Inventory.
3. findInventoryEntry(identifier)—the Inventory uses the ReservationRequest productIdentifier to locate the appropriate InventoryEntry.

4. canAcceptReservationRequest(request)—the Inventory checks that the InventoryEntry can accept a ReservationRequest (see Section 8.8 about availabilityPolicy).

5. getAnyProductInstance()—the Inventory gets a ProductInstance that is AVAILABLE from the InventoryEntry.

6. «create»—the Inventory creates a new Reservation.

7. reserve(reservationIdentifier)—the Inventory reserves the ProductInstance.

Just one ProductInstance is reserved in this example.

The Inventory may be able to resolve a ReservationRequest into a Reservation immediately. Where this isn't possible (i.e., requested items are not available), the Inventory maintains a waitingList of ReservationRequests that it will try to resolve into Reservations as inventory becomes available to meet the requests. It is quite common to have a waitingList for certain types of products, for example, a limited edition car or prepublication sales of an eagerly awaited book.

By comparing the ReservationRequest dateReceived with the dateReservationRequestActioned in the Reservation, you can track how well your business resolves ReservationRequests into actual Reservations.

8.10 Example—an inventory of books

In this section we take you through a very simple example of a book inventory to show how the Inventory archetype pattern can be used.

To maintain an inventory of books for sale, the first problem we have to solve is how to model a book. There are a couple of ways we could do this using the Product archetype pattern.

1. Use the IdenticalProduct pleomorph of the Product archetype pattern. Books are generally identical, so this is certainly a plausible approach. However, as we discuss in Section 7.27.2, it is also quite limiting.

2. Use the more general Product archetype pattern and some sort of MeasuredProduct (Section 7.24). This would certainly work, but it is probably overkill for such a simple problem.

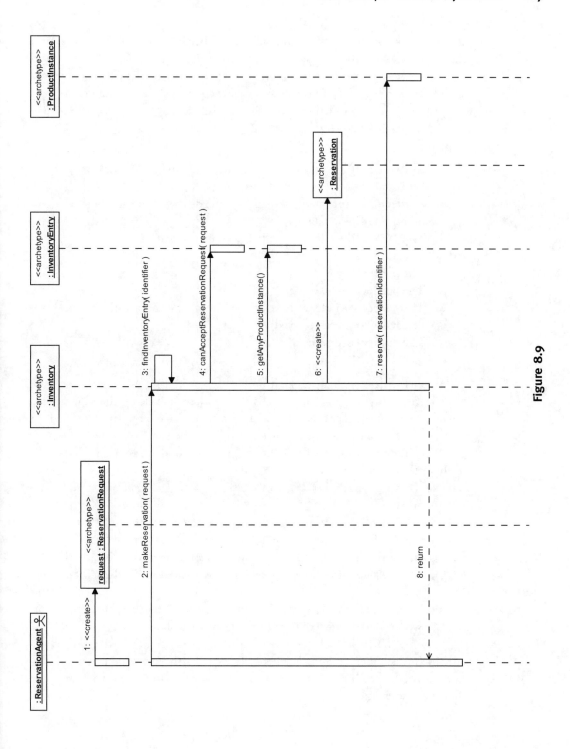

Figure 8.9

We'll take a compromise approach and subclass `ProductType` to give us a class that has semantics similar to `MeasuredProduct` but without the overhead of `Quantities` and `Metrics`, which do not really apply in this case. Our model is illustrated in Figure 8.10; the classes we have added are shown in gray.

We define a class called `Edition` that is a subclass of `ProductType`. An `Edition` specifies the following:

- The title of this edition (the `name` attribute inherited from `ProductType`)
- A brief `description` of this edition (the `description` attribute inherited from `ProductType`)
- The `ISBN` of the edition (a subclass of `ProductIdentifier`)
- The `authors`
- The `publisher`
- The `publicationDate`
- The `numberAvailable` (i.e., the total number of books still in stock that have not been reserved)
- The `numberReserved`

Because this is such a small, simple, and invariant set of features, we have modeled them as attributes of the `Edition`, rather than using the much more flexible `ProductFeatureType`/`ProductFeatureInstance` pattern described in Section 7.10. Again, this simplifies the model at the expense of flexibility.

We also define a class called `Book` that is an instance of an `Edition`. `Book` is really just a `flyweight` [Gamma 1995] that holds a reference to a `Reservation` (a `ReservationIdentifier`) and to its `Edition`—that is, it relates a `Reservation` to an `Edition`.

The class `BookInventoryEntry` is a type of `InventoryEntry` specialized for holding `Books`. It overrides `getAnyProductInstance()` so that instead of obtaining an existing `ProductInstance` it just asks for one from the `Edition`. In this model, a `ProductInstance` (i.e., a `Book`) is created only when a `Reservation` is made.

Because we are effectively dealing with identical products, the reservation process works slightly differently from the process shown in Figure 8.9—see Figure 8.11. When a `Book` is reserved, the `numberAvailable` attribute of the `Edition` is decremented and the `numberReserved` attribute is incremented. Notice that we had to make only relatively small changes to the model to support these new reservation semantics!

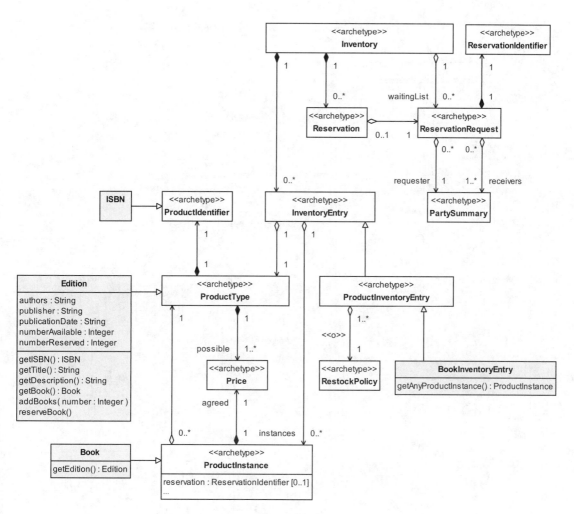

Figure 8.10

We have stripped the Inventory model right down to only the parts required. This is exactly how you should use archetype patterns—only use the bits you need. In particular we have lost the link to outstandingPurchase-Orders (see Section 8.5) because we assume that in this simple example we are not bothering to track books on order. However, it would be very easy to put this feature back in if you decided that you needed it—the archetype pattern shows you exactly where to add it.

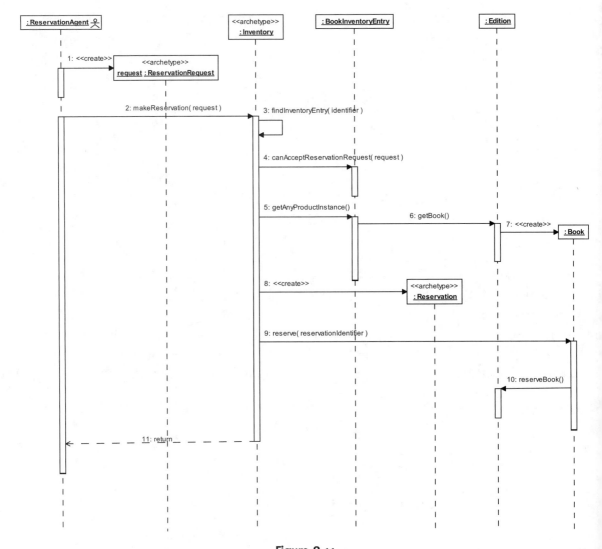

Figure 8.11

Despite the fact that we have stripped the model down, it still has some advanced features.

- Rules-based pricing (as discussed in Section 7.22.2)
- Rules-based reordering (using a `restockPolicy`, as discussed in Section 8.5)

- The ability to handle `Reservations` for `Books`
- The ability to handle `waitingLists` for `Books`

See Chapter 12 on `Rules` for more information about how business rules may be encoded in practice.

8.11 Book inventory revisited

In this section we look at a more complex instantiation of the `Inventory` pattern. If you are not interested in model transformations, you can skip this.

In the example in Section 8.10, we performed the simplest possible transformation on the `Inventory` archetype pattern—we just removed those bits we decided we didn't need and treated the archetypes as classes. As we discuss in Section 1.16, this is an isomorphism or translation of the archetype pattern.

Transformations that are more complex than this are also possible, *provided* the transformation preserves consistency and the business semantics of the pattern.

We transform the archetype pattern in a different way below to create a much simplified `BookInventory` model.

First, let's take the basic `Inventory` archetype pattern and turn it into a parameterized collaboration as described in Section 1.16. This is shown in Figure 8.12 (we have hidden the attributes and operations for clarity).

We can then instantiate this pattern by supplying classes for the parameters, as shown in Figure 8.13. This instantiation gives rise to the model shown in Figure 8.14 on page 294.

You can see that this is a much simpler model because we have been able to collapse the inheritance hierarchies of `InventoryEntry`, `ProductType`, `ProductInstance`, and `ProductIdentifier`. However, this simplicity comes at a cost— the instantiated pattern can now store only an inventory of books.

Although the model is simpler, each of the classes in it maps onto one or more archetypes in the `Inventory` archetype pattern—that is, it is homomorphic with that pattern. Having this traceability back to the original pattern is very desirable. In particular it allows you to:

- Understand the semantics of the instantiation based on the detailed descriptions in the archetype pattern
- See exactly what design compromises the instantiation makes and how those compromises limit it
- See exactly where you can add more features from the original pattern if you need them

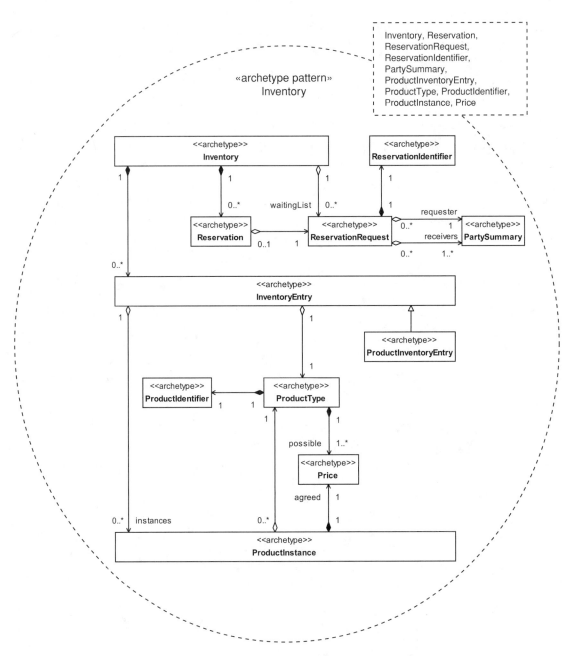

Figure 8.12

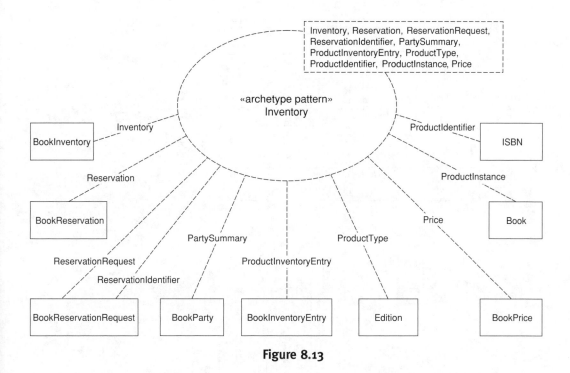

Figure 8.13

In terms of Model Driven Architecture (MDA—see Chapter 2), this sort of homomorphic transformation is a PIM-to-PIM transformation. It is one of the most powerful MDA transformations.

8.12   Example—an inventory of train journeys

In this example, we look at how the Inventory archetype pattern can be applied to an inventory of railway services.

Imagine that you are going on a train journey from Zürich to the alpine resort of Kandersteg. The situation is shown diagrammatically in Figure 8.15.

To create an Inventory for this service, you must first work out exactly what it is that you are selling. This is not always straightforward!

Let's start by looking at this from the operational perspective. The railway company wants to operate a service from Zürich to Kandersteg, with a stop at Bern.

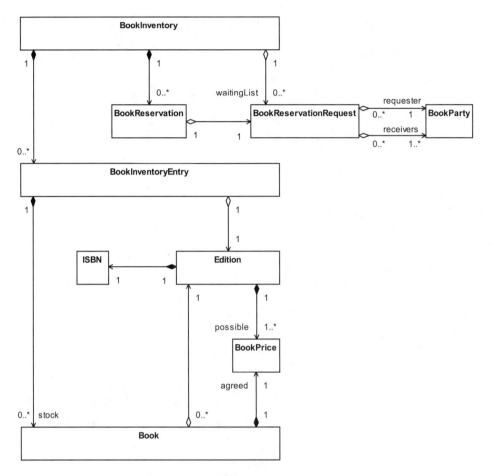

Figure 8.14

This route is made up of two legs, Zürich to Bern and Bern to Kandersteg. When the railway company schedules a train to traverse these legs at a particular point in time, it creates capacity that can be sold. The train has two carriages; one carriage provides 20 first-class seats, and the other provides 40 second-class seats. The total capacity is 60 seats, distributed as described across the two classes of travel.

In fact, each carriage may be physically divided by bulkheads into compartments. So a carriage may, in principle, have more than one compartment with a different class of travel in each. But in this simple example, we have restricted

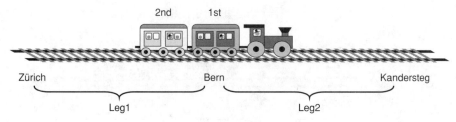

Figure 8.15

ourselves to one compartment per carriage, which is normal practice for smaller trains. However, you should note that the class of travel is associated with a *compartment* rather than with a *carriage*.

From the marketing perspective, the railway company would like to sell trips from Zürich to Bern, from Bern to Kandersteg, and from Zürich to Kandersteg for the three-month peak period of December 2003 through February 2004 in two classes, first and second.

You can see that there are three elements to this service:

1. The possible segments that passengers may travel—from Zürich to Bern, from Bern to Kandersteg, and from Zürich to Kandersteg
2. The date range for the service—December 2003 through February 2004
3. The class of travel—first class and second class

Note that segments are different from legs—a leg is an *operational* concept that describes travel between two consecutive stops that the train makes, whereas a segment is a *marketing* concept that describes the possible journeys that the railway company wishes to sell along a route. The relationship between segments and legs is shown in Figure 8.16.

In our example, there are only two legs, but there are three segments and two possible classes of travel. This makes a total of six possible types of service, as shown in Table 8.7.

The railway company may choose to offer all or just some of these types of service. For example, in order to maximize revenue, they might only offer the first-class compartment to travelers going all the way from Zürich to Kandersteg. However, in this example, we will assume that these services are *all* offered for *all* possible journeys.

You can model each of these six types of service as an instance of a CompartmentSegmentType class. A CompartmentSegmentType represents a specific

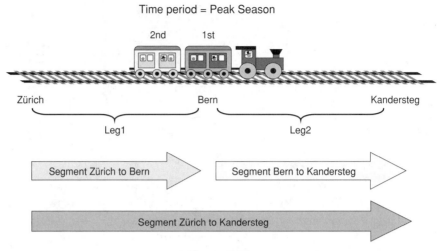

Figure 8.16

Table 8.7

	First class	Second class
Zürich/Bern	X	X
Bern/Kandersteg	X	X
Zürich/Kandersteg	X	X

journey across one or more legs in a specific compartment (i.e., class of travel) within some predefined time window such as "Peak Season."

Each individual leg of this journey is modeled as a CompartmentLegType, which represents travel over a particular LegType in a specific compartment.

The relationship between these classes is shown in Figure 8.17, with the added classes shown in gray. (Modelers, please note that the relationship between CompartmentSegmentType and CompartmentLegType is a *derived relationship*—it is actually an inherited relationship from the superclasses. For more information about derived relationships, see [Arlow 2001].)

Notice how we build up the information in the model in layers. The most basic element is the LegType—this just specifies an originStation and a des-

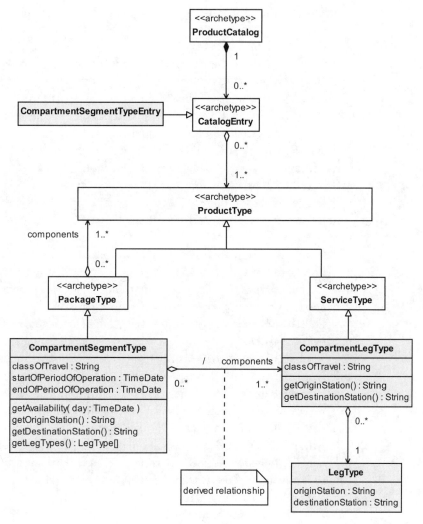

Figure 8.17

tinationStation (e.g., Bern to Kandersteg). The next level is the Compart-mentLegType. This adds the class of travel to the LegType. In this particular example, there are two classes of travel, so there are two CompartmentLegTypes for each LegType. Finally, we arrive at last at what we sell, the Compartment-SegmentType. This is a sequence of one or more CompartmentLegTypes in a particular period of operation (e.g., the spring or summer season). This is the

ProductType that must appear in the ProductCatalog. The CompartmentLeg-
Types are just components and are never sold on their own, so they should be
omitted from the ProductCatalog.

We have modeled CompartmentSegmentType as a kind of PackageType and
a CompartmentLegType as a ServiceType—that is, a kind of ProductType. This
gives us all the benefits of the Product archetype pattern that we discuss in
Chapter 7. In particular, we get rules-based package specification, which is very
useful for complex packages such as journeys.

In order to make this a complete model of what we have for sale, we added
ProductCatalog and CatalogEntry (see Sections 7.11 and 7.12, respectively)
and introduced a new type of CatalogEntry, CompartmentSegmentTypeEntry,
which is specialized to represent CompartmentSegmentTypes only. In fact, in this
simple example, each CompartmentSegmentTypeEntry represents exactly one
CompartmentSegmentType object.

Having discussed what we sell, we now have to consider what we deliver.

The Product archetype pattern tells us exactly how to model this—for
every ProductType, there is a corresponding ProductInstance, and for every
Package type, there is a corresponding PackageInstance.

Thus, CompartmentLegType needs a CompartmentLegInstance, and CompartmentSegmentType needs a CompartmentSegmentInstance.

Similarly, we might expect LegType to need a LegInstance, which adds a
time of departure and arrival to its origin and destination information. The
model of the delivery side of the system is shown in Figure 8.18.

We store two different things in Inventory. The CompartmentLegInstances are the "raw materials" that constitute the smallest units of service we
can deliver. However, because we sell only CompartmentSegmentTypes (not CompartmentLegTypes), the unit of service we actually deliver to a specific customer is always a CompartmentSegmentInstance, which is a collection of
CompartmentLegInstances. In other words, we only deliver CompartmentLeg-
Instances in packages of one or more.

This Inventory should work in a very particular way: as CompartmentSegmentTypes are sold, CompartmentSegmentInstances are created in the Inventory.
These consume the stock of CompartmentLegInstances. The Compartment-
SegmentInstances record what we have sold (or at least reserved), and the remaining CompartmentLegInstances record our unused capacity to deliver more
services.

The two classes CompartmentSegmentInstanceEntry and CompartmentLeg-
InstanceEntry have no interesting semantics—they are just an artifact of the
constraint we earlier applied to InventoryEntries that each InventoryEntry
should be for *exactly one* ProductType.

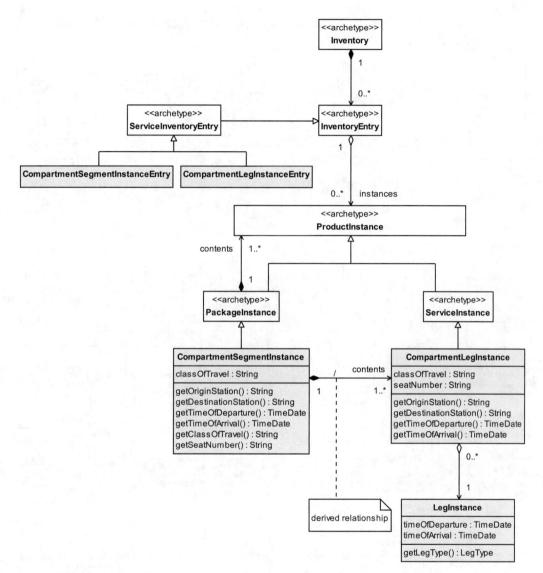

Figure 8.18

Putting the two halves of the model (what we sell and what we deliver) together, we arrive at the final model shown in Figure 8.19.

Clearly, you would have to do more work to make this into a usable system, but it does illustrate a realistic application of the Inventory pattern for complex services.

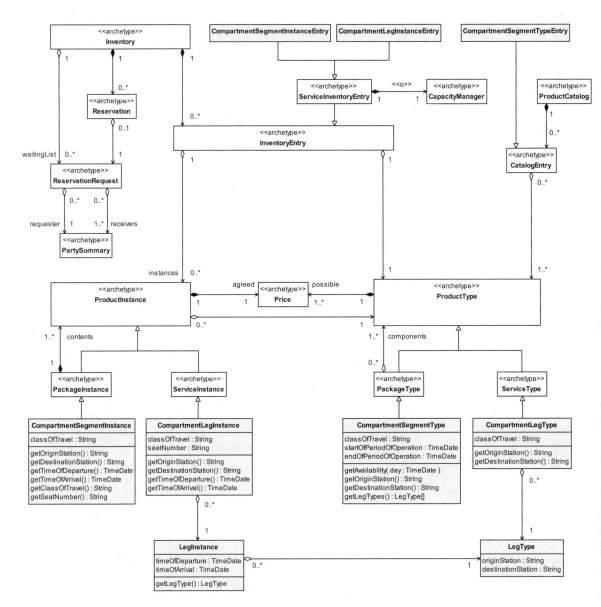

Figure 8.19

8.13 Summary

In this chapter we looked at the Inventory archetype pattern. This is a pattern for representing an inventory—a stock or store of goods. We covered the topics listed below.

- Inventory and the Product archetype pattern: how the Inventory archetype pattern interacts with the Product archetype pattern

- Inventory: how to represent a stock or store of goods or services as a collection of InventoryEntries

- InventoryEntry: how to represent the number of instances of a type of good or service that are available for sale or use

- ProductInventoryEntry: how to represent inventory information for a set of ProductInstances all of the same ProductType
  - RestockPolicy: how to represent the policy for restocking the items specified in a ProductInventoryEntry

- ServiceInventoryEntry: how to represent inventory information for a set of ServiceInstances all of the same ServiceType
  - Capacity planning and management:
    - Capacity: how to represent a service provider's ability to provide a specific service
    - CapacityManager: how to represent the management of capacity through controlling the release of ServiceInstances

- Availability: how to decide whether a ProductInstance is available for sale

- Reservation: how to represent the arrangement by which a ProductInstance is reserved for a specific Party
  - ReservationRequest: how to represent a request for a reservation
    - ReservationIdentifier: how to uniquely identify a ReservationRequest
  - ReservationStatus: how to identify whether a ProductInstance is available to be reserved or has already been reserved

- Example of an inventory of goods

- Example of an inventory of services

Chapter 9

Order
archetype pattern

9.1 Business context

When a customer decides to make a purchase, you need to have some way to record exactly what is required. This record is known as an *order*. It is a request by a buyer for a seller to deliver some goods or services. In return the seller normally receives some payment or other compensation.

Orders are archetypal. Orders, in one shape or another, have existed for a very long time, from verbal requests and agreements, through more permanent forms once writing was invented, to the modern electronic orders we discuss in this chapter.

You can use an order whenever you need to capture the details of the relationship between the various parties, goods, and services that come together in a particular sales transaction.

When a buyer creates an order and submits it to a seller to request some goods or services, this is known as a *purchase order*.

When a seller creates an order to record goods or services to be supplied to a buyer, this is known as a *sales order*.

As you'll see, these are really just two different perspectives on the same thing, and the informational content of purchase and sales orders is virtually identical.

The act of creating an order is often referred to as *raising* an order. This is the term we use throughout the rest of this chapter.

As well as recording key relationships, orders are used to track the stages in the sales process. This gives orders a complex lifecycle. However, you can make things conceptually very simple if you consider this lifecycle to be event driven. Things happen to the order (events) that drive it through its lifecycle. We will explore this in detail in Sections 9.11 through 9.20.

Both buyers and sellers may need to keep copies of orders for accounting purposes, so orders usually have a long life.

9.2 Order **archetype pattern and roadmap**

The Order archetype pattern is shown in Figure 9.1 and the contents of the OrderEvent package in Figure 9.2.

9.3 **The** Order **archetype**

> The Order archetype represents a record of a request by a buyer for a seller to supply some goods or services.

An Order links goods and services (represented by OrderLines) and Parties (represented by PartySummaries) in a record of a sales transaction. We discuss OrderLines in Section 9.5 and PartySummaries in Section 5.11.

Every Order is uniquely identified by an OrderIdentifier (see Figure 9.3).

> The OrderIdentifier archetype represents a unique identifier for an Order.

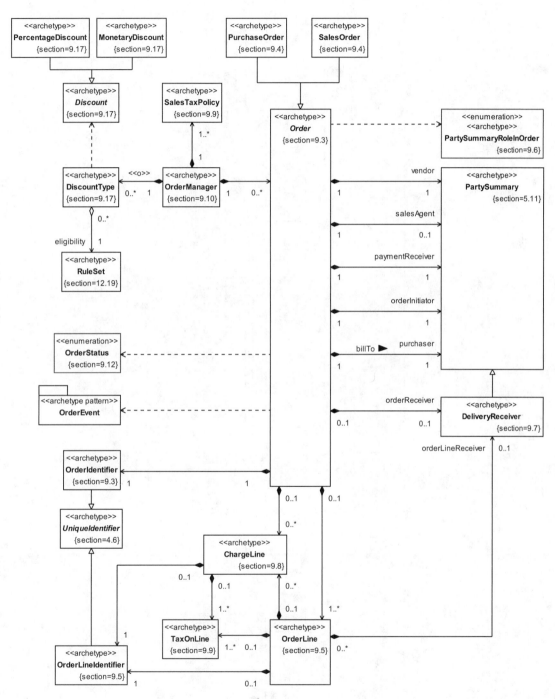

Figure 9.1

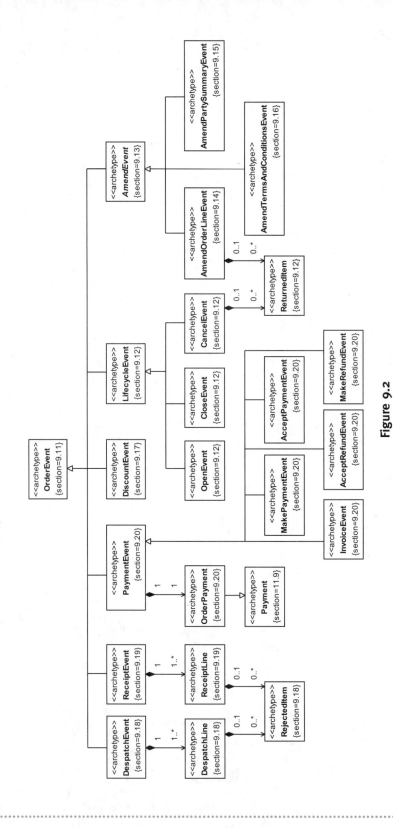

Figure 9.2

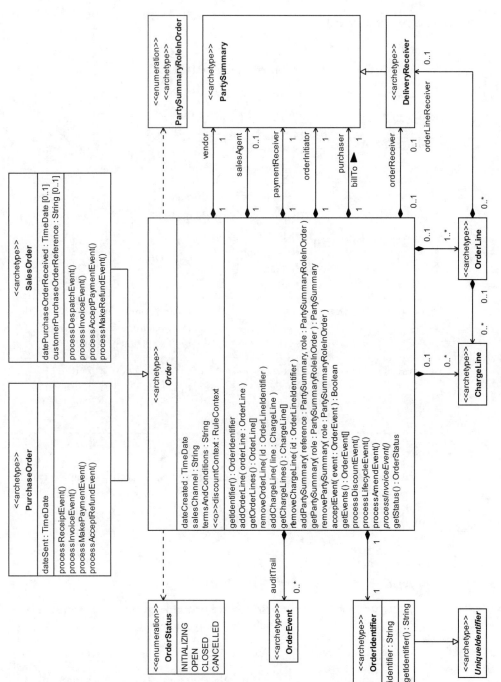

Figure 9.3

Every Order has the attributes shown in Table 9.1.

Table 9.1

Order **attributes**	
dateCreated	The TimeDate when the Order was created
salesChannel	The sales channel through which the Order was raised Examples of sales channels are • Internet • Telephone • Mail • Shop
termsAndConditions	A summary of the terms and conditions associated with this Order—a typical example might be "delivery within 28 days" or details of payment terms
«o»discountContext	If a rules-based Discount (see Section 9.17) is to be applied to the Order, this contains all the information necessary to calculate whether the Order is eligible for the Discount or not

Order has quite a few responsibilities. These responsibilities may be categorized into *manager responsibilities* and *event responsibilities*, as shown in Table 9.2.

Table 9.2

The manager responsibilities of Order		
Responsibility	**Operation**	**Semantics**
Manage identification	getIdentifier()	Returns the OrderIdentifier—this is the unique identifier for the Order
Manage OrderLines	addOrderLine(...)	Adds an OrderLine to the Order (see Section 9.5)
	getOrderLines()	Returns the collection of OrderLines that constitute the Order
	removeOrderLine(...)	Removes the specified OrderLine from the Order

Table 9.2   (Continued)

The manager responsibilities of Order		
Responsibility	**Operation**	**Semantics**
Manage ChargeLines	addChargeLine(...)	Adds a ChargeLine to the Order (see Section 9.8)
	getChargeLines()	Returns the collection of ChargeLines for the Order
	removeChargeLine(...)	Removes the specified ChargeLine from the Order
Manage Parties	addPartySummary(...)	Adds a PartySummary playing the specified PartySummaryRoleInOrder (see Section 9.6)
	getPartySummary(...)	Gets the PartySummary playing the specified PartySummaryRoleInOrder
	removePartySummary(...)	Removes the PartySummary playing the specified PartySummaryRoleInOrder

The event responsibilities of Order		
Handle OrderEvents	acceptEvent(...)	Accepts an OrderEvent (see Section 9.11)
	getEvents()	Returns all the OrderEvents that have been applied to this Order
	processDiscountEvent()	Adds or removes a Discount from the Order
	processLifecycleEvent()	Processes events that drive the Order through its lifecycle (see Section 9.12)
	processAmendEvent()	Makes an amendment to the Order
	processInvoiceEvent()	Is overridden by the Order subclasses, Purchase-Order and SalesOrder (see Section 9.4)
Get OrderStatus	getStatus()	Returns the OrderStatus (see Section 9.12)

The manager responsibilities are simple responsibilities concerned with Order construction through adding and maintaining the collections of Order-Lines and PartySummaries associated with the Order and with establishing the Order's unique identity and current state. Other, more complex responsibilities are associated with Order's two subclasses, PurchaseOrder and SalesOrder (see Section 9.4).

The event responsibilities are about managing the complex lifecycle of the Order. We discuss these in depth in Sections 9.11 through 9.20.

9.4   PurchaseOrder **and** SalesOrder

There are two types of Orders.

> The PurchaseOrder archetype represents a type of Order raised by a buyer and sub-mitted to a seller as a request for goods or services in return for an agreed payment.
>
> The SalesOrder archetype represents a type of Order used by a seller to track delivery of goods or services to a buyer in return for an agreed payment.

As you saw in Figure 9.3 on page 307, PurchaseOrder and SalesOrder are very similar—you can correctly consider PurchaseOrder and SalesOrder to be buyer- and seller-specific views, respectively, of a single thing called Order. While a PurchaseOrder records the date it was sent to the seller, details of an initiating PurchaseOrder can be recorded on a SalesOrder as datePurchaseOrderReceived and customerPurchaseOrderReference.

You also saw in Section 9.3 that Order has manager and event responsibilities. The two subclasses PurchaseOrder and SalesOrder have tracking responsibilities (see Table 9.3). These are more complex responsibilities about keeping track of ProductInstances received or despatched and of Payments made on the Order. We explore the detailed semantics of these responsibilities in depth in Sections 9.25 and 9.28.

In Table 9.3, we have organized the PurchaseOrder and SalesOrder operations by subclass in order to compare and contrast them. You can see that the tracking responsibilities of PurchaseOrder involve receiving ProductInstances, while those of SalesOrder involve despatching ProductInstances.

Similarly, PurchaseOrder is responsible for tracking Payments made and re-funds received, while SalesOrder is responsible for tracking Payments received and refunds made.

9.5   OrderLine

> The OrderLine archetype represents part of an Order that is a summary of particu-lar goods or services ordered by a buyer.

Table 9.3

Archetype	Responsibility	Operation	Semantics
PurchaseOrder	Track ProductInstances	processReceiptEvent()	Records that a number of ProductInstances have been received and accepted or rejected
	Track Payments	processInvoiceEvent()	Records that an invoice has been received for this PurchaseOrder
		processMakePaymentEvent()	Records that a Payment has been made against this PurchaseOrder
		processAcceptRefundEvent()	Records that a refund has been received against this PurchaseOrder
SalesOrder	Track ProductInstances	processDespatchEvent()	Records that the specified number of Product-Instances have been despatched
	Track Payments	processInvoiceEvent()	Records that an invoice has been raised for this SalesOrder
		processAcceptPaymentEvent()	Records that a Payment has been received for this SalesOrder
		processMakeRefundEvent()	Records that a refund has been made against this SalesOrder

Each type of item ordered by the buyer is represented on the Order by an Order-Line. If you think about an order printed out on paper, then an OrderLine is equivalent to a single line on such an order. Each OrderLine is uniquely identified within the Order by an OrderLineIdentifier (this may be as simple as assigning a sequence number).

The OrderLineIdentifier archetype represents a unique identifier for an OrderLine or a ChargeLine.

OrderLine is shown in Figure 9.4 and its attributes described in Table 9.4. OrderLine has to deal with two distinctly different types of ProductInstances:

1. ProductInstances of the same type that can be considered to be identical
2. ProductInstances of the same type that are each separately identifiable and have a SerialNumber that needs to be tracked through the sales process

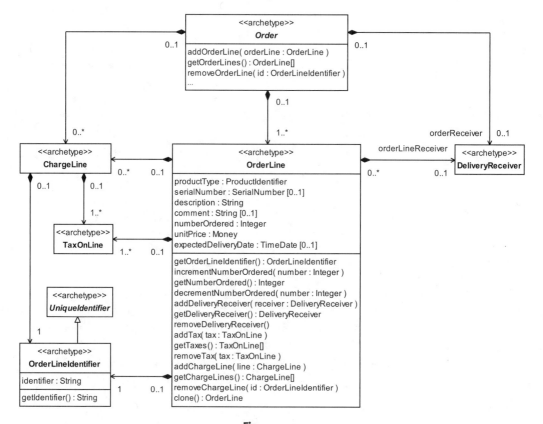

Figure 9.4

Table 9.4

OrderLine **archetype attributes**	
Attribute	**Semantics**
productType	The type of product (ProductType) to which this OrderLine refers
serialNumber [0..1]	The SerialNumber of the ProductInstance. This is only needed if the OrderLine refers to a ProductInstance that is separately identifiable and must be tracked individually
description	A short description of the product or service, including its name
comment [0..1]	Any comments about the OrderLine
numberOrdered	The number of ProductInstances ordered, of the type specified by the productType attribute. If the OrderLine represents a ProductInstance that is separately identifiable and must be tracked individually, this number is 1
unitPrice	The price per unit
expectedDeliveryDate [0..1]	The TimeDate by which the items on the OrderLine are expected to be delivered

We can represent a collection of identical ProductInstances of the same type as a single OrderLine with a numberOrdered >= 1 and no serialNumber. However, for a collection of individually tracked ProductInstances of the same type, we must have an OrderLine *for each instance*, with a numberOrdered of exactly 1 and the serialNumber of each ProductInstance recorded. (In practice, the serialNumber may not be known at the time the OrderLine is created but would be captured by the time the item is despatched.) For example, we may order five ProductInstances all of the same type, but if each needs to be separately tracked, we would have an OrderLine for each instance.

You can see in Table 9.5 how the attributes of OrderLine may be used to support both these cases.

Table 9.5

OrderLine **attribute values**		
Attribute	**Identical** `ProductInstances`	**Separately tracked** `ProductInstances`
`productType`	The `ProductType` of the `ProductInstances`	The `ProductType` of the `ProductInstance`
`serialNumber`	`null`	The `SerialNumber` of the `ProductInstance`
`numberOrdered`	`numberOrdered >= 1`	`numberOrdered = 1`

`OrderLine` has a number of manager responsibilities, as listed in Table 9.6.

Table 9.6

OrderLine **responsibilities**		
Responsibility	**Operation**	**Semantics**
Manage identification	`getOrderLineIdentifier()`	Returns the `OrderLineIdentifier`—this is the unique identifier for the `OrderLine`
Manage number ordered	`incrementNumberOrdered(...)`	Increments the number of `ProductInstances` recorded by the `OrderLine`
	`getNumberOrdered()`	Returns the number of `ProductInstances` recorded by the `OrderLine`
	`decrementNumberOrdered(...)`	Decrements the number of `ProductInstances` recorded by the `OrderLine`
Manage Parties	`addDeliveryReceiver(...)`	Adds a `DeliveryReceiver` to the `OrderLine` (see Section 9.7)
	`getDeliveryReceiver()`	Returns the `DeliveryReceiver` for this `OrderLine`
	`removeDeliveryReceiver()`	Removes the `Delivery-Receiver` from the `OrderLine`

Table 9.6 (Continued)

OrderLine responsibilities

Responsibility	Operation	Semantics
Manage tax	addTax(...)	Adds tax (represented by a TaxOnLine) to the OrderLine (see Section 9.9)
	getTaxes()	Returns all the TaxOnLines for this OrderLine
	removeTax(...)	Removes a TaxOnLine from the OrderLine
Manage ChargeLines	addChargeLine(...)	Adds a ChargeLine to the OrderLine (see Section 9.8)
	getChargeLines()	Returns all the ChargeLines associated with this OrderLine
	removeChargeLine(...)	Removes a ChargeLine from the OrderLine
Clone itself for amendment purposes	clone()	Makes a copy of the OrderLine and any associated objects that can be used to create an amended OrderLine (see Section 9.14)

9.6 PartySummaryRoleInOrder

Orders generally refer to at least two different Parties. One Party plays a "buying" role in the relationship, and the other Party plays a "selling" role. (We discuss the Party archetype in detail in Chapter 4 and PartyRoles in Chapter 5.)

The Order needs to record several things about a Party:

- The unique identifier for the Party (can be achieved by using the PartyIdentifier or the PartyRoleIdentifier)
- The unique reference (the PartyRoleIdentifier) to a specific role that the Party might be playing with respect to your business (optional; you need this only if you are using PartyRoles as described in Chapter 5)
- Summary information about the Party that *must* be recorded on the Order

The summary information is a snapshot of the `Party` information at the time the `Order` was raised. It contains a couple of mandatory attributes, `name` and `address`, and may contain `telephoneNumber` and `emailAddress`.

You need to record this summary information directly on the `Order` because `Party` information can change over time, but the `Order`, once raised, acts as a permanent record of the selling process and can be changed only by applying an `AmendEvent` (see Section 9.13).

You can represent this summary `Party` information by using the `PartySummary` archetype shown in Figure 9.5 (see also Section 5.11).

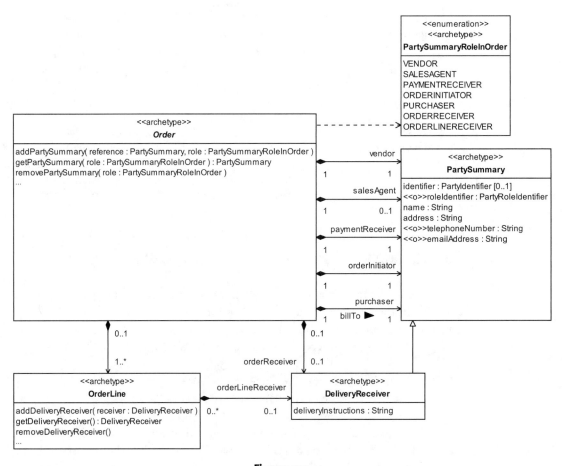

Figure 9.5

There are many roles that PartySummary may play with respect to the Order. These roles fall into two broad categories (see Table 9.7).

1. Buying roles—roles on the buying side of the sales transaction
2. Selling roles—roles on the selling side of the sales transaction

The PartySummaryRoleInOrder archetype represents a role within the Order process that can be played by a PartySummary.

Table 9.7

Type of role	PartySummary role in the Order	Semantics
Buying role	orderInitiator	Details of the Party that raises the Order
	purchaser	Details of the Party that pays for the Order
	orderReceiver orderLineReceiver	Details of the Party that receives one or more items from the Order
Selling role	vendor	Details of the Party that supplies the goods or services
	salesAgent	Details of a third Party that accepted the Order on behalf of the vendor
	paymentReceiver	Details of the Party that raises invoices and receives payment against the Order

A single PartySummary may play many of these roles. Minimally, there will usually be at least one PartySummary playing the buying roles and a *different* PartySummary playing the selling roles. Otherwise, a single PartySummary would be purchasing something from itself! It's hard to imagine a circumstance where this would make sense.

You can see that the buying roles consist of orderInitiator, purchaser, and orderReceiver or orderLineReceiver roles. It is quite common in business for one PartySummary to initiate the Order, a different PartySummary to pay for the Order, and a different PartySummary again to receive the goods or services.

Similarly, on the selling side, it is possible for different PartySummaries to create a SalesOrder and receive payments against that Order.

9.7 DeliveryReceiver

For any Order, the goods and services specified by the OrderLines may be sent to:

- The same receiver
- Different receivers

We represent receivers of the items specified in the Order by the Delivery-Receiver archetype.

> The DeliveryReceiver archetype represents a special type of PartySummary that also includes deliveryInstructions.

In Figure 9.5, each Order has zero or one orderReceiver. This is the De-liveryReceiver to whom the ProductInstances specified by the Order will be despatched.

Each OrderLine may also have zero or one orderLineReceiver. This is the DeliveryReceiver to whom the ProductInstances specified by the OrderLine will be despatched.

There are three constraints that make this model work.

1. If an Order specifies an orderReceiver, this is the default receiver for all of the items specified on the Order.
2. If an OrderLine specifies an orderLineReceiver, this overrides any orderReceiver that may be specified by the Order.
3. Each OrderLine must have a DeliveryReceiver of some sort. So, if an orderReceiver is not specified at the Order level, an orderLineRe-ceiver *must* be specified for each individual OrderLine.

This approach also ensures that deliveryInstructions appropriate to each DeliveryReceiver are applied (e.g., "Deliver between 10 a.m. and 4 p.m.").

9.8 ChargeLine

You may associate zero or more ChargeLines with each OrderLine and/or with each Order, as shown in Figure 9.6.

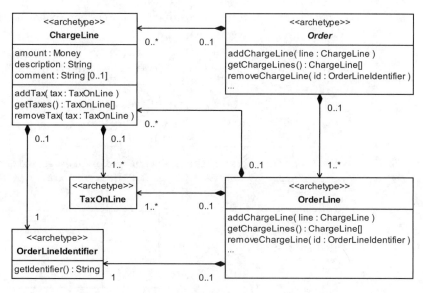

Figure 9.6

> The ChargeLine archetype represents an additional charge for an OrderLine over and above the OrderLine value *or* an extra charge added to an Order.

Each ChargeLine is identified by an OrderLineIdentifier and specifies an amount of Money, a description, and an optional comment. The description indicates what the additional charge is for (e.g., packaging, handling, shipping).

There may be other types of charges depending on the goods or services you are selling. For example, ChargeLine could specify the commission for exchanging an amount of Money in one Currency into another Currency.

In some cases, additional charges are applied to each OrderLine individually and summed at the end. In other cases, they are calculated for the whole Order and are not associated with any specific OrderLine.

ChargeLines may be liable to tax, as represented by TaxOnLine.

9.9   TaxOnLine

You should assume that each OrderLine and ChargeLine will have tax applied to it at least once. This needs to be recorded even if a zero rate of tax applies or the item is exempt from tax, so that you know that tax has been taken into account for everything you buy or sell.

ProductInstances on an OrderLine may be taxed several times. For example, in the United States, both federal sales taxes and state sales taxes may be applied to a given OrderLine.

Tax on an OrderLine or ChargeLine is represented in our model as one or more TaxOnLine objects, as shown in Figure 9.7.

The TaxOnLine archetype represents tax charged on an OrderLine or a ChargeLine.

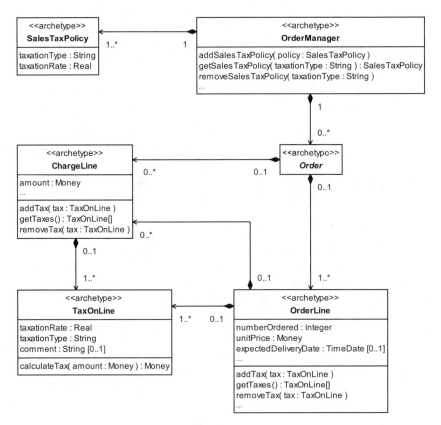

Figure 9.7

TaxOnLine records what taxationType has been applied to the OrderLine and what the taxationRate is. The taxationRate is expressed as a percentage of the price paid for the OrderLine.

Notice that the OrderManager (Section 9.10) is responsible for managing the prevailing SalesTaxPolicy, while TaxOnLine provides a *snapshot* of the tax that has been applied to a particular OrderLine or ChargeLine and so does not change if tax authorities alter the prevailing rates.

> The SalesTaxPolicy archetype records the prevailing taxation rate for a particular category of sales tax.

Table 9.8 shows an example of the values of the SalesTaxPolicy attributes for Value Added Tax (VAT) payable on goods and services in the United Kingdom (www.hmce.gov.uk). With VAT the zeroRate type means that the item has a zero VAT rate even though it *is* part of your taxable turnover. The exempt rate means that the item *is not* part of your taxable turnover at all.

Table 9.8

SalesTaxPolicy attribute values for VAT (October 2003)	
taxationType	taxationRate (%)
standardRate	17.5
reducedRate	5
zeroRate	0
exempt	0

9.10 OrderManager

> The OrderManager archetype manages a collection of Orders.

The OrderManager (Figure 9.8) provides a single point where Orders can be stored and accessed. It has operations for:

- Managing Orders in its collection
- Finding specific Orders

- Managing `DiscountTypes` and applying `Discounts` to `Orders` if a rules-based approach is taken to discounting (see Section 9.17)
- Managing the prevailing `SalesTaxPolicy`, for use when calculating `TaxOnLine` (see Section 9.9)

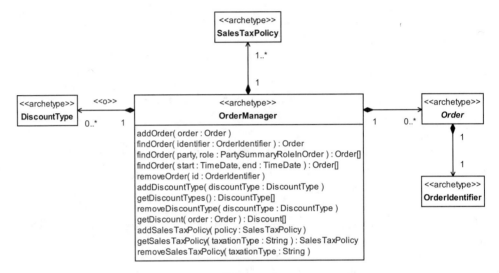

Figure 9.8

9.11 OrderEvents

Because `Orders` are used both to record the details of an order and to track the delivery of goods and services against it, each `Order` goes through a fairly complex lifecycle. This dynamic behavior is definitely the most difficult aspect of `Orders` and is an area where many software systems go wrong.

Our view is that the lifecycle of the `Order` is driven by certain notable occurrences or events. We model these events as different types of `OrderEvent`.

The `OrderEvent` archetype represents a notable occurrence in the lifecycle of an `Order`.

This event-driven view of the `Order` lifecycle gives you a very simple conceptual framework for capturing all of the different things that can happen to an `Order`. It also gives you a very simple approach to `Order` processing—the `Order` accepts and processes different types of OrderEvent generated by the business. This is illustrated in Figure 9.9.

Figure 9.9

The Order stores every OrderEvent sent to it. This creates an auditTrail for the Order processing activity.

Lots of things can happen to an Order during its lifecycle, and consequently there are lots of different types of OrderEvent. These are shown in Figure 9.10.

The attributes of OrderEvent are shown in Table 9.9.

Table 9.9

OrderEvent **archetype**	
Attribute	**Semantics**
orderIdentifier	The OrderIdentifier for the Order to which the Order-Event applies
authorization [0..*]	Zero or more PartySignatures authorizing the Order-Event (business rules dictate what authorizations are required for a particular type of event)
dateAuthorized	The TimeDate when all required authorizations have been obtained
processed	An indicator to show that the OrderEvent has been fully processed

You can categorize OrderEvents as shown in Table 9.10. Note that some events apply to PurchaseOrders only, some to SalesOrders only, and some to both.

We will look at each of these categories of events in the next few sections.

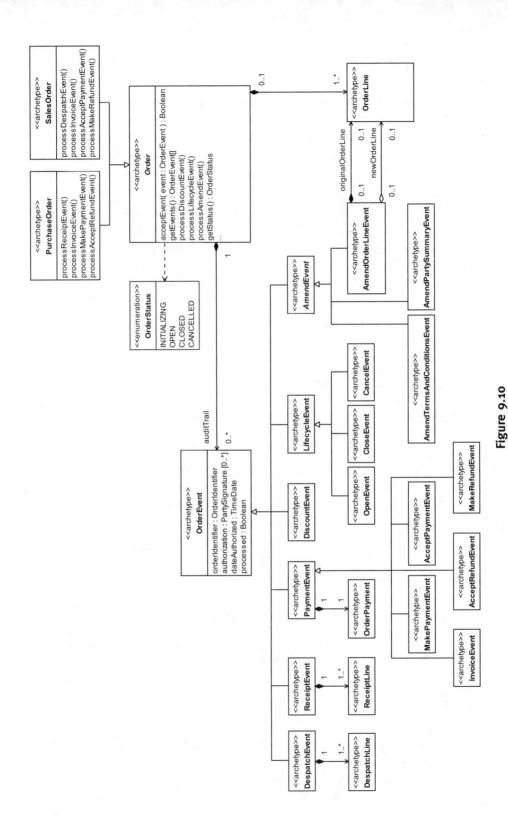

Figure 9.10

Table 9.10

Categories of OrderEvent

Category	Category semantics	Section	Events	Type of Order	Multiplicity
Lifecycle events	These are the basic events in the Order lifecycle, common to both Purchase-Orders and SalesOrders	9.12	OpenEvent	Both	0..1
			CloseEvent	Both	0..1
			CancelEvent	Both	0..1
Discount event	This event occurs when a Discount is agreed on an Order	9.17	DiscountEvent	Both	0..*
Amendment events	These events occur when the Order needs to be amended	9.13–9.16	AmendOrderLineEvent	Both	0..*
			AmendPartySummaryEvent	Both	0..*
			AmendTermsAndConditionsEvent	Both	0..*
Payment events	These events occur when payments and refunds are accepted or made against an Order	9.20	InvoiceEvent	Both	0..*
			MakePaymentEvent	PurchaseOrder	0..*
			AcceptRefundEvent	PurchaseOrder	0..*
			AcceptPaymentEvent	SalesOrder	0..*
			MakeRefundEvent	SalesOrder	0..*
Despatch event	This event occurs when the despatch of goods and services is recorded against a SalesOrder	9.18	DespatchEvent	SalesOrder	0..*
Receipt event	This event occurs when the receipt of goods and services is recorded against the PurchaseOrder	9.19	ReceiptEvent	PurchaseOrder	0..*

9.12 OrderStatus **and** LifecycleEvents

The OrderStatus archetype represents a particular state of the Order that constrains what activities can be performed against the Order.

The LifecycleEvent archetype represents an event sent to an Order that changes its OrderStatus.

The four values of OrderStatus and the three LifecycleEvents are shown in Figure 9.11.

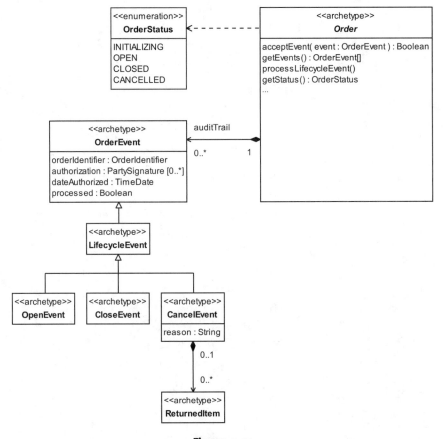

Figure 9.11

OrderStatus is determined by the Order, according to what LifecycleEvents the Order has received (see Table 9.11). For example, an Order that has no LifecycleEvents is in the INITIALIZING state, while one that has received an OpenEvent but not a CancelEvent or CloseEvent is in the OPEN state.

Table 9.11

Type of LifecycleEvent	Processed by		Archetype definition
OpenEvent	PurchaseOrder and SalesOrder		The OpenEvent archetype represents an event sent to an Order that changes its OrderStatus to OPEN.
CloseEvent	PurchaseOrder and SalesOrder		The CloseEvent archetype represents an event sent to an Order that changes its OrderStatus to CLOSED.
CancelEvent	PurchaseOrder and SalesOrder		The CancelEvent archetype represents an event sent to an Order that changes its OrderStatus to CANCELLED.

If you think very generally about Order processing, all Orders go through the same basic lifecycle shown in Figure 9.12.

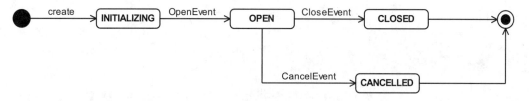

Figure 9.12

When the Order is first created, it is in the INITIALIZING state. In this state the Order is being assembled by adding and removing OrderLines, PartySummaries, ChargeLines, and TaxOnLines.

Once the Order has been assembled, it may be opened for processing. This occurs on receipt of an OpenEvent. You can think of the OPEN state as the state in which the Order is being processed. This may involve making amendments, despatching, receipting (i.e., formally recording the receipt of goods or services), and accepting payments. In fact, most of the OrderEvents occur while the Order is in the OPEN state.

The Order may be transitioned to CLOSED on receipt of a CloseEvent; processing of the Order then stops.

Alternatively, it may be transitioned to CANCELLED on receipt of a Cancel-Event along with a reason for the cancellation. Depending on the history of an Order at the point when it is cancelled, further action may be required to correct for items despatched or payments made (see Section 9.24 for PurchaseOrders, Section 9.27 for SalesOrders). Overpayment can be corrected by a refund (see Sections 9.25.5 and 9.28.6), while an item received by the buyer that must be returned is recorded as a ReturnedItem (see Sections 9.25.4 and 9.28.5).

> The ReturnedItem archetype represents an item that has been received by a DeliveryReceiver and must be returned to the vendor because a CancelEvent or AmendOrderLineEvent has rendered it surplus to requirements.

LifecycleEvents are generated by whatever purchase or sales process your business uses. This process may be described or constrained by business rules. For example, in some companies, the Order may be automatically transitioned to OPEN as soon as it has been initialized. In other companies, this transition may require an authorization process to occur. Either way, in our event-driven model, an OpenEvent will be generated.

9.13 AmendEvents

A fact of life in virtually every selling or purchasing scenario is that Orders will, on occasion, need to be amended.

The simplest way to handle this is to cancel the existing Order with a CancellationEvent, then raise a new Order with the required details. However, if you decide to allow direct amendment to Orders in your business systems, you can do this by sending the Order an AmendEvent.

The AmendEvent archetype represents an event sent to an OPEN Order that captures an amendment to the Order.

Note that AmendEvents are used to amend an Order only once it is OPEN. They are not used to amend an Order that is still INITIALIZING because the add and remove operations on Order and OrderLine are available to achieve this, and no audit trail is normally required at this early stage.

Business rules determine the circumstances under which amendments can be allowed—for example, a particular vendor may not allow amendments to OrderLines once despatching has begun but may still be willing to accept an amendment to the purchaser's details as long as no invoice has been issued.

You can see our model of AmendEvents in Figure 9.13.

There are only three ways in which an Order can be amended.

1. An OrderLine, PartySummary, or set of termsAndConditions is changed.
2. An OrderLine, PartySummary, or set of termsAndConditions is added.
3. An OrderLine, PartySummary, or set of termsAndConditions is removed.

To simplify the Order amendment process, we can apply the constraint that a change to an OrderLine, PartySummary, or set of termsAndConditions will *always* be implemented by replacing it with a new one. In other words, we don't allow an OrderLine, PartySummary, or set of termsAndConditions to be changed in place—it must be first removed from the Order and then replaced with a new one. Although other approaches are certainly possible (e.g., recording incremental changes to Order components in a change log), replacement has the right semantics while being conceptually very simple.

Applying this constraint, the model has to support only two actions:

1. Adding an OrderLine, PartySummary, or set of termsAndConditions
2. Deleting an OrderLine, PartySummary, or set of termsAndConditions

You can deal with these cases by introducing three subclasses of AmendEvent. The AmendOrderLineEvent deals with amendments to OrderLines, the Amend-PartySummaryEvent with amendments to PartySummaries, and the AmendTerms-AndConditionsEvent with amendments to termsAndConditions. We discuss these events in detail in the next three sections.

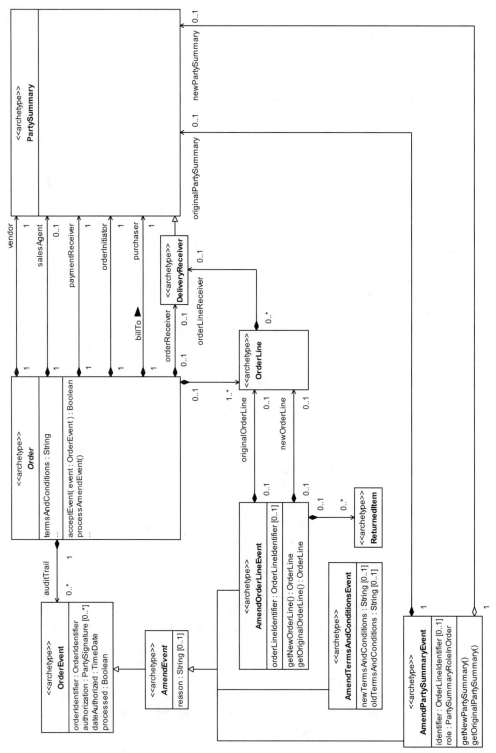

Figure 9.13

9.14 AmendOrderLineEvent

One type of amendment you can make to an `Order` is to its `OrderLines`. We model this as an `AmendOrderLineEvent` (see Figure 9.13).

> The `AmendOrderLineEvent` archetype represents an event that, when applied to an `OPEN` `Order`, results in a change to a specific `OrderLine`, the addition of a new `OrderLine`, or the deletion of an existing `OrderLine`.

Depending on the attribute values of the `AmendOrderLineEvent`, you can easily accommodate changes, additions, and deletions of `OrderLines`. This is illustrated in Table 9.12. We will look at each of these three cases in the following subsections.

Table 9.12

AmendOrderLineEvent **semantics**

	Attributes		
Action	`orderLineIdentifier`	`newOrderLine`	**Semantics**
Changing an OrderLine	Valid `OrderLineIdentifier`	Valid `OrderLine`	Replace `orderLine` specified by `orderLineIdentifier` with `newOrderLine`
Adding an OrderLine	null	Valid `OrderLine`	Add `newOrderLine` to `Order`
Deleting an OrderLine	Valid `OrderLineIdentifier`	null	Delete specified `OrderLine` from `Order`

Depending on the details of the `OrderLine` amendment, further action may be required to correct for items already despatched or payments made (see Section 9.25.3 for `PurchaseOrders`, Section 9.28.4 for `SalesOrders`). `ReturnedItem` represents an item that has been received by the `DeliveryReceiver` and must be returned to the vendor because an `AmendOrderLineEvent` has rendered it surplus to requirements (see Sections 9.25.4 and 9.28.5). Overpayment can be corrected by a refund (see Sections 9.25.5 and 9.28.6).

9.14.1 **Changing an** OrderLine

Changing an OrderLine is accomplished by replacing it with a new one that incorporates the desired changes. This is illustrated in Figure 9.14.

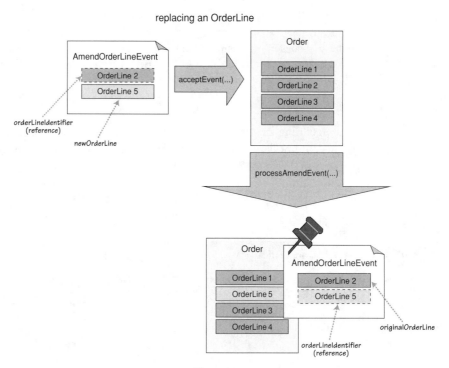

Figure 9.14

The process relies on the creation of a newOrderLine that replaces the Order-Line specified by the AmendOrderLineEvent's orderLineIdentifier.

1. Create the newOrderLine as follows.
    1.1. Make a copy of the specified OrderLine by using clone(). This clone must include all its associated objects.
    1.2. Amend the clone with the required changes. The amended clone is the newOrderLine.
2. When the Order processes the AmendOrderLineEvent, it marks the event as processed, exchanges the original OrderLine in the Order with the newOrderLine, and saves a reference to this new OrderLine in the AmendOrderLineEvent's orderLineIdentifier.

The end result of this process is that the new OrderLine is now attached to the Order. A reference to this new OrderLine is saved in the AmendOrderLine-Event, and the originalOrderLine is now attached to the event. This establishes an audit trial for the change.

9.14.2 Adding an OrderLine

This process is illustrated in Figure 9.15.

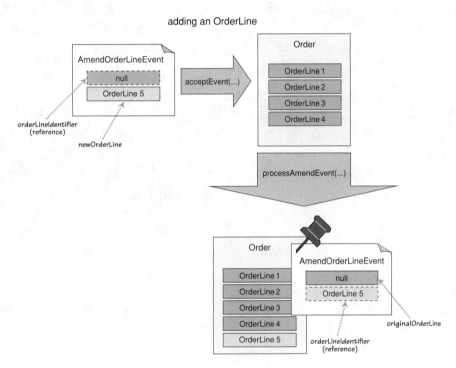

Figure 9.15

In this case, initially there is no orderLineIdentifier and the newOrder-Line contains the OrderLine to be added to the Order.

When the Order processes the AmendOrderLineEvent, it simply adds the new OrderLine to the Order. A reference to the new OrderLine is stored in the AmendOrderLineEvent, and the AmendOrderLineEvent is attached to the Order. This maintains an audit trail for the change.

9.14.3 **Deleting an** OrderLine

This process is illustrated in Figure 9.16.

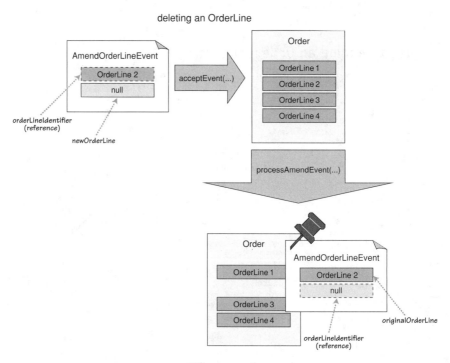

Figure 9.16

In this case, the orderLineIdentifier initially contains a reference to the OrderLine that will be deleted. The newOrderLine is null because nothing is going to be added.

When the Order processes the AmendOrderLineEvent, it simply removes the OrderLine referenced by the orderLineIdentifier in the Order and saves it in the AmendOrderLineEvent. The AmendOrderLineEvent is attached to the Order to maintain an audit trail for the change.

9.15 AmendPartySummaryEvent

Another type of amendment you can make to an Order is to its PartySummaries. We model this as an AmendPartySummaryEvent.

> The `AmendPartySummaryEvent` archetype represents an event that, when applied to an `OPEN` `Order`, results in a change to a specific `PartySummary`, the addition of a new `PartySummary`, or the deletion of an existing `PartySummary`.

The amendment mechanism is essentially the same as that for `OrderLines`. However, to identify the `PartySummary` to be amended, you need to specify the role the `PartySummary` plays. Also, if the `PartySummary` is the `orderLineReceiver`, you need to specify the `OrderLine` to which it is attached (see Figure 9.13 on page 330).

As with `AmendOrderLineEvent`, depending on the attribute values of the `AmendPartySummaryEvent`, you can accommodate changes, additions, and deletions. This is illustrated in Table 9.13.

Table 9.13

`AmendPartySummaryEvent` **semantics**			
`identifier`	`role`	`newPartySummary`	**Semantics**
Valid `OrderLineIdentifier`	Must be `ORDERLINERECEIVER`	Valid `DeliveryReceiver`	Replacement—if a `DeliveryReceiver` already exists in the `orderLineReceiver` role, replace that `orderLine-receiver` with the `newPartySummary` (i.e., `DeliveryReceiver`)
			Addition—if a `DeliveryReceiver` does *not* already exist in the `orderLineReceiver` role, add the `newPartySummary` (i.e., `DeliveryReceiver`)
Valid `OrderLineIdentifier`	Must be `ORDERLINERECEIVER`	`null`	Deletion—delete the `orderLineReceiver` from the specified `OrderLine`

Table continued on next page

Table 9.13   (Continued)

AmendPartySummaryEvent **semantics**			
identifier	role	newPartySummary	**Semantics**
null	Must be one of VENDOR SALESAGENT PAYMENTRECEIVER ORDERINITIATOR PURCHASER ORDERRECEIVER	Valid PartySummary	Replacement—if a PartySummary already exists in the specified role, replace that PartySummary with the newPartySummary Addition—if a Party-Summary does *not* exist in the specified role, add the newPartySummary in that role
null	Must be one of VENDOR SALESAGENT PAYMENTRECEIVER ORDERINITIATOR PURCHASER ORDERRECEIVER	null	Deletion—delete the PartySummary in the specified role from the Order

9.16   AmendTermsAndConditionsEvent

Finally, you can amend the termsAndConditions on an Order. We model this as an AmendTermsAndConditionsEvent (see Figure 9.13 on page 330).

> The AmendTermsAndConditionsEvent archetype represents an event that, when applied to an OPEN Order, results in a change to its termsAndConditions, the addition of termsAndConditions if these were previously absent, or the deletion of existing termsAndConditions.

The amendment mechanism is similar to that for OrderLines and Party-Summaries and can accommodate changes, additions, and deletions.

To effect a change, existing `termsAndConditions` in the `Order` are replaced by the `newTermsAndConditions` specified by an `AmendTermsAndConditions-Event`. If there are no `termsAndConditions` on an `Order`, these can be added by specifying `newTermsAndConditions` in an `AmendTermsAndConditionsEvent`. An `Order`'s `termsAndConditions` can be removed by applying an `AmendTermsAndConditionsEvent` with `null` `newTermsAndConditions`.

If the change is an amendment or a deletion, when the `Order` processes the event, the original `termsAndConditions` are saved as `oldTermsAndConditions` in the `AmendTermsAndConditionsEvent`, to provide an audit trail.

9.17 DiscountEvent

Each `Order` may have zero or more `Discounts` applied to it.

> The `Discount` archetype represents a discount to be applied to the total price of an `Order`.

The `Discount` archetype has two subclasses. These are `MonetaryDiscount` and `PercentageDiscount`.

> The `MonetaryDiscount` archetype represents an amount of `Money` to be deducted from the total price of an `Order`.
>
> The `PercentageDiscount` archetype represents a percentage to be deducted from the total price of an `Order`.

In our event-driven view of `Orders`, a `Discount` may be applied to an `Order` by sending the `Order` a `DiscountEvent`.

> The `DiscountEvent` archetype represents an event that, when applied to an `Order`, causes one or more `Discounts` to be recorded against the `Order`.

You can see our model of `Order` discounting in Figure 9.17.

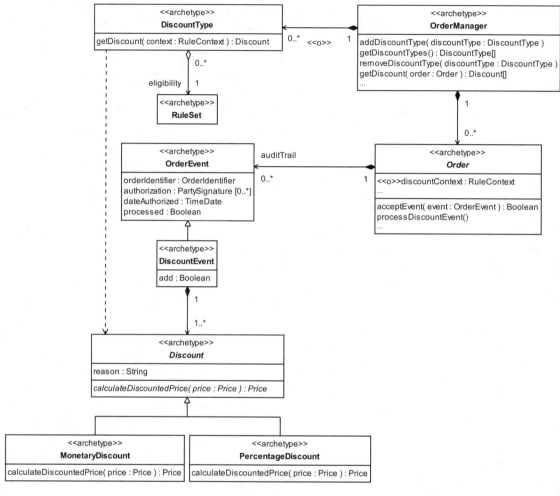

Figure 9.17

A Discount has a reason and may need to be authorized by a PartySigna-ture (on OrderEvent). Discounts on Orders may be granted based on considerations such as the following.

- *Who* is doing the buying—you may grant discounts to high-value customers, to encourage future business, or offer trade discounts to wholesale customers.
- *Where* the Order is raised—you may apply discounts to encourage sales in specific geographic regions.

- *How* the Order is raised—you may apply discounts to encourage sales through a specific sales channel such as the Internet.
- *When* the Order is raised—for example, "5% discount on total order value until end of the month."
- *How much* the Order is worth—for example, "Spend $50 or more, and get a 5% discount."

Discounts allow for variation of the *total* price that a purchaser pays for an Order.

If the price reduction is for just *part* of the Order (e.g., a single OrderLine or even a single ProductInstance), a Discount should *not* be applied to the Order itself. This is because price reductions for a ProductInstance can be modeled as one of its associated ProductType's Prices (see Section 7.22.1). Furthermore, quantity discounts can be effectively covered by package pricing (see Section 7.23).

You can see from Figure 9.17 that it is possible to record more than one DiscountEvent against an Order. Because only the DiscountEvent with the most recent dateAuthorized is in force, this provides a mechanism to amend Discounts if required, as well as a change history.

Discounts may be applied at the discretion of the vendor or salesAgent, or their application may be automated. As you can see in the model, the Order-Manager (Section 9.10) optionally maintains a collection of DiscountTypes.

> The DiscountType archetype contains a set of rules that describes the conditions under which a particular Discount may be applied.

Orders may optionally have a discountContext. This contains a set of information that the DiscountType can use to determine whether it will allow a Discount or not.

Although this rules-based approach to discounting can work in many circumstances, you should remember that if arbitrary Discounts are applied, these *can't* be captured by sets of Rules.

9.18 DespatchEvent

The business activity of sending goods or services to a receiver and reconciling those things against an OPEN SalesOrder is known as *despatching*.

We can model the despatch of goods or services by a DespatchEvent.

The DespatchEvent archetype represents an event that, when applied to an OPEN
SalesOrder, records goods or services sent to a DeliveryReceiver.

Our model of DespatchEvent is shown in Figure 9.18.

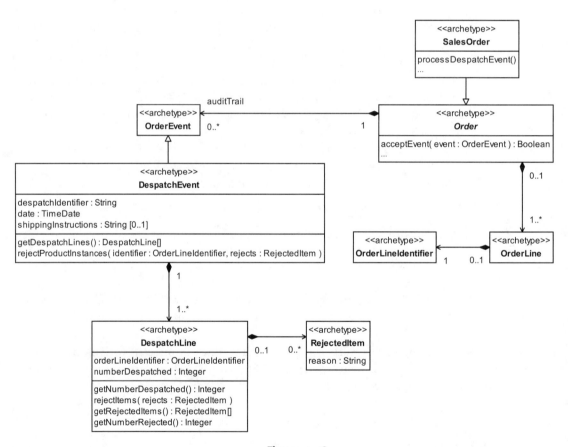

Figure 9.18

The DespatchEvent contains a despatchIdentifier that uniquely identifies it and the date on which the despatch was made. We have made simple provision for shippingInstructions on the DespatchEvent—depending on your business requirements, shipping can range from a straightforward activity to one requiring considerable information and processing. This is not modeled here because it is outside the scope of the Order itself.

The despatched goods or services are represented by DespatchLines.

> The DespatchLine archetype provides a record of the number of items despatched against a specified OrderLine as part of a particular DespatchEvent.

The DeliveryReceiver may reject some of the items received as damaged or otherwise unfit for purpose and inform the vendor accordingly. The appropriate number of RejectedItems, each including a reason, can be associated with the DespatchLine to record this (see Section 9.28.2).

> The RejectedItem archetype represents a delivered item that is rejected by a DeliveryReceiver as unfit for purpose.

9.19 ReceiptEvent

The business activity of receiving goods or services from a seller and reconciling those things against an OPEN PurchaseOrder is known as *receipting*.

We can model the receipt of goods or services with a ReceiptEvent.

> The ReceiptEvent archetype represents an event that, when applied to an OPEN PurchaseOrder, records goods or services received from a vendor.

Our model of ReceiptEvent is shown in Figure 9.19.

The ReceiptEvent contains a deliveryIdentifier that links it to a specific delivery of goods or services and the date on which the delivery was received.

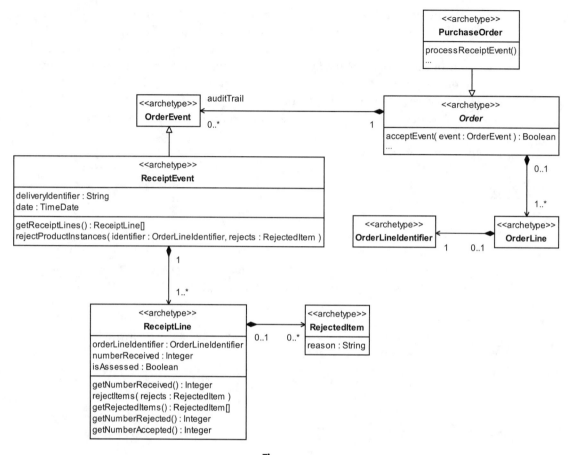

Figure 9.19

The receipted goods or services are represented by ReceiptLines.

The ReceiptLine archetype provides a record of the number of items received against a specified OrderLine as part of a particular ReceiptEvent.

The DeliveryReceiver assesses the items represented by each Receipt-Line. He or she may reject some of the delivered items as damaged or otherwise unfit for purpose and record these as RejectedItems against the appropriate ReceiptLine (see Section 9.25.1).

The `ReceiptLine` can `getNumberAccepted` by comparing the number of `RejectedItems` to the `numberReceived`.

9.20   OrderPayment **and** PaymentEvents

> The `OrderPayment` archetype represents a `Payment` made or accepted against an `Order`.

We discuss `Payments` in detail in Section 11.9.

You can represent the making or accepting of an `OrderPayment` by using a `PaymentEvent`.

> The `PaymentEvent` archetype represents an event that, when applied to an OPEN `Order`, records a `Payment` requested, made, or accepted against the `Order`.

`OrderPayments` and `PaymentEvents` are shown in Figure 9.20. `OrderPayment` optionally has two attributes additional to those it inherits from `Payment`—`toAccount` and `fromAccount` allow a snapshot to be taken of the accounts involved in the payment transaction.

Where `Orders` are concerned, there are five types of `PaymentEvents`; their semantics are described in Table 9.14.

A `PaymentEvent` represents a `Payment` against an `Order` that may optionally be for a specific `OrderLine` on that `Order`. If the `PaymentEvent` doesn't specify an `OrderLine`, you should consider the payment to be against the `Order` as a whole.

An `InvoiceEvent` doesn't represent an actual `Payment` but a request for a `Payment` to be made. An invoice (see Section 9.28.7) can be issued either for full or partial payment against the `Order` itself (e.g., as a request for prepayment—see Section 9.21) or may be issued in respect of a particular `Despatch-Event` referenced by its `despatchIdentifier`. Other types of `PaymentEvents` (e.g., `MakePaymentEvent`) can be matched to the relevant `InvoiceEvent` using the `invoiceIdentifier`.

Refunds are a special type of `Payment` and may be made in a variety of circumstances, including when a purchaser has made a payment against an `Order` that ends up as an overpayment because of subsequent cancellation or amendment of the `Order`.

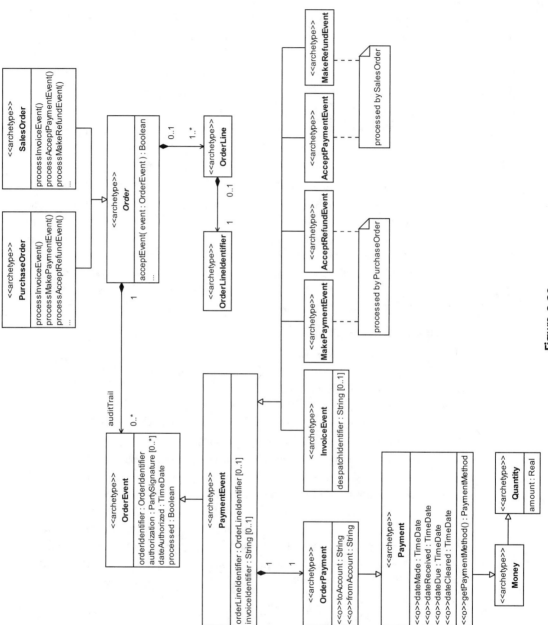

Figure 9.20

Table 9.14

Type of PaymentEvent	Processed by	Archetype definition
InvoiceEvent	PurchaseOrder and SalesOrder	The InvoiceEvent archetype represents an event that records an invoice sent by a paymentReceiver or received by a purchaser. If the invoice relates to a particular DespatchEvent, this can be recorded in the InvoiceEvent's despatchIdentifier
MakePaymentEvent	PurchaseOrder	The MakePaymentEvent archetype represents an event that records Money paid by a purchaser to a paymentReceiver against an OPEN PurchaseOrder.
AcceptRefundEvent	PurchaseOrder	The AcceptRefundEvent archetype represents an event that records Money refunded by a paymentReceiver to a purchaser against an OPEN PurchaseOrder.
AcceptPaymentEvent	SalesOrder	The AcceptPaymentEvent archetype represents an event that records Money received by a paymentReceiver from a purchaser against an OPEN SalesOrder.
MakeRefundEvent	SalesOrder	The MakeRefundEvent archetype represents an event that records Money refunded by a paymentReceiver to a purchaser against an OPEN SalesOrder.

9.21 Payment **strategies**

In this section we take a quick look at some of the strategies your business may use to handle Payments against outstanding PurchaseOrders. We think it is worthwhile to look at this because it is a central part of Order processing. It is also an area that can be confusing.

The basic use case (process) is PayForPurchaseOrder. It has four common variants, as illustrated in Figure 9.21.

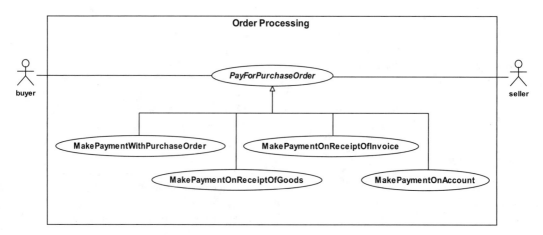

Figure 9.21

We discuss these variants in the next few subsections.

9.21.1 MakePaymentWithPurchaseOrder

This is the simplest case and is quite common in transactions between an individual and a business or when the customer is unknown and therefore has no relationship of trust with the business. This is often the case in e-commerce systems.

Main flow:

1. The vendor receives a PurchaseOrder along with full Payment.
2. The vendor opens a SalesOrder.
3. The paymentReceiver sends a receipt to the purchaser.

4. The vendor delivers the goods or services to the DeliveryReceivers.
5. The vendor closes the SalesOrder.

9.21.2 MakePaymentOnReceiptOfGoods

This is a very common case in business-to-business (B2B) transactions. The purchaser settles the full amount by an agreed period *after* the receipt of the goods or services.

Main flow:
1. The vendor receives a PurchaseOrder.
2. The vendor opens a SalesOrder.
3. The paymentReceiver sends an invoice to the purchaser.
4. The vendor delivers the goods and services to the DeliveryReceivers. (The order of steps 3 and 4 may vary.)
5. If the goods or services have been received by the DeliveryReceivers:
   5.1. The purchaser settles the invoice within an agreed time (e.g., 30 days) of receipt of the invoice or the goods, whichever is later.
   5.2. The vendor closes the SalesOrder.
   5.3. The paymentReceiver sends a receipt to the purchaser.

9.21.3 MakePaymentOnReceiptOfInvoice

In this case, the purchaser pays after the PurchaseOrder has been received by the vendor and in advance of receipt of the goods. The vendor agrees to deliver the goods to the DeliveryReceivers within an agreed time period.

Main flow:
1. The vendor receives a PurchaseOrder.
2. The vendor opens a SalesOrder.
3. The paymentReceiver sends an invoice to the purchaser.
4. The purchaser settles the invoice.
5. The vendor delivers the goods and services to the DeliveryReceivers within an agreed time period.
6. The vendor closes the SalesOrder.
7. The paymentReceiver sends a receipt to the purchaser.

9.21.4 MakePaymentOnAccount

This case occurs in both B2B transactions and in individual-to-business transactions when the individual has an account with the business.

Main flow:

1. The vendor receives a PurchaseOrder.
2. The vendor opens a SalesOrder.
3. The paymentReceiver sends an invoice to the purchaser.
4. The paymentReceiver debits the purchaser's account.
5. If the debit transaction succeeds:
   5.1. The vendor delivers the goods and services to the DeliveryReceivers.
   5.2. The vendor closes the SalesOrder.
   5.3. The paymentReceiver sends a receipt to the purchaser.

At any point in time:

1. Under circumstances agreed between the vendor and the orderInitiator, the purchaser makes Payments into the buyer's account with the seller, to maintain its balance at an agreed level.

9.21.5 Variants on MakePaymentOnAccount

Many possible variants on how an Order may be processed arise from the wide range of possible agreements that the vendor and the orderInitiator may enter into regarding payment and delivery of goods and services. Most of these variants can be accommodated as particular cases of MakePaymentOnAccount.

For example, if you are having construction work done on your house, you often pay a certain amount down and then pay the balance in installments and/or on completion of the work. At first glance this seems to be a case different from MakePaymentOnAccount. However, one way to look at this is that you have an account outstanding with your builder and an agreement that the service will be delivered against a partial payment of the Order, with the remaining payments at arranged intervals against the account.

9.22 Modeling the business process for Orders

In the following sections we take a look at how OrderEvents are raised by the business. To do this, we present a simple, universal business process for Order handling. This process is compatible with the processes currently outlined in ebXML (see www.ebxml.org).

Presenting such a model of the Order process is a challenge because our model must accomplish the following tasks.

- Capture the main activities involved in processing Orders.
- Capture logical dependencies between these main activities.
- Show the conditions under which the various types of OrderEvents are generated.
- Remain independent of any particular Order processing workflow.

While businesses tend to perform the same general activities to process Orders, the specific sequence of those activities (the workflow) may vary greatly from business to business. For example, one business may not allow cancellation of an Order once items have been despatched, while another may allow cancellation at any point while the Order is still OPEN, subject to the constraint that all despatched items will be returned.

In the next sections we present process archetypes for PurchaseOrders and SalesOrders. By applying specific business constraints to these archetypes, you can generate an Order processing workflow appropriate to your business.

9.23 The PurchaseOrder process archetype

Our archetypal PurchaseOrder business process is illustrated in Figure 9.22. The key activities in this process are described in Table 9.15.

Table 9.15

Activity	Semantics
create PurchaseOrder	The PurchaseOrder process begins when the orderInitiator creates a new PurchaseOrder
	Once any required authorization to proceed is obtained, the orderInitiator will open PurchaseOrder
open PurchaseOrder	An OpenEvent (with any authorizations obtained) is added to the Purchase-Order to record the fact that the PurchaseOrder is now OPEN for processing, then the orderInitiator will send PurchaseOrder to vendor

Table continued on next page

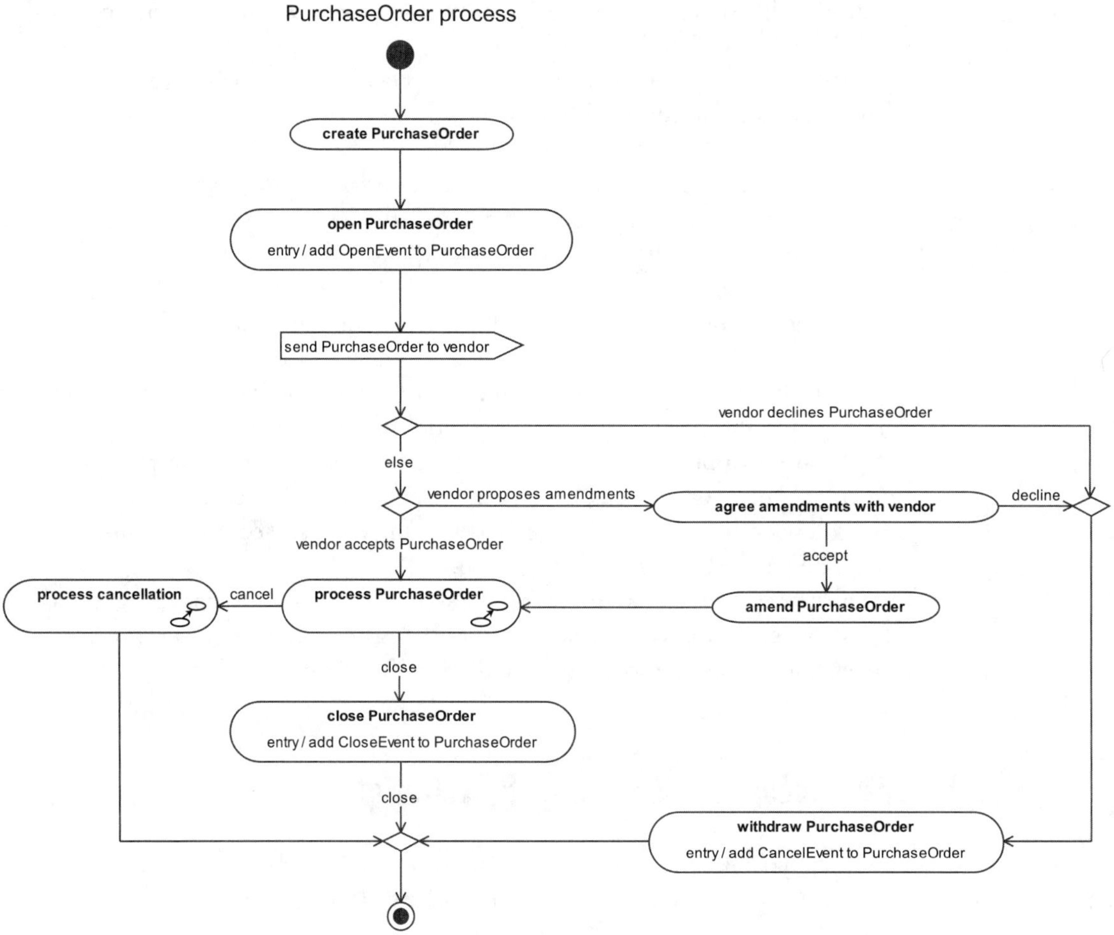

PurchaseOrder process

Figure 9.22

Table 9.15   (Continued)

Activity	Semantics
send PurchaseOrder to vendor	The PurchaseOrder is sent to the vendor
	If the vendor declines the PurchaseOrder (Section 9.26), then the orderInitiator must withdraw PurchaseOrder
	If the vendor proposes amendments, then the orderInitiator must agree amendments with vendor
	Else process PurchaseOrder

Table 9.15 (Continued)

Activity	Semantics
agree amendments with vendor	In this activity the vendor communicates with the orderInitiator to agree on a policy about further processing of the Order
	The orderInitiator may accept amendments, propose changes, or withdraw the PurchaseOrder; likewise, the vendor may choose to either accept or decline amendments
	If no agreement can be reached, then the orderInitiator will withdraw PurchaseOrder
	If agreement is reached, then the orderInitiator will amend PurchaseOrder
withdraw PurchaseOrder	The orderInitiator withdraws the PurchaseOrder and informs the vendor if necessary; the orderInitiator appends a CancelEvent to the PurchaseOrder
	The process terminates
amend PurchaseOrder	The orderInitiator updates the PurchaseOrder in line with the amendments agreed with the vendor, then will process PurchaseOrder
process PurchaseOrder	See Section 9.25
	At any point during processing (subject to the business rules applied by the particular business), the orderInitiator may cancel the PurchaseOrder—if this happens, then process cancellation
	If the PurchaseOrder is not cancelled, then at some point the orderInitiator will close the PurchaseOrder (e.g., because it has been paid for and delivered) by performing the activity close PurchaseOrder
process cancellation	See Section 9.24
	The process terminates
close PurchaseOrder	In this activity, the orderInitiator appends a CloseEvent to the PurchaseOrder to mark its closure
	The process terminates

9.24 PurchaseOrder—process cancellation

Our model for process cancellation is shown in Figure 9.23.
The activities that make up this process are described in Table 9.16.

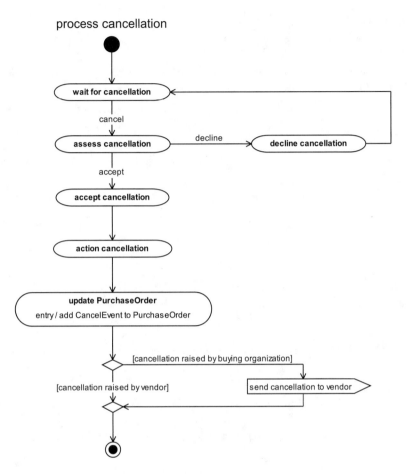

Figure 9.23

Table 9.16

Activity	Semantics
wait for cancellation	The process waits in this state until a cancellation is received for the PurchaseOrder, then assess cancellation
assess cancellation	In accord with the agreed Order termsAndConditions, the orderInitiator may choose to decline cancellation or accept cancellation

Table 9.16   (Continued)

Activity	Semantics
decline cancellation	The orderInitiator declines the cancellation and notifies the appropriate parties; if there are objections to this course of action, then the orderInitiator will have to resolve this conflict The process returns to wait for cancellation
accept cancellation	The orderInitiator accepts the cancellation and will action cancellation
action cancellation	If no deliveries have been received and no payments have yet been made against the Order, then the orderInitiator will just update PurchaseOrder However, if the cancellation results in a need to return goods (Section 9.25.4) or to refund an overpayment (Section 9.28.6), then the orderInitiator must inform and possibly negotiate with the vendor; the orderInitiator must then update PurchaseOrder
update PurchaseOrder	The orderInitiator appends a CancelEvent to the PurchaseOrder to mark it as cancelled If the cancellation was initiated by the buying organization, then send cancellation to vendor; if the cancellation came from the vendor, then the orderInitiator may send a confirmation to the vendor The process terminates
send cancellation to vendor	A cancellation note is sent to the vendor The process terminates

9.25   process PurchaseOrder

There are many ways in which a business may choose to process a PurchaseOrder. However, all of these approaches involve some or all of the activities shown in Figure 9.24.

We describe each of these activities in the following subsections.

process PurchaseOrder

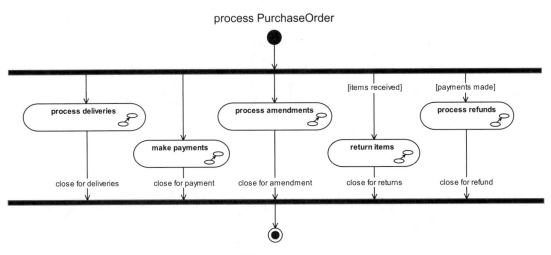

Figure 9.24

Notice that all of the activities are shown running in parallel, but some are logically contingent on others. For example, you don't need to start the process return items until at least one delivery has been received. Similarly, there is no need to start to process refunds until at least one Payment has been made.

As well as these logical dependencies between the parallel activities, each business may define its own PurchaseOrder process workflow that sequences the activities in a particular way, according to its specific business requirements.

For example, some companies may introduce a business rule constraining the PurchaseOrder process such that under a particular set of circumstances, no Payments can be made until the PurchaseOrder has been fully delivered, including the replacement of any rejected items. However, this sort of workflow rule is outside the scope of our archetypal process model.

Each activity is brought to an explicit close.

9.25.1 process deliveries

This activity is about receiving items from the vendor. Our model for process deliveries is shown in Figure 9.25.

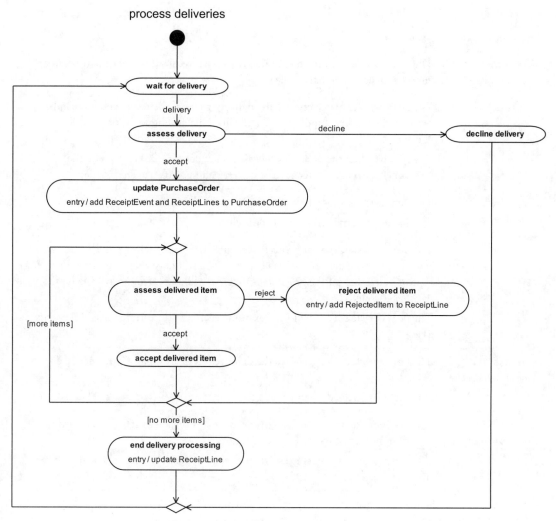

Figure 9.25

Note that this represents a two-stage receipting process—first, the receipt of a delivery is recorded, then the delivered items are assessed and either accepted or rejected.

The activities that make up this process are described in Table 9.17.

Table 9.17

Activity	Semantics
wait for delivery	The process waits in this state until a delivery is received for all or part of the PurchaseOrder, then assess delivery
assess delivery	The DeliveryReceiver assesses the delivery to see if the received items can be reconciled with any shipping note and with outstanding items on the PurchaseOrder
	If they can't, then the DeliveryReceiver may decline delivery; else the DeliveryReceiver will accept the delivery and update PurchaseOrder
decline delivery	The DeliveryReceiver refuses delivery of the shipment
	The process returns to wait for delivery
update PurchaseOrder	The DeliveryReceiver appends a ReceiptEvent to the PurchaseOrder to record the receipt of the delivery—this ReceiptEvent will have a ReceiptLine for each type of item received (i.e., each ReceiptLine will map to an OrderLine on the PurchaseOrder)
	The DeliveryReceiver will then examine each item in turn (assess delivered item)
assess delivered item	The DeliveryReceiver assesses the delivered item and may either reject or accept it
	If the item is rejected, then reject delivered item; else accept delivered item
reject delivered item	The DeliveryReceiver adds a RejectedItem to the ReceiptLine to record the rejection, noting a reason for the rejection
	If there are more items to assess, then assess delivered item; else end delivery processing
accept delivered item	The item is accepted
	If there are more items to assess, then assess delivered item; else end delivery processing
end delivery processing	The DeliveryReceiver updates each ReceiptLine to mark it as assessed (isAssessed = true)
	If there are any RejectedItems, then the DeliveryReceiver informs the vendor and returns the items
	If required, the DeliveryReceiver sends a receipt advice to the vendor
	The process returns to wait for delivery

9.25.2 make payments

Our model for make payments is shown in Figure 9.26.

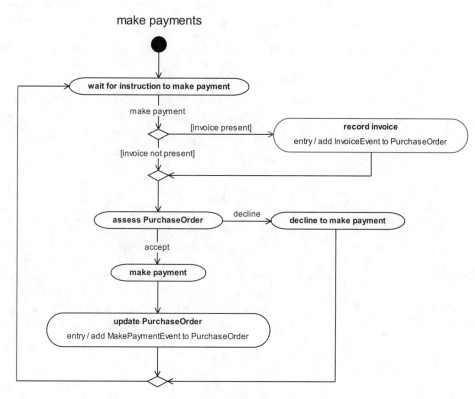

Figure 9.26

The activities that make up this process are described in Table 9.18.

Table 9.18

Activity	Semantics
wait for instruction to make payment	The process waits in this state until it receives an instruction (normally, receipt of an invoice) to make payment against the PurchaseOrder; then record invoice if invoice present, else assess PurchaseOrder

Table continued on next page

Table 9.18 (Continued)

Activity	Semantics
record invoice	The purchaser appends an InvoiceEvent to the PurchaseOrder to record the receipt of an invoice, then assess PurchaseOrder
assess PurchaseOrder	The purchaser assesses the PurchaseOrder to see what Payments are outstanding and when payment is due according to the termsAndConditions of the Order
	If there are no Payments due or there is some outstanding dispute about the Order, then the purchaser may decline to make payment
	If Payments are due, the purchaser accepts the instruction and will make payment—this may be immediately or after waiting for some period in accord with the Order termsAndConditions
decline to make payment	The purchaser declines to make the Payment—the purchaser may have to follow a specified business procedure to agree this outcome internally and/or with the vendor
	The process returns to wait for instruction to make payment
make payment	The purchaser makes a Payment against the PurchaseOrder—this involves sending money to the paymentReceiver by an agreed mechanism such as an automated bank transfer
	The purchaser must then update PurchaseOrder
update PurchaseOrder	The purchaser appends a MakePaymentEvent to the PurchaseOrder to record that a Payment has been made against it; if the Payment relates to a particular invoice, this can be noted in the MakePaymentEvent invoiceIdentifier
	The process returns to wait for instruction to make payment

9.25.3 process amendments

Our model for process amendments is shown in Figure 9.27.

The activities that make up this process are described in Table 9.19.

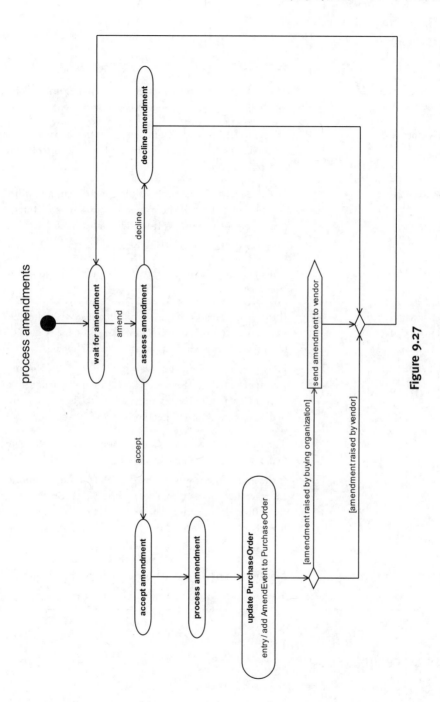

Figure 9.27

Table 9.19

Activity	Semantics
wait for amendment	The process waits in this state until an amendment is received for the PurchaseOrder, then assess amendment
assess amendment	In accord with the agreed Order termsAndConditions, the orderInitiator may choose to decline amendment or to accept amendment
decline amendment	The orderInitiator declines the amendment and notifies the appropriate parties; if there are objections to this course of action, then the orderInitiator will have to resolve this conflict The process returns to wait for amendment
accept amendment	The orderInitiator accepts the amendment and will process amendment
process amendment	If the amendment does not result in a need to return delivered items or to refund an overpayment against the Order, then the orderInitiator will just update PurchaseOrder However, if items must be returned (Section 9.25.4) or an overpayment refunded (Section 9.28.6), then the orderInitiator must inform and possibly negotiate with the vendor; the orderInitiator must then update PurchaseOrder
update PurchaseOrder	The orderInitiator appends an AmendEvent to the PurchaseOrder to record the amendment If the amendment was initiated by the buying organization, then send amendment to vendor; if the amendment came from the selling organization, the orderInitiator may send confirmation of acceptance to the vendor The process returns to wait for amendment
send amendment to vendor	Notification of the amendment is sent to the vendor The process returns to wait for amendment

9.25.4   return items

Our model for return items is shown in Figure 9.28.

The activities that make up this process are described in Table 9.20.

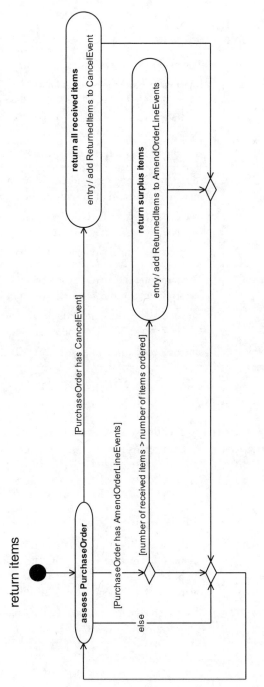

Figure 9.28

Table 9.20

Activity	Semantics
assess PurchaseOrder	The orderInitiator assesses the PurchaseOrder
	If the PurchaseOrder has a CancelEvent, then return all received items; if the PurchaseOrder has AmendOrderLineEvents and the number of received items > number of items ordered, then return surplus items
	Else the process returns to assess PurchaseOrder
return all received items	Any items already received are returned to the vendor—this may involve negotiation with the vendor for the returns
	The orderInitiator records the returns by adding ReturnedItems to the CancelEvent
	The process returns to assess PurchaseOrder
return surplus items	The items are returned to the vendor—this may involve negotiation with the vendor for the returns
	The orderInitiator records the returns by adding ReturnedItems to the AmendOrderLineEvent
	The process returns to assess PurchaseOrder

9.25.5 process refunds

Our model for process refunds is shown in Figure 9.29.

The activities that make up this process are described in Table 9.21.

Table 9.21

Activity	Semantics
wait for refund	The process waits in this state until a refund against the PurchaseOrder is received from the paymentReceiver—this might be because the SalesOrder has been overpaid (e.g., as the result of an amendment to the Order)
	The purchaser must then assess refund against PurchaseOrder
assess refund against PurchaseOrder	If the refund doesn't seem to apply to the PurchaseOrder, then the purchaser may decline refund, else the purchaser will accept refund

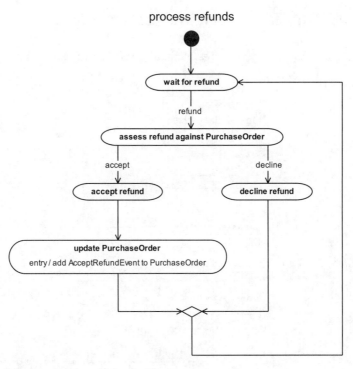

process refunds

Figure 9.29

Table 9.21   (Continued)

Activity	Semantics
decline refund	The purchaser declines the refund
	The purchaser must then agree with the vendor what action to take—usually, the refund is returned to the paymentReceiver
	The process returns to wait for refund
accept refund	The purchaser accepts the refund as being valid and must update PurchaseOrder
update PurchaseOrder	The purchaser appends an AcceptRefundEvent to the PurchaseOrder to record the refund accepted against it; if the refund relates to a particular invoice, this can be noted in the AcceptRefundEvent invoiceIdentifier
	The process returns to wait for refund

9.26 The SalesOrder **process archetype**

Our archetypal SalesOrder business process is illustrated in Figure 9.30.

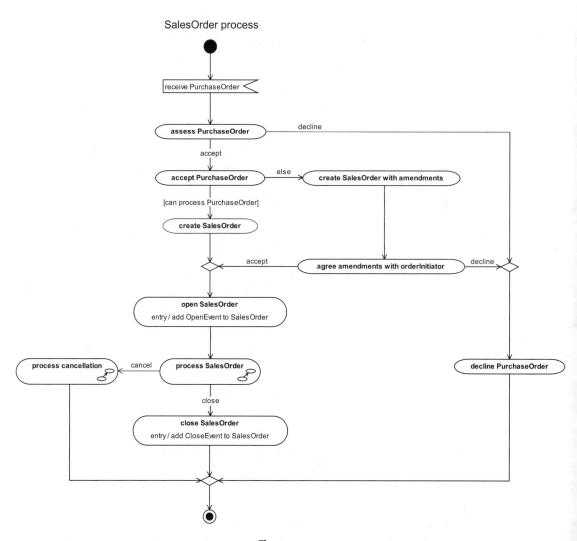

Figure 9.30

The key activities in this process are described in Table 9.22.

Table 9.22

Activity	Semantics
receive PurchaseOrder	The SalesOrder process begins when the vendor receives a PurchaseOrder from an orderInitiator, then the vendor will assess PurchaseOrder
assess PurchaseOrder	The vendor will have to answer the following sorts of questions to arrive at a decision as to whether or not to accept the order: • Is the PurchaseOrder comprehensible? • Is it feasible to deliver what the PurchaseOrder specifies? • Is the vendor confident of the customer's ability to pay? • Does the vendor want this piece of business? If the PurchaseOrder is accepted by the vendor, then accept PurchaseOrder If the PurchaseOrder is declined by the vendor, then decline PurchaseOrder
accept PurchaseOrder	At this point, the vendor has decided to work with the PurchaseOrder and to deliver all or part of it The goal of this activity is to convert the PurchaseOrder into a SalesOrder for further processing If the PurchaseOrder is complete and feasible, the vendor will create SalesOrder; else, the vendor will create SalesOrder with amendments
create SalesOrder	The SalesOrder is created as an exact mirror of the PurchaseOrder—i.e., there are no amendments
create SalesOrder with amendments	If the PurchaseOrder is incomplete in some respect, the vendor might attempt to complete missing details or might have to go back to the orderInitiator for more information; any corrected or additional information is merged into the SalesOrder If the vendor is unable to deliver against the PurchaseOrder as it stands (e.g., is unable to deliver everything specified or must substitute some items with others), a SalesOrder can be created with appropriate amendments In either case, the vendor must then agree amendments with orderInitiator

Table continued on next page

Table 9.22 (Continued)

Activity	Semantics
agree amendments with orderInitiator	In this activity the vendor communicates with the orderInitiator to agree on a policy about further processing of the Order
	The orderInitiator may accept amendments, propose changes, or withdraw the PurchaseOrder; likewise, the vendor may choose to either accept or decline amendments
	If no agreement can be reached, the vendor will decline PurchaseOrder
	If agreement is reached, the vendor will open SalesOrder
decline PurchaseOrder	The vendor informs the orderInitiator that the PurchaseOrder has been declined
	The process terminates
open SalesOrder	The vendor appends an OpenEvent to the SalesOrder to record the fact that the SalesOrder is opened for processing and will then process SalesOrder
process SalesOrder	See Section 9.28
	At any point during processing (subject to the business rules applied by the particular business), the vendor may cancel the SalesOrder—if this happens, process cancellation
	If the SalesOrder is not cancelled, then at some point the vendor will close the SalesOrder (e.g., because it has been paid for and delivered) by performing the activity close SalesOrder
process cancellation	See Section 9.27
	The process terminates
close SalesOrder	In this activity, the vendor appends a CloseEvent to the SalesOrder to mark its closure
	The process terminates

9.27 SalesOrder—process cancellation

Our model for process cancellation is shown in Figure 9.31.
The activities that make up this process are described in Table 9.23.

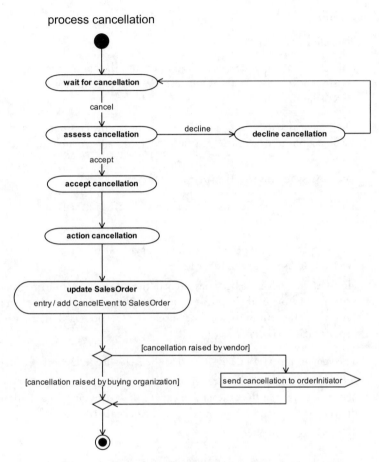

process cancellation

Figure 9.31

Table 9.23

Activity	Semantics
wait for cancellation	The process waits in this state until a cancellation is received for the SalesOrder, then assess cancellation
assess cancellation	In accord with the agreed Order termsAndConditions, the vendor may choose to decline cancellation or accept cancellation—for example, some vendors will accept a cancellation only if there have been no despatches, while others may accept cancellations at any point until the SalesOrder is closed

Table continued on next page

Table 9.23   (Continued)

Activity	Semantics
assess cancellation (continued)	If the cancellation request was raised internally, the contractual implications must be assessed (it is rare for the selling organization to initiate the cancellation of an OPEN Order)
decline cancellation	The vendor declines the cancellation and notifies the appropriate parties; if there are objections to this course of action, then the vendor will have to resolve this conflict
	The process returns to wait for cancellation
accept cancellation	The vendor accepts the cancellation and will action cancellation
action cancellation	If no despatches have been made and no payments have yet been received, then the vendor will just update SalesOrder
	However, if goods have been despatched, then the vendor must negotiate with the orderInitiator for their return; if payments have been received, then the payment-Receiver must refund these to the purchaser (Section 9.28.6); the vendor must then update SalesOrder
update SalesOrder	The vendor appends a CancelEvent to the SalesOrder to mark it as cancelled
	If the cancellation was initiated by the vendor, then send cancellation to orderInitiator; if the cancellation came from the buying organization, then the vendor may send a confirmation to the orderInitiator
	The process terminates
send cancellation to orderInitiator	A cancellation note is sent to the orderInitiator
	The process terminates

9.28 process SalesOrder

There are many ways in which a business may choose to process a SalesOrder. However, all of these approaches involve some or all of the activities shown in Figure 9.32.

We describe each of these activities in the following subsections.

Notice that all the activities are shown running in parallel, but some are logically contingent on others. For example, you don't need to start to process returned items until at least one despatch has been made. Similarly, there is

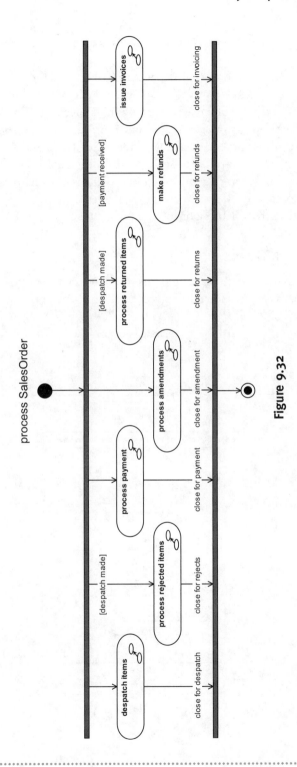

Figure 9.32

no need to start the make refunds process until at least one Payment has been received.

As well as these logical dependencies between the parallel activities, each business may define its own SalesOrder process workflow that sequences the activities in a particular way, according to its specific business requirements.

For example, some companies may introduce a business rule constraining the SalesOrder process such that under a particular set of circumstances, despatch can't occur until the SalesOrder has been paid for in full and is closed for payment. However, this sort of workflow rule is outside the scope of our archetypal process model.

Each activity is brought to an explicit close.

9.28.1   despatch items

This activity is about sending items to the DeliveryReceivers. Our model for despatch items is shown in Figure 9.33.

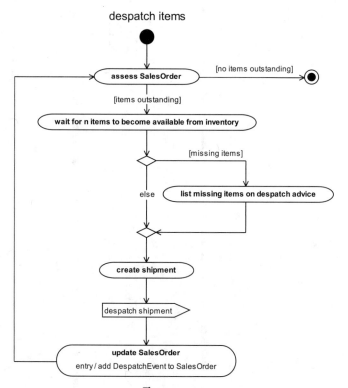

Figure 9.33

The activities that make up this process are described in Table 9.24.

Table 9.24

Activity	Semantics
assess SalesOrder	The vendor assesses the SalesOrder to see what items need to be despatched If there are items outstanding, then wait for n items to become available from inventory; else the process terminates
wait for n items to become available from inventory	The vendor queries the Inventory and, if necessary, waits for several of the items to become available before despatching them—the exact details of this step depend on the vendor's business practice and agreement with the orderInitiator: • Items may be individually despatched as they become available • Items may be despatched in lots (e.g., a quantity that is economically viable to handle, or all items specified on a SalesOrder OrderLine) • Items may be despatched only when everything specified on the Order becomes available For example, if you order from Amazon.com, you are given the option for items to be despatched as each becomes available or, to save postage, only when all items are available If there are missing items (i.e., not all items required for the despatch can be obtained from inventory), then list missing items on despatch advice; else create shipment
list missing items on despatch advice	Any items that are not currently available from inventory (and therefore can't be despatched) are listed on a despatch advice, perhaps with an estimated availability date Once the note has been created the vendor must create shipment
create shipment	A shipment is created that includes all of the items obtained from inventory, accompanied normally by a despatch advice (see Section 9.29) The next step is to despatch shipment
despatch shipment	The vendor sends the shipment to the DeliveryReceivers The vendor must then update SalesOrder
update SalesOrder	The vendor appends a DespatchEvent to the SalesOrder to record the despatch of the items to the DeliveryReceivers The process returns to assess SalesOrder

9.28.2 process rejected items

Our model for process rejected items is shown in Figure 9.34.
The activities that make up this process are described in Table 9.25.

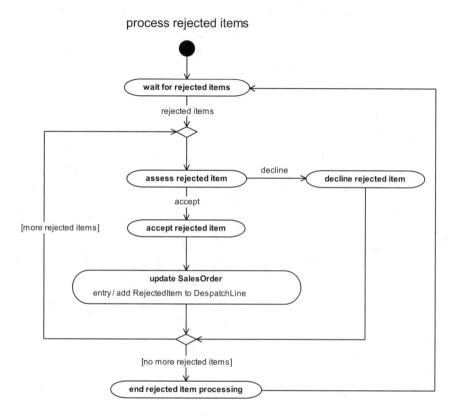

Figure 9.34

Table 9.25

Activity	Semantics
wait for rejected items	The process waits in this state until the vendor receives one or more rejected items against the SalesOrder (a rejected item is one that has been sent back by the DeliveryReceiver because it is damaged, defective, or otherwise unfit for purpose)
	The vendor must then cycle through each of the rejected items and assess rejected item

Table 9.25 (Continued)

Activity	Semantics
assess rejected item	The vendor assesses the rejected item and the reason it has been rejected and may decline rejected item or accept rejected item
decline rejected item	A vendor may choose to decline a rejected item for several reasons: • The rejected item has been damaged by the DeliveryReceiver • The rejected item isn't defective (the DeliveryReceiver is in error) • There may be other reasons depending on the rejected item and the termsAndConditions on the Order If there are more rejected items, then assess rejected item; else end rejected item processing
accept rejected item	The rejected item is accepted as valid for return, then update SalesOrder
update SalesOrder	For each accepted rejected item, the vendor adds a RejectedItem to the DespatchLine of the appropriate DespatchEvent If there are more rejected items, then assess rejected item; else end rejected item processing
end rejected item processing	The details of this activity vary from business to business If there are any rejected items that have been declined, then the vendor will usually contact the orderInitiator to notify them that the rejected items have been received, but not accepted; the vendor must negotiate with the orderInitiator to resolve any dispute over the declined items If there are any rejected items that have been accepted, then the vendor may contact the orderInitiator to confirm the rejects and may contact the manufacturer to get a refund or replacement item The process returns to wait for rejected items

9.28.3 process payment

Our model for process payment is shown in Figure 9.35.

The activities that make up this process are described in Table 9.26.

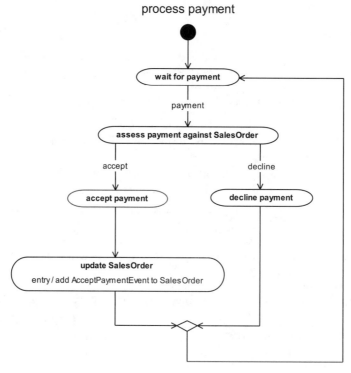

process payment

Figure 9.35

Table 9.26

Activity	Semantics
wait for payment	The process waits in this state until a Payment against the SalesOrder is received from the purchaser
	The paymentReceiver must then assess payment against SalesOrder
assess payment against SalesOrder	The Payment is assessed against the sum outstanding on the SalesOrder
	If no payment is due against the SalesOrder, then the paymentReceiver will decline payment; else the paymentReceiver will accept payment

Table 9.26 (Continued)

Activity	Semantics
assess payment against SalesOrder (continued)	(Sometimes the business has no choice but to accept the Payment—for example, payment by bank transfer will automatically credit the business's account without the business's explicit participation—if this is the case, then accept payment)
decline payment	The paymentReceiver declines the Payment—for example, the paymentReceiver returns a check to the purchaser or refuses to debit the purchaser's PaymentCard The process returns to wait for payment
accept payment	The paymentReceiver accepts the Payment and may send a payment receipt to the purchaser There are three accept payment cases to consider: • The Payment exactly covers the outstanding sum against the SalesOrder—in this case, the SalesOrder can be considered to be closed for payment • The Payment is less than the outstanding sum against the SalesOrder—in this case, the SalesOrder remains partially paid for • The Payment is more than the outstanding sum against the SalesOrder—in this case, the SalesOrder can be considered to be closed for payment, and a refund of the surplus amount paid will be made to the purchaser at some point (see Section 9.28.6) After accepting a Payment, the paymentReceiver must update SalesOrder
update SalesOrder	The paymentReceiver appends an AcceptPaymentEvent to the SalesOrder to record the Payment; if the Payment relates to a particular invoice, this can be noted in the AcceptPaymentEvent invoiceIdentifier The process returns to wait for payment

9.28.4 process amendments

Our model for process amendments is shown in Figure 9.36.
The activities that make up this process are described in Table 9.27.

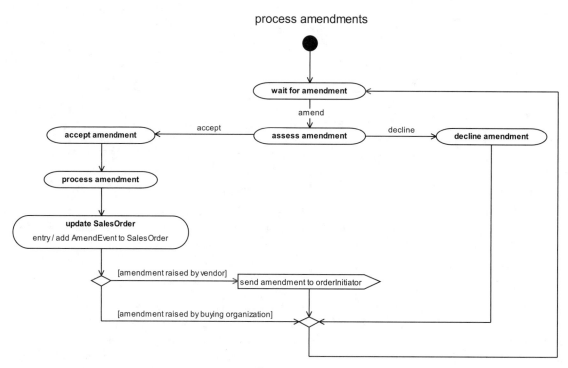

Figure 9.36

Table 9.27

Activity	Semantics
wait for amendment	The process waits in this state until an amendment is received for the SalesOrder, then assess amendment
assess amendment	In accord with the agreed Order termsAndConditions, the vendor may choose to decline amendment or to accept amendment

Table 9.27 (Continued)

Activity	Semantics
assess amendment (continued)	If the amendment request was raised internally, the contractual implications must be assessed
decline amendment	The vendor declines the amendment and notifies the appropriate parties; if there are objections to this course of action, then the vendor will have to resolve this conflict

The process returns to wait for amendment |
| accept amendment | The vendor accepts the amendment and will process amendment |
| process amendment | If the amendment does not mean that items must be returned by the DeliveryReceivers or that a refund is due, then the vendor will just update salesOrder

However, if items must be returned, then the vendor must inform and possibly negotiate with the orderInitiator; if the SalesOrder is overpaid, then the paymentReceiver may need to make a refund to the purchaser (Section 9.28.6); the vendor must then update SalesOrder |
| update SalesOrder | The vendor appends an AmendEvent to the SalesOrder to record the amendment

If the amendment was initiated by the selling organization, then send amendment to orderInitiator; if the amendment came from the buying organization, then the vendor may send confirmation of acceptance to the orderInitiator

The process returns to wait for amendment |
| send amendment to orderInitiator | Notification of the amendment is sent to the orderInitiator

The process returns to wait for amendment |

9.28.5 process returned items

Our model for process returned items is shown in Figure 9.37.

The activities that make up this process are described in Table 9.28.

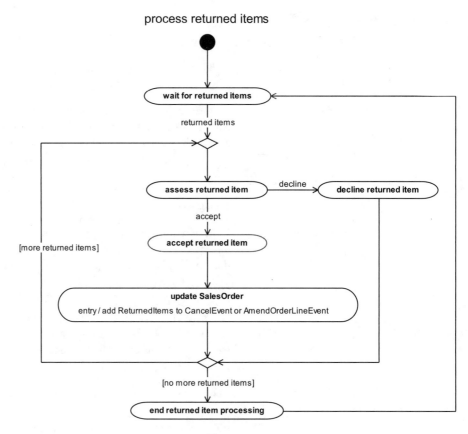

process returned items

Figure 9.37

Table 9.28

Activity	Semantics
wait for returned items	The process waits in this state until the vendor receives one or more returned items against the SalesOrder
	A returned item is one that has been returned by the orderInitiator as a result of:
	• An amendment to the PurchaseOrder • A cancellation of the PurchaseOrder
	(Returned items are semantically different from rejected items, which are items that are not fit for purpose)

Table 9.28   (Continued)

Activity	Semantics
wait for returned items (continued)	The vendor must then cycle through each of the returned items and assess returned item
assess returned item	The vendor assesses the returned item and may decline returned item or accept returned item
decline returned item	The vendor may choose to decline a returned item for several reasons: • The Order termsAndConditions specify that returns are not allowed • The returned items can't be returned to inventory—for example, the items may be damaged or some security seal on them may have been broken If there are more returned items, then assess returned item; else end returned item processing
accept returned item	The item is accepted as valid for return, then update SalesOrder
update SalesOrder	For each accepted returned item: • The vendor adds a ReturnedItem to the CancelEvent if the returned items were the result of an Order cancellation • The vendor adds a ReturnedItem to the appropriate AmendOrderLineEvent if the returned items were the result of an Order amendment If there are more returned items, then assess returned item; else end returned item processing
end returned item processing	The details of this activity vary from business to business If there are any returned items that have been declined, then the vendor will usually contact the orderInitiator to notify them that the returned items have been received, but not accepted; the vendor must negotiate with the orderInitiator to resolve any dispute over the declined items If there are any returned items that have been accepted, then the vendor may contact the orderInitiator to confirm the returns The process returns to wait for returned items

9.28.6 make refunds

Our model for make refunds is shown in Figure 9.38.

The activities that make up this process are described in Table 9.29.

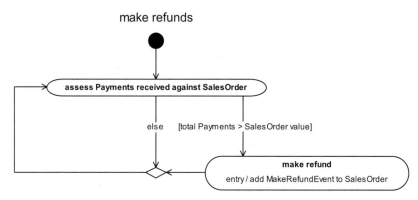

Figure 9.38

Table 9.29

Activity	Semantics
assess Payments received against SalesOrder	The paymentReceiver assesses the Payments received to date against the total cost of the SalesOrder There are three possible cases: • The Payments received to date exactly cover the total cost of the SalesOrder—in this case, the SalesOrder is fully paid for and no refund action is required, so return to assess Payments received against SalesOrder • The Payments received to date come to less than the total cost of the SalesOrder—in this case, the SalesOrder is only partially paid for and no refund action is required, so return to assess Payments received against SalesOrder • The Payments received to date come to more than the total cost of the SalesOrder—in this case, the paymentReceiver must make refund

Table 9.29 (Continued)

Activity	Semantics
make refund	The paymentReceiver makes a refund to the purchaser—this involves sending money to the purchaser by an agreed mechanism such as an automated bank transfer (alternatively, a credit note can be sent to the purchaser)
	The paymentReceiver appends a MakeRefundEvent to the SalesOrder to record the refund; if the refund relates to a particular invoice, this can be noted in the MakeRefundEvent invoiceIdentifier
	The process returns to assess Payments received against SalesOrder

9.28.7 issue invoices

Our model for issue invoices is shown in Figure 9.39.

The activities that make up this process are described in Table 9.30.

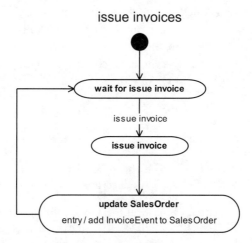

Figure 9.39

Table 9.30

Activity	Semantics
wait for issue invoice	The process waits in this state until an instruction is received to issue an invoice, then issue invoice
issue invoice	The paymentReceiver issues an invoice in the appropriate amount and sends it to the purchaser (business rules determine whether the invoice is for the whole or part of the SalesOrder value or relates to a particular DespatchEvent), then update SalesOrder
update SalesOrder	The paymentReceiver appends an InvoiceEvent to the SalesOrder to record the issue of the invoice and the invoiceIdentifier; if the invoice relates to a particular DespatchEvent, this can be noted in the InvoiceEvent despatchIdentifier The process returns to wait for issue invoice

9.29 Order **process documentation**

The Order archetype pattern contains information that can be used to generate a variety of paper or electronic documents associated with order processes. (See www.oasis-open.org for work done by the OASIS Universal Business Language Technical Committee on developing a standard library of XML for use in electronic business documents.)

We summarize the most common documents in Table 9.31.

Table 9.31

Document type	Created by	Purpose
Purchase order	Buyer	Requests a seller to provide goods or services in return for a specified payment
Order response (simple)	Seller	Sent to a buyer either to confirm the acceptance of a purchase order as it stands or to reject a purchase order
Order response (complex)	Seller	Sent to a buyer and effectively replaces the purchase order; provides missing details or notifies the buyer about necessary changes or substitutions

Table 9.31 (Continued)

Document type	Created by	Purpose
Sales order	Seller	Itemizes the goods or services to be provided to a buyer in return for a specified payment (this is common where no formal purchase order has been sent by the buyer to the seller)
Order cancellation	Buyer	Cancels an order, subject to contractual terms and conditions, business rules, and so on
Order picking list	Seller (internal document)	Used by warehouse staff to put together the required items for a despatch
Despatch advice	Seller	Provided to the buyer to facilitate checking of a consignment—can also include shipping and handling information Note that lines on the despatch advice may not have a one-to-one relationship to lines on the order (e.g., due to a partial despatch)
Receipt advice	Buyer	Sent to the seller to confirm receipt of items Can also be used to notify the seller about shortages or rejected items
Invoice	Seller	Sent to a buyer to request payment, either against the entire order (on a whole or partial basis) or in relation to a particular despatch event
Payment receipt	Seller	Sent to a buyer to confirm receipt of payment against an invoice

Combination documents are also often produced—for example, a sales order and despatch advice, or an invoice and payment receipt.

All these documents can be readily generated from the information captured in the Order archetype pattern.

9.30 Variation in Order processes

Across the commercial world, there can be enormous variation in order processes. In the remainder of this chapter, we briefly survey some different order environments.

9.30.1 Retail versus B2B sales

In the retail environment, a simplified order process is often used for face-to-face transactions, with documents reduced to a minimum—perhaps to just a payment receipt and implicit sales order.

More complex processes and more formal order documentation are used where greater detail about transactions is required. This typically involves the following aspects.

- Identification—the vendor needs to record who is buying.
- Delivery—the vendor needs to record where to deliver goods or services.
- Payment—the vendor needs to track payment on account or other deferred payments.

Almost all B2B transactions require this greater degree of formality and tracking.

9.30.2 Purchasing in large organizations

Large organizations commonly exercise considerable control over purchases, providing a formal process to raise a purchase requisition and to authorize the expenditure. The purchase requisition is effectively a PurchaseOrder in the INITIALIZING state, while one or more appropriate authorizations can be captured on the OpenEvent (i.e., the OpenEvent signals that the PurchaseOrder has been authorized).

9.30.3 Orders in e-commerce systems

We don't address e-commerce systems in detail in this book, but it is still worth having a brief look at how Orders interact with these systems. A typical e-commerce interaction proceeds as shown in Figure 9.40. The customer places items in a shoppingBasket and at some point either abandons the basket or buys the items at checkout.

What we want to illustrate is that when the customer has finished shopping and proceeds to checkout, the shoppingBasket is passed into the checkout activity, where it is transformed into a SalesOrder. An electronic copy of the SalesOrder may be sent to the customer as a record and receipt for the sales transaction, while the SalesOrder is sent to the seller's order processing system, where it is actioned.

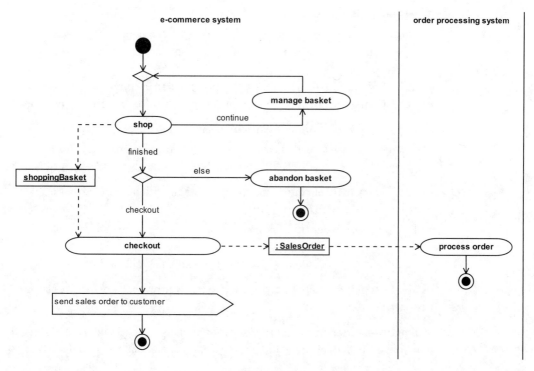

Figure 9.40

A common mistake we see in e-commerce systems is to confuse the ShoppingBasket with the Order. In fact, the ShoppingBasket is just a transient record of the items that the customer *may buy*. The Order, however, is a persistent record of the items that the customer *has bought*. We feel that this difference in semantics is sufficient to warrant modeling ShoppingBaskets and Orders as two different things.

9.31 Summary

In this chapter we looked at the Order archetype pattern. This is a pattern for representing an order. We covered the topics listed below.

- The Order archetype: how to represent a request by a buyer for a seller to supply some goods or services
  - OrderIdentifier: how to uniquely identify an Order

- PurchaseOrder and SalesOrder:
  - PurchaseOrder: how to represent the type of Order raised by a buyer and submitted to a seller as a request for goods or services in return for an agreed payment
  - SalesOrder: how to represent the type of Order used by a seller to track delivery of goods or services to a buyer in return for an agreed payment
- OrderLine: how to represent particular goods or services in an Order
  - OrderLineIdentifier: how to uniquely identify an OrderLine or a ChargeLine
- PartySummaryRoleInOrder: how to represent the different roles that a PartySummary may play in the order process
  - Buying roles: orderInitiator, purchaser, orderReceiver, orderLineReceiver
  - Selling roles: vendor, salesAgent, paymentReceiver
- DeliveryReceiver: how to represent the receiver of goods or services specified in an Order
- ChargeLine: how to represent an additional charge for an OrderLine over and above the OrderLine value or an extra charge added to an Order
- TaxOnLine: how to represent the tax charged on an OrderLine or ChargeLine
  - SalesTaxPolicy: how to record the taxation rate for a particular category of sales tax
- OrderManager: how to represent and manage a collection of Orders
- OrderEvents: how to represent notable occurrences in the Order lifecycle
- OrderStatus and LifecycleEvents:
  - OrderStatus: how to represent the status of an Order as it is being processed
  - LifecycleEvent: how to represent events that change the OrderStatus
    - OpenEvent: how to represent the opening of an Order for processing
    - CloseEvent: how to represent the completion of Order processing
    - CancelEvent: how to represent the cancellation of an Order
- AmendEvents: how to represent events that change an OPEN Order in some way
  - AmendOrderLineEvent: how to represent an event that changes or deletes an existing OrderLine or adds a new OrderLine to an Order
    - ReturnedItem: how to represent an item that must be returned to a vendor because a CancelEvent or AmendOrderLineEvent has rendered it surplus to requirements

- AmendPartySummaryEvent: how to represent an event that changes or deletes an existing PartySummary or adds a new PartySummary to an Order
- AmendTermsAndConditionsEvent: how to represent an event that changes or deletes existing termsAndConditions or adds termsAndConditions to an Order if these were previously absent

● DiscountEvent: how to represent an event that causes one or more Discounts to be recorded against an Order
  ■ Discount: how to represent a discount to be applied to the total price of an Order
    – MonetaryDiscount: how to represent a Discount as an amount of Money
    – PercentageDiscount: how to represent a Discount as a percentage of the total price
  ■ DiscountType: how to represent the set of rules governing the application of a Discount

● DespatchEvent: how to represent the action of sending goods or services to a DeliveryReceiver
  ■ DespatchLine: how to represent the number of items despatched against a specified OrderLine as part of a particular DespatchEvent
  ■ RejectedItem: how to represent an item rejected by a DeliveryReceiver as unfit for purpose

● ReceiptEvent: how to represent the action of receipting goods or services
  ■ ReceiptLine: how to represent the number of items received against a specified OrderLine as part of a particular ReceiptEvent

● OrderPayment and PaymentEvents:
  ■ OrderPayment: how to represent a Payment made or accepted against an Order
  ■ PaymentEvent: how to represent the action of making or receiving a payment against an Order
    – InvoiceEvent: how to represent the action of issuing or receiving an invoice (i.e., a request for payment)
    – MakePaymentEvent: how to represent the action of making a payment against a PurchaseOrder
    – AcceptRefundEvent: how to represent the action of accepting a refund against a PurchaseOrder
    – AcceptPaymentEvent: how to represent the action of accepting a payment against a SalesOrder
    – MakeRefundEvent: how to represent the action of making a refund against a SalesOrder

- Payment strategies:
  - `MakePaymentWithPurchaseOrder`
  - `MakePaymentOnReceiptOfGoods`
  - `MakePaymentOnReceiptOfInvoice`
  - `MakePaymentOnAccount`

- Modeling the business process for `Orders`: how `OrderEvents` are raised by the business

- `PurchaseOrder` process archetype: this consists of the activities:
  - create and open `PurchaseOrder`
  - process `PurchaseOrder`
    - process deliveries
      - reject items
    - make payments
    - process amendments
    - return items
    - process refunds
  - process cancellation
  - close `PurchaseOrder`

- `SalesOrder` process archetype: this consists of the activities:
  - receive and assess `PurchaseOrder`
  - create and open `SalesOrder`
  - process `SalesOrder`
    - despatch items
    - process rejected items
    - process payment
    - process amendments
    - process returned items
    - make refunds
    - issue invoices
  - process cancellation
  - close `SalesOrder`

- Order process documentation: an overview of the paper or electronic documents that may be generated by the order process:
  - Purchase order
  - Order response (simple)
  - Order response (complex)
  - Sales order

- Order cancellation
- Order picking list
- Despatch advice
- Receipt advice
- Invoice
- Payment receipt

● Variation in order processes: how the order process may vary in some common business contexts:

- Retail versus business-to-business sales
- Purchasing in large organizations
- Orders in e-commerce systems

Chapter 10

Quantity archetype pattern

10.1 Business context

In various places in this book, we have mentioned quantities of things. In this chapter we provide a simple pattern for capturing quantities.

> A quantity is an amount of something measured according to some standard of measurement.

Another way to say this is that a quantity of something is a number expressed in a particular metric.

> A metric is a standard of measurement.

For example, a bag of sugar in the store contains 1 (the number) kilogram (the metric) of sugar (the something). To express a quantity, you always need to specify both the number *and* the metric. You may optionally specify the thing to which the quantity refers.

The metric always has a name (e.g., kilogram) and often has a standard symbol (e.g., kg). You can talk about quantities in the abstract sense (e.g., "1 kg"), or you may associate the quantity with something (e.g., "1 kg of sugar").

There are many systems of measurement in the world, including the American system of measurement. However, these systems are generally defined in terms of the International System of Units that we discuss in Section 10.6.

Full source code for a Python implementation of our Quantity pattern is available from our Web site (www.businessarchetypes.com).

10.2   Compliance with existing standards

The models presented in this chapter comply with the standard listed in Table 10.1.

Table 10.1

Standard	Contents	Reference
SI	International System of Units—Bureau International des Poids et Mesures (BIPM)	www.bipm.fr

The pattern presented here is an extension of that presented in [Fowler 1996].

10.3   Quantity archetype pattern and roadmap

Our model for the Quantity pattern is shown in Figure 10.1.

10.4   Money and Currency

In the business environment, Money is one of the most important types of Quantities, and Currency is one of the most important types of Metrics. We have devoted Chapter 11 to the Money archetype pattern, so we do not discuss it further here.

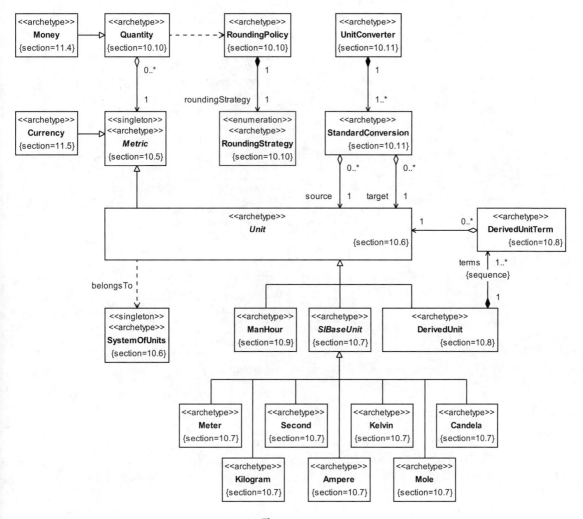

Figure 10.1

10.5 Metric

The Metric archetype represents a standard of measurement.

`Metric` is shown in Figure 10.2.

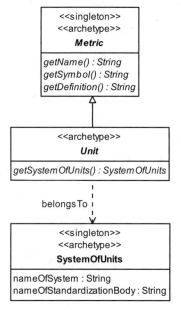

Figure 10.2

`Metric` has the operations described in Table 10.2.

Table 10.2

`Metric` **archetype operations**	
Operation	**Semantics**
`getName()`	Returns the name of the `Metric`, e.g., "meters"
`getSymbol()`	Returns `null` or the standard symbol for the `Metric`, e.g., "m"
`getDefinition()`	Returns the formal definition of the `Metric`, e.g., "The meter is the length of the path travelled by light in vacuum during a time interval of 1/299792458 of a second"

10.6 Unit **and** SystemOfUnits

> The Unit archetype represents a type of Metric that is part of a SystemOfUnits.
>
> The SystemOfUnits archetype represents a set of related Units defined by a standard such as SI.

These archetypes are shown in Figure 10.2.

A good example of a SystemOfUnits is the International System of Units or SI. This is an international standard for weights and measures adopted by the 11th General Conference on Weights and Measures in 1960. The standardization body for SI is the Bureau International des Poids et Mesures (BIPM). The BIPM Web site is at www.bipm.fr.

Taking SI as an example, the nameOfSystem attribute of SystemOfUnits has the value "SI" and the nameOfStandardizationBody attribute has the value "BIPM".

10.7 SIBaseUnit

> The SIBaseUnit archetype represents one of the base units defined in the International System of Units (SI). The different SIBaseUnits are mutually independent.

SI defines seven base units, shown in Figure 10.3.

Each of the SIBaseUnits is defined in Table 10.3.

Table 10.3

SIBaseUnit	**Semantics**	getName()	getSymbol()	getDefinition()*
Meter	Unit of length	"meter"	"m"	"The meter is the length of the path travelled by light in vacuum during a time interval of 1/299792458 of a second"

Table continued on next page

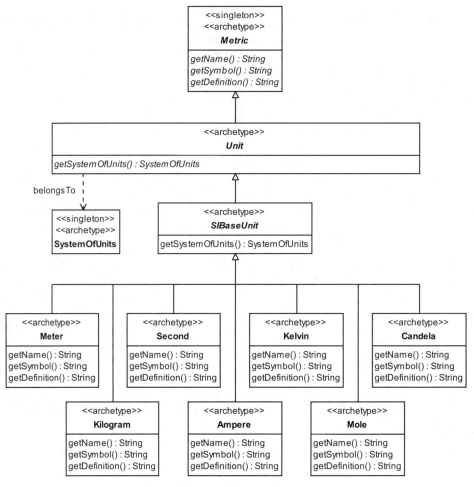

Figure 10.3

Table 10.3 (Continued)

SIBaseUnit	**Semantics**	getName()	getSymbol()	getDefinition()*
Kilogram	Unit of mass	"kilogram"	"kg"	"The kilogram is the unit of mass; it is equal to the mass of the international prototype of the kilogram"

Table 10.3 (Continued)

SIBaseUnit	Semantics	getName()	getSymbol()	getDefinition()*
Second	Unit of time	"second"	"s"	"The second is the duration of 9,192,631,770 periods of the radiation corresponding to the transition between the two hyperfine levels of the ground state of the cesium 133 atom"
Ampere	Unit of electric current	"ampere"	"A"	"The ampere is that constant current which, if maintained in two straight parallel conductors of infinite length, of negligible circular cross-section, and placed 1 meter apart in vacuum, would produce between these conductors a force equal to 2 x 10^{-7} newton per meter of length"
Kelvin	Unit of thermodynamic temperature	"kelvin"	"K"	"The kelvin, unit of thermodynamic temperature, is the fraction 1/273.16 of the thermodynamic temperature of the triple point of water"
Mole	Unit of amount of substance	"mole"	"mol"	"The mole is the amount of substance of a system which contains as many elementary entities as there are atoms in 0.012 kilogram of carbon 12"
Candela	Unit of luminous intensity	"candela"	"cd"	"The candela is the luminous intensity, in a given direction, of a source that emits monochromatic radiation of frequency 540 x 10^{12} hertz and that has a radiant intensity in that direction of 1/683 watt per steradian"

* Definitions from the Bureau International des Poids et Mesures (www.bipm.fr).

10.8 DerivedUnit

All unit systems have derived units.

> The DerivedUnit archetype represents a combination of one or more base Units according to a specific equation.

A derived unit always has the form:

$$A^a B^b C^c \ldots$$

where A, B, C... are units and a, b, c... are powers.

SI defines several derived units. For example, speed is defined as the number of meters travelled in one second. The unit of speed is therefore meters per second. Expressed in SI symbols, this is m/s or ms^{-1}.

So, in the case of speed, the DerivedUnit is:

$$ms^{-1} \text{ or } m^1s^{-1} \quad (\text{because } m = m^1)$$

A DerivedUnit is always made up of a sequence of one or more Derived-UnitTerms. In the example above of speed, the two DerivedUnitTerms are m^1 and s^{-1}.

> The DerivedUnitTerm archetype represents part of a DerivedUnit comprising a single Unit and its power.

Our model of DerivedUnit and DerivedUnitTerm is shown in Figure 10.4. Table 10.4 shows some examples of SI DerivedUnits.

Table 10.4

SI DerivedUnit	DerivedUnitTerm(s)	Represents
m^2	m^2	Area
m^3	m^3	Volume
ms^{-1}	m^1, s^{-1}	Speed, velocity
ms^{-2}	m^1, s^{-2}	Acceleration
m^{-1}	m^{-1}	Wave number

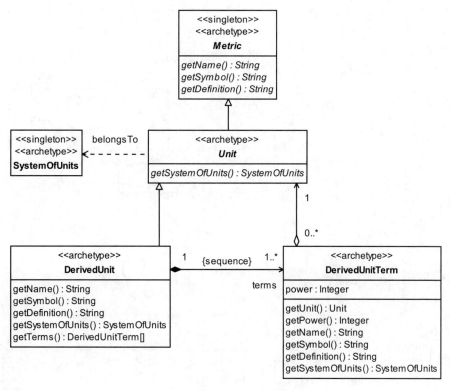

Figure 10.4

10.9 ManHour

Our model shows a type of Unit called ManHour (see Figure 10.5).

The ManHour archetype represents an amount of work corresponding to one person working for one hour.

Notice that this Unit is not part of the SI or any other international standard. We introduce it simply to illustrate that there may be many types of Units. In the case of these nonstandard Units, the operation getSystemOfUnits() should return null. With ManHour, getSymbol() also returns null.

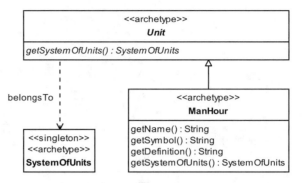

Figure 10.5

10.10 Quantity

The Quantity archetype represents an amount measured in some Metric.

This archetype is shown in Figure 10.6.

Quantity provides a set of functions to perform the following types of operations:

- Arithmetic
- Comparison
- Rounding

We'll look at each of these sets of operations in turn. In the following subsections, the term *target* always refers to the Quantity object that the operation is applied to, and *parameter* always refers to the Quantity object that is passed into the operation.

10.10.1 Arithmetic operations

The Quantity archetype has the arithmetic operations listed in Table 10.5.

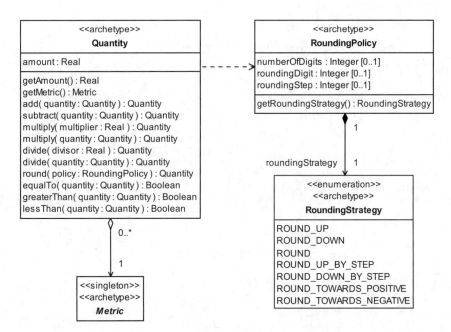

Figure 10.6

Table 10.5

Quantity **archetype arithmetic operations**	
Operation	**Semantics**
add(quantity : Quantity) : Quantity	Adds two Quantity objects
	Precondition: both the target and the parameter Quantity objects must be in the same Metric
	Returns a new Quantity object that has an amount equal to the sum of the amounts of the target Quantity object and the parameter Quantity object
subtract(quantity : Quantity) : Quantity	Subtracts one Quantity object from another
	Precondition: both the target and the parameter Quantity objects must be in the same Metric
	Returns a new Quantity object that has an amount equal to the amount of the target Quantity object minus the amount of the parameter Quantity object

Table continued on next page

Table 10.5   (Continued)

Quantity **archetype arithmetic operations**	
Operation	**Semantics**
multiply(multiplier : Real) : Quantity	Multiplies the Quantity object by the multiplier
	Returns a new Quantity object that has an amount equal to the amount of the target Quantity object multiplied by the multiplier
multiply(quantity : Quantity) : Quantity	Multiplies two Quantity objects
	Returns a new Quantity object that has an amount equal to the product of the amounts of the target Quantity object and the parameter Quantity object
	The Metric of the returned Quantity object is a DerivedUnit given by the following equation:
	TP
	where T is the Unit of the target object and P is the Unit of the parameter object
divide(divisor : Real) : Quantity	Divides the Quantity object by the divisor
	Returns a new Quantity object that has an amount equal to the amount of the target Quantity object divided by the divisor
divide(quantity : Quantity) : Quantity	Divides one Quantity object by another
	Returns a new Quantity object that has an amount equal to the amount of the target Quantity object divided by the amount of the parameter Quantity object
	The Metric of the returned Quantity object is a DerivedUnit given by the following equation:
	TP^{-1}
	where T is the Unit of the target object and P is the Unit of the parameter object

An important point about these arithmetic operations is that they leave both the target Quantity object and the parameter Quantity object *unchanged*. For example, if you have three Quantity objects, q1, q2, and q3, and you perform the following operation:

```
q1 = q2.add( q3 )
```

neither q2 *nor* q3 change in value. The variable q1 gets the new Quantity object returned as a result of the add(...) operation.

10.10.2 Comparison operations

The Quantity archetype has the comparison operations listed in Table 10.6.

Table 10.6

Quantity **archetype comparison operations**	
Operation	**Semantics**
equalTo(quantity : Quantity) : Boolean	Precondition: both the target and the parameter Quantity objects must be in the same Metric
	Returns true if both Quantity objects have the same amount; otherwise, returns false
greaterThan(quantity : Quantity) : Boolean	Precondition: both the target and the parameter Quantity objects must be in the same Metric
	Returns true if the target Quantity object has an amount greater than the amount of the parameter Quantity object; otherwise, returns false
lessThan(quantity : Quantity) : Boolean	Precondition: both the target and the parameter Quantity objects must be in the same Metric
	Returns true if the target Quantity object has an amount less than the amount of the parameter Quantity object; otherwise, returns false

10.10.3 Rounding operation

It is important that all arithmetic and comparison operations occur with well-defined precision. This precision is determined by the requirements of your business application. For example, calculations involving Money (a type of Quantity—see Chapter 11) usually are done at very high precision to avoid cumulative rounding errors. However, at some point, a result needs to be returned that has a realistic precision, and this may involve rounding.

Rounding *reduces* the precision of the amount of a Quantity by approximating it with an amount of lower precision.

For example, if you are in the United Kingdom and you calculate the Value Added Tax (VAT) at a rate of 17.5% on a purchase costing £1, the amount of VAT is £0.175 or 17.5p. As the penny (p) is the smallest unit of coinage in the U.K., this value must be rounded to a whole number of pence before it is presented to the customer.

How rounding occurs is determined by a `RoundingPolicy` (see Figure 10.6) that is passed as a parameter to the `Quantity` archetype's `round(...)` operation.

> The `RoundingPolicy` archetype determines the mathematical semantics of the `Quantity` archetype's `round(...)` operation.

`RoundingPolicy` has the attributes listed in Table 10.7.

Table 10.7

RoundingPolicy **attributes**	
Attribute	**Semantics**
numberOfDigits	The number of digits before or after the decimal place (i.e., the precision that is required)
	The following examples show the result when different levels of rounding are applied to the number 142.312

numberOfDigits	Rounds to
2	Two places to the right of the decimal point (hundredths): 142.31
1	One place to the right of the decimal point (tenths): 142.3
0	No decimal places (the nearest integer): 142
–1	One place to the left of the decimal point (tens): 140
–2	Two places to the left of the decimal point (hundreds): 100

roundingDigit	A test digit with which a digit within the number being rounded is compared— see ROUND in Table 10.8
roundingStep	The multiple to which you want to round
	For example, to round a price of $3.1412 to an accuracy of 5 cents, use a roundingStep of 0.05—see ROUND_UP_BY_STEP in Table 10.8

The RoundingPolicy also has a RoundingStrategy.

 The RoundingStrategy archetype represents an aspect of a RoundingPolicy that determines the type of rounding to be applied.

There are seven RoundingStrategies, described with examples in Table 10.8.

Table 10.8

RoundingStrategy	Semantics
ROUND_UP	Rounds a number to the specified numberOfDigits, moving its value away from zero This means that positive numbers get more positive and negative numbers get more negative <table><tr><th>Number</th><th>Result when numberOfDigits = 1</th></tr><tr><td>4.45</td><td>4.5</td></tr><tr><td>−4.45</td><td>−4.5</td></tr></table>
ROUND_DOWN	Rounds a number to the specified numberOfDigits, moving its value towards zero (i.e., effectively truncates the number at the specified precision) This means that positive numbers get less positive and negative numbers get less negative <table><tr><th>Number</th><th>Result when numberOfDigits = 1</th></tr><tr><td>4.45</td><td>4.4</td></tr><tr><td>−4.45</td><td>−4.4</td></tr></table>
ROUND	Behaves like ROUND_UP if the digit following the specified numberOfDigits is greater than or equal to the specified roundingDigit; otherwise, behaves like ROUND_DOWN Note: the roundingDigit in most common use is 5

Table continued on next page

Table 10.8 (Continued)

RoundingStrategy	Semantics		
	Number	**Result when** numberOfDigits = 1	
ROUND (continued)	4.45	roundingDigit = 5, answer = 4.5	
		roundingDigit = 6, answer = 4.4	
	−4.45	roundingDigit = 5, answer = −4.5	
		roundingDigit = 6, answer = −4.4	
ROUND_UP_BY_STEP	Rounds a number up to the nearest multiple of the specified rounding-Step, moving its value away from zero		
	Allows numbers to be rounded in specified steps—e.g., if prices are to be rounded up to the nearest 25 cents		
	Note that because the roundingStep also dictates the required precision, a separate numberOfDigits is not required		
	Number	**Result when** roundingStep = 0.25	
	4.45	4.50	
	−4.45	−4.50	
ROUND_DOWN_BY_STEP	Rounds a number down to the nearest multiple of the specified roundingStep, moving its value towards zero		
	Allows numbers to be rounded in specified steps—e.g., if prices are to be rounded down to the nearest 25 cents		
	Note that because the roundingStep also dictates the required precision, a separate numberOfDigits is not required		
	Number	**Result when** roundingStep = 0.25	
	4.45	4.25	
	−4.45	−4.25	
ROUND_TOWARDS_POSITIVE	Behaves like ROUND_UP for positive numbers and like ROUND_DOWN for negative numbers		
	This means that positive numbers get more positive and negative numbers get less negative (see Figure 10.7)		
	Number	**Result when** numberOfDigits = 1	
	4.45	4.5	
	−4.45	−4.4	

Table 10.8   (Continued)

RoundingStrategy	Semantics
ROUND_TOWARDS_NEGATIVE	Behaves like ROUND_DOWN for positive numbers and like ROUND_UP for negative numbers This means that positive numbers get less positive and negative numbers get more negative (see Figure 10.7)

Number	Result when numberOfDigits = 1
4.45	4.4
–4.45	–4.5

Because RoundingStrategies can be quite hard to understand, we have diagrammed them in Figure 10.7. This figure shows the number line, centered on zero, and the effects of each RoundingStrategy on a positive and a negative number.

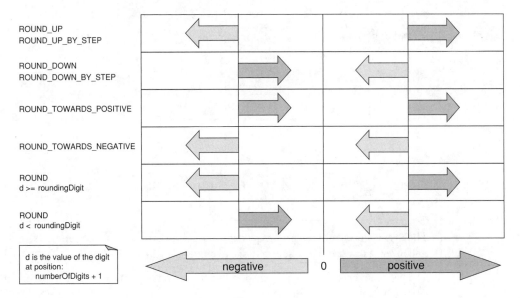

Figure 10.7

The rounding capability we describe here is a superset of that found in spreadsheets such as Microsoft Excel and in business system packages such as SAP. You can see how our rounding approach maps onto Excel functions in Table 10.9.

Table 10.9

RoundingStrategy	Equivalent Excel function
ROUND_UP	ROUNDUP(...)
ROUND_DOWN	ROUNDDOWN(...)
ROUND	ROUND(...) Uses implicit roundingDigit of 5
ROUND_UP_BY_STEP	CEILING(...) The sign of the significance must match that of the number being rounded
ROUND_DOWN_BY_STEP	FLOOR(...) The sign of the significance must match that of the number being rounded
ROUND_TOWARDS_POSITIVE	N/A
ROUND_TOWARDS_NEGATIVE	N/A
RoundingPolicy attribute	**Excel parameter**
numberOfDigits	num_digits
roundingDigit	N/A
roundingStep	significance

10.11 StandardConversion **and** UnitConverter

The StandardConversion archetype defines a conversionFactor that can be used to convert a Quantity in a source Unit to a Quantity in a target Unit.

The UnitConverter archetype is responsible for converting a Quantity in a source Unit to a Quantity in a target Unit.

UnitConverter provides a single operation, convert(...) which tries to find a StandardConversion that references the correct Units for its quantity and targetUnit parameters.

The conversion process is very simple. The amount of the Quantity of the source Unit is multiplied by the conversionFactor to produce a Quantity of the target Unit.

StandardConversion and UnitConverter are shown in Figure 10.8.

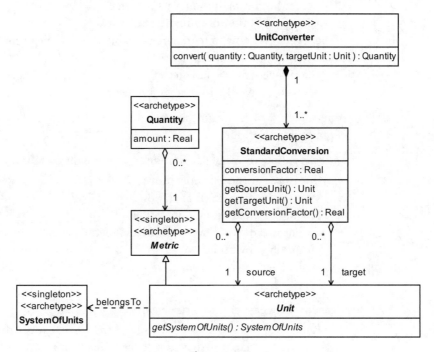

Figure 10.8

10.12 Summary

In this chapter we looked at the Quantity archetype pattern. This is a pattern for representing quantities of things. We covered the topics listed below.

- Metric: how to represent a standard of measurement for quantities
- Unit: how to represent a type of Metric that is part of a SystemOfUnits

- SystemOfUnits: how to represent a set of related Units defined by a standard such as the International System of Units (SI)
  - SIBaseUnit: how to represent one of the base units defined in SI
    - Meter: SI unit of length
    - Kilogram: SI unit of mass
    - Second: SI unit of time
    - Ampere: SI unit of electric current
    - Kelvin: SI unit of temperature
    - Mole: SI unit of amount of substance
    - Candela: SI unit of luminous intensity
  - DerivedUnit: how to represent a combination of one or more base Units according to a specific equation
    - DerivedUnitTerm: how to represent a term (i.e., a single Unit and its power, e.g., s^{-1}) within a DerivedUnit

- ManHour: how to represent the amount of work corresponding to one person working for one hour

- Quantity: how to specify an amount that is measured in some Metric
  - How to use arithmetic operations
  - How to use comparison operations
  - How to use the rounding operation
    - RoundingPolicy: how to define the mathematical semantics of the rounding operation
    - RoundingStrategy: how to represent the type of rounding to be applied

- StandardConversion and UnitConverter:
  - StandardConversion: how to define a conversionFactor that can be used to convert a Quantity in a source Unit to a Quantity in a target Unit
  - UnitConverter: how to represent the conversion process

Chapter 11

Money archetype pattern

11.1 Business context

In this chapter we describe the Money archetype pattern.

The purpose of money is to allow trade to take place without barter. Instead of a direct exchange of goods or services for other goods or services, these are exchanged for some token that represents purchasing power. This token is money.

Nowadays, money consists of a number of floating currencies whose exchange rates are set by the money markets. The value of a unit of currency depends on the degree of trust that the world money markets place on the government, or other body, that issues that currency.

The value of each currency moves up and down relative to all the other currencies, according to supply and demand speculation. Because of this, modern money has little *intrinsic* value—as we note above, it is primarily a social convention based on trust. For example, coins have some small value as scrap metal, but this value is usually *much* less than their face value. Bank notes really have no intrinsic value because they are made of paper or plastic that typically has little or no recycling value.

This wasn't always the case—in the West, money has been based on gold and silver (the bimetallic standard), silver (the silver standard), and gold (the gold standard). All of these standards guaranteed that an amount of money in a standard currency could be exchanged (at least in principle) for a defined weight of one of these precious metals. In metal standard currencies, money is a token representing a weight of precious metal.

There has recently been a small resurgence of currencies based on precious metal standards on the Internet. For example, www.e-gold.com offers four Internet currencies, e-gold, e-silver, e-platinum, and e-palladium, that are backed by weights of gold, silver, platinum, and palladium, respectively. Each unit of these currencies represents a weight (either a troy ounce or a gram) of one of these precious metals that is stored in vaults in Europe or Dubai. You can find an exchange rate for weights of these precious metals to/from any currency in the world, so any of these e-metal currencies may be used as a universal currency, subject only to the condition that it is recognized by all parties involved in a particular financial transaction.

There have been recent attempts to set up universal Internet currencies (e.g., beenz and flooz). However, at the time of writing, both of these currencies have been withdrawn. Without the backing of a government or of precious metal, consumer confidence in these currencies never reached a sufficiently high level to sustain them. Also, given that money is based on trust, their slightly flippant "new economy" names probably did little to inspire the necessary customer confidence.

Despite the overwhelming prevalence of money as a means of conducting trade, barter is still alive and has found a home on the Internet. Check out sites such as www.barterwww.com for more details.

There are now even completely virtual currencies that exist only in virtual worlds and yet still have an exchange rate against "real" currencies. For example, in the adventure role-playing game Asheron's Call (www.microsoft.com/games/zone/asheronscall), a unit of currency called the Platinum Scarab can be used to buy virtual equipment for a player's characters. Through a mechanism in the game known as Secure Trade, items and currency may be exchanged between players. This opens the door for the virtual world to reach out into the real world of commerce, and as we write this, on eBay, you can buy (or sell) 1,000 Platinum Scarabs for about $200. This gives this completely virtual currency an exchange rate of 5 Platinum Scarabs to the dollar in the real world.

In the rest of this chapter, we will discuss a fairly mainstream notion of money. Nevertheless, you will find that the archetypes we present here may also be applied, perhaps with modification, to some of the newer types of money that are emerging.

11.2 Compliance with existing standards

The models presented in this section comply with the standards listed in Table 11.1.

Table 11.1

Standard	Contents	Reference
OMG Currency Specification	A standard to support international currency	www.omg.org/technology/documents/formal/currency
ISO 4217	Three- and two-letter currency codes, currency numbers, and currency names	www.iso.org
ISO 3166	Two-letter country codes and country names	www.iso.org

11.3 Money **archetype pattern overview and roadmap**

The complete model for the Money archetype pattern is shown in Figure 11.1.

11.4 Money

Money is an official or commonly accepted medium of exchange that can be used to buy goods and services.

> The Money archetype represents an amount of a specific Currency. This Currency is acceptedIn one or more Locales.

The Money, Currency, and Locale archetypes are shown in Figure 11.2. In Section 11.7, we'll look at how the operations that Money inherits from Quantity work. For convenience, Money has an operation, getCurrency(), that has the same semantics as the getMetric() operation it inherits from Quantity.

Although we are concerned with archetypes in this book and *not* implementation details, we'd like to point out that you have to think quite carefully about implementing the Money archetype. In particular you need to consider the maximum amount of Money to represent. In banking applications, this can be very large.

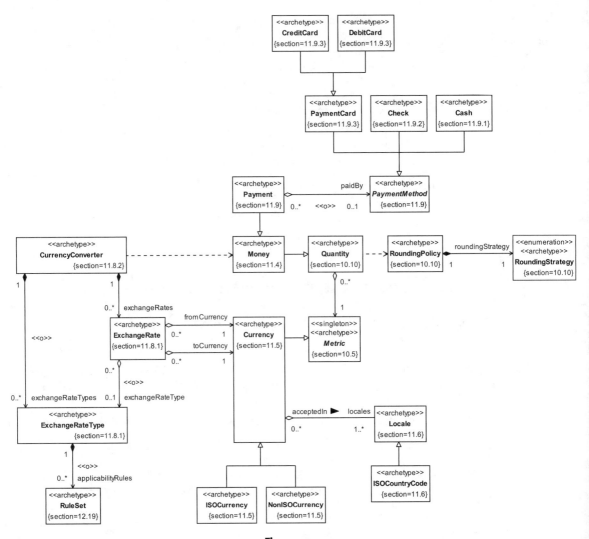

Figure 11.1

11.5 Currency

 The Currency archetype represents a Metric or standard of value for measuring Money.

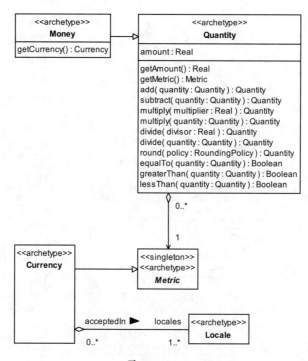

Figure 11.2

The Currency archetype represents a generalized notion of currency, as shown in Figure 11.3.

Currency implements the three abstract operations of Metric and adds getLocales(). Note that getSymbol() returns the majorUnitSymbol.

Currency has the attributes shown in Table 11.2.

Table 11.2

Currency **archetype**	
Attribute	**Semantics**
name	The name of the Currency, e.g., "Pound Sterling"
definition	A description of the Currency, e.g., "The monetary unit of the U.K."—null if a description is not required

Table continued on next page

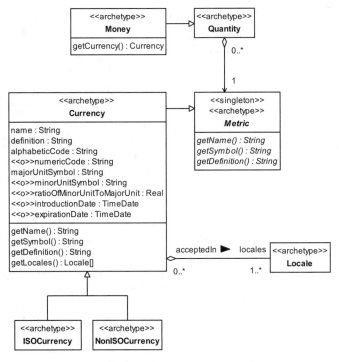

Figure 11.3

Table 11.2 (Continued)

Currency **archetype**	
Attribute	**Semantics**
alphabeticCode	An alphabetic code that represents the currency, e.g., "EUR" for the Euro
«o»numericCode	A numeric code optionally assigned to the Currency For example, the ISO 4217 standard assigns the numeric code "826" to the pound sterling (U.K.) and "840" to the U.S. dollar
majorUnitSymbol	The symbol used to denote the major unit of the currency, e.g., in the U.K., the major unit is the pound, symbol "£"

Table 11.2 (Continued)

Currency **archetype**	
Attribute	**Semantics**
«o»minorUnitSymbol	The symbol used to denote the minor unit of the currency, e.g., in the U.K., the minor unit is pence, symbol "p"
	If the currency does not have a minor unit (e.g., the Turkish Lira), this attribute should have the value null
«o»ratioOfMinorUnitToMajorUnit	The ratio of the value of the minor unit to that of the major unit
	For example, for dollars there are 100 cents to 1 dollar; so the ratio of the minor unit to the major unit is
	100/1 = 100
	If the currency does not have a minor unit, this attribute should have the value 1
«o»introductionDate	The date on which the Currency became valid
«o»expirationDate	The date after which the Currency is no longer valid

The unique identifier for a Currency is its alphabeticCode.

At present, there are two fundamentally different types of currency—those that are specified by ISO and those that are not. The ISO currencies are standard international currencies, whereas the non-ISO currencies may be arbitrary currencies such as American Airlines AAdvantage Miles or Platinum Ounces.

You can model this situation with two subclasses of Currency, ISOCurrency and NonISOCurrency, as shown in Figure 11.3.

> The ISOCurrency archetype represents a type of Currency whose name, alphabetic-Code, and numericCode are defined in ISO 4217.
>
> The NonISOCurrency archetype represents a type of Currency that is not defined in ISO 4217.

You can find an example implementation of ISOCurrency, and hyperlinks to the appropriate ISO standards, on our Web site (www.businessarchetypes.com).

11.6 Locale **and** ISOCountryCode

> The Locale archetype represents a general notion of place, location, or context.

Each Currency may be acceptedIn one or more Locales.

- The pound sterling (an ISO currency) is accepted primarily within the United Kingdom.
- The Euro (an ISO currency) is accepted throughout most of the European Community.
- The AAdvantage Mile (a non-ISO currency) is accepted only within the American Airlines Mileage program.

As far as a Currency is concerned, a Locale simply provides a context in which amounts of the Currency have value.

The Locale archetype is illustrated in Figure 11.4. This may have many subclasses that represent different types of locales.

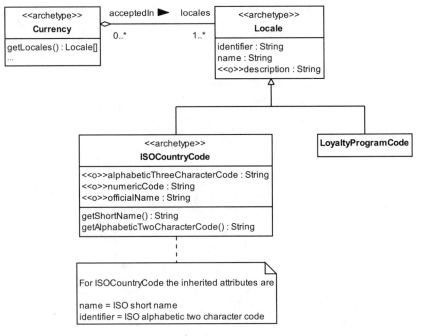

Figure 11.4

Each `Locale` has a unique `identifier`, a name, and an optional description. The semantics of these attributes are summarized in Table 11.3.

Table 11.3

Locale **archetype**	
Attribute	**Semantics**
`identifier`	A unique identifier for the `Locale`
`name`	The name of the `Locale`
`«o»description`	A brief description of the `Locale`

Many types of `Locale` are possible. For example, in Figure 11.4 we show a subclass called `LoyaltyProgramCode`. This class represents the code for a `Locale` such as the American Airlines AAdvantage loyalty program.

`ISOCountryCode` is the most significant subclass of `Locale`. Because it represents an ISO standard, we consider it to be an archetype.

> The `ISOCountryCode` archetype is a type of `Locale` that represents an identifier for a country as defined in ISO 3166.

Table 11.4 summarizes the semantics of the attributes of `ISOCountryCode`.

Table 11.4

ISOCountryCode **archetype**	
Attribute	**Semantics**
`Identifier`	The alphabetic two-character code (alpha 2 code) that represents the country, e.g., "DE" for Germany
	This attribute is inherited from `Locale`

Table continued on next page

Table 11.4 (Continued)

ISOCountryCode **archetype**	
Attribute	**Semantics**
name	The short name of the country as listed in ISO 3166, e.g., "Germany" This attribute is inherited from Locale
«o»description	A brief description of the country (this isn't provided by ISO 3166) This attribute is inherited from Locale
«o»alphabeticThreeCharacterCode	The alphabetic three-character code (alpha 3 code) that represents the country, e.g., "DEU" for Germany
«o»numericCode	The numeric three-digit code that represents the country, e.g., "276" for Germany and "008" for Albania—note that this number may have leading zeros and should therefore be represented by a string
«o»officialName	The official name of the country as listed in ISO 3166, e.g., "Federal Republic of Germany"

You can find an example implementation of ISOCountryCode, and hyperlinks to the appropriate ISO standards, on our Web site (www.businessarchetypes.com).

11.7 Working with Money

In the following sections, we'll look briefly at how Money implements each type of operation that it inherits from Quantity (see Figure 11.5). A full description of Quantity's operations is provided in Section 10.10.

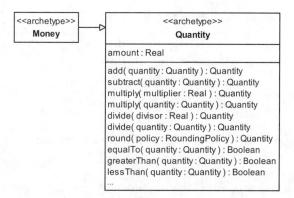

Figure 11.5

11.7.1 Arithmetic operations

Details of how Money implements the arithmetic operations inherited from Quantity are summarized in Table 11.5.

Table 11.5

Money **archetype—implementation of** Quantity **archetype arithmetic operations**	
Operation	**Implementation**
add(quantity : Quantity) : Quantity subtract(quantity : Quantity) : Quantity	Target and parameter Quantities must be of type Money and in the same Currency
multiply(multiplier : Real) : Quantity divide(divisor : Real) : Quantity	Identical to the implementations in Quantity
multiply(quantity : Quantity) : Quantity	Not implemented—not meaningful to multiply two Money objects or Money with any other Quantity
divide(quantity : Quantity) : Quantity	Money cannot apply this operation where the target and parameter Quantities are both Money objects Can be applied where the target Quantity is a Money object of a particular Currency and the parameter Quantity is a nonmonetary Metric—this allows you to express a cost per unit, e.g., Euros per kilo

11.7.2 Comparison operations

Details of how Money implements the comparison operations inherited from Quantity are summarized in Table 11.6.

Table 11.6

Money **archetype—implementation of** Quantity **archetype comparison operations**	
Operation	**Implementation**
equalTo(quantity : Quantity) : Boolean greaterThan(quantity : Quantity) : Boolean lessThan(quantity : Quantity) : Boolean	Target and parameter Quantities must be of type Money and in the same Currency

11.7.3 Rounding operation

Money implements the rounding operation inherited from Quantity without changes.

11.8 ExchangeRate **and** CurrencyConverter

Although there are parallels between ExchangeRate and StandardConversion, and between CurrencyConverter and UnitConverter (see Section 10.11), the semantic and practical differences are sufficient for us to model ExchangeRate and CurrencyConverter as independent archetypes rather than as subtypes of StandardConversion and UnitConverter, respectively.

11.8.1 ExchangeRate

> The ExchangeRate archetype represents the price of one type of money relative to another.

For example, at the time we're writing this paragraph, 1 EUR = 0.860453 USD. This means that we can buy 1 Euro for about 86 cents.

There are several important points about ExchangeRates.

1. ExchangeRates may vary rapidly with time. In fact, the Euro to dollar rate has changed in the time it took us to write this sentence. It is now 1 EUR = 0.860502 USD.
2. ExchangeRates vary according to who is making the transaction. Banks and Bureaux de Change get different (better) exchange rates than individuals. So can businesses, depending on the amount or frequency of the exchange transactions.
3. ExchangeRates have a history.

The ExchangeRate archetype is shown in Figure 11.6.

Each ExchangeRate has a period of validity. This is determined by the following attributes:

- validFrom: specifies the point in time after which the ExchangeRate becomes valid
- validTo: specifies the point in time at which the ExchangeRate is no longer valid

An ExchangeRateType may be optionally associated with each ExchangeRate.

> The ExchangeRateType archetype represents a category of ExchangeRate that determines its applicability.

For many applications, there may be only a single ExchangeRateType in operation, but for others, there may be multiple ExchangeRateTypes in force. An ExchangeRateType may have a set of rules that determines the conditions under which it may be offered—see our Rule archetype pattern in Chapter 12 for a complete discussion of rules.

11.8.2 CurrencyConverter

> The CurrencyConverter archetype converts an amount of a source Currency into an equivalent amount of a target Currency by applying an ExchangeRate.

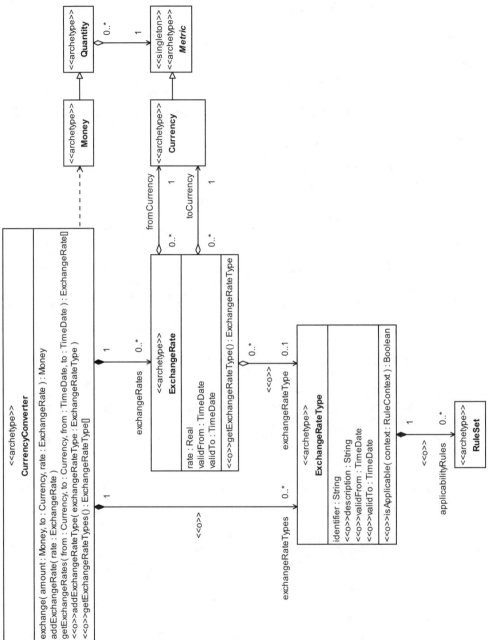

Figure 11.6

You can see that CurrencyConverter (Figure 11.6) has a number of responsibilities, including the following:

- Converting amounts of a source Currency into equivalent amounts of a target Currency by applying an ExchangeRate
- Managing a set of current and historic ExchangeRates
- Managing a set of ExchangeRateTypes (optional)

Essentially, the CurrencyConverter archetype provides a Bureaux de Change service.

The CurrencyConverter maintains a list of ExchangeRates. The ExchangeRates need to be kept up to date according to the specific requirements of your business. This may be a real-time update (for currency traders) or hourly or daily updates (for Bureaux de Change and travel agents). When an ExchangeRate changes, the old rate can be kept as history.

Note that if you buy an amount of a Currency, an Order is raised (either explicitly or implicitly), and a charge or commission may be added to the Order by the organization providing the exchange service (see Section 9.8).

11.9 Payment

The Payment archetype represents Money paid by one Party to another, in return for goods or services.

For much of human history, Payments involved moving large amounts of physical money around. This was (and is) both expensive and risky. In recent times this practice increasingly is giving way to Payments that are electronic in nature.

Although, in principle, electronic Payments can travel at close to the speed of light, they generally travel much slower than that in practice. Sometimes it can take several days for an electronic Payment to find its way from one account to another, even within the same bank. Electronic Payments can generate large amounts of revenue by resting in holding accounts as "float" on their way between source and target accounts.

The Payment archetype is shown in Figure 11.7 and has the attributes shown in Table 11.7.

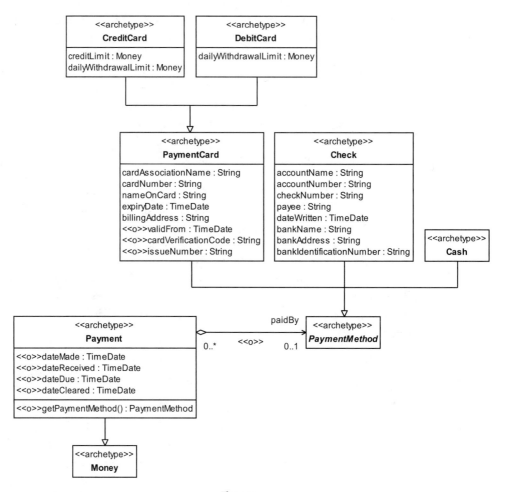

Figure 11.7

Table 11.7

Payment **archetype**	
Attribute	**Semantics**
«o»dateMade	The date on which the Payment was made by the payer (this attribute is most likely to be required by the payer's electronic systems)
«o»dateReceived	The date on which the Payment was received by the payee (this attribute is most likely to be required by the payee's electronic systems)

Table 11.7 (Continued)

Payment **archetype**	
Attribute	**Semantics**
«o»dateDue	The date on which the payee expects to receive the Payment
«o»dateCleared	The date on which the Payment is cleared by a banking system or other payment processing mechanism

Optionally, Payment may also have a PaymentMethod.

> The PaymentMethod archetype represents the medium by which a Payment may be made.

There are many types of PaymentMethod, and we show some examples in Figure 11.7. The semantics of the Cash, Check, and PaymentCard payment methods are very familiar to most people and are discussed below.

Other PaymentMethods also exist, including various automatic bank payments. In the United Kingdom, for example, standing orders and direct debits are in common use. With standing orders, the payer gives instructions for specified sums to be transferred at specified intervals from their account to a payee's account. With direct debits, the payer authorizes a payee to request variable sums at specified intervals from the payer's account to the payee's account.

We intend to discuss alternative payment methods in a future book.

11.9.1 Cash

> The Cash archetype represents a Payment made in a physical amount of a Currency.

This is the simplest type of PaymentMethod. It has no attributes and simply acts as a flag to indicate that a particular Payment is paidBy an amount of physical money such as U.S. dollars.

The advantage of Cash is its anonymity. You can see that the archetype holds no information about Parties or accounts. If you are concerned about privacy, a Cash transaction is the best way to achieve this. These transactions are difficult to trace.

Thus the disadvantage of Cash is also its anonymity. It can be moved from place to place with no record. This is why it is the favored medium of commerce for criminals and "black economy" workers who avoid government taxes and regulations.

It's interesting to note that since 1969, the highest denomination bill in circulation in the United States has been the $100 bill. These notes are produced by the Bureau of Engraving and Printing (www.bep.treas.gov), which produces about 37 million notes a day with a face value of about $696 million. The reason for the absence of higher denomination notes is partly because they were never that popular and partly to make it difficult for criminals to move large quantities of U.S. currency around the world.

U.S. bank notes of denominations $500, $1,000, $5,000, and $10,000 were last printed in 1945 and were issued until 1969. Although they are still legal tender, most of these notes are now in the hands of collectors or dealers.

11.9.2 Check

> The Check archetype represents a bill of exchange drawn on a bank and payable on demand—in other words, a written order to pay Money to a Party.

Each Check holds the key information listed in Table 11.8.

Table 11.8

Check **archetype**	
Attribute	**Semantics**
accountName	The name of the account on which the Check is drawn
accountNumber	The number of the account on which the Check is drawn
checkNumber	The number of the Check This is a unique identifier for the Check within the context of the account on which it is drawn

Table 11.8 (Continued)

Check **archetype**	
Attribute	**Semantics**
payee	The name of the Party to which the Check is made payable
dateWritten	The date on which the Check was written Usually Checks are valid only for a set time after this date
bankName	The name of the bank that issued the Check
bankAddress	The address of the bank that issued the Check
bankIdentificationNumber	The unique identifier of the bank that issued the Check This is also known as a *bank routing number* in the U.S. and is called a *bank sort code* in the U.K.

Most Checks are *not* redeemed as Cash but rather in a transfer of Money between two bank accounts. We hope to look at Accounts in a future book.

11.9.3 PaymentCard

The first credit card was introduced by Diner's Club, Inc., in 1950. Since then, the notion of an identifying card as a mechanism of payment has, in our opinion, become sufficiently pervasive to be considered archetypal despite its short history. (There are now over one billion payment cards in use around the world.)

> The PaymentCard archetype represents a physical token such as a plastic card that authorizes the Party identified on it to charge the cost of goods or services to an account.

Attributes of the PaymentCard archetype are listed in Table 11.9.

Table 11.9

PaymentCard **archetype**	
Attribute	**Semantics**
cardAssociationName	The name of the card association that manages the card network to which the PaymentCard belongs, e.g., "MasterCard", "Visa"
cardNumber	The number on the PaymentCard
nameOnCard	The name of the Party authorized to use the PaymentCard
expiryDate	The date after which the PaymentCard is no longer valid
billingAddress	The address to which account statements are sent
«o»validFrom	An optional date from which the PaymentCard is valid
«o»cardVerificationCode	A verification code printed on the back of the PaymentCard At present, this is a three-digit number
«o»issueNumber	A number used by the issuing authority to uniquely identify the issue of the PaymentCard

In face-to-face transactions where a PaymentCard is present, point-of-sale machines can read a verification code directly from the card. At present, this is encoded in the card's magnetic stripe and is known as the Card Verification Value (CVV) by Visa and as the Card Validation Code (CVC) by MasterCard. When the PaymentCard is *not* present, the cardholder can supply a cardVerificationCode as an anti-fraud measure. This code is usually a three-digit number written on the back of the card. For Visa the code is known as the CVV2, and for MasterCard it is known as the CVC2.

There are many different types of PaymentCard. In Figure 11.7 you can see two specific examples, CreditCard and DebitCard. These are so widely used that we have modeled them as archetypes. There are also many other types of PaymentCard that are specific to particular payment scenarios and are not in any meaningful sense archetypal.

The CreditCard archetype represents a PaymentCard that comes with a line of credit.

The DebitCard archetype represents a PaymentCard where Payments are immediately debited from a source account.

In this section we have provided just enough information so that you can represent `PaymentCards` in selling systems. We defer a more complete discussion of `PaymentCard` and the different types of `PaymentCards` to a future book.

11.10 Summary

In this chapter we looked at the `Money` archetype pattern. This is a pattern for representing money. We covered the topics listed below.

- `Money`: how to represent money as an amount of a specific `Currency`
- `Currency`: how to represent a currency
  - `ISOCurrency`: how to represent a type of currency whose details are defined in ISO 4217
  - `NonISOCurrency`: how to represent a currency whose details are not defined in ISO 4217
- `Locale`: how to represent a location or context within which a `Currency` is accepted (i.e., has value)
  - `ISOCountryCode`: how to represent an identifier for a country as defined in ISO 3166
- Working with `Money`:
  - How to use arithmetic operations
  - How to use comparison operations
  - How to use the rounding operation
- `ExchangeRate` and `CurrencyConverter`:
  - `ExchangeRate`: how to represent the price of one type of money relative to another
    - `ExchangeRateType`: how to represent a category of `ExchangeRates`
  - `CurrencyConverter`: how to represent the function of converting `Money` in one `Currency` into an equivalent amount of another `Currency`
- `Payment`: how to represent `Money` paid by one `Party` to another
- `PaymentMethod`: how to represent the medium by which a `Payment` may be made
  - `Cash`: how to represent a `Payment` made in a physical amount of a `Currency`
  - `Check`: how to represent a bill of exchange drawn on a bank and payable on demand

■ PaymentCard: how to represent a physical token such as a plastic card that authorizes the Party identified on it to charge the cost of goods or services to an account
  – CreditCard: how to represent a PaymentCard that comes with a line of credit
  – DebitCard: how to represent a PaymentCard where Payments are immediately debited from a source account

Chapter 12

Ru1e **archetype pattern**

12.1 **Business context**

In various places in this book, we have mentioned rules. In this chapter, we explain exactly what we mean by rules and provide a simple Ru1e pattern.

When we first thought of presenting a Ru1e model, we expected it to be a normal pattern rather than an archetype pattern. However, as you will see, we have been able to establish a one-to-one correspondence between this pattern and the concepts of formal logic. As such, we believe that the pattern really represents mathematical, and therefore archetypal, notions of rules in a very direct way.

Our main purpose in providing this Ru1e pattern is to give you a concrete basis for understanding and working with the various kinds of rules you will encounter in business analysis and system development. You may also be able to use it to implement simple rules-based systems.

You can download complete Python source code for a working implementation of our Ru1e pattern from our Web site (www.businessarchetypes.com). This is made available to you as open source under the GNU Lesser General Public License (LGPL—www.opensource.org).

You can find a related rules pattern in the paper "A Pattern Language for Adaptive and Scalable Business Rule Construction" by Ali Arsanjani. This paper can be found at www.cbdiforum.com in the patterns section and describes different ways of implementing rules in some detail.

12.2 Ru1e **archetype pattern and roadmap**

Figure 12.1 shows our Ru1e archetype pattern.

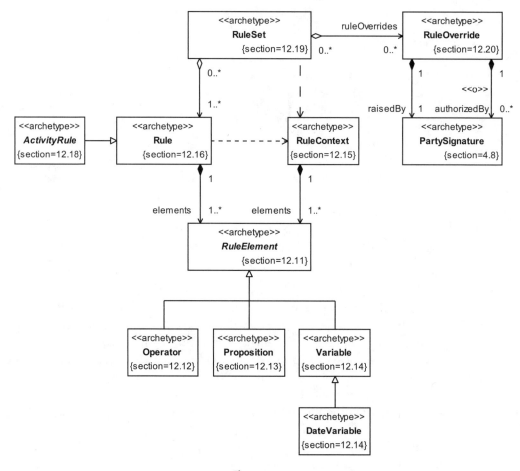

Figure 12.1

12.3 What are rules?

Rules are constraints. The typical dictionary definition of a rule is:

- A code or principle that governs or constrains action or behavior (i.e., a constraint on an action)
- An established or normal quality or condition of things (i.e., a constraint on the state of something)

So some rules are simple statements of fact about the state of something, while others may be used explicitly to trigger actions. These two aspects of rules are of equal importance.

12.4 Business rules and system rules

You may find it useful to distinguish between the business and system aspects of rules. In the rest of this chapter, we will use the following terms.

A rule is a constraint on something.

A business rule is a constraint on the operation of the business.

A business system rule is a constraint on the operation of the software systems of the business.

We will use the term *rule* when we are talking generally about rules and the terms *business rule* and *business system rule* when we need to be more specific.

12.5 Business rules

A business rule may constrain the business in two fundamentally different ways.

1. It may constrain the *structure* of the business. For example, business rules may determine the relationship between various subunits of the organization, such as marketing and manufacturing.
2. It may constrain the *operation* of the business. For example, business rules determine the sequence of actions in business workflows such as order processing.

Business rules are pervasive and exist at all levels of the organization. For example, every company incorporated in the United Kingdom must have a Memorandum and Articles of Association that contain a series of statements about how the company will operate and the business activities in which the company will be involved. These statements are high-level business rules that determine, in a very broad way, what the company can and can't do. There are also much more specific business rules, such as policies about product returns.

In a sense, business rules form a hierarchy from the very general to the very specific. This hierarchy is itself subject to the constraint that all of its rules must be consistent with each other. However, because organizations generally don't capture their business rules in any formal way, this consistency is often absent. Clearly, being able to capture and formalize business rules can have a very positive effect on the activities of a business.

A detailed discussion of business rules is beyond the scope of this book. We refer you to [von Halle 2002] for more information.

12.6 Business system rules

Business system rules are specific constraints on the operation of the software systems of the business. They are derived from business rules via a software engineering process, as illustrated in Figure 12.2.

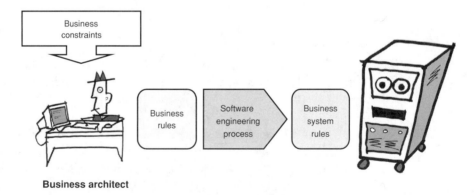

Figure 12.2

This looks like a fairly simple process, but it can be fraught with difficulty. For example, many organizations find it difficult to distinguish between real business rules and rules that arise only as artifacts of existing software systems.

This can lead to the situation in Figure 12.3, where the systems themselves constrain the activities of the whole business.

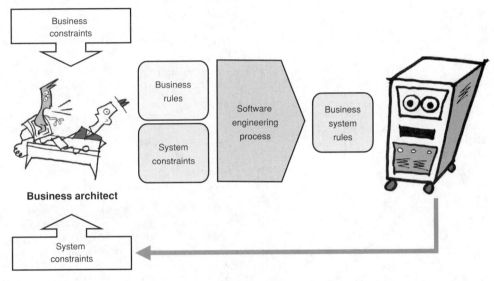

Figure 12.3

Organizations that have many legacy software systems can be particularly prone to this sort of problem. Indeed, some companies may predicate their entire business process on outdated business rules encoded in legacy systems. This can lead to many missed business opportunities.

12.7 Rules and business processes

A business process is a sequence of business activities that, when executed, is designed to lead to some business benefit.

You can model a business process using UML activity diagrams. These diagrams contain business activities, business events, transitions, decisions, guard conditions, and states. The semantics for these elements are summarized in Table 12.1.

Table 12.1

Component	Example in Figure 12.4	Semantics
Business activity	A1	A piece of work performed in pursuit of some business benefit
Business event	e1	A notable occurrence in the operation of the business
Transition	The arrow joining A2 and A4	The movement from one business activity to another
Decision	The diamond shape	A branch in the process where one of two or more transitions is chosen
Guard condition	[c1]	A Boolean expression based on some aspect of the state of the business A transition can occur only if its guard condition evaluates to true
Start state	The filled circle	The beginning of the business process
Stop state	The bull's-eye	The end of the business process

Figure 12.4 shows the UML syntax for a business process made up of four business activities.

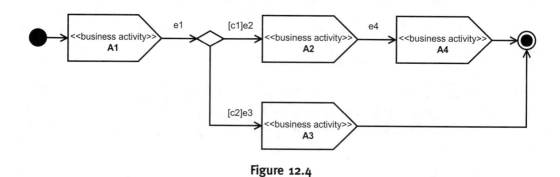

Figure 12.4

Activity diagrams have a very rich syntax—see [Arlow 2001] for full details.

Rules can affect business processes in two ways.

1. They can embody information about the state of the business.
2. They can conditionally trigger business activities based on that information.

By *state of the business*, we mean all of the information relevant to the business at a particular time, that is, any piece of information that the business may use in making a particular decision (e.g., the number of sales transactions pending, the number of active customers, the specific details of those customers, and so on).

Figure 12.5 shows a very simple example of how business rules and business system rules can control a business process.

Figure 12.5

The business process here is about selling an insurance policy to a customer. This process can be summarized as:

```
if customerAge >= minimumAge then
        sellPolicy()
```

The process requires three rules for its operation. Two of these rules just embody information, while the third rule triggers a business activity. The three rules are listed in Table 12.2.

Table 12.2

ID	Rule	Type	Semantics
1	`customerAge = 17`	Information	A fact about the customer
2	`minimumAge = 18`	Information	A fact about the business (here, the circumstances under which it is prepared to do business)
3	`if customerAge >= minimumAge then` `    sellPolicy()`	Activity	A rule that triggers a business activity All rules that trigger activities take this `if/then` form

The informational context provided by rules 1 and 2 determines the outcome of rule 3. We call this informational context the *rule context*.

Typically, the `minimumAge` rule will *not* change (or will change only slowly), so this type of rule is often known as an *invariant*.

Because rule 3 may trigger a business activity, it is called an *activity rule*. This distinguishes it from rules such as `minimumAge = 18` that do not, by themselves, trigger any activities. The expression `sellpolicy()` indicates a business activity that is contingent on the expression `customerAge >= minimumAge` being true. In fact, the latter expression acts as a precondition for the `sellPolicy()` business activity.

This simple example highlights the essence of business rules. Business rules determine the direction of a business process by constraining the range of possible business activities at any particular time, based on the current state of the business.

12.8 The physical location of rules

If you are working with rules of any type, you need to decide where they should be located.

In most organizations, business rules tend to exist implicitly in legal documents, business process and activity guidelines, policies, and even vision statements. It is unfortunately still quite rare for a business to make its rules explicit in any way.

Business system rules can exist in three places:

1. In the source code
2. As database triggers
3. As explicit rules managed and manipulated by a rules engine

Each of these locations has its advantages and disadvantages, as summarized in Table 12.3.

Table 12.3

Location	Advantages	Disadvantages
Source code	Applications have good performance	Rules are *very* hard to change, and it is expensive to make the change Rules are generally not reusable across applications Applications are inflexible
Database triggers	Rules are more accessible to change Applications are more flexible	Rules are coupled to data Rules are not reusable across data sets Not all rules can be encoded in this way
Explicit rules managed by a rules engine	Rules are completely accessible to change, and it is easy and inexpensive to make the change Rules are made explicit and so are open to inspection and review Rules are separate from applications and data Applications are very flexible	Applications may not perform as well as they would with hard-coded rules—this depends on the rules engine

You can see from the table that there are a lot of advantages to making business system rules as explicit as possible and in keeping them separate from applications and data. This is the approach we discuss in the rest of this chapter.

12.9 Rules and formal logic

In our opinion, the best way to model rules is to use the principles of formal logic.

The formal (or symbolic) logic we use in this chapter appeared in 1847 when George Boole published *The Mathematical Analysis of Logic* [Boole 1998]. It has since become a very well established branch of mathematics and provides the basis for modern computers.

In the next subsections we introduce the key concepts in formal logic, propositions and variables, as a basis for creating our Rule archetype pattern.

12.9.1 Propositions

The building block of logic is the *proposition*.

A proposition is a statement that has a truth value.

Two examples of propositions are shown in Table 12.4.

Table 12.4

Propositions	
Statement	**Truth value**
customer002923IsPlatinumCardHolder	true
account001234IsOverdrawn	false

Each proposition has two parts—the *statement* is the part that contains the semantics of the proposition, and the *truth value* is the truth or falsehood of that statement. A typical rules engine maintains a database (*factbase*) of such statements and uses their values to trigger business activities.

Propositions can be used to capture Boolean (i.e., true/false) facts about the business. As events occur in the business, some of these propositions change their truth values. Other propositions remain largely unchanged—as mentioned earlier, these are invariants.

At any particular time, a set of propositions provides a snapshot of Boolean facts about the business.

Because propositions are Boolean, you can apply Boolean algebra to them to create new propositions called *compound propositions*.

If you consider two propositions, P1 and P2, applying the Boolean operators AND, OR, and NOT to them gives the results in Tables 12.5, 12.6, and 12.7, respectively. These tables are known as *truth tables*.

Table 12.5

Logical AND		
P1	P2	**Value of** (P1 AND P2)
true	true	true
false	true	false
true	false	false
false	false	false

Table 12.6

Logical OR		
P1	P2	**Value of** (P1 OR P2)
true	true	true
false	true	true
true	false	true
false	false	false

Table 12.7

Logical NOT	
P1	**Value of** NOT(P1)
true	false
false	true

There is also another operation, XOR, which is often provided for convenience, although it can be derived from combinations of AND, OR, and NOT. This is shown in Table 12.8.

Table 12.8

Logical XOR		
P1	P2	**Value of** (P1 XOR P2)
true	true	false
false	true	true
true	false	true
false	false	false

You can combine any number of terms to create compound propositions that make quite complex statements about the state of the business at a specific point in time.

12.9.2 Variables and predicates

Propositions deal with Boolean information, but much of the information about the business is *not* Boolean. Many notable events in the business involve a change in the value of some quantity. We represent these values as *variables*.

> A variable is a symbol that represents the value of something and can assume any of a set of values.

The second proposition shown in Table 12.4 could just as easily be expressed in terms of the current balance of the account:

(account001234IsOverdrawn) is equivalent to (account001234.balance < 0.0)

In formal logic, the statement (account001234.balance < 0.0) is called a *predicate*.

> A predicate is a statement containing variables related by quantifiers that is either true or false depending on the values of the variables.

Quantifiers are comparison operators such as =, >, <, >=, and <=. When two variables are related by a quantifier, the result is a predicate. When evaluated, a predicate generates a new proposition about the business.

12.10 Logic and the `Rule` archetype pattern

Using propositions, Boolean operators, predicates, and quantifiers, you can construct a pattern that describes a simple rules engine that works according to the principles of formal logic.

In our pattern, the engine's database is broken into two parts. The first part contains the `Rules` themselves, and the second part (the `RuleContext`) contains the factbase on which the `Rules` operate.

`Rules` are evaluated against a `RuleContext` to return a Boolean result, which may be used to trigger an activity. You can think of this mechanism as being like a lock and a key. The "lock" is a `Rule` that is triggered only if the right conditions are met. The "key" is the `RuleContext` that contains the factbase required by the `Rule`.

In the field of artificial intelligence, our `Rule` pattern would be formally classified as a forward chaining inference engine with the factbase (the `RuleContext`) separated from the rulebase (the `Rules`). Although it might sound fearsome, you'll soon see that inference engines are very simple things. You can read more about inference engines and their applications in artificial intelligence in [Negnevitsky 2001] and [Haggarty 2002].

12.11 `RuleElement`

`Rules` and `RuleContexts` are both made up of a sequence of one or more `RuleElements`. You can see the `RuleElement` archetype in Figure 12.6.

> The `RuleElement` archetype is an abstract class that represents an element of a `Rule` or a `RuleContext`.

`RuleElement` has a name that indicates the semantics of the element and an abstract operation `getType()` that returns the type of the `RuleElement`. This operation is overridden by `RuleElement` subclasses to return a string representation

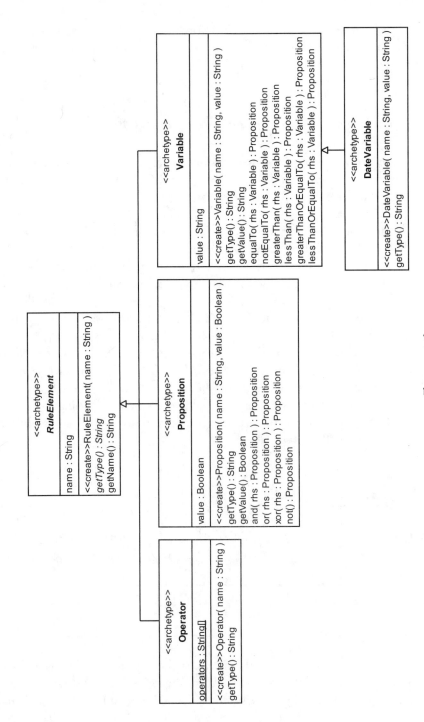

Figure 12.6

of their type. In our pattern, valid types are "Operator", "Proposition", "Variable", and "DateVariable". You may extend this pattern to add your own types.

12.12 Operator

> The Operator archetype represents a Boolean operator or a quantifier operator.

The operation getType() inherited from RuleElement (see Figure 12.6) is overridden to always return "Operator".

The name attribute inherited from RuleElement indicates the semantics of the Operator and may have one of the following values:

"AND", "OR", "XOR", "NOT", "EQUALTO", "NOTEQUALTO", "GREATERTHAN", "LESSTHAN", "GREATERTHANOREQUALTO", "LESSTHANOREQUALTO"

These values are stored in the class scope attribute, operators.

12.13 Proposition

> The Proposition archetype represents a proposition in formal logic.

The operation getType() inherited from RuleElement (see Figure 12.6) is overridden to always return "Proposition".

The name attribute inherited from RuleElement indicates the semantics of the Proposition, for example, "account001234IsOverdrawn".

The value attribute of Proposition may have values true or false.

Proposition defines operations for the Boolean operators AND, OR, and XOR. These operations take another Proposition as a parameter to represent the right-hand side of the equation being executed (rhs) and return a new Proposition with a value of true or false, according to the truth tables given in Section 12.9.1.

Proposition also defines an operation for the Boolean operator NOT, which returns a new Proposition that has a value of true if the original Proposition was false or a value of false if the original Proposition was true (see Table 12.7).

12.14 Variable **and** DateVariable

> The Variable archetype represents a variable in formal logic.

The operation getType() inherited from RuleElement (see Figure 12.6) is overridden to always return "Variable".

The name attribute inherited from RuleElement indicates the semantics of the Variable. The value attribute contains a string representation of the value of the Variable.

Variable defines operations for the quantifiers listed in Table 12.9. Each of these operations returns a Proposition.

Table 12.9

Quantifier	Operation	Value **of returned** Proposition
=	v1.equalTo(v2)	v1.value == v2.value
!=	v1.notEqualTo(v2)	v1.value != v2.value
>	v1.greaterThan(v2)	v1.value > v2.value
<	v1.lessThan(v2)	v1.value < v2.value
>=	v1.greaterThanOrEqualTo(v2)	v1.value >= v2.value
<=	v1.lessThanOrEqualTo(v2)	v1.value <= v2.value

v1 and v2 are Variables

Each operation has the precondition (v1.getType() == v2.getType())—i.e., mixed mode expressions between Variables of different types are *not* allowed

There can be many different types of Variables. As an example, our model shows DateVariable.

> The DateVariable archetype is a type of Variable that represents dates and times.

The operation getType() inherited from RuleElement is overridden to always return "DateVariable".

DateVariable can be used to compare two different dates or times.

12.15 RuleContext

The RuleContext archetype contains the informational context for the execution of a Rule. It represents this information as a collection of RuleElements that may be Propositions, Variables, or DateVariables but *not* Operators.

RuleContext is shown in Figure 12.7.

RuleContext has operations to add and find the RuleElements that comprise it, as well as an operation to append another RuleContext to itself. RuleContext can add RuleOverrides (see Section 12.20) that arise within the specific context.

As you'll see shortly, the Rule itself also contains Propositions and Variables, but these only have names and *no* values. The names refer to Propositions and Variables in the factbase provided by the RuleContext.

12.16 Rule

The Rule archetype represents a constraint on the operation of the software systems of the business. Its semantics are defined by a sequence of RuleElements.

Rule is shown in Figure 12.8.

Rule has operations to add the various RuleElements that comprise it, as well as one to evaluate the Rule using the information provided by a particular RuleContext (see Section 12.17 for the mechanics of rule evaluation).

Perhaps the best way to understand how the Rules engine actually functions is to examine the code available from our Web site (www.businessarchetypes.com). To help you do this, we also give a brief description here.

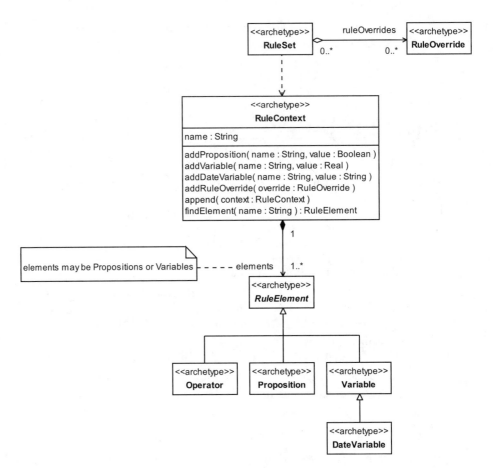

Figure 12.7

In this simple pattern, we have decided that Rules will always be expressed *without* using parentheses. A good way to do this is to express the Rule in Reverse Polish Notation (RPN).

To understand RPN, you first need to know that normal mathematical notation is known as *infix notation*, where the operators are placed between the operands, for example:

```
1 + 2
```

Standard infix notation requires the use of brackets and precedence rules. For example, in standard infix notation the expression 1 + 2 × 2 evaluates to 5

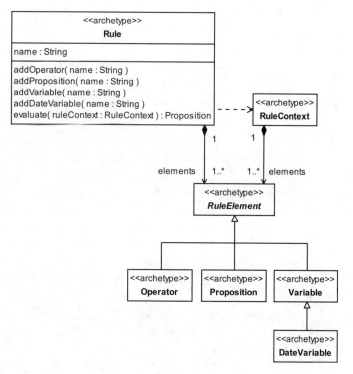

Figure 12.8

if × has a higher precedence than +. If + has a higher precedence than ×, the expression evaluates to 6. Precedence rules are so common that we apply them almost unconsciously.

In the 1920s Jan Lukasiewicz (www.fmag.unict.it/PolPhil/Lukas/Lukas.html) developed a way to write mathematical expressions using *prefix notation*, where the operators are placed before the operands, for example:

+ 1 2

He also used *postfix notation*, where the operators are placed after the operands, for example:

1 2 +

Neither of these notations requires the use of brackets or precedence rules.

The postfix variant is known as *Reverse Polish Notation* in honor of Luka-siewicz and is widely used in HP pocket calculators. We have chosen RPN for our simple rules engine.

RPN uses a simple last in, first out (LIFO) stack to process expressions. For example, the expression

```
1 2 +
```

may be processed as follows, from left to right. 1 is placed on the stack, 2 is placed on the stack. The + operator is a binary operator that requires two parameters, so 2 is popped off the stack, 1 is popped off the stack, and + is executed. The result of + is pushed back onto the stack.

A very good reason to use RPN is that it is *very* quick and easy to process. However, if you prefer to use infix notation, it's easy to write a simple prepro-cessor that converts infix rules to the postfix rules required by our engine.

Let's look at an example of a rule expressed in infix notation and then in RPN.

For operational reasons, airlines may sometimes need to select passengers for upgrade. Here is a rule from this scenario, `suitableForUpgrade`, expressed in infix notation:

```
passengerIsEconomy AND ( passengerIsGoldCardHolder OR
passengerIsSilverCardHolder )
AND ( passengerCarryOnBaggageWeightKg LESSTHANOREQUALTO
carryOnBaggageAllowanceKg ) AND passengerDressIsSmart
```

This can be expressed in RPN:

```
passengerIsEconomy passengerIsGoldCardHolder
passengerIsSilverCardHolder
OR AND passengerCarryOnBaggageWeightKg carryOnBaggageAllowanceKg
LESSTHANOREQUALTO AND passengerDressIsSmart AND
```

In our `Rule` pattern, a rule such as the simple example above is expressed as a `Rule` object with a collection of `RuleElement` objects. The object diagram for this rule is shown in Figure 12.9.

Notice that the `Rule` does *not* contain values for the `Variables` or `Propo-sitions`. This information is supplied by a `RuleContext` during the process of rule evaluation.

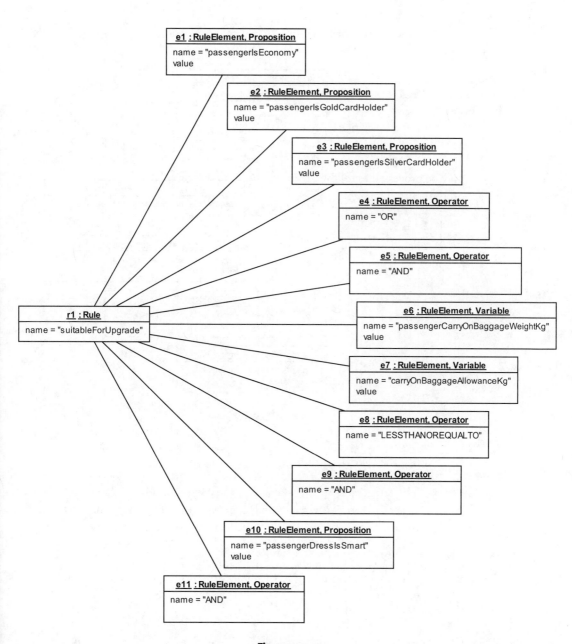

Figure 12.9

A RuleContext for the above Rule might look something like Figure 12.10.

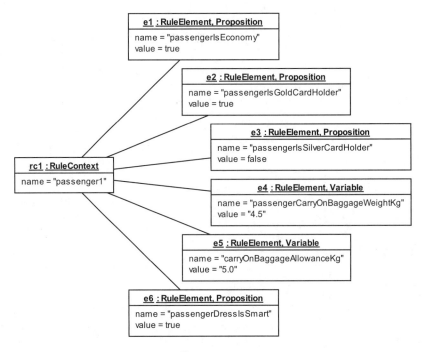

e1 : RuleElement, Proposition
name = "passengerIsEconomy"
value = true

e2 : RuleElement, Proposition
name = "passengerIsGoldCardHolder"
value = true

e3 : RuleElement, Proposition
name = "passengerIsSilverCardHolder"
value = false

rc1 : RuleContext
name = "passenger1"

e4 : RuleElement, Variable
name = "passengerCarryOnBaggageWeightKg"
value = "4.5"

e5 : RuleElement, Variable
name = "carryOnBaggageAllowanceKg"
value = "5.0"

e6 : RuleElement, Proposition
name = "passengerDressIsSmart"
value = true

Figure 12.10

Notice the following about this RuleContext.

- The RuleContext has a Proposition corresponding to each Proposition in the related Rule and a Variable corresponding to each Variable in the Rule. (The Rule doesn't assume any value for a missing Proposition or Variable.)
- The Propositions and Variables now have values.
- The RuleContext contains only information—it does not contain any Operators.

12.17 Rule **evaluation**

A UML activity diagram that illustrates how Rule evaluation works is shown in Figure 12.11.

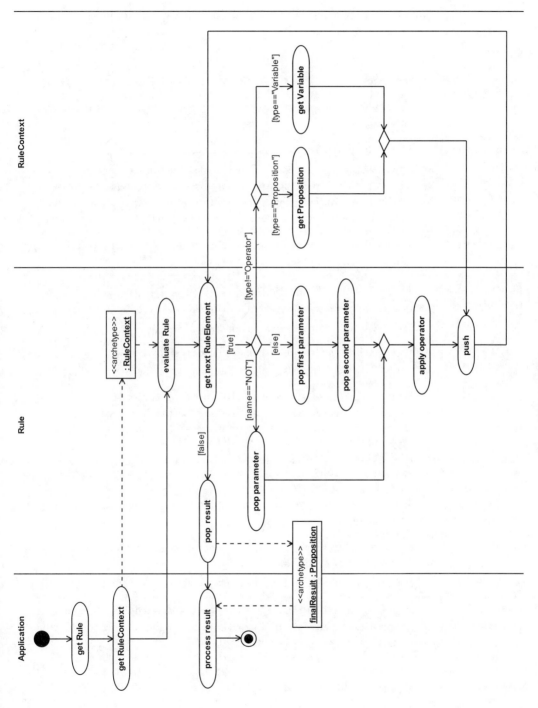

Figure 12.11

Table 12.10 provides a walkthrough of the activity diagram in Figure 12.11.

Table 12.10

Activity	Semantics
get Rule	The application creates a `Rule` object or gets one from a database or some other persistent store
get RuleContext	The application creates a `RuleContext` object
	The `RuleContext` is generally created by the application because it contains a mix of data from persistent stores and from the application itself—for example, a `RuleContext` may contain customer information retrieved from a database and information that the customer has entered directly into the application
evaluate Rule	The application calls the `evaluate(...)` operation of the `Rule` object, passing in the `RuleContext` object as a parameter
get next RuleElement	This gets the next `RuleElement` from the `Rule`
	If there are no more `RuleElements`, then `pop result`
	If the type of the `RuleElement` is not "Operator", then
	• If type is "Proposition", then `get Proposition`
	• If type is "Variable", then `get Variable`
	If the name of the `RuleElement` is "NOT", then `pop parameter`, else `pop first parameter` (i.e., this is some `Operator` other than "NOT")
pop result	Peek (copy) the top of the stack to get the `finalResult`
	Return this `Proposition` as the result of the `evaluate(...)` operation, then `process result`
process result	The application processes the `Proposition` returned from the `evaluate(...)` operation of the `Rule`
pop parameter	The current `RuleElement` is the "NOT" `Operator`—this is a unary operator that requires exactly one parameter
	Pop the next `RuleElement` off the stack and `apply operator` to the parameter
pop first parameter	The current `RuleElement` is a binary operator—this requires two parameters, so pop the first parameter off the stack (i.e., the right-hand side of the expression), then `pop second parameter`
pop second parameter	Pop the second parameter for the binary operator (i.e., the left-hand side of the expression), then `apply operator` to the two parameters

Table 12.10 (Continued)

Activity	Semantics
apply operator	Apply the operator to the parameter or parameters from the stack, then push
push	Push the resultant RuleElement back onto the stack Go to get next RuleElement
get Proposition	The RuleElement being processed by the Rule is a Proposition Look up this Proposition in the RuleContext and assign its value to the value of the RuleElement, then push
get Variable	The RuleElement being processed by the Rule is a Variable Look up this Variable in the RuleContext and assign its value to the value of the RuleElement, then push

12.18 ActivityRule

The ActivityRule archetype represents a type of Rule that automatically executes an activity when it evaluates to true.

ActivityRule has an abstract operation called activity() that must be overridden by subclasses (see Figure 12.12). Typically, subclasses would override activity() to perform some business activity, trigger a business event, or perhaps generate a new Rule.

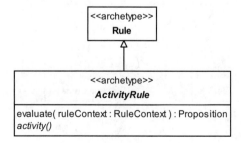

Figure 12.12

When the evaluate(...) operation of an ActivityRule subclass is called, the activity() operation is automatically called next *only* if the ActivityRule evaluates to true.

ActivityRule is really just a convenience archetype. It captures the common case where an activity is executed when a Rule evaluates to true. Clearly, you could achieve the same result by using an if...then statement to execute code based on the result of a Rule evaluation.

12.19 RuleSet

> The RuleSet archetype represents a set of Rules (no duplicates allowed).

A RuleSet can be evaluated to a Proposition that is true if and only if every Rule in the set also evaluates to true. It therefore performs a logical AND on all of the Rules it contains.

The RuleSet is useful for grouping Rules. It also allows RuleOverrides to be applied to one or more of the Rules. RuleSet and RuleOverride are shown in Figure 12.13.

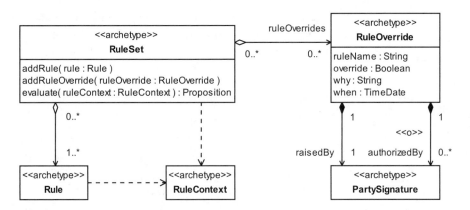

Figure 12.13

12.20 RuleOverride

Sometimes you need to break a Rule.

As an example, business rules may be in place to determine the price of a hotel room. Suppose an important customer phones to ask for a Price to which he or she is not really entitled. This may be because one of the customer's staff or contacts, who is entitled to that price, has told him or her about it.

On the one hand, to refuse the customer may lose a lot of valuable business, but on the other hand, to meet the customer's demand necessitates breaking one of the pricing rules. To do this, you use a RuleOverride that allows you to break Rules in a RuleSet in a structured way, leaving behind a clear audit trail.

> The RuleOverride archetype overrides a Rule in a RuleSet.

RuleOverride (see Figure 12.13) records the ruleName of the Rule that it overrides, the value of the override (i.e., whether the Rule was overridden to true or false), why the override was made, when it happened, and who the override was raisedBy and optionally authorizedBy.

12.21 Summary

In this chapter we looked at the Rule archetype pattern. This is a pattern for representing simple rules based on formal logic. We covered the topics listed below.

- What are rules: a brief explanation of the concept of rules
- Rules and business processes: how rules interact with business processes
- Business rules and system rules: why it is useful to distinguish between these
  - Business rules: rules that constrain the structure or operation of a business
  - Business system rules: rules that constrain business software systems
- The physical location of business system rules:
  - Source code
  - Database triggers
  - Explicit rules

- Rules and formal logic:
  - Propositions: statements that have a truth value:
    - AND, OR, NOT, XOR
  - Variables and predicates:
    - Variable: a symbol that represents the value of something
    - Predicate: a statement containing variables related by quantifiers
    - Quantifier: the comparison operators =, >, <, >=, and <=
- How the `Rule` archetype pattern functions as a simple rules engine:
  - Consists of `Rules` and the factbase (`RuleContext`) on which they operate
- `Rule`: how to represent a constraint on the operation of the software systems of a business
  - Defined by a sequence of `RuleElements`
  - Expressed using Reverse Polish Notation, a mathematical notation that does not require brackets or precedence rules
- `RuleContext`: how to represent the database of facts on which a `Rule` operates
  - Made up of a sequence of `RuleElements` that may be `Propositions`, `Variables`, or `DateVariables` but *not* `Operators`
- `RuleElement`: how to represent an element of a `Rule` or `RuleContext` using four types (you can also extend the pattern with your own types)
  - `Operator`: how to represent operators
    - "AND", "OR", "XOR", "NOT", "EQUALTO", "NOTEQUALTO", "GREATERTHAN", "LESSTHAN", "GREATERTHANOREQUALTO", "LESSTHANOREQUALTO"
  - `Proposition`: how to represent propositions
  - `Variable`: how to represent variables
  - `DateVariable`: how to represent dates and times
- `Rule` evaluation: how to process a `Rule` and a `RuleContext`
- `ActivityRule`: how to represent a `Rule` that automatically triggers an activity when it evaluates to `true`
- `RuleSet`: how to represent a set of `Rules`
- `RuleOverride`: how to override a specific `Rule` in a `RuleSet` in a structured way, leaving a clear audit trail

Summary

In this book we brought together a lot of existing ideas and introduced some new ones.

In Part 1, we introduced the theory of archetype patterns that enabled us to construct the detailed patterns in Part 3. We also considered how to automate the use of these patterns by using MDA modeling tools.

In Part 2 we looked at how to increase the value of UML models by making them accessible to a wider audience through literate modeling. This part also explained how we documented the archetype patterns in Part 3 and how you can document your own UML models and patterns.

In Part 3 we presented a valuable pattern catalog. We hope that these patterns will prove to be very useful to you and that they will save you a lot of time and effort.

What is the future of archetype patterns? As we go to press, our work on archetype patterns could move in several interesting directions.

- We would like to create another volume of archetype patterns covering other aspects of the business domain. This is very likely.
- We may work with one or more of the MDA modeling tool vendors to incorporate archetype patterns directly into their MDA modeling tools. We have already done some proof-of-concept work with Interactive Objects on this.
- We may do some work with standards bodies such as the OMG to apply archetype patterns to existing and emerging standards.
- We have wanted (for many years) to do more work on literate modeling. In particular, we would like to formalize it and integrate it into modeling tools by using XML-based technologies.

- Because this is a practical book, we have covered only the key aspects of archetype theory rather than exploring it in detail. For example, we have left the relationship between archetype patterns, ontologies, and the Semantic Web largely unexplored. But these theoretical areas might be best explored through papers in journals rather than in practical books like this!

Because the creation of archetype patterns requires detailed domain knowledge, we are happy to work with domain experts who would like to create these patterns in their specific domain. We are also happy to work with academics who might like to take archetype pattern theory or the literate modeling technique further. You can contact us via our Web site (www.businessarchetypes.com).

Finally, we hope you have enjoyed this book! As we stated in the Introduction, we have tried to make it as readable and useful to you as we can.

Archetype glossary

Archetype	Definition	Page number
AcceptPaymentEvent	Represents an event that records Money received by a paymentReceiver from a purchaser against an OPEN SalesOrder	345
AcceptRefundEvent	Represents an event that records Money refunded by a paymentReceiver to a purchaser against an OPEN PurchaseOrder	345
Action	Represents a description of something that can happen	198
ActivityRule	Represents a type of Rule that automatically executes an activity when it evaluates to true	457
Address	Represents information that can be used to contact a Party	132
AddressProperties	Specifies information about an Address assigned to a specific Party	132
AmendEvent	Represents an event sent to an OPEN Order that captures an amendment to the Order	329
AmendOrderLineEvent	Represents an event that, when applied to an OPEN Order, results in a change to a specific OrderLine, the addition of a new OrderLine, or the deletion of an existing OrderLine	331

Archetype	Definition	Page number
AmendPartySummaryEvent	Represents an event that, when applied to an OPEN Order, results in a change to a specific PartySummary, the addition of a new PartySummary, or the deletion of an existing PartySummary	335
AmendTermsAndConditionsEvent	Represents an event that, when applied to an OPEN Order, results in a change to its termsAndConditions, the addition of termsAndConditions if these were previously absent, or the deletion of existing termsAndConditions	336
ArbitraryPrice	Represents an ad hoc Price applied to a specific ProductInstance that overrides all other possible Prices	249
AssignedResponsibility	Represents an instance of a Responsibility assigned to a specific PartyRole	181
Batch	Describes a set of ProductInstances of a specific ProductType that are all to be tracked together, usually for quality control purposes	215
BodyMetrics	Provides a way to store information about the human body such as size, weight, hair color, eye color, measurements, and so on	141
CancelEvent	Represents an event sent to an Order that changes its OrderStatus to CANCELLED	327
Capabilities	Represents a collection of facts about what a Party is capable of doing	182
CapacityManager	Manages the utilization of capacity by releasing ServiceInstances	280
Cash	Represents a Payment made in a physical amount of a Currency	427
CatalogEntry	Represents information about a specific type of product held in a ProductCatalog	224

Archetype	Definition	Page number
ChargeLine	Represents an additional charge for an OrderLine over and above the OrderLine value *or* an extra charge added to an Order	319
Check	Represents a bill of exchange drawn on a bank and payable on demand—in other words, a written order to pay Money to a Party	428
CloseEvent	Represents an event sent to an Order that changes its OrderStatus to CLOSED	327
Communication	Represents a type of PartyRelationship that captures details of a communication between two PartyRoles	193
CommunicationRouting	Is a special type of Communication that represents a handover between CustomerServiceRepresentatives	194
CommunicationThread	Represents a sequence of Communications about a particular topic	197
Company	Represents an Organization created to make money by selling goods or services, with a legal identity that is separate from its owners	144
CompanyGroup	Represents an Organization comprising a collection of Companies that have a legal relationship	144
CompatibleWith	Provides a way to show that the client in a ProductRelationship is compatible with all of the suppliers	244
ComplementedBy	Provides a way to show that the client in a ProductRelationship may be complemented in some way by one of the suppliers	244
ConditionalPropositionOfInclusion	Determines the ProductTypes of the ProductInstances that may be included in a PackageInstance based on selections from a ProductSet—the inclusion can occur only if the condition PropositionOfInclusion is true	234

Archetype	Definition	Page number
CreditCard	Represents a PaymentCard that comes with a line of credit	430
Currency	Represents a Metric or standard of value for measuring Money	414
CurrencyConverter	Converts an amount of a source Currency into an equivalent amount of a target Currency by applying an ExchangeRate	423
Customer	Is a type of PartyRole that a Party may play on the purchasing side of a sales process	190
CustomerAgent	Represents a PartyRole played by someone who acts on behalf of a Customer	197
CustomerCommunicationManager	Manages all Customer Communications as a set of CustomerServiceCases	192
CustomerServiceCase	Represents a collection of all Communications about a specific topic related to a specific Customer	195
CustomerServiceCaseIdentifier	Represents a unique identifier for a CustomerServiceCase	197
CustomerServiceRepresentative	Represents a PartyRole played by someone who acts on behalf of, and with the authorization and authority of, the customer services department	197
DateVariable	Is a type of Variable that represents dates and times	448
DebitCard	Represents a PaymentCard where Payments are immediately debited from a source account	430
DeliveryReceiver	Represents a special type of PartySummary that also includes deliveryInstructions	318
DerivedUnit	Represents a combination of one or more base Units according to a specific equation	398

Archetype	Definition	Page number
DerivedUnitTerm	Represents part of a DerivedUnit comprising a single Unit and its power	398
DespatchEvent	Represents an event that, when applied to an OPEN SalesOrder, records goods or services sent to a DeliveryReceiver	340
DespatchLine	Provides a record of the number of items despatched against a specified OrderLine as part of a particular DespatchEvent	341
Discount	Represents a discount to be applied to the total price of an Order	337
DiscountEvent	Represents an event that, when applied to an Order, causes one or more Discounts to be recorded against the Order	337
DiscountType	Contains a set of rules that describes the conditions under which a particular Discount may be applied	339
EmailAddress	Specifies a way of contacting a Party via e-mail	136
Ethnicity	Represents a classification of one or more People according to common racial, national, tribal, religious, linguistic, or cultural origin or background	140
ExchangeRate	Represents the price of one type of money relative to another	422
ExchangeRateType	Represents a category of ExchangeRate that determines its applicability	423
GeographicAddress	Represents a geographic location at which a Party may be contacted—is a postal address for the Party	132
IncompatibleWith	Provides a way to show that the client in a ProductRelationship is not compatible with any of the suppliers	244

Archetype	Definition	Page number
Inventory	Represents a collection of InventoryEntries held in stock by a business	271
InventoryEntry	Records a type of good or service and the number of instances of that good or service that are available	271
InvoiceEvent	Represents an event that records an invoice sent by a paymentReceiver or received by a purchaser	345
ISOCountryCode	Is a type of Locale that represents an identifier for a country as defined in ISO 3166	419
ISOCurrency	Represents a type of Currency whose name, alphabeticCode, and numericCode are defined in ISO 4217	417
ISOGender	Represents a classification of a Person according to their gender using the ISO 5218 standard	140
LifecycleEvent	Represents an event sent to an Order that changes its OrderStatus	326
Locale	Represents a general notion of place, location, or context	418
MakePaymentEvent	Represents an event that records Money paid by a purchaser to a paymentReceiver against an OPEN PurchaseOrder	345
MakeRefundEvent	Represents an event that records Money refunded by a paymentReceiver to a purchaser against an OPEN SalesOrder	345
ManHour	Represents an amount of work corresponding to one person working for one hour	399
MeasuredProductInstance	Represents a kind of ProductInstance that specifies an amount of some Metric (a Quantity) of the product to be sold	254

Archetype	Definition	Page number
MeasuredProductType	Represents a kind of ProductType that specifies possible Metrics and a single preferred Metric for measuring Quantities of the product	254
Metric	Represents a standard of measurement	393
MonetaryDiscount	Represents an amount of Money to be deducted from the total price of an Order	337
Money	Represents an amount of a specific Currency—this Currency is acceptedIn one or more Locales	413
NonISOCurrency	Represents a type of Currency that is not defined in ISO 4217	417
OpenEvent	Represents an event sent to an Order that changes its OrderStatus to OPEN	327
Operator	Represents a Boolean operator or a quantifier operator	447
Order	Represents a record of a request by a buyer for a seller to supply some goods or services	304
OrderEvent	Represents a notable occurrence in the lifecycle of an Order	322
OrderIdentifier	Represents a unique identifier for an Order	304
OrderLine	Represents part of an Order that is a summary of particular goods or services ordered by a buyer	310
OrderLineIdentifier	Represents a unique identifier for an OrderLine or a ChargeLine	312
OrderManager	Manages a collection of Orders	321
OrderPayment	Represents a Payment made or accepted against an Order	343
OrderStatus	Represents a particular state of the Order that constrains what activities can be performed against the Order	326

Archetype	Definition	Page number
Organization	Represents an administrative and functional structure	143
OrganizationName	Represents a name for an Organization	143
OrganizationUnit	Represents an Organization that is part of another Organization	143
Outcome	Describes the possible or actual result of an Action (the description) and an optional reason for that specific Outcome	200
PackageInstance	Represents a collection of one or more ProductInstances sold together to increase the business benefit generated by the sale—a PackageInstance is a kind of ProductInstance	226
PackageType	Specifies a set of component ProductTypes and rules about how these may be combined to create PackageInstances—a PackageType is a kind of ProductType	226
Party	Represents an identifiable, addressable unit that may have a legal status and that normally has autonomous control over (at least some of) its actions	122
PartyAuthentication	Represents an agreed and trusted way to confirm that a Party is who they say they are	129
PartyIdentifier	Represents a unique identifier for a Party	125
PartyManager	Manages a collection of Parties	153
PartyRelationship	Captures the fact that there is a semantic relationship between two Parties in which each Party plays a specific role	160
PartyRelationshipConstraint	Specifies the names of PartyRoles that may adopt the client and supplier sides of a PartyRelationship of a specific PartyRelationshipType	176

Archetype	Definition	Page number
PartyRelationshipType	Provides a way to store all of the common information for a set of PartyRelationship instances	173
PartyRole	Captures the semantics of the role played by a Party in a particular PartyRelationship	160
PartyRoleConstraint	Specifies the typeOfParty that is allowed to play a PartyRole of a specific PartyRoleType	175
PartyRoleIdentifier	Represents a unique identifier for a PartyRole	160
PartyRoleType	Provides a way to store all of the common information for a set of PartyRole instances	173
PartySignature	Represents the identifying mark of a Party	128
PartySummary	Represents a snapshot of summary contact information about a Party, in relation to a particular context	184
PartySummaryRoleInOrder	Represents a role within the Order process that can be played by a PartySummary	317
Payment	Represents Money paid by one Party to another, in return for goods or services	425
PaymentCard	Represents a physical token such as a plastic card that authorizes the Party identified on it to charge the cost of goods or services to an account	429
PaymentEvent	Represents an event that, when applied to an OPEN Order, records a Payment requested, made, or accepted against the Order	343
PaymentMethod	Represents the medium by which a Payment may be made	427
PercentageDiscount	Represents a percentage to be deducted from the total price of an Order	337
Person	Represents information about a human being	137

Archetype	Definition	Page number
PersonName	Represents a name for a Person	141
Preference	Represents a Party's expressed choice of (or liking for) something, often from a set of possible or offered options	150
PreferenceOption	Specifies the name of a possible option and its description	150
PreferenceType	Specifies the name, a description, and a range of PreferenceOptions for a Preference	150
Price	Represents the amount of money that must be paid in order to purchase a good or service	245
PricingStrategy	Determines how a Price is calculated for a PackageType	252
ProductCatalog	Represents a persistent store of product information used in the selling process	221
ProductFeatureInstance	Represents a specific feature (such as color) of a good or service and its value (e.g., blue)	219
ProductFeatureType	Represents a type of feature (such as color) of a good or service and its range of possible values (e.g., {blue, green, yellow, red})	219
ProductIdentifier	Represents a unique identifier for a type of product (a ProductType)	210
ProductInstance	Represents a specific instance of a ProductType	208
ProductInventoryEntry	Represents an InventoryEntry that holds a set of ProductInstances all of the same ProductType	275
ProductRelationship	Represents a fixed relationship between ProductTypes that is not a packaging or containment relationship	242
ProductSet	Represents a set of ProductIdentifiers that refer to ProductTypes	233

Archetype	Definition	Page number
ProductType	Describes the common properties of a set of goods or services	208
Proposition	Represents a proposition in formal logic	447
PropositionOfInclusion	Determines the ProductTypes of the ProductInstances that may be included in a PackageInstance based on selections from a ProductSet	233
PurchaseOrder	Represents a type of Order raised by a buyer and submitted to a seller as a request for goods or services in return for an agreed payment	310
Quantity	Represents an amount measured in some Metric	400
ReceiptEvent	Represents an event that, when applied to an OPEN PurchaseOrder, records goods or services received from a vendor	341
ReceiptLine	Provides a record of the number of items received against a specified OrderLine as part of a particular ReceiptEvent	342
RegisteredIdentifier	Represents an identifier for a Party that has been assigned by a recognized or statutory body	127
RejectedItem	Represents a delivered item that is rejected by a DeliveryReceiver as unfit for purpose	341
ReplacedBy	Provides a way to show that the client in a ProductRelationship has been superseded by the suppliers—this means that the client is now obsolete and must be replaced by one of the suppliers	243
Reservation	Represents the assignment of one or more ProductInstances to one or more Parties via PartySummaries—that is, an arrangement by which a ProductInstance is kept for the use of a specific Party at some point in time	283

Archetype	Definition	Page number
ReservationIdentifier	Represents a unique identifier for a ReservationRequest	283
ReservationRequest	Represents a request for a Reservation to be made	283
ReservationStatus	Indicates whether a ProductInstance is AVAILABLE to be reserved or has already been RESERVED	283
Responsibility	Represents a description of an activity that a PartyRoleType may be expected to perform	179
RestockPolicy	Represents a set of rules determining when inventory items need to be reordered	275
ReturnedItem	Represents an item that has been received by a DeliveryReceiver and must be returned to the vendor because a CancelEvent or AmendOrderLineEvent has rendered it surplus to requirements	328
RoundingPolicy	Determines the mathematical semantics of the Quantity archetype's round(...) operation	404
RoundingStrategy	Represents an aspect of a RoundingPolicy that determines the type of rounding to be applied	405
Rule	Represents a constraint on the operation of the software systems of the business—its semantics are defined by a sequence of RuleElements	449
RuleContext	Contains the informational context for the execution of a Rule—it represents this information as a collection of RuleElements that may be Propositions, Variables, or DateVariables but *not* Operators	449
RuleElement	Is an abstract class that represents an element of a Rule or a RuleContext	445
RuleOverride	Overrides a Rule in a RuleSet	459

Archetype	Definition	Page number
RuleSet	Represents a set of Rules (no duplicates allowed)	458
SalesOrder	Represents a type of Order used by a seller to track delivery of goods or services to a buyer in return for an agreed payment	310
SalesTaxPolicy	Records the prevailing taxation rate for a particular category of sales tax	321
SerialNumber	Represents a unique identifier for a specific instance of a product (a ProductInstance)	214
ServiceDeliveryStatus	Records the status of the delivery of a particular ServiceInstance	257
ServiceInstance	Represents an instance or execution of a ServiceType delivered to one or more Parties	256
ServiceInventoryEntry	Represents an InventoryEntry that holds a set of ServiceInstances all of the same ServiceType	277
ServiceType	Is a kind of ProductType that represents a type of service	256
SIBaseUnit	Represents one of the base units defined in the International System of Units (SI)—the different SIBaseUnits are mutually independent	395
StandardConversion	Defines a conversionFactor that can be used to convert a Quantity in a source Unit to a Quantity in a target Unit	408
SubstitutedBy	Provides a way to show that an instance of the client in a ProductRelationship may be substituted by an instance of one of the suppliers	243
SystemOfUnits	Represents a set of related Units defined by a standard such as SI	395
TaxOnLine	Represents tax charged on an OrderLine or a ChargeLine	320

Archetype	Definition	Page number
TelecomAddress	Represents a number that can contact a telephone, mobile phone, fax, pager, or other telephonic device	134
UniqueIdentifier	Represents an identifier that is unique within a given context	125
Unit	Represents a type of `Metric` that is part of a `SystemOfUnits`	395
UnitConverter	Is responsible for converting a `Quantity` in a source `Unit` to a `Quantity` in a target `Unit`	408
UpgradableTo	Provides a way to show that the `suppliers` in a `ProductRelationship` represent upgrades to the `client`	243
Variable	Represents a variable in formal logic	448
WebPageAddress	Represents the URL for a Web page related to the `Party`	137

Bibliography

[Alexander 1977]   *A Pattern Language—Towns, Buildings, Construction.* Christopher Alexander, Sara Ishikawa, and Murray Silverstein. Oxford University Press, 1977, ISBN 0-195-01919-9.

[Arlow 2001]   *UML and the Unified Process—Practical Object-Oriented Analysis and Design.* Jim Arlow and Ila Neustadt. Addison-Wesley, 2001, ISBN 0-201-77060-1.

[Arlow 1998]   "Literate Modelling—Capturing Business Knowledge with the UML." Jim Arlow, Wolfgang Emmerich, and John Quinn. «UML» '98 Conference Proceedings (see www.businessarchetypes.com/literatemodeling/literatemodeling.htm).

[Bandler 1990]   *The Structure of Magic.* Richard Bandler and John Grinder. Science & Behavior Books, 1990, ISBN 0-8314-0044-7.

[Bishop 2002]   *Computer Security.* Matthew A. Bishop. Addison-Wesley, 2002, ISBN 0-201-44099-7.

[Boole 1998]   *The Mathematical Analysis of Logic.* George Boole. St. Augustine's Press, 1998, ISBN 1-85506-583-5.

[Buzan 1996]   *The Mind Map Book.* Tony Buzan. Plume, 1996, ISBN 0-452-27322-6.

[Chappell 2001]   *Professional ebXML Foundations.* David A. Chappell et al. Wrox, 2001, ISBN 1-861-00590-3.

[Coad 1999]   *Java Modeling in Color with UML—Enterprise Components and Process.*
                   Peter Coad, Eric Lefebvre, and Jeff De Luca. Prentice Hall, 1999,
                   ISBN 0-13-011510-X.

[Dupré 1998]   *Bugs in Writing.* Lyn Dupré. Addison-Wesley, 1998, ISBN 0-201-
                   37921-X.

[Dyché 2001]   *The CRM Handbook.* Jill Dyché. Addison-Wesley, 2001, ISBN 0-201-
                   73062-6.

[Fowler 1996]   *Analysis Patterns—Reusable Object Models.* Martin Fowler. Addison-
                   Wesley, 1996, ISBN 0-201-89542-0.

[Frankel 2003]   *Model Driven Architecture.* David S. Frankel. Wiley & Sons, 2003,
                   ISBN 0-471-31920-1.

[Gamma 1995]   *Design Patterns—Elements of Reusable Object-Oriented Software.* Erich
                   Gamma, Richard Helm, Ralph Johnson, and John Vlissides. Addison-
                   Wesley, 1995, ISBN 0-201-63361-2.

[Garfinkel 1995]   "Inside Risks" (column). Simson Garfinkel. *Communications of the
                   ACM*, October 1995.

[Haggarty 2002]   *Discrete Mathematics for Computing.* Rod Haggarty. Addison-Wesley,
                   2002, ISBN 0-201-73047-2.

[Hubert 2001]   *Convergent Architecture.* Richard Hubert. Wiley & Sons, 2001, ISBN
                   0-471-10560-0.

[Jung 1981]   *The Archetypes and the Collective Unconscious.* Carl Gustav Jung.
                   Princeton University Press, 1981, ISBN 0-691-01833-2.

[Kleppe 2003]   *MDA Explained.* Anneke Kleppe, Jos Warmer, and Wim Bast.
                   Addison-Wesley, 2003, ISBN 0-321-19442-X.

[Knuth 1984]   "Literate Programming." D. Knuth. *The Computer Journal*,
                   27:97–111, 1984.

[Mellor 2002]   *Executable UML.* Stephen J. Mellor and Marc J. Balcer. Addison-
                   Wesley, 2002, ISBN 0-201-74804-5.

[Negnevitsky 2001]   *Artificial Intelligence.* Michael Negnevitsky. Addison-Wesley, 2001, ISBN 0-201-71159-1.

[Stevenson 2001]   *Operations Management.* William J Stevenson. McGraw-Hill Higher Education, 2001, ISBN 0-07-247670-2.

[Succi 2001]   *Extreme Programming Examined.* Giancarlo Succi and Michele Marchesi. Addison-Wesley, 2001, ISBN 0-201-71040-4.

[Taylor 1995]   *Business Engineering with Object Technology.* David A Taylor. Wiley & Sons, 1995, ISBN 0-471-04521-7.

[von Halle 2002]   *Business Rules Applied.* Barbara von Halle. Wiley & Sons, 2002, ISBN 0-471-41293-7.

Index

Also Available from Addison-Wesley

MDA Explained
The Model Driven Architecture™: Practice and Promise

by Anneke Kleppe, Jos Warmer, and Wim Bast

0-321-19442-X
Paperback
192 pages
© 2003

Written by three members of OMG's MDA standardization committee, **MDA Explained** gives readers an inside look at the advantages of MDA and how they can be realized. This book begins with practical examples that illustrate the application of different types of models. It then shifts to a discussion at the meta-level, where developers will gain the knowledge necessary to define MDA tools.

Highlights of this book include:

• The MDA framework, including the Platform Independent Model (PIM) and Platform Specific Model (PSM)

• OMG standards and the use of UML

• MDA and Agile, Extreme Programming, and Rational Unified Process (RUP) development

• How to apply MDA, including PIM-to-PSM and PSM-to-code transformations, for relational, Enterprise JavaBean (EJB), and Web models

• Transformations, including controlling and tuning, traceability, incremental consistency, and their implications

• Metamodeling

• Relationships between different standards, including Meta Object Facility (MOF), UML, and Object Constraint Language (OCL)

The advent of MDA offers concrete ways to dramatically improve productivity, portability, interoperability, maintenance, and documentation. With this groundbreaking book, IT professionals can learn to tap this new framework to deliver enterprise systems most efficiently.

Register
Your Book
at www.awprofessional.com/register

You may be eligible to receive:

- Advance notice of forthcoming editions of the book
- Related book recommendations
- Chapter excerpts and supplements of forthcoming titles
- Information about special contests and promotions throughout the year
- Notices and reminders about author appearances, tradeshows, and online chats with special guests

Contact us

If you are interested in writing a book or reviewing manuscripts prior to publication, please write to us at:

Editorial Department
Addison-Wesley Professional
75 Arlington Street, Suite 300
Boston, MA 02116 USA
Email: AWPro@aw.com

Visit us on the Web: http://www.awprofessional.com